This book investigates the way in which tax systems affect economic efficiency and the distribution of welfare. It examines within a unified framework questions that are usually treated in different areas of the literature: institutional economics, positive economics, normative economics, and political economics. It adheres to the rigorous standards of pure theory while paying careful attention to the policy relevance of the arguments. Tax systems are viewed as information extracting devices that generate sets of equilibria of complex geometry. A tax reform methodology is proposed that sheds light on optimal taxes. Social conflicts in the determination of taxes are shown to have effects on social cohesion.

# A contribution to the pure theory of taxation

# A contribution to the pure theory of taxation

ROGER GUESNERIE

CAMBRIDGE
UNIVERSITY PRESS

Published by the Press Syndicate of the University of Cambridge
The Pitt Building, Trumpington Street, Cambridge CB2 1RP
40 West 20th Street, New York, NY 10011-4211, USA
10 Stamford Road, Oakleigh, Melbourne 3166, Australia



First published 1995

Printed in Great Britain at the University Press, Cambridge

*A catalogue record for this book is available from the British Library*

*Library of Congress cataloguing in publication data*
Guesnerie, R.
A contribution to the pure theory of taxation / Roger Guesnerie.
p. cm.
Includes bibliographical references.
ISBN 0 521 23689 4
1. Taxation. I. Title.
HJ2305 G84 1995
336.2–dc20 94-1872
CIP

ISBN 0 521 23689 4 hardback

SE

# Contents

# Foreword

This book attempts to contribute to what Walras called 'théorie pure' (in opposition to 'économie appliquée'). 'Pure theory' focuses attention on stylized models in which some features of the real world are ignored while others are accentuated. Choosing the appropriate idealized features on which to focus attention is a part of the modeller's art: the construction should be amenable to the analysis and attract attention to some key elements of real world mechanisms. Also, the collection of polar models of pure theory should define a set of anchoring points, a basis (in the usual sense of the word as well as in analogy with the sense of linear algebra) for analysing and recomposing the various dimensions of the real world's economic complexity.

With these criteria in mind, this book clearly is (or attempts to be) a 'contribution to the pure theory of taxation'. It analyses an idealized world where public policies in general, taxation in particular, are simply constrained by incomplete asymmetric information. Clearly the understanding of complex realities eventually will have to appeal not only to thc teachings of this model, but also to the analysis of other stylized models. But, in line with the pure theory options, attention is here voluntarily restricted to one polar world.

A vivid tradition of normative economics is associated with the names of Dupuit, George, Walras, Pareto, Hotelling, Allais, Samuelson (among others). Along the lines of this tradition, the design of public policies can separate efficiency and equity issues. For example, the most eloquent advocate of this tradition, the second theorem of welfare economics, asserts that an efficient allocation of resources can be obtained via a system of decentralized competitive markets once an appropriate redistribution of income has been achieved. Such a redistribution of income can be achieved however only if the government has access to full information regarding the individuals and firms. In particular, a detailed knowledge of the individual's characteristics that determine both his (her) tastes and the extent and profitability of his (her) market activities is required. Observation together with reflection suggest that such a knowledge considerably exceeds the actual knowledge of tax authorities. Indeed the starting point of this book is that the government has only partial information on the agents' characteristics.

The facts retained in the model are primarily the standard stylized facts both of static general equilibrium and of the economics of incomplete information. In an abstract economy à la Arrow–Debreu, the agents' characteristics relevant for taxation decisions are (partly) hidden from the government: technically, they are private information. Our polar world has two complementary features. On the one hand, the organization of the productive activities of the economy is a simple problem in the sense that it could be solved by using the solutions suggested by the second theorem of welfare economics. Then, in the production sector, the model abstracts from the difficulties that parallel the (informational) difficulties emphasized in the household sector. On the other hand, the model adopts a set of rather extreme observability assumptions about transactions.

In a world where the (three) just described ingredients are combined, lump-sum transfers are impossible and the (second) best tax institutions involve the use of commodity and income taxes according to arrangements that are indeed more reminiscent of the actual arrangements of modern economies than of the idealized first-best lump-sum tools. The study of such tax systems, clearly second-best tax systems, is the central subject of this book.

This rather brief assessment of the general perspective of the book suggests that it aims at two different audiences: the audience of theorists and the audience of 'public' economists.

One of the main objectives, and maybe the first one, is to convince theorists, and general equilibrium theorists in particular, that second-best taxation is not only a useful subject for policy makers but also a theoretically sound subject. Both the general construction of the book and the detailed organization of the argument are aimed at this objective.

The general construction follows a strict, and hopefully clear and logical, scheme: the analysis of the basic theoretical status of the model – in chapter 1 – precedes the 'positive' investigation of the subject – chapter 2, the 'normative' analysis – in chapter 3 – provides a basis for the 'political' economics perspective. Indeed, such a basic frame fits the needs of the present study. It is likely to have more general scope and provide useful guidelines to those economic theory studies that have both second-best features and a general equilibrium perspective.

The content also reflects the pure theory option. Chapter 1 contains a reflection on the foundations of the tax institutions that are studied in the rest of the book. It is shown that these tax institutions are indeed appropriate in the polar world we are considering. These stylized institutions lead us far away from the polar world of the second welfare theorem but closer to the actual taxation problematic of practitioners. The incentives argument that is developed here will be more familiar to specialists of incentives or contracts than to general equilibrium theorists. However, taxation is a truly general equilibrium subject as chapter 2 shows; the understanding of the structure of tax equilibria requires the full power of the best tools developed for analysing the Walrasian general equilibrium problem. Furthermore, new theoretically attractive problems emerge (as for example the connectedness problem), the solution of which challenges intuition as well as, possibly, actual procedures of practitioners. Chapter 3 adopts a basic perspective in tackling the optimization taxation problem: the tax reform approach provides a local normative analysis that exploits the knowledge of the local structure of tax equilibria; the study of the corresponding tax reform algorithms underline the significance and the limits of optimal tax formulas. The problem of the relationship between social values and prices is lengthily discussed in chapter 4 as a central second-best taxation problem, and, more generally, as a theoretical key second-best problem. Also, the analysis in chapter 5 of the structure of second-best Pareto optima provides insights that have a broad theoretical appeal. Finally the game theoretical analysis of the so-called 'political economics of taxation' within the framework of a very simple model raises points that have specific implications for the analysis of the size of economic organizations, but are also of general theoretical interest.

It is hoped that theorists will find not only a satisfactory framework for analysis, familiar techniques, but also, as just suggested, interesting results. During the 1970s the theory of public economics made substantial advances in our understanding of policy optimization under constraints beyond those of technology and resource availability: the so-called second best. These advances have not been digested by practitioners of public economics or by theorists outside of public economics. Indeed some elements of what can be called the second-best culture have been rediscovered: for example the theory of contracts stresses some normative properties paradoxical to the first-best intuition, but familiar to specialists of optimal taxation. The theory of incomplete markets has reproduced the methodology of local normative analysis of tax equilibria in order to assess the inefficiency of (incomplete) market equilibria. These facts (among others) provide slightly worrying examples of inefficient cross fertilization. This book explicitly aims at favouring the circulation of ideas indispensable to the vitality of the profession.

The pure theory option of the study is also reflected in the presentation of the argument and the comments: emphasis is put on the coherency and theoretical unity of the whole construction and this option is often detrimental to the recognition of the richness of applications and interpretations. In order to attenuate the effects of such a 'monist' option, a more eclectic view of the content of each of the chapters is offered in the conclusion, that stresses independent interpretations rather than theoretical unity. But until then our comments stick to the initial pure theory option.

Having insisted on the pure theory option (the less obvious when the subject is taxation), I should recall the more obvious: the study is a study in public economics and then, as such, it aims at the audience of public economists. The reasons why public economists should be concerned with the subject of this book are obvious: first the model under consideration is the classical taxation model, the study of which has been pioneered by Diamond and Mirrlees: indeed the second part of chapter 3 gathers a large set of classical results in optimal taxation; also, the same chapter provides a rather comprehensive analysis – within the same framework but with a rather broader ambition – of the tax reform methodology that has often replaced in applied studies the optimal taxation approach. Nowadays, besides optimal taxation and tax reform, alternative methods using computable general equilibrium models have become standard in applied taxation studies. The content of the book also relates with this now most important alternative methodology. Chapter 2 in particular provides a number of insights and results that are of direct relevance to the mastering of computable general equilibrium models.

The pure theory option already emphasized may also be a second reason why public economists should be concerned by the content of the book: it was stressed above that theorists have to learn from the results of second-best theory; one can also safely conjecture that public economists can benefit from confronting their models with the demanding tests of pure theory as they have been set, for example, by general equilibrium theory. My emphasis is not so much here on rigor or generality tests but on what I would be tempted to call 'perspective' tests; by forcing us to assess as exactly as possible the significance and the limits of each result, the pure theory viewpoint helps to put these results in the right perspective. Often, such an assessment of perspective is a prerequisite to prudent and appropriate use. It is also preparation for a better appraisal of the theoretical progresses needed for the development of the field.

It is sometimes argued that public economics is in crisis. It is not the purpose of the present introduction to discuss the extent and reasons of this crisis (if there is such a crisis); one may however conjecture that a better, and hopefully mutually beneficial, dialogue between pure theory and public economics – to which this book attempts to contribute – is most desirable.

Three more points should be underlined.

The first remark applies to the delimitation of the subject of the book; I have argued above that it was strongly determined by the consistency requirements of the pure theory option; it is also clear that it reflects my own interests: conformably to the rules of the monograph game, the selection of subjects is much influenced by proximity with my own work through personal or co-authored contributions. It will be explained in the conclusion what are, in my view, the main gaps in this book as well as in present theory. Let me only stress here that the two explanatory factors, theoretical consistency and personal interest are not necessarily contradictory.

The second remark concerns the prerequisites of this book's reading. This book has been written as a monograph and not as a textbook; this option is in line with the objectives of the series as well with the initial intellectual contract. Consequently, the book uses mathematical techniques that are not necessarily elementary; also, as stressed by one referee, the discussion often supposes a good deal of intellectual maturity from the reader. A reader's guideline provides however different reading schemes: the first scheme (indicated*) refers to the most elementary – technically or conceptually – parts, providing a broadly accessible introduction to the issues covered in this book. The second scheme (indicated**) retains the central message of the monograph, and can be used as an advanced textbook, which should be accessible to graduate students who have acquired through good education enough conceptual and technical maturity, whatever their field of specialization. The third scheme (indicated***) includes subjects that are closer to research and/or that correspond to ramifications of the central line of argument. A fourth scheme (****) adds subjects that are more distant to our preoccupations and that have been included for the sake of completeness. The letters T or C signal that the corresponding (sub) section has a mainly technical (T) or conceptual (C) character (they are only used for (***) or (****) sections). Finally the indications given in the table of contents provide, when necessary, rough aggregates, for sections, of the different difficulties of subsections.

The last remark concerns the mathematical prerequisites. The book assumes a knowledge of algebra, calculus and topology that is provided by most internationally recognised graduate programs in economics. The Mathematical appendix has two parts: the first one gives definitions and results in differential topology that are outside the scope of standard graduate programs but that are useful in chapter 2. The second one is a selected remainder of results that are either intensively used here or possibly less well known.

# Acknowledgements

The writing of this monograph has been a long venture with which three editors of the series F. Hahn, J.M. Grandmont and A. Dixit have been associated. I am grateful to them for their support. I have a particular debt to F. Hahn and A. Dixit. F. Hahn convinced me to undertake this project, read several early pieces and went on encouraging it all along. I was most sensitive, here as elsewhere, to his intellectual enthusiasm. The pure theory style of the output reflects his initial influence as well as my own inclination. This monograph also owes much to A. Dixit. His warm encouragement and expert suggestions were decisive in triggering the completion of the manuscript. Later, he provided generous and precious advice.

My interest in public economics, which this book exemplifies, certainly reflects an economic education much influenced by the tradition of the French 'ingénieurs économistes'. This tradition goes back at least to J. Dupuit. I was exposed to it directly through the reading of the work of M. Allais, E. Malinvaud and more particularly M. Boiteux and S. Kolm but also indirectly through the intellectual influence of a 'connoisseur' of the tradition, J.H. Drèze.

The pioneering work of P. Diamond and J. Mirrlees, who have applied the second best optimization techniques developed by Samuelson and Boiteux (among others) to taxation problems, is the main starting point of the reflection of this monograph. Indeed the model under consideration here is mainly the so called Diamond–Mirrlees model and Diamond–Mirrlees's early results on optimal taxation are reported, mainly in section 5 of chapter 3.

Although a more complete assessment of the relationship of the content of the book with the literature is postponed to the bibliographical note that appears at the end of each chapter, some direct preliminary acknowledgement of other key intellectual connections should be made at the outset.

First, this book relies much on a number of previous co-authored contributions. I have then a particular debt to my friends and co-authors

F. Fogelman, G. Fuchs, M. Jerison, C. Oddou, M. Quinzii, K. Roberts and J. Tirole. Working with them was for me both enjoyable and fruitful. They have some responsibility for the content of this book although the usual disclaimer, concerning mistakes, applies.

Second, my understanding of the issues covered here has much benefited from my familiarity with the written work of (but also often from discussion with) A. Atkinson, A. Dixit, J.H. Drèze, J. Stiglitz, S. Kolm for the public economic aspects, P. Dasgupta, J. Green, P. Hammond, L. Hurwicz, J.J. Laffont, E. Maskin for incentives theory, Y. Balasko, G. Debreu, E. Dierker and A. Mas Colell for general equilibrium.

Third, close relationships of the results reported here with the work of P. Hammond (chapter 1) and J. Greenberg–S. Weber (chapter 4) (besides Diamond–Mirrlees in chapter 3) should be stressed.

Thanks are also due to those who read parts or all the manuscript i.e. besides three anonymous referees and the editors, C. Blackorby, P.A. Chiappori, J. Cremer, E. Dierker, P. Hammond, M. Jerison, T. Piketty, J. Tirole. I am also grateful to students of my 1992 course in public economics at EHESS and particularly to S. von Coester and H. Heloui.

Finally, many have contributed to the efficient typing of the manuscript at various stages including C. Eudet, H. Monot, M.T. Pillet but special thanks are due to M.H. Kaufmann and E. Lemeille. I am grateful to A. Rix for editorial and linguistic assistance.

# Introduction

This introduction aims at presenting an overview of the content of the book. For each chapter it presents the problem, the model and the main results. Whenever possible, an analysis or even a sketch of the proof is given within an appropriately simplified version of the model. The information can also be read by section, each section, or overview, acting as an extended introduction to the corresponding chapter. Finally, it provides a summary to which the reader may want to refer after reading the whole book. Naturally, these are not mutually exclusive uses of the Introduction!

As stressed in the foreword, and as emphasized in the title, the monograph is a contribution to pure theory. As such, it aims at exploring the logic of an abstract model, the stylized features of which describe a (so-called) polar world. Within such a model – again 'théorie pure' à la Walras – derivations and also comments concern the polar world under consideration and not the specific issues, debates, and controversies that the analysis of the polar world aims at clarifying. Although the separation of theory and policy analysis is a standard modern procedure, it has the inconvenience of making the theorist's logic and motivation more obscure to practitioners than it should be. As an attempt to overcome this difficulty, at the beginning of each overview a subsection, entitled 'Motivation of the chapter: issues, studies and debates', sketches a description of background materials, underlying issues, related applied studies and possible controversies that put each chapter in a better perspective. Throughout the book bibliographical references are kept to a minimum. In fact, they are gathered as much as possible in the bibliographical note appearing at the end of each chapter.

## 1 An overview of chapter 1: the institutional economics of taxation

### 1.1 Motivation of the chapter: related issues, studies and debates

*Chapter 1* mainly attempts to answer a question that is primarily theoretical. To what extent and under what conditions are taxation schemes of the kind commonly observed – consumption taxes such as VAT, income tax, etc. – appropriate means of solving the tax problem?

This question has a long history: an influential segment of the profession has argued that personalized transfers perform better than distortionary taxes. This issue still creeps into current debates on policy (it will for example be referred, in the introduction to chapter 1, to the French debate on housing subsidies in the 1970s). It can however be put into better perspective by the modern theory of incentives. This theory puts at the forefront the informational problems of public organizations and suggests for example the reconsideration of the controversies surrounding the relative merits of lump-sum taxation and distortionary taxes in the light of these informational problems. This is what chapter 1 is aimed at.

To some extent, the basic message gives support to a reasonable intuition: that the taxation base may include all the (easily) observable variables or actions of individuals but need not include too complex considerations – such as making somebody's taxes depend on somebody else's taxes or depend on a complex set of announcements. In this sense, the standard tax system of the theory of second best, that mixes linear taxes and non-linear taxes, can be justified by incentive theory arguments, those that relate to the so-called taxation principle.

This message, satisfactory from the intuitive or practioner's viewpoint, has however to be reconciled with the fact that incentives theory has designed powerful mechanisms that seem to perform better, at least in some contexts, than standard taxation devices. It is shown, at the end of chapter 1, that one key issue is correlation. More complex incentives devices will not perform better when the agents' 'hidden' characteristics – those that would be fully relevant for taxation purposes – are uncorrelated. Indeed, the most spectacular tools of incentive theory – those associated with the so-called Nash, perfect Nash or even Bayesian Nash implementation – exploit to a considerable extent correlation of the information held by individual agents.

Hence chapter 1 attempts to base a theory of tax institutions on informational and incentive considerations. It does not claim to be exhaustive: the actual tax base should depend on the objectives of the 'government', i.e., on optimization (see chapter 3), but also on the 'administrative' costs of including such-or-such variable in the tax base (in the present analysis these costs are zero or plus infinity). However chapter 1, besides providing a background to the recent contributions in public finance that stress self-selection problems[1] (particularly for studying anti-poverty mechanisms) presents a starting point for a more comprehensive

[1] See for example Blackorby–Donaldson (1988), Besley–Coates (1992).

look at the tax institutions (such as the one sketched in the conclusion of this book).

## 1.2 The problematic from a simple model

The aim of chapter 1 is to provide one (not necessarily the only one) coherent justification of the model that will be considered later. This model is a taxation model in which commodity and factor taxes introduce wedges between the prices faced by the production sector and the prices faced by the consumption sector. An obvious objection to such taxation schemes is that they distort the choice of economic units and create inefficiencies. From the second welfare theorem, these inefficiencies could be removed if distorting taxes were replaced by lump-sum transfers. To put it in another way, the model can be justified only (i) if lump-sum transfers are unavailable, (ii) if commodity taxes are the right substitutes for lump-sum taxes. Chapter 1 indeed argues that there are circumstances where for some basic reasons conditions (i) and (to some extent) (ii) are fulfilled.

The following discussion of a simple model provides an introduction to the core of the argument of chapter 1.

Let us consider here a two-good economy. Commodity 1 is labour, commodity 2 is the 'consumption good'. The economy has a large number of final agents (consumers) which we represent as a continuum of agents. Each agent has preferences depending upon a one-dimensional characteristic described by a parameter $\theta (\theta \in [0,1])$. Then, household $\theta$'s preferences over the bundle consumption–labour $(c,l)$ are represented by a concave utility function $u(c, l, \theta)$. At this stage of the analysis, the exact nature of $\theta$ and $l$ is not essential. For example, $\theta$ might be a personal productivity parameter,[2] which multiplied by the labour time effectively supplied (effective labour) would determine the quantity $l$ of 'efficient labour'. The production sector is in charge of constant returns to scale techniques which, in the setting just sketched, transform one unit of labour into one unit of consumption. Let $(c(\theta), l(\theta))$ be the consumption – labour bundle of $\theta$. If there is a continuum of characteristics distributed as described by some probability measure $\mu$, then the scarcity constraint can be written

$$\int c(\theta) d\mu \leq \int l(\theta) d\mu \tag{1}$$

Again, the fact that the individual utility function depends upon $\theta$ may describe differences in tastes but may also reflect – as in the just sketched productivity setting – the fact that agents of different productivities find it

[2] As in Mirrlees (1971).

unequally difficult to supply a given amount of 'efficient labour' (since this amount involves different numbers of hours of effective labour time).

Consider a utilitarian planner, whose social optimization problem would consist in maximizing $\int u(c(\theta), l(\theta), \theta) d\mu$ under the scarcity constraint(s).

The solution consists of a vector function that associates to every $\theta$ a bundle consumption – (efficient) labour. It is a **first-best optimum** in the sense that it is only constrained by scarcity of resources and technological limitations.

In fact, it is well known – since this follows from the second welfare theorem – that the optimum can be decentralized, i.e., can obtain as the outcome of a market organization. This market solution necessarily has the following features. First, the market price of the consumption good being set equal to one, the wage (of 'efficient labour') is also one. Equivalently in the productivity interpretation of the model the wage of 'efficient labour' is one and the wage of a unit of effective labour equals $\theta$, i.e., its productivity. Second, the income of every agent does not only consist of his labour income but also incorporates some income transfer; here income transfer $R$ is naturally indexed on $\theta$ and then necessarily satisfies $\int R(\theta) d\mu = 0$ (the net total transfer is zero).

As is well known, the basic message behind this 'simple' story has a broad validity: it holds true in a world with many commodities and with public goods: the attainment of the first-best optimum does not require and is in general incompatible with distorting taxes.

The simple story however makes it clear that the decentralization of the first-best solution requires the modification of the primary income distribution determined by market forces. Transfers, positive or negative that depend upon $\theta$, have to be implemented. Their implementation requires that either the planner knows $\theta$ or, if it is not the case, that the agents – having information on their own $\theta$ – are willing to transmit it truthfully. In other words, the implementation of the first-best optimum requires either that the information on which lump-sum transfers are based is public information or, in the case where it is not public information, that it can be costlessly acquired, for example through an appropriate **incentive compatible device**.

We have not yet introduced the tools that allow the analysis of incentive compatibility. However we may already note that the revelation of the information on $\theta$ – assuming it is private – is unlikely. For example, if the above productivity interpretation is specified in such a way that the initial preferences between consumption and effective labour of all agents are assumed to be similar – although utility functions that trade off between consumption and efficient labour are different – then it can be shown that not only is taxation redistributive ($R$ decreases when $\theta$ increases) but also that the welfare finally achieved by the agents is negatively correlated with their productivity.[3] In such a case it is easy to understand that highly productive agents have little incentive to confess their productivity!

## 1.3 The core of the argument

First-best organization of the economy would rule out commodity taxes. Informational problems make such a first-best infeasible and will force us to rely on taxes. To see that, let us come back to the above simple world. But let us explicitly assume that information on $\theta$ instead of being public – as the reference to the second welfare theorem implicitly supposes – is private: each agent knows its own characteristic. Let us suppose however that the centre – the planner – knows the probability distribution of characteristics.

In this setting, economic organization must take into account not only the technological and scarcity constraints but also the **informational constraints**. Its study should be viewed as a subject of the so-called theory of incentives.[4] In the light of this theory, let us consider incentive mechanisms that can be used by a planner. Let us restrict attention to a special kind of such incentive mechanisms, those that are direct, anonymous and truthful. A mechanism is direct when the agent's announcements only consists of his own characteristics instead of more abstract (and possibly complex) messages; a mechanism is anonymous when it depends upon the announcement of the agent and the distribution of the announcements of the others; a mechanism is truthful when it is designed in such a way that it is in each agent's interest to truthfully reveal his characteristics.

The reader may inquire about the significance of the restriction that the consideration of the above class of mechanisms induces. A complete answer cannot be given without an exposition of the theory of incentives that is out of the scope of this introduction (or even of this book). To shorten the story, the restriction to truthful direct mechanisms is innocuous in our setting: this is the celebrated revelation principle (that holds given the informational assumptions – which themselves affect our choice of solution concept) that we make more precise in chapter 1. Also, the study of the limitations induced by anonymity is discussed in chapter 1 (particularly section 1.6).

Formally, a **direct anonymous truthful mechanism** consists of a mapping $F$

[3] This (insufficiently known) result is due to Mirrlees (1986); see also Guesnerie (1980).

[4] Following Gibbard (1973), Hurwicz (1973), economic organization should be analysed from the study of 'game forms'. One important ingredient for the study of game forms is the choice of a solution concept. The present conventional wisdom in incentive theory is that the choice of the solution concept (dominant strategy, Bayesian–Nash, or Nash) should reflect the basic informational assumptions that are made (agents ignore the others' characteristics, know it statistically, know it exactly). For obvious reasons, this introduction remains rather loose on these questions.

which associates a vector of consumption and (efficient) labour as a function of an announcement of characteristics and of a distribution of announcements

$$F:(\theta,\nu)\in\Theta\times\mathscr{P}(\Theta)\to F(\theta,\nu)=\{F_1(\theta,\nu),F_2(\theta,\nu)\}\in\mathscr{R}^2$$

(where $\mathscr{P}(\Theta)$ designates the set of probability distributions over $\Theta$) and which satisfies the following condition

$$\theta\in\arg\max_{\hat{\theta}} u(F(\hat{\theta},\nu),\theta), \forall\theta, \text{ for every } \nu \tag{2}$$

Condition (2) formally expresses that truthful revelation will obtain whatever the agent's characteristic, but also, here, whatever the announcement of others: in other words $\theta$ is a dominant strategy. Then we refer to the concept of dominant strategy implementation (in chapter 1 a less demanding Bayesian–Nash concept of implementation will be adopted).

Furthermore the mechanism $F$ is **admissible** whenever it satisfies

$$\int_\Theta F_1(\theta,\nu)d\nu=\int_\Theta F_2(\theta,\nu)d\nu \tag{3}$$

i.e., when it induces the equality of total consumption with total supply of efficient labour. This equality is supposed to hold whatever the distribution of characteristics $\nu$; in fact, the true distribution $\mu$ will necessarily be discovered so that it is enough, in a sense, to have (3) met with $\nu=\mu$. For that reason, we will often forget (here) about the dependence of $\nu$ on the mechanism.[5]

In this setting, the planner's problem is drastically different from the first-best problem: it is a second-best problem that consists of maximizing social welfare over the set of mechanisms that are truthful and admissible, i.e., that satisfy (2) and (3).

There is however a less sophisticated way to allocate resources when the information on characteristics is private: it is to rely upon **taxation systems**.

Here, $l$ is the amount of efficient labour: if labour is valued in a competitive setting and if the price of the consumption good is one, $l$ is identical to labour income. Assuming that $l$ is observable – as it has been implicitly assumed in the definition of the above mechanism – the planner can consider implementing an income tax schedule.

Formally an **income tax schedule** is a mapping $\psi$ which, for every positive labour income (pre-tax income), associates some (positive) consumption level (post-tax income).

Given the income tax schedule $\psi$, a householder with productivity $\theta$

[5] However in the terminology of incentive theory, 'admissibility' will only hold at equilibrium and not outside equilibrium.

chooses his bundle consumption–efficient labour $c_\psi(\theta)$, $l_\psi(\theta)$ as a solution of the following programme $P(\theta,\psi)$

$$\begin{aligned}&\max u(c,l,\theta) \\ &c \leq \psi(l)\end{aligned} \tag{4}$$

The tax schedule $\psi$ is admissible if

$$\int_\Theta c_\psi(\theta)d\mu = \int_\Theta l_\psi(\theta)d\mu \tag{5}$$

i.e., if total consumption equals total labour supply.

The planner's problem when he considers the implementation of income tax schedules is still a **second-best problem**: to maximize social welfare over the set of admissible income tax schedules.

It is natural now to look at a **sophisticated planner** – or the incentive mechanism planner – and an **unsophisticated** one – or the tax schedule planner – and to compare their performances.

The comparison is strikingly simple: the set of allocations that can be achieved by, on the one hand, the sophisticated and, on the other hand, the unsophisticated planner are **the same** (and consequently both can achieve the same level of social welfare).

The proof of this **equivalence result** is simple and can be sketched as follows:

(i) Consider some tax schedule $\psi$ and let $c_\psi(\theta)$, $l_\psi(\theta)$ be one corresponding outcome (obtained as the solution of programme (4) $P(\theta,\psi)$). Then the mapping $\theta \rightarrow c_\psi(\theta)$, $l_\psi(\theta)$ defines a direct anonymous truthful mechanism that is admissible when the true distribution is $\mu$.[6] This statement is easy to check. Assume that it is wrong, i.e., that there exists $\theta$ and $\hat{\theta}$ such that $c_\psi(\hat{\theta})$, $l_\psi(\hat{\theta})$ is better for household $\theta$ than $c_\psi(\theta)$, $l_\psi(\theta)$; but $c_\psi(\hat{\theta})$, $l_\psi(\hat{\theta})$ is a point on the income tax schedule – the one chosen by $M.\hat{\theta}$ – that would have been preferred by household $\theta$ to $c_\psi(\theta)$, $l_\psi(\theta)$ in the solution of programme (4), a contradiction.

(ii) Consider now some truthful incentive mechanism $c(\theta,\mu)$, $l(\theta,\mu)$ (restricted to the given distribution $\mu$). We can show that there is an income tax schedule $\psi$ that leads to the same outcome.

For that it is enough to consider $Z = U_\theta\{c(\theta,\cdot), l(\theta,\cdot)\}$ a subset of $\mathscr{R}^2_+$ and then the north-east frontier of the set $Z - \mathscr{R}^2_+$. This frontier is the graph of a

[6] In the spirit of the previous remarks, we focus attention on the actual distribution $\mu$. Naturally, the analysis of chapter 1 is much more explicit on the significance of the choice of what incentive theory terms the 'domain of environments'.

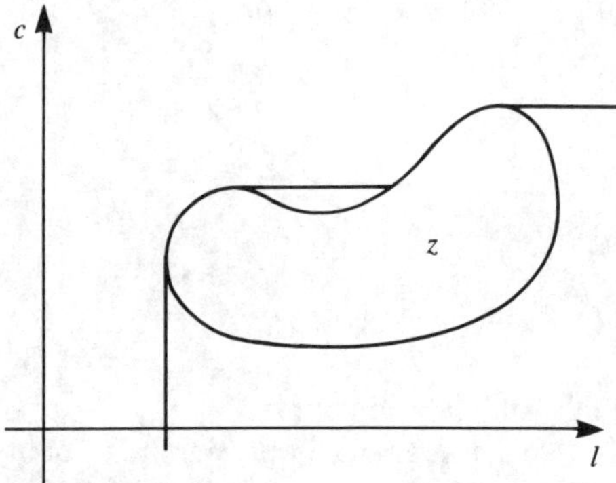


Figure 1

function $\psi$ (Figure 1). Arguing as above by contradiction, one concludes that a solution of household $\theta$'s maximization problem when it faces the income tax schedule $\psi$ is indeed $c(\theta,\cdot)l(\theta,\cdot)$.[7]

The conclusion is clearcut: 'sophisticated' incentive mechanisms can do no better in our problem than 'unsophisticated' income tax schedules. (Note however that although unsophisticated our tax schedules are not linear and can only be approximated by linear tax schedules.)

## 1.4 Developments of the argument

The preceding equivalence result is at the core of the argument of the first part of chapter 1; this argument is however more intricate for at least two reasons. On the one hand, one considers an $n$-commodity world instead of a two-commodity model; on the other hand, one distinguishes two kinds of private commodities: the first ones cannot be exchanged by households once they have been allocated by the planner, but the second ones are outside the planner's control. Consequently the unsophisticated planner is restricted to using linear taxation for the 'tradable' goods, keeping non-linear taxation for the 'non-tradable' ones.

In the just sketched setting chapter 1 establishes an equivalence result that generalizes the equivalence result briefly described here. Again the sophisticated planner, using direct anonymous truthful admissible mechanisms subject to the tradability constraint, and the unsophisticated planner using tax systems that are partly linear and partly non-linear, can implement the same final allocations.

[7] Such a property has a general counterpart, called by Rochet (1986) the taxation principle, see Hammond (1979) and Guesnerie (1981a).

The equivalence result is however conditional on two key ingredients of the analysis that have to be discussed further.

First, the equilibrium concept adopted for the analysis of the game form is the concept of Bayesian–Nash equilibrium.

This condition is clearly restrictive: adopting the concept of a perfect-Nash equilibrium, recent work[8] that applies to the present setting has argued that 'almost every performance function' could be implemented. There is however no contradiction between this conclusion and that of chapter 1: Nash implementation makes complete sense only when agents know their own characteristics as well as the characteristics of other agents. The concept of a Bayesian–Nash equilibrium adopted here reflects a more restrictive informational hypothesis, i.e., that each agent knows his own characteristics and only the distribution of characteristics of others.

Second, the sophisticated planner is supposed to use direct anonymous truthful mechanisms rather than mechanisms that will rely upon a more complex set of messages and/or will not be anonymous.

As mentioned, a general principle of incentive theory, the revelation principle, holds (for Bayesian–Nash implementation) and indicates that there is no loss of generality in taking direct truthful mechanisms. There is however a problem with anonymity: it is discussed at length in the last section of chapter 1. The main conclusion is that the kind of anonymity assumed here involves no loss of generality for the analysis of incentives only when there is **no correlation between the individual characteristics of agents**: this obtains if for example each agent's characteristics are the outcomes of independent drawings from the same basket. In that case the profile of characteristics is the realization of an infinite number of independent and identically distributed random variables and a variant of the equivalent result emphasized holds true here.

The above informal analysis gives the appropriate flavour of the content of chapter 1. However the intuition that is conveyed here cannot be made rigorous without some precautions: this involves distinguishing the names of agents from their characteristics, making assumptions of how goods are traded outside the planner's control, making explicit the implicit assumptions on observability etc. It follows that the reading of chapter 1 requires more caution than its informal summary suggests.

In conclusion chapter 1 establishes general conditions under which the kind of organization described in the model of this book – which we associated with unsophisticated planning – is the best that can be achieved. However, the model considered in this book only considers linear taxation – or 'affine' taxation when a uniform lump sum is considered – when the equivalence result supports the use of non-linear taxation for a subset of

[8] See for example Moore (1992).

commodities. In other words, the model of this book assumes the simplification **of linearization** (although some considerations of non-linearities are reintroduced at the end of chapter 4). But subject to this simplification, and under the basic conditions that the analysis in chapter 1 make explicit, the model is the right model to think about the allocation of resources in the world of private information we are considering.

## 2 A presentation of the model

Let us now introduce the basic model considered in this monograph, in particular in chapters 2 and 3. This model is a variant of the model of taxation studied by Diamond–Mirrlees in their pioneering study (1971); it is indeed known as **the Diamond–Mirrlees model**. It can be described as follows.

The economy has $n$ private commodities indexed by $l=1\ldots n$ and one public good. Consumers indexed by $i=1\ldots m$ have preferences represented by a strictly quasi-concave utility function $U_i(z_i, y_0')$, where $z_i$ is the vector of net trades of consumer $i$ and $y_0'$ the level of public good available in the society.

The economy consists of two firms with standard convex technologies: the first one is a private firm that has the standard competitive profit-maximizing behaviour, the second one is a semi-public firm that produces the specified level of public good $y_0'$ together with the input vector $-y_0''$ (in other words the net output vector is $y_0''$) that is chosen in order to minimize the production cost of $y_0'$ units of the public good.

The central feature of the model is that consumers, on the one hand, and producers, on the other, are faced with two different price systems. The first one, the **consumption price system**, is denoted $\pi$, the second one, the **production price system**, is denoted $p$. Both are vectors of $\mathscr{R}^n_+$. The difference $T=\pi-p$ is a vector of $\mathscr{R}^n$, called the tax vector or sometimes the vector of specific taxes.

Let us call $d_i(\pi, y_0')$ the excess demand of consumer $i$ when the public good level is $y_0'$ and the consumption price vector is $\pi$; let us call $\eta_1(p)$ and $\eta_0(y_0', p)$, respectively, the profit-maximizing and cost-minimizing supply function of the private and semi-public firm.

Formally:

$d_i(\pi, y_0')$ is the solution of the programme

$$\max U_i(z_i, y_0') | \pi . z_i \leq 0$$

$\eta_1(p)$ is the solution (also assumed to be unique) of

$$\max p.y_1'', y_1'' \in Y_1 \subset \mathscr{R}^n$$

where $Y_1$ is the private production set.
$\eta_0(y_0', p)$ is the solution of

$$\max p.y_0'', (y_0', y_0'') \in Y_0 \subset \mathscr{R}^{n+1}$$

where $Y_0$ is the semi-public production set.

By definition a **feasible state** of the model under consideration (still called a **tax equilibrium**) consists of consumption bundles $z_i$, a private production plan $y_1''$ and a semi-public net output vector $y_0''$, a public good level $y_0'$ and two price vectors $\pi$ and $p$ such that

$$z_i = d_i(\pi, y_0') \tag{6}$$

$$y_1'' = \eta_1(p) \tag{7}$$

$$y_0'' = \eta_0(y_0', p) \tag{8}$$

$$\sum_i z_i \leq y_1'' + y_0'' \tag{9}$$

Most often (7) and (8) will be aggregated in

$$y'' = \eta(y_0', p) \tag{7'}$$

where by definition $\eta$ will be $\eta_1 + \eta_0$. Then (9) will become

$$\Sigma_i z_i \leq y'' \tag{9'}$$

(when the equality is strict, we say that the equilibrium is tight or strict).

It should be noted here that the implementation of a tax equilibrium, as defined here, requires some kind of government intervention in order

- to decide upon the public good level
- to disconnect consumption and production prices: such a disconnection is operated, in the real world, through tax systems that allow for differentiated (linear) taxation of different goods. A VAT system (with differentiated rates) is the most obvious example of such tax systems. Note, however, that with a tax equilibrium of the kind considered here, tax 'rates' will generally differ across all commodities, so that the taxation complexity that is required for the implementation of such tax equilibria exceeds the real world complexity.
- to impose a 100 per cent tax on the pure profit of the production sector. This policy assumption is implicit to our formulation where the consumer's demand does not depend upon the producers' profit. Again this is a polar assumption which is however well in line with the more basic justifications of the model that are explored in chapter 1.

A more complex version of the model (incorporating other policy tools such as a uniform lump-sum transfer and several public goods) is presented at the beginning of chapter 2. This presentation includes a detailed discussion of the policy assumptions. In particular, it focuses attention on the question of the budget balance. Our definition of tax equilibrium does not refer to **budget balance** but only (through (9)) to market clearing. A simple but important proposition states that the budget – as usually defined, i.e., here as tax receipts (commodity plus profit taxes) minus cost of public good – is balanced whenever markets clear. This is proposition 1 in chapter 2. This fact may be viewed as the analogue in this model of Walras' law in an Arrow–Debreu general equilibrium model: Walras' law says that when $n-1$ markets clear, the $n^{\text{th}}$ also clears; proposition 1 says that when all markets clear then the government budget is balanced. In a world where resources are raised from the economy by the government, market clearing is possible only when the government subtracts from households, through taxation, the amount of purchasing power that is adequate to finance public goods.

An interesting feature of the tax equilibrium concept just defined is that quantities are unchanged through independent changes of **normalization** of production and consumption **prices**. This suggests interesting questions: is the concept of more taxed or less taxed commodities meaningful? Can we say that the tax distortion is higher in one tax equilibrium than in another one? Why is the budget balance property preserved when changes in normalization modify all the components of the budget? All these questions are carefully discussed at the beginning of chapter 2.

## 3 An overview of chapter 2: positive economics

### 3.1 Motivation of the chapter: related issues studies and debates

*Chapter 2* provides a standard theoretical study of a general equilibrium model. But this general equilibrium model which reflects the informational considerations analysed in chapter 1, is a model with taxes.

The standard theoretical questions of a positive economics study are raised here: does there exist an equilibrium? Is it unique? How is it modified when taxes change? The existence, uniqueness and comparative static properties more basically reflect the 'geometry' of the set of tax equilibria or, if one prefers, its so-called structure. Indeed the study of this structure, first locally and then globally, is the founding stone of the analysis of the chapter.

The questions raised in this chapter are familiar to theorists. They will find hopefully challenging problems and results – on the connectedness and the uniqueness questions. Theoretical interest should also be attracted by the fact that the model is well grounded and the fact that the simplicity of its structure is likely to make it a useful milestone for further generalizations.

The reasons why public finance economists should be concerned by the theoretical results of chapter 2 are twofold: the model in its present version encompasses specific models that have been used in different sectors of public finance – corporate income taxation, consumption taxation – thus in some cases enriching previously existing knowledge of these specific models. Also, the model encompasses many variants of the general equilibrium computable models which have been extensively used in applied studies in the last fifteen years. These computable general equilibrium models actually make a number of specific assumptions (for example they assume simple preferences) although the theoretical approach pursued here gives little attention to special cases. Even if there is some gap between the different perspectives, that is unfilled here, the general results of chapter 2 ought to be of concern to practitioners of computable general equilibrium models.

### 3.2 The local structure

Let us come back to the definition of a tax equilibrium in the simplified version of the Diamond–Mirrlees model that has been taken above. A more compact version of conditions (6) to (9) obtains if we identify an equilibrium with the two vectors of $\mathscr{R}^n_+$, and a number $y_0'$, i.e., the consumption and production price vectors and the public good level. Then a tax equilibrium consists of $(p, \pi, y_0')$ such that

$$\sum_i d_i(\pi, y_0') \leq \eta(y_0', p) \tag{10}$$

In fact, we are mainly interested in **tight** equilibria, i.e., those that satisfy

$$\sum_i d_i(\pi, y_0') = \eta(y_0', p) \tag{11}$$

The set of tight tax equilibria is then identified with the set of $(p, \pi, y_0')$ that satisfy (11).

One of the main objectives of the chapter is to analyse the structure of tax equilibria or in other words to understand the geometry – in the space of $p, \pi, y_0'$ – of the set of tax equilibria.

Section 2.2 makes the first step in this direction by focusing attention on the **local structure** of the set: its objective is to describe the set of tax equilibria that are 'close' to an initially given tight tax equilibrium.

The core of the argument of this section can be presented in an easy way if we simplify the model under consideration here. First, let us ignore the public good in such a way that the set of tax equilibria consists of $(\pi,p)$ satisfying

$$\sum_i d_i(\pi) - \eta(p) = 0 \tag{12}$$

or calling $d \overset{\text{def}}{=} \sum d_i$

$$d(\pi) - \eta(p) = 0 \tag{12'}$$

Second, let us assume – although it contradicts the previous hypothesis of a single valued supply correspondence – that the private production set coincides with a portion of a hyperplane – at least in the neighbourhood of the initial production plan we are considering. The normal vector of this hyperplane is $p_0$, the production price vector associated with our initial tax equilibrium.

An infinitesimal change $d\pi$ is feasible – in the sense that it leads from the initial tight equilibrium $(\pi^0, p^0)$ to another tax equilibrium $(\pi^0 + d\pi, p^0)$ if and only if

$$(p_1^0, \dots p_n^0) \begin{pmatrix} \frac{\partial d_1}{\partial \pi_1} \cdots \frac{\partial d_1}{\partial \pi_n} \\ \frac{\partial d_n}{\partial \pi_1} \cdots \frac{\partial d_n}{\partial \pi_n} \end{pmatrix}_{(0)} \begin{pmatrix} d\pi_1 \\ \vdots \\ d\pi_n \end{pmatrix} = 0 \tag{13}$$

In more compact form (13) is written

$$p^0.(\partial_\pi d)_{(0)}.d\pi = 0 \tag{14}$$

when $\partial_\pi d$ is the Jacobian matrix of total demand in $\pi^0$ (as made explicit in (13)).

Also considering the vector $\Phi(p^0, \pi^0) \overset{\text{def}}{=} p^0.(\partial_\pi d)_0$, we have

$$\Phi(\cdot)d\pi = 0 \tag{14'}$$

A consequence of (14′) is the existence of $(n-2)$ local degrees of freedom for picking up tax equilibria in a neighbourhood of a given tax equilibrium: $n-1$, the dimension of the consumption price vector when the normalization freedom is taken into account, minus one, because of (14′). Also (14) can be viewed as the **local equation** defining tax equilibria.

Section 2.2 extends the argument sketched here, making it clear that

> it does not depend on the local 'hyperplane' assumption: with a strictly convex production set, a local equation like (14′) is still

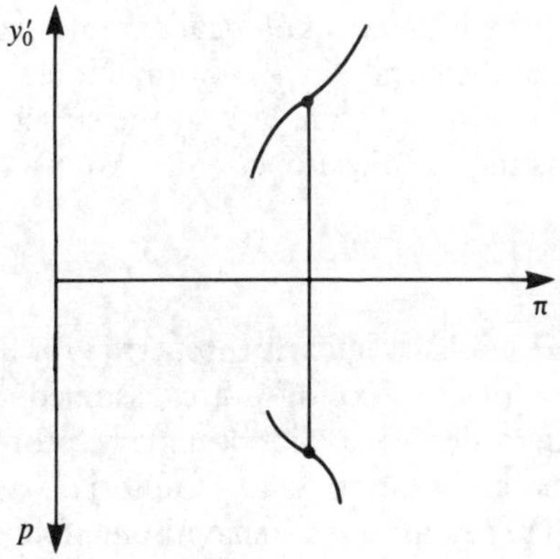


Figure 2

valid; however for each change in $d\pi$, an adequate change in $p$, $dp$ has to be implemented in order to match the change in demand (in accordance with an insight made rigorous in lemma 1).

Formula (14′) becomes more complex when public goods or other variables that enter utility functions are introduced into the model. For example with one public good, a term that can be interpreted as the generalized marginal cost of the public good enters into a formula similar to (14′).

The first formal results of section 2.2, the flavour of which has just been given, are detailed in theorem 1.

Theorem 2 considers the problem of the **local parametrization** of the set of tax equilibria. In our degenerate version of the problem the question is trivial: any subset of $n-2$ consumption prices constitute a set of parameters that allows us to describe 'locally' the set of equilibria. In the complete model, the appropriate choice of a subset of variables – the number of which is equal to the number of local degrees of freedom – that will act as parameters is subject to verification. For example, coming back to the model of equation (11), a consequence of theorem 2 is that the set of tax equilibria can be locally parametrized by the consumption prices – the number of degrees of freedom then being $n-1$, which is unsurprising since the model has one public good that was ignored in the above analysis – but the validity of this local parametrization is subject to the condition that some 'generalized marginal cost' – alluded to above – differs from zero.

The meaning of the local parametrization for the model (11) is illustrated by Figure 2 which uses a representation to which we will return later.

Finally, theorem 3 goes further into the analysis of local parametrization by making explicit the **derivatives** of the parametrization functions.

Section 2.2 provides a starting point for the analysis of the structure of tax equilibria; it is far from exhausting the question.

### 3.3 The global structure

A first objective of section 2.3 is to establish **regularity properties** for the set of tax equilibria. The basic data of the economy are assumed to be sufficiently differentiable, and, in order to avoid boundary problems, attention is focused on the set of so-called interior tax equilibria.

It is shown that the set of interior tax equilibria is a **smooth manifold** – that would have dimension $n-1$ in the case of the model associated with (11) – either when some specific assumptions on preferences are made (additivity between public and private goods) – this is theorem 4 – or 'generically', i.e., for almost all economies – this is theorem 5.

The results are in line with previous analysis: in some sense they say that the number of local degrees of freedom that was previously found remains constant over the set of equilibria. However, it is not necessarily straightforward to achieve these results: if theorem 4 could be deduced from theorem 2, theorem 5 requires the full strength of Sard's theorem – which is certainly not trivial![9]

Section 2.3.2 establishes the conditions for theorems 6 and 8 under which the local parametrizations of theorem 3 can be extended to global ones. In the model associated with equations (11), a **global parametrization** obtains when the set of tax equilibria can be defined by a function $\mathscr{Y}$ and a function $\mathscr{P}$, so that an equilibrium writes down $y_0'=\mathscr{Y}(\pi)$, $p=\mathscr{P}(\pi)$; the set of equilibria (in the space $(p,\pi,y_0')$) is nothing other than the graph of the functions $\mathscr{Y}$ and $\mathscr{P}$. Hence, the $(n-1)$ consumption prices – once normalization has been made – are not $(n-1)$ endogenous variables of the model among others. They play a special – and important – technical role as a mathematical device allowing us to 'describe' the set of equilibria! But as these prices are also key policy choices, the representation is interesting for assessing not only 'positive' but also the 'normative' issues of the model.

Let us visualize such a situation when the number of private commodities of model (11) is two. Then, after normalization, production and consumption prices can be identified with a single number. The space in which equilibria are described is three dimensional and can be represented, with a two-dimensional diagram: figure 3. This diagram obtains by representing

[9] For example, fixed point theorems can be easily derived from Sard's theorem (see Milnor (1965)).

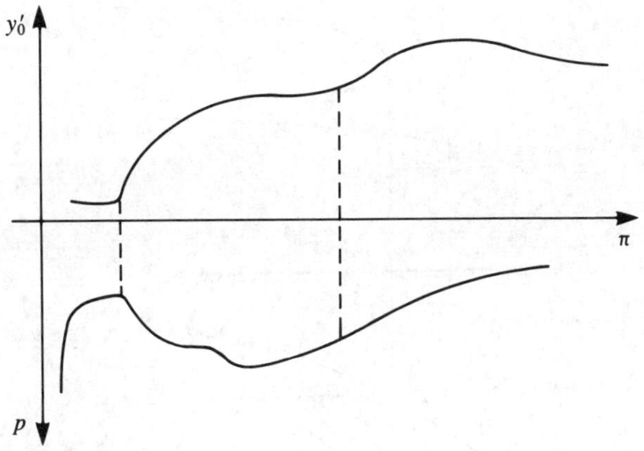


Figure 3

on the (same) plane the projection of the set both on the $(y_0', \pi)$ plane and on the $(p, \pi)$ plane and by relating them as shown above. Note that this follows the convention of a formerly active subfield of geometry called descriptive geometry.

In our example the manifold of tax equilibria is one-dimensional; the curve in the orthant $(\pi, y_0')$ is the projection of this manifold on the subspace $(\pi, y_0')$; the curve in the orthant $(p, \pi)$ is the projection of the manifold on the space $(p, \pi)$. The global parametrization result means that the projection on the space $(y_0', \pi)$ is the graph of a function of $\pi$, and the same is true for the projection on the space $(p, \pi)$. This is a remarkably simple structure that has in particular the consequence that the set of equilibria is **connected**: one can move continuously, over the set of tax equilibria, from one equilibrium to another one. Clearly connectedness is a feature of theoretical importance; in its absence, the set of tax equilibria will consist of several connected components and some of the algorithms that will be proposed later for exploring the set of tax equilibria necessarily remain in the same connected component; they may then be trapped in the wrong component . . .

A related question considered in section 2.3 is the connectedness of the set called, by reference to the terminology of the public finance literature, the set of '**equal yield tax alternatives**'. With respect to figure 3, this set consists of the equilibria that have the same $y_0'$; the diagram suggests that these points are in finite number, here one, two or three according to the value of $y_0'$. Hence, the set in this example is not always connected. It would be if the function $\mathscr{Y}(\pi)$ were always increasing, ruling out the possibility of local or global maxima that are associated in popular thinking with the '**Laffer curve**'. Indeed, theorem 7 shows that connectedness of the set of

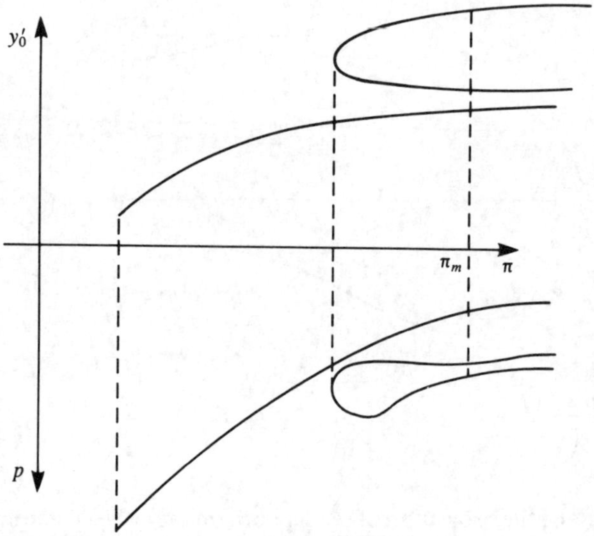


Figure 4

equal yield tax alternatives obtain when a (rather sharp) condition that rules out Laffer-type phenomena is fulfilled.

Section 2.3 is rather technical. This is unsurprising in view of the focus on connectedness. In particular, one has, for technical reasons, to extend the initial economy so that negative quantities of public goods can be produced. The consideration of the so '**extended**' economy introduces some complications but finally makes the analysis easier: in particular, it can be shown that the set of extended tax equilibria is homeomorphic to the consumption price space, a fact from which the results visualized in figure 3 are deduced.

An interesting question associated with section 2.3 is why connectedness may not obtain in this model? Indeed, an example is given in section 2.1 of the same chapter of a set of equilibria that is not connected: it is as shown in figure 4.

The set of tax equilibria consists of two connected components. It is remarkable that there are three equilibria above a point like $\pi_m$ and that they are Pareto-ranked: the equilibria only differ by the quantity of public good (and the higher, the better for everybody). In fact the example involves some interaction between labour supply and the quantity of public good available: in some sense more public good generates higher labour supply and the economy is more efficient; this synergy generates, in some sense again, different worlds. A world of high levels of public goods and high efficiency corresponding to the upper connected component and a world with a relatively low level of public goods and low efficiency corresponding to the lower connected component. This phenomenon[10] is reminiscent of a multiplicity phenomenon often emphasized in simpler models. Note also that the interaction between the level of public good and labour supply that is at the source of the phenomenon just described is ruled out in theorem 8 where preferences display separability between private and public goods.

### 3.4 Existence, continuity uniqueness

Section 2.4 switches attention from the structure of tax equilibria to the question of the **existence** of tax equilibrium with respect to a fixed tax system: a fixed tax system in our terminology establishes a rigid connection between consumption prices and production prices: formally, once $p$ and $\pi$ have been normalized, a fixed tax system is described by a mapping $\psi$, associating with every $p$, $\pi = \psi(p)$.

Hence an equilibrium with respect to a fixed tax system $\psi$ is an equilibrium, in the more general sense of the beginning of this chapter, which satisfies the relationship associated with $\psi$. The concept clearly fits experience: 'real world' tax systems – such as given *ad valorem* systems – are fixed tax systems in our sense.

Section 2.4 first focuses attention on the **continuity** properties of equilibria with respect to fixed tax systems when the fixed tax system is itself varied. Theorem 9 asserts that 'generically' the number of tax equilibria is a constant modulo 2 and that again 'generically' tax equilibria indeed vary continuously with tax systems.

Giving a precise meaning to the word 'generically' – while using finite dimensional mathematical tools – requires however some precaution and the statement of theorem 9 is made simple enough only after strong assumptions have been made.

After continuity, the **existence problem** is considered. Theorem 10 asserts that if we are in an economy when the manifold of tax equilibria is globally parametrizable in the sense of theorem 8, and if the image of $\psi$ – in model (11) this image belongs to the space of consumption prices – is compact, then there is an equilibrium with respect to $\psi$. Figure 5 gives some (low dimensional) flavour of theorem 10.

After a discussion of **tax incidence** that leads to the distinction of direct incidence and two types of indirect incidence (section 2.4.4), section 2.4

[10] It was stressed in Fuchs–Guesnerie (1983). It is reminiscent of a multiplicity phenomenon that was emphasized later in models involving strategic complementarities (see Cooper–John (1988)).

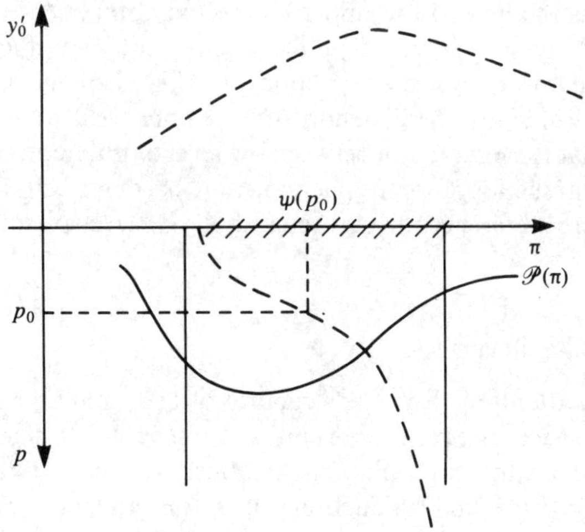


Figure 5

finishes with a discussion on uniqueness. It is first argued that the hypotheses that are sufficient, in a Walrasian framework, to assure uniqueness, are unlikely to assure uniqueness in the present framework. Theorem 11, building upon the existence result of theorem 10, gives a **uniqueness result** that holds when some comparative properties – involving the set of tax equilibria and the fixed tax system – hold true.

## 4 An overview of chapter 3: normative economics of taxation

### 4.1 Motivation of the chapter: related issues, studies and debates

*Chapter 3* gathers together a number of important and standard results for tax reform and optimal taxation. In line with the options of the whole monograph, these results have not been limited to specific cases (although later special preferences are considered in the one consumer case). However, they present a background reference that should meet the theorist and practioner's needs. The methodology for tax reform presented in sections 3.1, 3.2 and 3.3 follow guidelines of general scope. The problem is structured in such a way to make it rather easy so that it can serve as a simple reference point for more complex cases. Also, the content of the analysis challenges many tax reform ideas that were influential – either in the theoretical or in the applied sides of the profession – twenty years ago. The analysis then serves the purpose of grounding intuition on more adequate reasoning before using it later in simpler or on the contrary in more complex circumstances. The theoretical discussion of issues of practical importance, such as the performance of tax reform algorithms or the question of socially desirable cost–benefit analysis, hopefully place them in a better perspective and/or dissipates some of the conceptual confusion that the sole optimizing viewpoint may introduce. The importance of optimal taxation results needs no advocate: again, their derivation (here as a consequence of the local tax reform analysis) places them in an improved perspective. Although the analysis does not claim to be exhaustive, the corresponding sections present a comprehensive discussion of the consequences of the optimality condition both for cost–benefit analysis and the provision of pure public goods and for a desirable tax structure.

## 4.2 Tax reform

Chapter 3 is devoted to the study of normative economics. It first approaches the problem from a local viewpoint. Starting from a given tax equilibrium, one knows from chapter 2 the characteristics of the neighbouring tax equilibria; the question is then to realize which, if any, are better from a normative viewpoint. This is called here the **tax reform** problem.

The flavour of the analysis of tax reform developed in section 1 can be given by considering the simplistic version of the model that was used in the overview of chapter 2 to discuss the local structure. In this schematic variant, the public good is ignored and the private production set is locally a hyperplane with normal vector $p^0$.

Let us recall that, in this setting, the feasibility constraint, for infinitesimal changes, was

$$\Phi^0 \cdot d\pi = 0 \tag{14'}$$

where $\Phi^0 = p^0 \cdot (\partial_\pi d)_0$ is a vector of $\mathscr{R}^n$, the product of the row vector $p^0$ and of the jacobian matrix of total excess demand.

Hence, starting from $(p^0, \pi^0)$, neighbouring tight equilibria are here of the form $(p^0, \pi^0 + d\pi)$ where $d\pi$ satisfies (14′).

In order to include neighbouring equilibria that would not be tight, let us weaken the feasibility constraint (14′) to (15)

$$\Phi^0 \cdot d\pi \leq 0 \tag{15}$$

What about the normative properties of these equilibria? Let us consider the cost change of the net trade vector of household $i$: it is $z_i^0 \cdot d\pi$. Intuition, here supported by a straightforward argument in consumer theory, strongly suggests that the change $d\pi$ will improve household $i$'s welfare if

$$z_i^0 \cdot d\pi < 0 \tag{16}$$

Now an (infinitesimal) change $d\pi$ that satisfies (15) and (16) for every $i$ is both **feasible** and **Pareto-improving**, i.e., beneficial for all households.

We now denote

$$Q^0 = \{a \in \mathscr{R}^n | \Phi^0 \cdot a \leq 0\}$$

and

$$K^0 = \{a \in \mathscr{R}^n | z_i^0 \cdot a < 0\}$$

Note here that knowledge of the two sets $Q^0$, $K^0$ only requires knowledge of the production prices, the initial trade vectors of all consumers and the elasticities of total demand.

Three typical respective positions for $Q^0$, $K^0$ can be defined.

(a) $K^0 \cap Q^0 = \phi$
There exists no infinitesimal change that is both feasible and Pareto improving.

(b) $K^0 \cap Q^0 \neq \phi$ but $K^0 \cap FrQ^0 = \phi$

(c) $K^0 \cap FrQ^0 \neq \phi$
(where $FrQ^0$ designates the frontier of $Q^0$). There exists in this case infinitesimal changes that are feasible (more precisely, they maintain the equilibrium tight) and beneficial in the Pareto sense.

The second situation (b) is stranger on theoretical grounds: there are changes that are feasible and Pareto improving but they are incompatible with maintaining a tight equilibrium. This situation leads to what has been called '**temporary inefficiencies**' in the process of tax reform and only occurs when the distortion between $p$ and $\pi$ is sufficiently large. The operational significance of this situation has to be appreciated while taking into account the fact that it can often be ruled out in models involving a set of policy tools broader than the ones considered here. The possible existence of such a situation is however a challenge to first-best intuition. Undoubtedly, the phenomenon has theoretical significance.

The mathematical theory of duality (that underlies Kuhn Tucker or Lagrange optimization conditions) relates the fact that closed cones have an empty (or non-empty) intersection to the position of the set of 'normals' to these cones.

Then, let $Z^0$ be the cone generated by the vectors $z_i^0$ and let $-$ and $C$ respectively denote symmetry with respect to the origin and the complement of a set. It follows from the mathematical results alluded to above that:

case a is equivalent to $\Phi^0 \in -Z^0$
case b is equivalent to $\Phi^0 \in Z^0$
case c is equivalent to $\Phi^0 \in C[Z^0 U - Z^0]$.

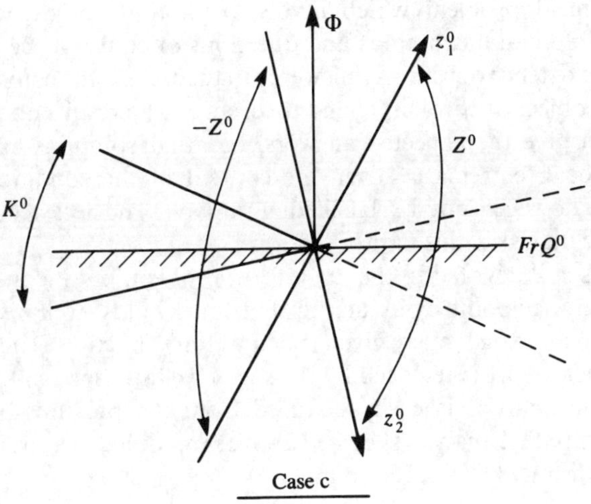


Figure 6

Theorem 1, the central statement of section 3.1, conveys a general message that preserves the essence of the analysis (of the very special case), that has just been sketched.

For the purpose of illustration, figure 6 visualizes what is called case (c) in the theorem, when the (normalized) price space is two dimensional. In section 3.2, a number of corollaries of theorem 1 are given for specific cases. In particular, the problem of cost–benefit analysis of the public sector, a problem that cannot be explicitly raised in our simplified framework, is envisaged from the reform viewpoint. The analysis, which is formally a consequence of theorem 1, emphasizes the role of production prices – those faced by the private production sector – in **cost–benefit analysis** of the 'public' sector: in particular, changes that are feasible and Pareto improving do exist whenever the production price vector and the shadow price vector of the public sector differ (corollary 4 of theorem 1).

## 4.3 Algorithms of tax reforms

Section 3.3 is devoted to the study of **algorithms of tax reform** based upon the principles that have been explored at the beginning of the section: the problem is to go from the analysis of infinitesimals, that give the directions of desirable changes, to the determination of finite changes that are feasible and Pareto improving. Roughly speaking, the local analysis leads to a differential equation (with a multi-valued right-hand side) which has to be integrated in order to generate an actual tax reform algorithm. This is clearly a technical problem which involves questions of existence of solutions for differential equations and questions of convergence of such solutions. The existence question is answered in theorem 2, the convergence question is the object of corollary 5 and theorem 3. The results do provide conditions that give the expected answers, i.e., that solutions exist and converge (to local 'extrema'). Given the content of the conditions, the results should however not be labelled intuitive! (The less technically oriented reader may skip this part of section 1.)

Section 3.4 is still devoted to the tax reform problem but it considers it from a different viewpoint by assuming that households' welfare can be aggregated with an exogenously given social welfare function. The Pareto viewpoint of section 3.1 is replaced by the **social welfare viewpoint**.

Formally, the analysis is easily deduced from the previous one: for example, the simplified analysis sketched above is modified in a straightforward way: condition (16) is replaced by

$$\left(\sum_{i}\lambda_i z_i^0\right)\cdot d\pi<0 \tag{17}$$

where the $\lambda_i$ are the social weights, attached to the given social welfare function, that aggregate individual cost changes.

The characterization result of welfare-improving tax reform can then be viewed only as a corollary of theorem 1 (corollary 6).

The social welfare viewpoint however leads to specific algorithms. When an initial tight equilibrium is not a social (local) maximum, there exist generally many directions of welfare improvement (as well as previously there existed many directions of Pareto-improvement). One specific algorithm can be designed by choosing one particular direction; it is tempting to select the direction of 'steepest ascent' in the sense given to this term by **gradient projection algorithms**. The main subject of section 3.4 is indeed the study of tax reform gradient projection algorithms.

Again, a flavour of a gradient projection algorithm can be given by referring to the stylized version of the model associated with equations (14′) and (17). The gradient projection direction of change of consumption prices $\dot{\pi}$ is of the form

$$\dot{\pi}=-\sum\lambda_i z_i-\mu\Phi \tag{18}$$

Intuitively the first term corresponds to the most socially desirable direction of change, when the second term is a correction that makes the change feasible (for it can be shown that $\mu$ must equal $\frac{(-\Sigma\lambda_i z_i)\cdot\Phi}{\|\Phi\|^2}$). This correction is in some sense the cheapest one.

The gradient algorithm described in theorem 5, indeed, builds upon ideas that generalize the argument just sketched. Theorem 6 proposes another algorithm of the gradient projection variety, that involves a cost–benefit analysis rule (for the public sector) of remarkable simplicity: it recommends a change in the public sector production plan in the direction which maximizes the speed of increase in profit, measured with the production prices faced by the private sector. Finally section 3.4 proposes an interpretation of the algorithms, with decisions on changes being taken by semi-independent offices – acting as a team – that is reminiscent of the well-known Musgravian views on economic policy. Also, theorem 7 transposes theorems 3 and 4 above to the case of the gradient projection algorithms.

Section 3.5, entitled 'Second best Pareto optima', is devoted to the study of what is often referred to as 'optimal taxation'.

A **second-best Pareto optimum** is a tax equilibrium such that there exists no other tax equilibrium that is Pareto preferred. In a second-best Pareto optimum, indeed, no Pareto improving tax reform of the kind discussed above can exist. Theorem 8, that characterizes second-best Pareto optima can be viewed as a very direct implication of theorem 1. Coming back to our simplified analysis of tax reform, we see that in a second-best Pareto optimum (denoted*) we are necessarily in the previously called case (a) i.e.: $\Phi^* = p^* \cdot (\partial_\pi d)_{(*)}$ belongs to $-Z^*$ when $Z^*$ is the cone generated by the vectors $z_i^*$.

In other words, this means that there exist positive numbers, call them $\lambda_i^*$, such that

$$-\sum_l p_l^* \left(\frac{\partial d_l}{\partial \pi_k}\right)_{(*)} = \sum_i \lambda_i^* z_{ik}^*, \qquad \forall k \tag{19}$$

Formula (19) is actually valid for our simplified problem and furthermore is shown to be valid, in general, at a second-best Pareto optimum of the complete model. Second-best Pareto optimality however involves other relationships that concern the production of public goods and the production of private goods by the public sector.

The second-best **optimal production of public goods** does not obey the first-best Samuelson rules. Second-best optimality introduces a discrepancy between the sum of the marginal willingnesses to pay and the marginal cost of the public good. The results of the analysis of this discrepancy are summarized in corollary 11.

The reform analysis has emphasized the role played by **production prices** in cost–benefit analysis of the public sector. This role is confirmed through the analysis of the conditions of second-best optimality. At a second-best optimum, the adequate shadow prices for cost–benefit analysis of the public sector are the production prices faced by the private sector (corollary 10).

This crucial fact has a number of consequences: for example, there is no loss of efficiency in assuming, as we did in the model presented at the outset, that public goods are produced by a so-called semi-public firm that minimizes cost, measured by production prices. Also, it is not desirable to introduce taxation schemes that would lead different firms in the production sector to face different price systems. Finally, production prices are the adequate shadow prices for social computations and can be considered as (proportional to) the social values of commodities.

With this latter interpretation of production prices, formula (19) can read as follows.

The social cost associated with a decrease of a tax on commodity $k$ (everything being equal) – this is the left-hand side of formula (19) – is equal to the social benefit, aggregated over households, of the tax decrease – this is the right-hand side of formula (19).

A further discussion of optimal taxes is facilitated by algebraic manipulations aimed at exhibiting compensated demand rather than uncompensated.

These manipulations lead to the so-called **Ramsey many-person tax rules** (corollary 12)

$$\frac{T\cdot(\partial_\pi d_l)^c}{z_l} = \sum_i \nu_i \frac{z_{il}}{z_l}, \ \forall l \qquad (20)$$

The left-hand side of (20) is the ratio of a numerator $T\cdot(\partial_\pi d_l)^c$ – which is the effect on total compensated demand of an increase in consumption prices proportional to the existing tax vector or the effect on total demand of an 'intensification' of the tax system – over a denominator, total demand of $l$. It is called the relative index of discouragement of commodity $l$. The right-hand side is the covariance between the net social values of income (the $\nu_i$) that sum up to zero and the consumption shares of commodity $l$.

One question about taxation formulations like (19) and (20) is whether, besides elegant interpretation, they can provide a more precise qualitative understanding of the optimal tax structure. For this purpose, the end of section 3.5 focuses attention on a simple economy with only two classes of consumers.

## 5 An overview of chapter 4: normative economics of taxation: further issues

### 5.1 Motivation of the chapter: related issues studies and debates

*Chapter 4* is mixed in content. Section 4.1 touches on what I (personally) view as the most theoretically important problem of the theory of second best: what can be said, outside the domain of validity of the second welfare theorem, of the 'social opportunity costs of commodities'? In other words, how should social cost–benefit analysis value commodities? The simple answer of chapter 3 (use production prices) relies on assumptions that are extreme. The analysis of section 4.1 is an attempt at testing the robustness of such simple conclusions. It is a step towards clarifying a key theoretical issue that has immediate relevance for the design of sound practical rules.[11] The second part of chapter 4 focuses attention on the usefulness of quotas policies often utilized in practice (redistribution in kind, rationing, etc.). It shows why in a second-best context agents will not generally select the socially appropriate amount of commodities, and offers simple and intuitively appealing criteria that allow for the assessment of the bias (from a 'social' viewpoint, the consumption is too high or too small). Without exhausting the question, it gives key insights on the real world desirability of quotas policies. The last part of chapter 4, by focusing attention on the single consumer case, provides some historical perspective on the optimization (Ramsey) and reform problems while presenting tools of (possibly) independent interest.

### 5.2 Sketch of analysis

Chapter 4 continues the normative theoretical study of taxation undertaken in chapter 3. It first moves on from the special framework of chapter 3 to the objectives of testing the robustness of some conclusions (4.1) but also to exploring other directions of applications (4.2) (4.4). Also, it comes back to the special one-consumer version of the original model (4.3).

*Section 4.1* examines directions of extension, with the objective of testing the robustness of the previous results.

It presents an essay on the concept of **social values of commodities**. We have argued that, in our model, the production prices were (up to proportionality) the appropriate social values. Section 4.1 considers a more abstract second-best model – that encompasses many existing or non-existing (!) models. Theorem 1 characterizes second-best optima in such an abstract setting. It still recognizes a central role to the concept of social values of commodities. However, the relationship of such social shadow prices with existing prices is complex. Can social values of commodities be anything? The end of subsection 1 argues that, as real prices do, they should reflect, to a certain extent, the technological conditions of production. The analysis relies on a crude envelope theorem (theorem 2) and its results are precisely stated in theorem 3 and its corollaries.

*Section 4.2* comes back to the linearity assumption that was a useful simplifying assumption of our model and considers the introduction of non-linearities of a very simple kind. They are due either to **rationing** that restricts consumption or on the contrary to forced consumption.

[11] See for example the chapter on cost–benefit analysis in the Handbook on Development, Drèze and Stern (1987).

Theorem 4 shows that in general **quota policies** of the kind just described are desirable in a second-best world. It provides a very simple criterion – involving the social values of commodities and a fictitious index of discouragement – for the desirability of rationing or on the contrary of forced consumption.

*Section 4.3* focuses attention on the case where there is only **one consumer** in the model. This interest in a one-consumer world has two justifications. First, historically, the one-consumer case has been extensively studied, either from an optimization viewpoint – this is the Ramsey contribution – or from a reform viewpoint – cf. the significant segment of literature on the reduction of distortions. Second, and because the one-consumer case has been much studied, one may expect that it will provide useful insights for the understanding of the more complex multi-consumer case.

The beginning of section 4.3 focuses attention on the Ramsey problem. One first specifies the above optimal taxation formulas in this case. Indeed these formulas can be inverted using Antonelli matrices. Particular cases where optimal taxation is proportional are exhibited (corollary 4). Also, corollary 5, relying upon appropriate composite commodities, shows that the simple Ramsey rules – tax rates inversely proportional to compensated elasticities – are generally true when commodities are adequately redefined.

Theorem 9, the last statement of section 4.3, provides detailed results on the reform problem in a one-consumer economy with offsetting lump-sum transfer.

Since the interest of the results of section 4.3 for understanding the general problem of redistributive taxation remains now unclear – whatever their specific interest – this section can be skipped by the reader at first reading.

*Section 4.4* proposes a bird's eye view on the effect of introducing **non-linear** taxation into our prototype model. Indeed the model is specialized to the case where there is only one factor, labour – subject to non-linear income taxation – and two households. The way our previous analysis is affected is briefly discussed and, in particular, theorem 6 shows how optimal tax formulas are modified. Corollary 6 and proposition 3 stress considerable, although implausible, simplifications of the analysis.

## 6 An overview of chapter 5: the political economics of taxation

### 6.1 Motivation of the chapter: related issues, studies and debates

*Chapter 5* has a more tentative character. It is true, for example, that the game-theoretical analysis of taxation that is presented competes with other alternative approaches for examining questions like the optimal size of a tax community. Ideas that emerge from the analysis, even if partial, seem however to be of relevance to policy debates on these questions. Also, in the begining of chapter 5, the assessment of the nature of the conflicts between agents or social groups delivers a simple but robust message of which tax experts, and not only social choice theorists, should be aware. Finally, the examination of the structure of tax equilibria in a one-dimensional version of the model provides an unambiguous and hopefully comprehensive picture of the theoretical scope of the famous Laffer argument.

Chapter 5 focuses attention on the **conflicts** between agents in the determination of taxation schemes. The analysis of chapter 4 has already made apparent the existence of such conflicts; but either it did not directly confront them – by referring only to the unanimity criterion – or it solved them in a rather arbitrary way – by introducing an exogenously given social welfare function. On the contrary the analysis of chapter 5 views the determination of the tax system as an endogenous problem, the solution of which is of a political nature. Hence the title, the political economics of taxation.

The content of the chapter may not meet the ambition of the title, since it (unsurprisingly!) falls short of providing a general political theory of taxation. The chapter consists in fact of different essays each of which has a different focus: the first ones provide an assessment of the geometry of the set of second-best Pareto optima, as a subset of the set of tax equilibria of our model; the third one is a tentative effort, within the framework of a model whose manifold of tax equilibria is one-dimensional, to endogenize the choice of a taxation scheme using game theoretical ideas – referring to the core concept.

## 6.2 The geometry of social conflicts

The first part of the chapter (*section 5.1*) is devoted to the analysis of the **geometry** of the set of second-best Pareto optima. The core of the argument can easily be communicated through the consideration of a low-dimensional problem. Consider again the model presented in this introduction with one public good and $n$ private commodities. According to theorem 2 of chapter 2, the set of tax equilibria is a manifold of dimension $n-1$ that can be globally parametrized as

$$y_0' = \mathscr{Y}(\pi) \tag{21}$$

$$p = \mathscr{P}(\pi) \tag{22}$$

It is remarkable that, in our problem, the analysis of welfare only requires knowledge of $\mathscr{Y}$ (since individual welfare does not depend upon $p$). Hence

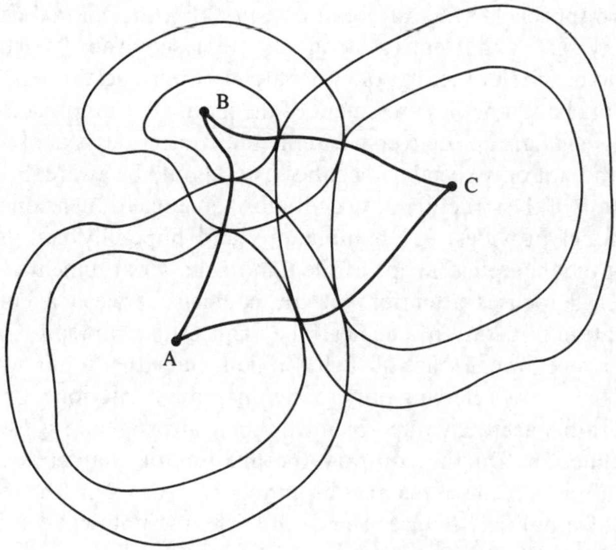


Figure 7

the social welfare problem can be entirely analysed from a reduced form consisting of the function $\mathscr{Y}$ and the individual indirect utility functions $V_i(\pi, y_0')$.[12] Using (21), indirect utility can be written as $V_i(\pi, \mathscr{Y}(\pi))$, i.e., as a function of the consumption prices. When the dimension of the private commodity space is 3, these (doubly) indirect utility functions can be visualized in a two-dimensional diagram. Figure 7 indeed depicts such indirect preferences for three consumers.

Each consumer's indirect preferences are associated with a bliss point, i.e., a most preferred tax scheme (such a tax scheme generally exists since indirect preferences trade off between the level of public good and its financing cost). Indifference curves delimit domains that have no reason to be convex.

From this diagram the reader will easily convince himself that the set of second-best Pareto optima is the curviline triangle ABC depicted on the diagram. Furthermore the diagram clearly suggests that the set of second-best Pareto optima is somewhat large (of measure non-zero) when the number of different households is greater than the dimension of the commodity space, and small (of measure zero) in the case where there are strictly fewer households than commodities. Theorem 1 of chapter 5 shows

[12] Whether this reduced form suffices to capture all the political aspects of taxation is debatable.

that this fact is true, at least 'generically'. (The genericity idea being conveyed in a rather crude way.)

The second part of chapter 5 specifies the general model to the case where the set of tax equilibria is a smooth manifold of dimension 1, i.e., when there are two private goods and one public good.

In *section 5.2*, the taxation problem is indeed viewed as a one-dimensional social choice problem. The question under consideration is the following: Is the profile of preferences over the set of tax equilibria that is generated in the tax problem somewhat restricted when compared to a 'general' social choice problem? In order to answer such a question, it is necessary to characterize first of all the possible sets of tax equilibria corresponding to well-behaved preferences and technologies. In some way, one has to characterize all (general equilibrium) Laffer curves of our tax problem. This is done in theorem 2, from which one can deduce that indeed there are few restrictions, coming from economic theory, on the social choice problem associated with tax decisions.

## 6.3 Taxation as a game

In the remainder of the chapter, we stick to the one-dimensional version. The political choice of taxation scheme is viewed as the outcome of a cooperative game: the taxation game. However here, and in contrast with other attempts to endogenize tax choices, the power of the agents is assessed from the analysis of secession threats of coalitions. In other words, reference is made to the game theoretical core concept (rather than to the concept of Shapley value).

The **taxation game** describes what the coalitions can do. For a given coalition one has then to assess the set of tax equilibria, the relevant part of which for welfare considerations is associated with a function $q^s$; hence, $y_0' = q^s(\pi)$ is the equation of the set of equilibria accessible to the coalition. Knowledge of the functions $q^s$ allows the definition of a game in characteristic form, i.e., the definition for each coalition of a subset of utilities accessible to the coalition. Note that, as usual in studies relying upon the core concept, the set of utilities accessible to the coalition only depends upon the resources of the coalition. A less classical feature of the game is the way it treats asymmetric information: it is implicitly assumed that all coalitions – including the grand coalition – can know at no cost the distribution of characteristics of their members (but do not know individual characteristics).

An important point to make is that the **taxation game may not be superadditive** in the sense that some levels of utilities achieved by the coalition members when these coalitions are disjointed cannot be achieved any longer when these coalitions are merged! In other words, the economies of scale in the production of the public good that obtain when two coalitions merge may not overcome diseconomies of scale in decision making: when coalitions join, the set of agents becomes more heterogeneous so that agents find it more difficult to agree on the public decision. This fact is a priori surprising and much at variance with first-best intuition where the surpluses due to increasing returns to scale can always be shared (thanks to lump-sum transfers) in a unanimously accepted way.

A consequence of the absence of superadditivity in the taxation game is that the core – in which it is supposed that the grand coalition forms – may not exist when some 'structure of coalitions' may be stable, i.e., immune to secession threats. The concept of C-stable solution (or Core-like stable solution) that describes such stable structures of coalitions is analysed at the end of section 5.1.

Section 5.3 provides an answer to the following questions:

(a) When is the taxation game **superadditive**?
Theorem 3 provides a remarkably simple answer; a necessary and sufficient condition for superadditivity – under a condition of quasi-concavity of the indirect utility function – is the existence of a complete set of **bilateral merging agreements** of the following kind: two agents who are 'dictators' in two disjointed coalitions find a mutually advantageous agreement in the coalition obtained after merging. Note that in reaching such an agreement the two agents ignore the welfare of other agents and that theorem 4 reduces the check of superadditivity to the check of a finite number of conditions.

(b) When is the grand coalition (consisting of all agents) unambiguously socially desirable?
The grand coalition is unambiguously socially desirable when there is always a social gain to merging a 2-partition of the set of all agents. Also, in our terminology the grand coalition is said to be '**universally efficient**'.

Theorem 4 has the same focus as theorem 3 and shows – under an additional assumption that makes explicit that larger coalitions are more efficient in producing public goods – that universal efficiency of the grand coalition is equivalent to the existence of a full set of bilateral merging agreements for two partitions of the grand coalition. Again a finite number of tests are sufficient to check universal efficiency.

(c) When has the taxation game a **non-empty core**?
The surprising result of theorem 5 asserts that when the grand coalition is universally efficient, then the game has a non-empty core.

Theorems 6, 7 and 8 provide other existence results for the core. Under the conditions of theorem 6, the Condorcet winner of the voting game belongs to the core, when, in theorem 7, the core belongs to some 'median' range of the taxation possibilities. Theorem 9 introduces an assumption that guarantees that, if the game is superadditive, it is Scarf balanced (and hence has a non-empty core); however the previous results on non-emptiness do not rely upon Scarf balancedness.

(d) When has the game a **stable structure of coalitions**?
Theorem 11, which provides a statement of existence of a stable structure of coalitions, is based upon a condition of unambiguous ranking of preferences that is reminiscent of the Spence–Mirrlees' condition in the theory of incentives.

# 1

# Institutional economics of taxation

## 1.1 Introduction (*)

The first chapter is concerned with an analysis of the rationale of the tax structure which we are going to study later. It presents a reflection on the design of fiscal tools, that gives a central role to informational constraints. The analysis has to be contrasted with the analysis of following chapters, which focus attention on tax incidence or tax design within given tax institutions.

This chapter addresses one question which should be of central relevance for those who are concerned with the foundations of the field and particularly for theorists. Indeed, pure theorists and mathematical economists have often viewed real tax systems either as pragmatic constructs which are not rooted in satisfactory theory or even as rough devices which could be advantageously replaced by more efficient systems. The underlying objection that applies, in particular, to the direct and indirect taxes that we are going to consider here often echoes the second theorem of welfare economics by stressing that, in the absence of lump-sum taxes, individual choices are distorted in an inefficient way.[1] Such a sceptical appraisal parallels a long tradition, associated in particular with the names of L. Walras, H. George, etc.[2] Again the debate is not purely intellectual. Notwithstanding the ambitious reform proposals à la Walras that advocate the switch to taxation schemes more neutral than the existing ones, the distortion issue creeps into many recurrent policy discussions.[3]

[1] The critical assessment of the hypothesis of the second-best taxation literature by F. Hahn (1973) also stresses that real tax arrangements display some elements of 'head' direct taxation. For another perspective on this question, the reader will refer to Mirrlees's chapter in *The Handbook of Mathematical Economics* (1986).

[2] The permanency of which is witnessed in the book of M. Allais (1977a).

[3] See, for example, the French debate on the modalities of housing subsidies. The issue is whether one should have 'subsidies to the stone' or 'subsidies to the person' ('aide à la pierre' or 'aide à la personne'), see R. Barre (1973).

The purpose of the first chapter of this book is to show that comparison of the different systems of taxation, which are actually in operation or which have been advocated, can be organized along the lines of a rigorous discussion. In the present setting, the (first-best) optimal compromise between efficiency, equity and financing considerations that is imbedded in the second welfare theorem does not serve as a realistic reference: its implementation would require a perfect knowledge of individual characteristics that is not accessible to 'tax authorities'. The analysis stresses the central role of these informational constraints. Relying on the modern theory of incentives, it views the design of tax institutions by tax authorities as the design of adequate 'game forms' by a planner à la Hurwicz. It exhibits conditions under which standard tax institutions are indeed the best possible – the second-best – institutions.

The core of the argument has been presented in the introduction and the reader may want to go back to this part of the introduction before proceeding with this chapter. The content of the chapter can be described as follows:

Section 1.2 presents the model. The framework is that of a general abstract economy where the consumption sector consists of a continuum of consumers. A central planner is in charge of the organization of the economy, facing informational and observational constraints: more specifically, he cannot observe any component of the vector of characteristics which determine the preferences and endowments of the consumers and he cannot observe transactions taking place between consumers within the consumption sector. However, he has full control of the production sector, and can detect any transaction between this sector and any consumer. Also, some intra-consumer transactions are too costly to be possible.

The purpose of the analysis is to compare the relative merits of two different planning conceptions. The first one, which is associated with a (highly) sophisticated planner (incentive mechanism planner), rests on the design of abstract incentives mechanisms. In the Hurwicz tradition, information is extracted from 'game forms', but a particular emphasis is put here on the observational constraints and on the imperfect control of the planner over the final allocation.

The (partly!) unsophisticated planner (tax setting planner) advocates economic organization based on the implementation of tax systems, taxes being linear for commodities which can be reallocated between consumers and non-linear for other commodities.

Sections 1.3 and 1.4 concentrate on the comparison of allocations obtained with game forms and tax systems in the case where the *distribution* of characteristics is public information and when game forms are restricted to be fully anonymous. The equivalence result which is obtained is in line with previous analysis.[4] The systematic approach which is taken (starting from the basic constraints and focusing on institutional comparisons) makes more precise the status of the result and extends it in several directions (particularly in order to explain the mixture of linear and non-linear taxes). Section 1.5 discusses it further.

Section 1.6 comes back to the comparison when the 'game form' is no longer restricted to be anonymous (anonymity being itself divided between recipient anonymity and anonymity in influence). It appears that difficulties will occur in the definition of tax systems and that the statistical correlation that may exist between the individual characteristics of different agents play a crucial role in the analysis. It is exhibited as a class of environments – which is in some sense the largest one where this phenomenon can occur – where the unsophisticated planner relying on non-anonymous tax systems can rival the sophisticated one using fully general incentive mechanisms.

## 1.2 The model (*)

### 1.2.1 Preferences, technological and informational constraints

We consider an economy with $n$ private commodities.[5]

Consumers are associated with a vector of characteristics $\theta$, which is finite-dimensional ($\theta \in \mathscr{R}^{\nu}$). (This vector summarizes all the information on consumers which is relevant for economic purposes.) So, $\theta$ describes the endowment of the consumer in each of the commodities of the abstract commodity space $\mathscr{R}^n$. It also describes all the taste parameters[6] and possibly some parameters that the planner might consider as relevant for the evaluation of social welfare (colour of the eyes, name of the agents might be included, . . .).

Once $\theta$ is known, the preferences of an agent over the set of **transactions**

[4] I.e., Hammond (1979) (see the bibliographical note at the end of the chapter). The conclusion here obtains when the game theoretical concept of Nash (Bayesian) equilibrium is used. In fact some results hold when dominant-strategy implementation is considered, but in general the timing of the game imposes reference to the Bayesian–Nash interpretation.

[5] The analysis is entirely unaffected if a fixed bundle of public goods has to be produced. It is not basically modified with variable levels of public goods as soon as the conditional distribution of taste parameters is known. (Compare, however, with the viewpoint of the Clarke, Vickrey, Groves literature; see Green–Laffont (1978).)

[6] Let us notice that the distinction between taste and endowment parameters is not as straightforward as it looks. For example, in the income tax problem, differences in ability can be formalized as differences of tastes (agents are more or less reluctant to provide one hour of 'efficient' labour) or through endowments parameters (agents have the same preferences and the same endowments, but in different types of labour, or still different endowments in the same type of abstract labour).

are known; they are represented by a utility function defined on a **transaction set** $Z(\theta)$ and depending upon the vector of transactions $z$; $U=U(z,\theta)$. $U$ is supposed to be monotonic in $z$.

Hence according to this formulation two agents who have the same vector $\theta$ have the same preferences over transactions and the same transaction set. The underlying assumption is rather weak: all the differences of the agents can be comprehensively described by a finite dimensional vector.

We suppose also that there are '**many agents**' in the economy. As an idealization of this assumption, we assume the existence of a continuum of agents indexed by $a \in [0,1]=A$; $a$ has to be interpreted as a distinctive personal feature of the agent which allows the planner to identify him: it may be for example the name of the agent, under the condition that such a name is not information relevant in the sense indicated above, or preferably a 'number' given to the agent.

We call the *profile of characteristics* the function $\theta(\cdot)$: $a \in A \rightarrow \theta(a)$ which associates to every agent his characteristics. The profile $\theta(\cdot)$ can be identified with $\prod_{a \in A} \theta(a)$ and will also be referred to later as a 'trajectory of characteristics' (in section 6). In the following sections 1.3, 1.4 and 1.5, this profile is entirely unknown to the planner. However, the planner knows exactly the distribution of characteristics in the society, as stated in assumption HI.

HI The distribution of characteristics is given by a probability measure $\mu$, the support of which is $\Theta$ a subset of $\mathscr{R}^{v}$ which is contained in a compact set.

Note that we assume that the distribution is known by the planner but also, when necessary, known from the agents.

As we shall see later, the abstract mechanisms that will be considered in the sequel may often be designed to discover the distribution even if it is unknown a priori. On the contrary, the design of a tax system – as we shall view it here – does require this knowledge or at least requires information (on the response of aggregate demand) which can be inferred from the distribution of $\theta$. In the absence of information on something like the distribution, the decision maker would be unable even to decide whether a tax system is admissible or not. HI is the simplest assumption which makes meaningful the comparison between admissible tax systems and admissible game forms.

On the production side, one will only be concerned with the aggregate production possibilities of the economy; they are described by a global production set $Y \subset \mathscr{R}^{n}$. The planner has **both full information and full control of production**; in particular, the implementation of any global production plan $y \in Y$ is subject to the planner's approval.

### 1.2.2 Observational constraints and transaction costs

Another crucial assumption concerns the observation of transactions in the economy.

First we suppose that transactions between the production side and the consumption side are observable and verifiable at no cost: precisely the planner can detect the trade vector between the production side of the economy and any consumer *a*. Such a trade vector is denoted $z(a)$.

Clearly the assumption is stronger than, although consistent with, the assumption of government control of the public sector. It implies that the government can discriminate between any two commodities[7] and recognize the amount of any trade between the production and the consumption sector, and identify the consumer engaged in the transaction.

Second we make a second polar assumption for transactions **within** the consumption sector: we assume that they are entirely unobservable to the government.

However, we complete this assumption by the hypothesis that some of the (unobservable) transactions are impossible within the consumption sector. Precisely, we suppose that commodities are partitioned into two groups, $L_1$, $L_2$, $L = L_1 \cup L_2$. A vector $z$ will be denoted $z = (z_1, z_2)$, where $z_1 \in \mathscr{R}^{|L_1|}, z^2 \in \mathscr{R}^{|L_2|}$. Trades in commodities of $L_1$ are unobservable and cannot be forbidden by the planner.

But trades in commodities in $L_2$ are **impossible** within the consumption sector. This impossibility has to be understood as resulting from very high transaction costs if transactions occur between consumers. A kind of commodity we think as belonging to $L_2$ is electricity. Transferring the electricity obtained from the electricity company to your neighbour involves rather complex operations and a rather high transaction cost (disregarding the fact that usually it is also illegal).

In fact all the above assumptions can be viewed as polar cases of observation and transaction costs and they can be summarized as follows:[8]

[7] In fact, the analysis is in part compatible with an imperfect discrimination between commodities; but results have to be reinterpreted accordingly. To give very briefly an intuitive illustration of this assertion, take the case of labour. Strictly speaking, the assumption means that different qualities of labour can be observed. However, if following the standard interpretation of income tax models, we interpret the existence of different productivities as different endowments in a homogeneous 'efficient labour', then the assumption does not imply that qualities and employment time can be observed, but only that the amount of efficient labour supplied – which is in fact the product of productivity by employment time, i.e., in this case income – is observed. With Maskin's categories (1980), both 'concealment' (or something like concealment) and 'destruction' of endowments can be incorporated into this framework.

[8] In fact, as the above electricity example suggests, for commodities $L_2$ one has in mind a mixture of high transaction costs and low enforcement costs (and hence low observation costs). So it is reasonable to expect that the last assumption (for transaction costs of $L_2$)

| | |
|---|---|
| Costs for the government of observing the individual $\theta$. | $+\infty$ |
| Costs for the government of observing the distribution of $\theta$. | 0 |
| Transaction costs between the production and the consumption sectors for any commodity. | 0 |
| Costs of observing trades between the production and the consumption sectors. | 0 |
| Costs of observing trades between consumers. | $+\infty$ |
| Transaction costs between consumers for commodities $l \in L_1$. | 0 |
| Transaction costs between consumers for commodities $l \in L_2$. | $+\infty$ |

## 1.3 Allocation via game forms (**)

Given the informational and observational constraints that we have just described, what is an adequate economic organization from the planner's point of view? To attempt to answer this question, we will follow the general framework initially proposed by Gibbard and Hurwicz for the comparative study of economic organizations. Following this framework, different types of organizations should be viewed as abstract allocation mechanisms operating in a specified class of environments. These allocation mechanisms are associated with a game or, to put it differently, have a 'game form'. For every realization of the environment, the game determines the allocation which prevails. Such an outcome depends upon the strategies available to the agents and also upon the nature of strategic interactions as reflected in the equilibrium concept which is adopted.

We should emphasize, at this point, one specific feature of the approach taken here: the equilibrium concept to which we refer in principle all along here is the one of **Bayesian–Nash** equilibrium.[9] In fact when $L_1 = \phi$, i.e., when side exchanges are impossible between consumers, the equilibria of the game form that we consider in the first sections are also dominant strategy equilibria. When $L_1 \neq \phi$, however, this is no longer true. We restrict attention to **truthful direct games** (or **revelation** games): the messages sent by agents are their characteristics and the game induces the agents to tell the truth. The literature on incentive compatibility has emphasized that such games were as efficient as the more general games when dominant strategy implementation was considered. The same holds true, in some weaker sense, for Bayesian–Nash implementation.

could be replaced by an assumption of zero observation costs for transactions in commodities $L_2$ within the consumption sector (but see section 1.4).

[9] As will be seen later, the fact that our game has two steps makes the discussion of our solution concept somewhat delicate: our implementation game has not a standard reduced form. Although one may formally interpret the equilibrium of this section (indifferently) as a Nash equilibrium or a Bayesian–Nash equilibrium, the Nash interpretation is somewhat misleading. (See, e.g., footnote 14 when this question is reconsidered.)

Although the general framework à la Hurwicz focuses on informational questions, it does not specifically take into account the observability problems that have been emphasized here. These observational limitations play a central role and impose the design of a two-step game. The first step, whose outcomes can be observed, are under the planner's control but the second step concerns trades of non-observables and is outside the planner's control.

Let us come to a more precise description, although still informal, of this two-step game:

> the first game (step $A$) is a revelation game where agents announce their characteristics and where observed outcomes are net trades ($z^A(a)$) with the production sector.
>
> The second game (step $B$) is played by the consumers and consists in exchange of commodities $l \in L_1$. We suppose that its outcomes will be additional net trades ($z^B(a)$) which **are competitive equilibria of the economy whose initial endowments are the commodity bundles obtained by the agents after the first stage**.

This assumption could be justified in different ways;[10] one will mainly stress that it is the simplest and most standard hypothesis on the outcome of an exchange process between many agents, assuming that the government has no control over this process. It should also be emphasized that we cannot avoid describing in an explicit way the second-step exchange process: for example, in order to avoid it, it would be tempting to retain the assumption that the first-step outcome bundle of commodities $L_1$ is constrained to be Pareto optimal (conditional on the allocation of commodities $L_2$). But, if people lie, opportunities of exchange appear and we are left with the problem of describing them.

Finally, we will suppose that in the first-step game, the agents as well as the centre, have perfect foresight on the outcome of the second step. This hypothesis is reasonable as soon as we do not want to make the design of the allocation dependent on forecasting mistakes by the agents. However, we have to face the usual problem created by the perfect foresight assumption when the outcome is multi-valued (as it may be here in the second step).

Let us switch to a more formal analysis in order to describe the first-step game.

In full generality, the rules of the game should relate the net trade of an

[10] A more basic view of the second step would be for example that it consists in a sophisticated exchange game that yields competitive outcomes when the incentive compatible solution is constrained to first-best Pareto optimality and when the set $\Theta$ is connected (see Champsaur–Laroque (1981) for an emphasis on this latter point). Also the requirements of incentive compatibility individual rationality and Pareto optimality imply competitive outcomes in the conditions made clear by Hurwicz (1979).

agent to his announced characteristics $\hat{\theta}$, to the announced characteristics of all the other players – here, to the announced profile that we can denote $\hat{\underset{\sim}{\theta}}(\cdot)$ – and possibly to the 'number' of the agent $a$. Hence, the net trade of agent $a$ should be a function $F(a, \hat{\theta}, \hat{\underset{\sim}{\theta}}(\cdot))$.[11]

We will restrict the generality of the description to three directions:

First, $F$ will not depend upon $a$: we will refer to this property as **recipient anonymity**.

Second, $F$ does not depend on the whole profile $\hat{\underset{\sim}{\theta}}$ but only on the probability distribution of $\hat{\underset{\sim}{\theta}}$ (that is here the same with or without $a$). We will refer to this property as **anonymity in influence**.

When both types of anonymity hold, we say that the game is **anonymous**.[12]

Third, noting that, under the restriction to truthful solutions, the argument in $F$ that will appear in equilibrium instead of $\hat{\underset{\sim}{\theta}}$ will be the known distribution $\mu$, we go one step further and assume that the mechanism does not explicitly depend upon the distribution.

We then define a **first-step anonymous game** as a single-valued measurable mapping $F$: $\Theta \to \mathscr{R}^n$ which associates to every announced characteristic a vector of net trades with the production sector.[13]

This mechanism is non-stochastic (the outcome is a deterministic function of the announcement) and makes individual net trades a function of individual announcements, independently of the announcements of others. Note that the planner is fully committed to match[14] the net trade $F(\hat{\theta})$ once the agent announces $\hat{\theta}$. Leaving the announced distribution as an argument of $F$ would allow both to extend the game to a broader set of environments

[11] Where $\hat{\underset{\sim}{\theta}}$ has to be understood as designating an 'equivalence class' of functions which includes as well the function $\theta(\cdot): a \in [0,1] \to \theta(a)$ or the same function restricted to $[0, a[ \cup ]a, 1]$.

[12] Note that the terminology differs from that of Hammond (1979) who calls such a property symmetry. The terminology is the one adopted by Mas Colell (1978).

[13] Let us notice that we could have required in the definition that $F(\theta) \in Z(\theta)$. This might not introduce significant changes in the analysis (since this property is required for 'admissibility' (see later)).

[14] As defined here, the mechanism will be admissible (in the sense made precise later) only if agents tell the truth. In the terminology of incentives theory, admissibility will be required only at the equilibrium of the game. In particular if the announced distribution were different from the true one, then, total net trades might be impossible to match with existing production possibilities. This will not occur, however, if the agents fully trust the relationship between announcements and net trades. Hence the present game rests on a credible commitment of the planner to match in any case the promises of the mechanism, e.g., by importing goods if necessary (see, however, section 1.5). Note that a commitment of a similar nature will be implicit in the definition of the tax system.

(see section 1.5) and to limit the commitment hypothesis implicit to the present formulation. However, the present option has the merit of being symmetric to the one adopted for the definition of tax systems.

Suppose now that agents are actually induced to truthfully announce their types in the first-step game. We can then compute the competitive equilibria of the second-step game. The price equilibria are vectors of $\mathscr{R}^{|L_1|}$ and the set of competitive price equilibria denoted $\Pi^F$ is defined as follows:

*Definition:* ***Set of second step price equilibria*** $\boldsymbol{\Pi^F}$

$\pi \in \Pi^F$ *if and only if* $\exists$ *a measurable function*
$z^B\colon \theta \to z^B(\theta) = (z_1^B(\theta), 0)$, *such that:*

(i) $z^B(\theta)$ *is a solution of*

$$\max_{z^B} U(z^B + F(\theta), \theta),\ \pi \cdot z_1^B \leq 0,$$
$$z_2^B = 0,\ z^B + F(\theta) \in Z(\theta),\ \forall \theta \in \Theta$$

(ii) $\displaystyle\int_{\Theta} z^B(\theta) d\mu = 0$

In the definition, whose ingredients are all classical, $z^B = (z_1^B, z_2^B)$, where $z_1^B$, $z_2^B$ are respectively vectors of $\mathscr{R}^{|L_1|}$, $\mathscr{R}^{|L_2|}$.

Let us now come to the maximization problem of a consumer of characteristic $\theta$; it depends upon the first step function $F$, the characteristics $\theta$, and the second-step price expectation $\pi$, and is denoted $P(F, \pi, \theta)$.

*Definition: Programme* $\boldsymbol{P(F, \pi, \theta)}$

$$\max_{\hat{\theta}} U(z, \theta)$$
$$z = z^A + z^B$$
$$z^A = F(\hat{\theta})$$
$$\pi \cdot z_1^B \leq 0,\ z_2^B = 0$$
$$z \in Z(\theta)$$

*(The control variable is the vector* $\hat{\theta}$ *of announced characteristics.)*

We will often adopt the following notation

$$L(\pi, 0) = \{z = (z_1, z_2) | \pi \cdot z_1 \leq 0,\ z_2 = 0\}$$

The constraints of the programme can then be written down more simply

$$z = z^A + L(\pi, 0),\ z \in Z(\theta),\ z^A = F(\hat{\theta})$$

We are now in a position to give a formal definition of the game form.

*Definition: Two-step **ARG***

*The two-step game F is an anonymous revelation game (ARG) if and only if:*

(i) $\exists \pi \in \Pi^F$ *such that* $\hat{\theta}=\theta$ *is a solution of the programme* $P(F,\pi,\theta)$, $\forall \theta \in \Theta$.

(ii) $\int_\Theta F(\theta)d\mu \in Fr\,Y$ *where* $Fr\,Y$ *is the frontier of the global production set* $Y$.

The first condition says that whatever the characteristic $\theta$ of the agents, the truth is an optimal strategy. In the case $L_1=\phi$ (impossibility of retrading) this optimal strategy is trivially a dominant strategy. But when $L_1 \neq \phi$, optimality is conditional on the fact that the second-step price equilibrium vector is $\pi$. This latter property holds true when all agents tell the truth in the first step, but would generally be wrong if a group of (positive measure) agents lied (even if these lies were restricted not to contradict the actual distribution of characteristics). Hence, in this latter case, the implementation concept we refer to is *Bayesian–Nash* (even if, as noted earlier, there is in the restricted set of environments under consideration, formal coincidence with truthful direct Nash implementation).[15]

The second condition expresses the technological feasibility (at the revealing equilibrium) of the first-step aggregate net trade: we restrict ourselves to productively efficient allocations by imposing that $y$ belongs to the frontier of $Y$.

Another comment on the definition:

For the model, the following fact is crucial: if a consumer lies in the first step, he is still able to achieve his desired second-step trade without affecting the second-step equilibrium price vector. If we think of the continuum assumption as an approximation of the large number, the asymptotic version of the property is that a consumer who lies will trade in the second step without 'much' modifying the equilibrium price vector. The fact that such an equilibrium possibly disappears with small changes of the economic data questions the asymptotic validity of the result. A solution

[15] Telling the truth when the others tell the (known) truth (Nash) or telling the truth when the others tell the (statistically known) truth (Bayesian–Nash) is here equivalent. Referring to Bayesian–Nash, that may look less natural here, has several advantages.

First, it is the concept that we use later on, where our basic informational assumptions are reconsidered. Indeed, the forthcoming discussion of section 1.6 will make it clearer that considering here indirect Nash implementation – to which the reference to the Nash concept leads – would be inconsistent with our basic informational assumptions. In other words, we have rightly appealed to the revelation principle.

Second, the reduced form of the implementation mechanism makes here the final allocation of an agent depend on his announcement, the announcement of others but also of the true profile. This is *not* a standard reduced form so that for example the (standard) property that direct Nash implementation implies dominant strategy implementation *does not* hold true.

(that we leave the reader to explore) would be to rule out such critical price vectors in the definition (this would leave the spirit of the equivalence theorems unaffected).

Note finally that if the outcome of the game is essentially unique in the absence of the possibility of retrading, we do not make such a claim in the general case. We only assert (in the terminology of incentives theory) that the outcome function $F(\theta)+z^B(\theta)$ is truthfully implementable[16] through the ARG $F$. This justifies the following definition:

*A **truthful outcome** of the ARG F is a vector function* $z$: $\Theta \to \mathscr{R}^n$ *of transaction s.t.* $z(\theta)=F(\theta)+z^B(\theta)$ *where* $z^B(\theta)=(z_1^B(\theta),0)$ *is the solution of* max $U(F(\theta)+z^B,\theta)$, $z^B \in L(\pi,0)$ *for some* $\pi \in \Pi^F$.[17]

## 1.4 Tax systems versus game forms (**)

### 1.4.1 Tax systems

We are now going to focus attention on institutional arrangements which look a priori less sophisticated than the two-step ARG just defined above.

The allocation is determined through decentralized procedures based on price adjustments. Transactions are made on markets where consumers and producers respectively behave as utility maximizers and (competitive) profit maximizers. Government intervention consists in taxing the transactions occurring between the production sector and the consumption sector. The tax system is designed in such a way that it is compatible with the basic observational constraints of the problem and that it takes into account the other assumptions concerning intra-consumers transactions.

Precisely, it consists of linear taxes for commodities $l \in L_1$ and non-linear taxes for commodities $l \in L_2$ and has the following implications:

the production sector is faced with linear prices.[18]
the budget set of the consumers has the following shape

$$q \cdot z_1 + \varphi(z_2) \leq 0$$

where $q$ is a vector of $\mathscr{R}^{|L_1|}$ describing the consumption (linear) prices of commodities $L_1$ and $\varphi$: $\mathscr{R}^{|L_2|} \to \mathscr{R} \cup \{+\infty\}$ is a function describing the

[16] In order to be able to discuss the uniqueness of Bayesian–Nash equilibria of this game, we should have defined the second-stage equilibrium as a function of the (possibly non-truthful) announcements of the first period. This is not done here. One may note, however, that uniqueness is unlikely (even in the absence of a multiplicity problem for the second-period equilibrium).

[17] Let us note that it follows from the definitions that $z$ is measurable.

[18] As production sets are convex, there is no need to use non-linear ones.

non-linear taxes on $L_2$.[19] The above budget constraint[20] means that a net trade vector $z_1$ has a cost which is linear, the coefficients being the consumption prices. It should be noted that the cost of the transaction vector $z_2 (z_2 \in \mathscr{R}^{|L_2|})$ is neither a linear nor a separable function. Hence, its enforcement requires the centralization of the information gathered on each market of $L_2$. In other words, when linear taxation of commodities $L_1$ can be implemented market by market, non-linear taxation requires a detailed knowledge of transactions on all markets $L_2$ by each consumer and hence a more complicated administrative organization.

The fact that we use linear prices for commodities $L_1$ is suggested by their economic nature (they are 'tradable', out of sight of the planner). This intuitive justification is formally confirmed in section 1.5 where the consequences of 'tradability' are examined with tax systems that are a priori fully non-linear.

Let us now define formally the demand for transactions of the consumer with characteristics $\theta$ (with obvious notation).

*Definition: Consumer programme* $\boldsymbol{P(q, \varphi, \theta)}$

$$\max U(z, \theta)$$
$$q \cdot z_1 + \varphi(z_2) \leq 0$$
$$z \in Z(\theta)$$

*The set of solutions of this programme is denoted* $D(q, \varphi, \theta)$.

So $D(\cdot)$ is the demand for transactions of an agent of characteristics $\theta$, faced with the budget constraint associated with $q$, $\varphi$.

Identifying a tax system with a couple of vectors $p \in \mathscr{R}^n_+$, $q \in \mathscr{R}^{|L_1|}_+$ and a function $\varphi$ we can define an admissible tax system.

*Definition:* ***Admissible tax system***

*An admissible tax system (ATS) consists of a triple* $(p, q, \varphi)$ *such that:*

(i) $\exists z(\theta) \in D(q, \varphi, \theta)$, *a measurable selection of* $D$, *with*

$$\int_{\Theta} z(\theta) d\mu \in Y$$

(ii) $p \cdot \int_{\Theta} z(\theta) d\mu \geq p \cdot y, \ \forall y \in Y$

[19] It should be noted that no assumption is made on $\varphi$. A measurability assumption will be made directly on the outcome associated with the tax system. This procedure might be criticized, but it contributes greatly to the simplicity of the results obtained here.

[20] Meaningful interpretation preferably refers to some numeraire (i.e., one commodity belonging to $L_1$ – say commodity 1 – of price 1).

Condition (i) indicates that the vector of total excess demand is (technologically) feasible, while condition (ii) indicates that it is profit maximizing with respect to $p$.[21]

**An outcome** of the ATS $(p, q, \varphi)$ is a function $z$ satisfying (i) and (ii).

Clearly, the class of tax systems which are called admissible is large. In particular we have no restriction on the function $\varphi$. However, when the set of commodities $L_2$ is empty, the set of ATS defined here coincides with the set of equilibria of a Diamond–Mirrlees type of model considered in optimal taxation theory.[22] Also, when $n=2$ and when $L_2$ reduces to the unique commodity 'effective labour' the ATS reduces to the set of admissible income tax systems of the income tax literature. Note that when $L_1 = \phi$, we will say that the tax system is **fully non-linear**, and when $L_2 = \phi$, we will say that it is **affine.**[23]

### 1.4.2 Game forms versus tax systems

In this section, we want to compare the class of allocations generated by two-step anonymous revelation games (ARG) and by admissible tax systems (ATS).

A first difficulty appears due to the fact that both the outcomes of the game and those of the tax system are not necessarily single valued.

More importantly, we cannot even expect a one to one relationship between truthful outcomes of ARG and outcomes of ATS. We will show, however, that the set of allocations attainable through ARG and ATS is basically the same. This is the consequence of the next two theorems.

**Theorem 1**

*Given any outcome of an admissible tax system, there exists a two-step anonymous revelation game which has the same outcome.*

*Proof*

Take the ATS $(p, q, \varphi)$.

We know that there exists $z: \Theta \to \mathcal{R}^n$ measurable selection of $D$ such that:

21 Note that as well as the earlier programme $P(F, \pi, \theta)$ relies on the planner's commitment to meet the demands corresponding to $F$, the programme $P(q, \varphi, \theta)$ relies on the planner's commitment to stick to $q$, $\varphi$. However, as soon as the planner commits himself to both $q$ and $\varphi$, the consumer $i$'s optimal strategy is here dominant when it is not necessarily in a true two-step game (see, however, the findings of subsection 4.1).

22 If the production sector is privately owned and does not have constant returns to scale, the definition of ATS given here supposes that pure profits are 100 per cent taxed. This assumption conforms both to the informational assumptions of this chapter and the dominant optimal taxation tradition.

23 It is important to note that in the case where $L_2 = \phi$, we do not suppress the function $\varphi$ from the definition; but it can only be a constant. The corresponding model is a Diamond–Mirrlees model with poll tax.

1 $\bar{y} = \int_{\Theta} z(\theta) d\mu \in Y$.
2 $\bar{y}$ is profit maximizing (with respect to $p$).

Define $\bar{F}$: $\Theta \to \mathscr{R}^n$ by $\bar{F}(\theta) = z(\theta) \quad \forall \theta \in \Theta$
We will show that $\bar{F}$ defines an ARG:

(i) $\bar{F}$ is measurable and $\int_{\Theta} \bar{F}(\theta) d\mu \in Fr\,Y$ (by definition).
(ii) $q \in \Pi^{\bar{F}}$: In fact, we are going to see that given the first-step transactions $\bar{F}$, if the price vector is $q$ there is an equilibrium with no transactions in the second step.
For that, let us consider $\bar{F}(\theta) + L(q, 0)$, the sum of the vector $\bar{F}(\theta)$ and of the set $L(q, 0)$ (cf. definition p. 42). This latter set is necessarily included in $B(q, \varphi) = \{z = (z_1, z_2) | q \cdot z_1 + \varphi(z_2) \leq 0\}$.
Hence, as $\bar{F}(\theta)$ is a solution of max $U(z, \theta)$, $z \in B(q, \varphi) \cap Z(\theta)$, $\bar{F}(\theta)$ is also a solution of max $U(z, \theta)$, $z \in \{\bar{F}(\theta) + L(q, 0)\} \cap Z(\theta)$. There is actually a no-transactions equilibrium associated with $q$.
(iii) The truth is an optimal strategy of $P(\bar{F}, \theta, q)$.
Let us denote $C^{\bar{F}} = \bigcup_{\Theta} \bar{F}(\theta)$ and let $C^{\bar{F}} + L(q, 0)$ be the sum of the sets $C^{\bar{F}}$ and $L(q, 0)$.
The fact that $\theta$ is a solution of

$$\max_{\hat{\theta}} U(z, \theta), z = z^A + z^B, z^A = \bar{F}(\hat{\theta}), q \cdot z_1^B \leq 0, z_2^B = 0, z \in Z(\theta)$$

is equivalent to the fact that $\bar{F}(\theta)$ is a solution of

$$\max U(z, \theta)\ z \in \{C^{\bar{F}} + L(q, 0)\} \cap Z(\theta)$$

This latter property results itself from the fact that $\bar{F}(\theta) \in D(q, \varphi, \theta)$ and that, as it follows from the above argument in (ii) $\{C^{\bar{F}} + L(q, 0)\} \subset B(q, \varphi)$. □

We have then proved that the outcome of any admissible tax system is the truthful outcome of a revelation game. This property is reminiscent of the revelation principle (that holds true both for dominant strategy implementations and for Bayesian–Nash implementation). According to this principle any abstract game is equivalent to a direct game (where agents announce their characteristics). The tax system 'game' can be viewed here as the abstract game, where strategies are announcements of net trades. Indeed, when retrading is impossible, theorem 1 is only a straightforward restatement of the revelation principle for dominant strategy implementation.

The problem is more complex when retrading is possible. The proof given here shows in particular that ATS are associated with a special subclass of ARG; precisely those where no transactions take place in the second round.

We will show now the converse: two-step ARG are equivalent, in the sense defined above, to ATS.

**Theorem 2**

*Given any truthful outcome of a two-step anonymous revelation game, there exists an admissible tax system which has the same outcome.*

*Proof*

Take $F$ a two-step ARG and a $\pi \in \Pi^F$ and consider the truthful outcome $z$; $z(\theta)=F(\theta)+z^B(\theta)$, with $z^B(\theta)$ a solution of max $U(z^B+F(\theta),\theta)$, $\pi \cdot z_1^B \leq 0$, $z_2^B=0$, $z^B+F(\theta)\in Z(\theta)$, where $\pi \in \Pi^F$.

Consider $C^Z=\bigcup_{\theta\in\Theta}\{z(\theta)\}$

We are going to show that taking $q=\pi$, we can find $\varphi$ such that the associated budget set $B(q,\varphi)=C^Z+L(q,0)$.

Take $\bar{z}=(\bar{z}_1,\bar{z}_2)\in C^Z$; $\bar{z}=F(\bar{\theta})$ for some $\bar{\theta}$ in $\Theta$.

I argue first that $\bar{z}_1(=F_1(\bar{\theta}))$ is necessarily a solution of the following programme $P(\bar{z}_2)$

$$P(\bar{z}_2)\text{: max } \pi \cdot z_1,\ (z_1,\bar{z}_2)\in C^Z$$

Suppose the contrary. Then $\exists z_1'$ s.t. $(z_1',\bar{z}_2)\in C^Z$ and $\pi\cdot z_1' > \pi\cdot\bar{z}_1$. But, as $(z_1',\bar{z}_2)\in C^Z$, there exists $\theta'\in\Theta$ such that $(z_1',\bar{z}_2)=F(\theta')$. But considering the programme $P(F,\pi,\bar{\theta})$, it follows from the monotonicity of preferences that the announcement of $\theta'$ dominates the announcement of $\bar{\theta}$ (for an agent of characteristic $\bar{\theta}$).

Now let us call $V(\bar{z}_2)$ the value of the programme $P(\bar{z}_2)(=\pi\cdot\bar{z}_1)$ and define $\varphi$ as follows:

If the set $\{z=(z_1,\bar{z}_2)\in C^Z\}$ is empty, we put $\varphi(\bar{z}_2)=+\infty$.
If not, we put $\varphi(\bar{z}_2)=-V(\bar{z}_2)$.

The construction shows that for any $\bar{z}_2$ $(\bar{\theta})$ satisfying $\bar{z}_2=F_2(\bar{\theta})$, we have now

$$F(\bar{\theta})+L(\pi,0)=B(\pi,\varphi)\cap\{z_2=\bar{z}_2\}$$

Taking the union of both sides, it follows that $B(\pi,\varphi)=C^Z+L(\pi,0)$ so that $z(\theta)$, the ARG outcome belongs to $D(\pi,\varphi,\theta)$.

It remains to note that in $\bar{y}=\int_\Theta z(\theta)d\mu$, which belongs to $Fr\,Y$, the convex set $Y$ has a supporting hyperplane with respect to some vector $p$. $(p,\pi,\varphi)$ so defined are actually associated with an ATS. □

The above statements show that the sophisticated planner (the adept incentive mechanisms) and the less sophisticated one (the tax designer) face

[24] Note that the relationship would still be more intricate if instead of the convenient definition of tax systems taken here, we use more standard definitions. The relationship is

the same set of opportunities in the sense that they can reach the same set of allocations. However, it is not true that there is a one to one correspondence between games and tax systems.[24] Essentially for a given outcome of a tax system there are in general an infinity of games $F$ which yield similar outcomes.

Several corollaries of the theorems deserve to be stated.

**Corollary 1** *Suppose* $L_1 = \phi$ or $|L_1| = 1$.

*A function z is a truthful outcome of some ARG if and only if it is an outcome of some fully non-linear ATS.*

**Corollary 2** *Suppose* $L_2 = \phi$.

*A function z is a truthful outcome of some ARG if and only if it is an outcome of some affine ATS.*

These two corollaries are close in spirit to Hammond's propositions evoked in the bibliographical note. The first one provides an extension of the conclusion that has been suggested in the argument of the introductory chapter. The second one provides a basic justification to the model considered from the beginning of the next chapter.

It is interesting to compare the outcomes stressed by the two corollaries, with standard competitive outcomes. This is the purpose of next corollary.

**Corollary 3** *If* $L_2 = \phi$, *and Y is a cone which contains 0, an outcome of some ARG is first-best Pareto optimal only if it is a competitive allocation.*

*Proof*

From corollary 2, the considered outcome is the outcome of some affine ATS. From Pareto optimality we can choose $p = q$. As $Y$ is a cone, one shows that $\varphi$, which is necessarily a constant, equals zero. Conclusion follows.[25] □

The conclusion that first-best Pareto optimality implies competitiveness has to be contrasted with previous results with the same flavour. In particular standard conditions implying a similar conclusion are that $L_1 = \phi$ and $\Theta$ is connected. Intuitively these conditions follow from the fact that the agents should face, because of Pareto optimality, the same price vector,

simple, only if sticking to the present framework, we compare tax systems with the subclass of games restricted to inducing no net trade in the second period (so that $F_1(\theta)$ is Pareto optimal conditional to $F_2(\theta)$).

25 Note how the conclusion is modified when $Y$ is not a cone.

and that the value of their bundles measured with this price vector should be the same (and hence zero for the same reason as in the above proof). This latter fact – constancy of income – is itself a consequence of connectedness: an agent would choose his neighbour's income if this income were higher. On the contrary, in our context, connectedness does not play any role. Here agents have the same budget set because of incentive compatibility constraints and it is affine because of the existence of the second-step competitive exchange.

In some sense, the view taken here is more basic (since it considers the possibilities of side exchanges which are themselves related to some intrinsic characteristics of the economy); but in another sense it is less basic since it has been assumed (and not derived) that the second-step exchange conforms to competitive principles (a fact that may indeed refer to connectedness if we consider the second step from the viewpoint of incentives theory). Again, the reader is invited to refer to the bibliographical note that attempts to put these issues in a better perspective.

## 1.5 More on game forms versus tax systems (**)

In this section, we will come back to some assumptions adopted in the model of the previous section. We shall consider the effect of relaxing the hypothesis of the linearity of taxes for commodities $L_1$ and shall briefly evoke alternative assumptions on the observability of characteristics and the domain of characteristics.

### 1.5.1 The linearity of taxes on commodities of $L_1$

In the definition of the tax system in section 1.4, we assumed, without further discussion, that the planner restricts himself to use linear taxes for commodities $l \in L_1$. Is that actually a restriction? Or equivalently could the planner do better by imposing non-linear taxes on all commodities? If we maintain the basic hypothesis according to which the reallocation of commodities $l \in L_1$ cannot be forbidden and takes place according to the competitive mechanism, intuition inclines us to believe that the answer to the preceding question is negative, i.e., that the planner can gain nothing by using non-linear taxes on commodities $L_1$. We can actually substantiate this intuition and hence show that the formulation of the tax systems of section 1.2 implied no loss in generality.

Before sketching briefly the argument, let us define a fully non-linear tax system (FNLTS) as a function $\psi: \mathscr{R}^n \to \mathscr{R}$. With the FNLTS $\psi$, the budget set of every consumer is $\{z \mid \psi(z) \leq 0\}$.

**A fully non-linear admissible tax system** (FNL ATS) is then naturally associated with a function $\psi$, a price vector $\pi \in \mathscr{R}^{|L_1|}$, a price vector $p$, and two measurable functions $z^A(\Theta \to \mathscr{R}^n)$, $z^B(\Theta \to \mathscr{R}^{|L_2|} \times \{0\})$ such that:

1 The couple $(z^A(\theta), z^B(\theta) = (z_1^B(\theta), 0))$ is a solution of

$$\max U(z,\theta),\ z = z^A + (z_1^B, 0),\ \psi(z^A) \leq 0,\ \pi \cdot z_1^B \leq 0,\ z \in Z(\theta)$$

2 $\bar{y} = \int_\Theta z^A(\theta) d\mu \in Y$
3 $p \cdot \bar{y} \geq p \cdot y, \forall y \in Y$
4 $\int_\Theta z_1^B(\theta) d\mu = 0$

We leave it to the reader to check that the definition corresponds to the idea that a reallocation of commodities $L_1$ between consumers takes place, according to the competitive mechanism (with zero taxes) after the implementation of the non-linear tax system.

We also leave it to the reader to define a precise concept of outcome of FNL ATS (in a way similar to that in sections 1.3, 1.4 for outcomes of ARG and ATS).

The 'equivalence' between FNL ATS and ATS takes precisely the following form:

**Theorem 3**
*Given any outcome of a FNL ATS there exists an ATS which has an identical outcome.*

*Proof*
Rather than proving the statement directly, we will show that it derives straightforwardly from the previous theorems.

Take an FNL ATS $\psi$, $\pi$, $p$, and the outcome associated with the measurable functions $z^A$, $z^B$. Take the function $F$ defined by $F(\theta) = z^A(\theta)$, $\forall \theta \in \Theta$. We first claim that $F$ is an ARG with $\pi \in \Pi^F$ (come back to the definition and check that $\pi \in \Pi^F$ and that $\theta$ is an optimal strategy); and that $z(\theta) = F(\theta) + z^B(\theta)$ is an outcome of the ARG. According to theorem 2, $z(\theta)$ is also an outcome of some ATS. □

As announced, by imposing linear taxes on commodities $L_1$, we do not change the power of the tax setting planner of previous sections. In some sense, one may even argue that the procedure has reinforced his control over the economy, by giving him a control on the multiplicity problem that the incentive mechanism planner did not necessarily have.

### 1.5.2 Partial observability of the characteristics and universal domain

Suppose that some coordinates of the vector of characteristics are observable. Both the designer of the game and the designer of the tax system can take into account the possibilities offered by this new information. We let the reader define the concepts of a two-step ARG conditional on the observation and a tax system conditional on the observation. With this straightforward extension of previous definitions, an equivalence result generalizing theorems 1 and 2 can easily be derived.

### 1.5.3 Extending the domains on which the game form is defined

We have assumed at the outset that the distribution of characteristics of the agents (over $\Theta$) was known. However, the direct anonymous mechanism $F$ under consideration in sections 1.2, 1.3 and 1.4 can straightforwardly be extended to the case in which the distribution of characteristics is not a priori known (at least when retrading is impossible).

To see that, let us make the net trade depend on the announced characteristics $\hat{\theta}$ and the probability distribution of announced characteristics $\hat{\nu}$. In that framework, the game $F$ is an anonymous revelation game if and only if (again $L_1 = \phi$):

(i) $\hat{\theta} = \theta$ is a solution of max $U(z, \theta)$, $z = F(\hat{\theta}, \nu)$, $\forall \theta$, $\forall \nu$ the announced distribution of characteristics

(ii) $\int_{\Theta} F(\theta, \nu) d\nu \in Fr\, Y$, $\forall \nu$

In other words, announcing the truth is an optimal strategy, whatever the distribution resulting from the announcement of others ((*i*)); for the announced distribution (whatever it may be), the corresponding net trades are feasible and the mechanism is admissible. The just defined ARG extends the previous game (that was associated with $\nu = \mu$, the fixed distribution) and is implementable in dominant strategies.

A simple variant of the argument given above shows that the outcome of an ARG is the one that would obtain if each agent were faced with the budget set $B(\nu) = \bigcup_{\Theta} F(\theta, \nu)$, when the true distribution is $\nu$. Naturally, if this true distribution is not known to the tax setting planner; he cannot design a tax system that depends on it.

Hence the incentive mechanism planner has here an obvious advantage over the less sophisticated tax designer:

> When he does not know the true distribution, he can, by making the mechanism dependent on the announced distribution, discover it.[26]
>
> When he knows the true distribution, he can extend an admissible mechanism in such a way that admissibility obtains even out of equilibrium.

[26] This advantage is exaggerated in the static framework under consideration here. In a dynamic setting, the TSP would be able to learn information on the distribution through trials.

However, these remarks do not simply extend to the case where retrading is possible in a second step. Then, the case where the planner knows the true distribution (and then extends the mechanism for obtaining admissibility over a larger domain) and the case where he ignores it have to be distinguished.

In the former case, an ARG ($F(\theta)$) of the previous section can be transformed into an ARG on an extended domain ($F(\theta, \nu)$) so that it remains admissible on this broader domain. (Again, take $\int F(\theta, \nu) d\nu \in Fr\, Y$.) Then if the agents also know the true distribution, the truthful announcement is still a (Bayesian) Nash equilibrium. However there is more scope for multiplicity (for non-truthful equilibria).

In the latter case, the fact that the agents now face uncertainty in the second period (even under the conjecture of truthful announcements by others) makes the problem more difficult. A similar difficulty will be faced more fully in the next section.

## 1.6 Coming back on the anonymity assumption (TC***)

The preceding analysis has hopefully clarified the relationship between abstract games and tax systems. The comparison has raised the issue of the initial information on the agents' characteristics (particularly at the end of the previous section). In the present section we shall come back on this question, from a more basic perspective. We will then be in a position to reconsider the main restriction that we imposed on the incentive mechanism planner, i.e., the anonymity of mechanisms.

Before doing that, let us give a more detailed account of what determines the choice of characteristics.

Let us view now the set of agents $A = [0,1]$ as a measure space associated with the $\sigma$-algebra of Borelians and the Lebesgue measure $\alpha$.

Let us recall that a profile of characteristics is a mapping $\theta(\cdot)$: $A \to \Theta$. Equivalently one may refer to the trajectory of characteristics $\omega = \prod_{a \in A} \theta(a)$.

In the following, the words profile or trajectory will be used as synonyms.[27]

The set of a priori possible trajectories (profiles) is denoted $\Omega$. We assume that nature chooses randomly one of them. Hence we identify $\Omega$ as the basic space of states of nature of probability theory and we associate with it a $\sigma$-algebra $\mathcal{S}$ and a measure $\nu$.

In the following, the conditions of the random choice of a trajectory of characteristics by nature – as described through $\mathcal{S}$ and $\nu$ – will most often be assumed to be common knowledge (between the planner and the agents).

[27] Although the function $\theta$ and the trajectory $\omega$ are identical mathematical objects, it may be convenient to give them two different names.

Also (subsets of) states of nature will also be referred to as environments and $\Omega$ as the universal domain of environments or the universal domain.[28]

Finally, we define an equivalence relation on trajectories as follows: $\omega_1$ and $\omega_2$ are said to be equivalent if they coincide except possibly on a subset of measure zero of $A$. The set of equivalence classes associated with this relation is denoted $\underset{\sim}{\Omega}$ and an element is noted $\underset{\sim}{\omega}$.

### 1.6.1 General revelation games

In this subsection, we shall define a class of revelation games that are general in the sense of being non-anonymous and of having 'universal domain'.

However we will limit the analysis to the **case where retrading is impossible**. A game then will be associated with a measurable function $\psi$

$$\psi: A \times \Theta \times \underset{\sim}{\Omega} \rightarrow \mathscr{R}^n$$

that describes the net trade as a function of the name, the agent's announcement and the announcements of others.

In order to decide whether this function is truthfully implementable let us introduce the following programme of the consumer. This consumer's programme depends upon his name $a$, his characteristics $\theta$ and on $\omega$: it is denoted $P(a, \psi, \omega, \theta)$

$$\max_{\hat{\theta}} \int U[\psi(a, \hat{\theta}, \underset{\sim}{\omega}), \theta] dv_a(\underset{\sim}{\omega} | \theta)$$

The consumer's choice does involve here Bayesian conjectures that are associated with $dv_a(\underset{\sim}{\omega}|\theta)$, a conditional density function assumed to exist. In the objective probability interpretation of the choice of nature presented above and which we stick to from now, this density is itself derived from the basic probability measure $\nu$ (or its density $d\nu$).

*Definition*[29]*: The outcome function $\psi$ is* ***truthfully implementable***[30] *if and only if*

$$\forall \omega \in \Omega, \forall a, \forall \theta, \theta \text{ is a solution of } P(a, \psi, \omega, \theta) \quad (1)$$
$$\forall \omega = \prod_{a \in A} \theta(a) \in \Omega, \int_A \psi(a, \theta(a), \underset{\sim}{\omega}) da \in Fr\, Y \quad (2)$$

[28] The rationale for the terminology is clear: there are however some difficulties mentioned later: does $\Omega$ also contain the set of all possible announcements (see next footnote).

[29] The definition is fully satisfactory only if the set $\Omega$ is 'big enough'. However, even when it is not, the class of truthfully implementable mechanisms that we consider will induce profiles of responses in $\underset{\sim}{\Omega}$. In that case, admissibility can be reinterpreted as involving the planner's commitment to meet demand outside these cases.

[30] Clearly we are referring here to Bayesian–Nash implementation. Thus the ambiguity mentioned earlier (footnote 11) disappears. However, again the game associated with $F$ may have other equilibria that are no longer truthful.

In principle $\int_A f d\alpha$ denotes the Lebesgue integral with respect to the Lebesgue measure $\alpha$. However in the following we will consider cases in which the function $\theta(\cdot)$ is not necessarily a measurable function of $a$; we will refer then to an unusual concept of integral.

Note also that when $\psi$ does not depend on $a$, then $\int_A \psi(\theta(a))d\alpha$ equals $\int_\Theta \psi(\theta)d\mu$ where $\mu = \alpha \circ \theta^{-1}$ is the probability measure induced on $\Theta$ by the profile $\theta(\cdot)$.

As we saw above, the anonymity assumption of section 2 had two different dimensions which we referred to as recipient anonymity and anonymity in influence.

If the above outcome function $\psi$ does not depend on $a$, we will say that the corresponding game is a recipient anonymous revelation game (RARG).

When the outcome function depends on $a$ but only depends on $\omega$ through the induced distribution $\mu = \alpha \circ \theta^{-1}$, we will call the corresponding game an anonymous in influence revelation game (AIRG).

When both restrictions hold true, the game is called an anonymous revelation game with universal domain (ARGUD): it can be viewed as extending the anonymous revelation game of section 1.3 to the whole domain of characteristics.

When none of these restrictions hold true, the game is only referred to as a (general) revelation game (G)RG.

In order to compare tax systems with GRG, it seems appropriate to allow tax systems to be non-anonymous. This leads to the introduction of NAATS (non-anonymous admissible tax systems).

The more natural idea in defining NAATS is to transpose the definition of ATS based on observable characteristics suggested above, the observable feature being now $a$, the name of the agent. However, we will introduce another ingredient in order to take into account the fact that the tax system designer can only rely on a crude information (at most the distribution of $\theta$).

A NAATS will be associated with a function $\varphi$ describing non-linear taxation depending upon $(a, z)$, and the price system $p$. The consumer programme will be denoted $P(a, \varphi, \theta)$ and its set of solutions $D(a, \varphi, \theta)$, i.e.

$$D(a, \varphi, \theta) = \arg\max U(z, \theta)$$
$$\varphi(a, z) \leq 0,\ z \in Z(\theta)$$

We say that $(p, \varphi)$ defines a NAATS with respect to the set of environments $\bar{\Omega}$ if and only if:

1 $\exists z(a, \theta)$, a measurable selection of $D(a, \varphi, \theta)$ such that $\bar{y} = \int_A z(a, \theta(a))d\alpha$ is independent of $\omega = \prod_{a \in A} \theta(a) \in \bar{\Omega} \subset \Omega$ and $\bar{y} \in Fr\, Y$

2 $p \cdot \bar{y} \geq p \cdot y,\ \forall y \in Y$

In 1 the important change with respect to previous definitions is that we make it clear that feasibility must hold in some given class of environments which is not (necessarily) the class of environments with a fixed distribution of characteristics.

We are now in a position to come back to our basic comparison of the (ultra) sophisticated planner relying on GRG and the (partly) unsophisticated planner relying on NAATS. We will proceed in two steps: in the first one, we will make some basic remarks (1.6.2); in the second step, we will exhibit a class of economic environments in which NAATS are as good as GRG (1.6.3).

### 1.6.2 Preliminary analysis

The comparison of the mechanisms GRG with tax systems NAATS is now rather complex.

1. Let us compare first mechanisms anonymous in influence (AIRG) with non-anonymous tax systems (NAATS).
   The problem with NAATS is that they may be defined (admissible) over a relatively small set of trajectories. However, as soon as the domain of some NAATS is large enough in order to include a set of trajectories with a given distribution of characteristics, a variant of the 'taxation principle' repeatedly used above shows that there is an AIRG that gives the same outcome over this subset.[31] However, the converse of this straightforward relationship is not true. An outcome of an AIRG, even restricted to a subset of trajectories $\Omega_\mu$ with a fixed distribution $\mu$ of characteristics is not necessarily the outcome of some NAATS. Over the set, an AIRG would allow the aggregate production vector to vary (it has to meet the condition $\forall \omega = \prod_a \theta(a) \in \Omega_\mu$, $\int \psi(a, \theta(a), \underset{\sim}{\omega})\, d\alpha \in Fr\, Y$) when a NAATS leads to a fixed aggregate outcome (we have assumed $\int z(a, \theta(a))\, d\alpha = \bar{y}$). The difference in definition is supposed to reflect the (debatable) fact that the unsophisticated planner chooses the production price vector as part of his choice of the tax system. Naturally, the difficulty here is partly semantic.
2. Let us now (briefly) discuss a more difficult issue, the usefulness of RARG.
   Consider a recipient anonymous mechanism (RARG) $\psi(\theta, \omega)$. Assume that the planner insists on the fact that the mechanism should be implementable in dominant strategy. To make the point more simply, consider the case of sections 1.2 to 1.4 when the

[31] We leave it to the reader to precisely state and prove this property.

distribution of characteristics $\mu$ is given and known. Let $\Omega_\mu = \{\omega \in \Omega / a \circ \theta^{-1} = \mu\}$, the set of trajectories for which the distribution of characteristics is $\mu$. For $\omega = \bar{\omega} \in \Omega_\mu$, $\int \psi(\theta, \bar{\omega}) d\mu \in Fr\, Y$ so that, in the terminology of section 1.3, $\psi(\cdot, \bar{\omega})$ is an ARG (over $\Omega_\mu$). Hence the choice of an RARG which is *not* anonymous in influence – when compared to an RARG that would be anonymous in influence – amounts to randomizing the outcome over $\Omega_\mu$. Consider a planner whose social welfare only depends on the function that associates individual welfare to characteristics. Even with such an anonymous social welfare function such a randomization may be beneficial.[32] However, each of the mechanisms $\psi(\theta, \cdot)$ can be mimicked by the tax setting planner who would know the distribution associated with $\omega$. In other words, the randomization associated with the mechanism can be mimicked by *ex ante* randomization over tax systems. The just sketched argument then suggests again that the advantage of the incentive mechanism planner (IMP) over the tax setting planner (TSP) is partly semantic: our definition of mechanisms allows some randomness that is not allowed by our definition of tax systems.

However the above argument relies on our requirement of dominant strategy implementation. Within Bayesian–Nash implementation, an IMP using RARG that are *not* anonymous in influence can do 'better' than the TSP (even if he randomizes over tax systems). In order to clarify this point let us consider the RARG $\psi(\theta, \omega)$.

Again we must have $\int_\Theta \psi(\theta, \omega) d\mu \in Fr\, Y, \forall \omega \in \Omega_\mu$. But $\psi(\theta, \omega)$ is not (necessarily) a RARG over $\Omega_\mu$ (since we only have $\theta \in \arg\max \int \psi(\hat{\theta}, \omega) d\nu(\omega)$) and thus cannot be associated with an ATS.

The reason why the TSP offering a random menu of tax systems cannot mimick any longer the IMP is that the mechanism does not lead to proposing a collection of independent budget sets contingent on the realization of $\omega$ (something that a stochastic ATS could mimick), but a unique budget set in the space of contingent allocations. In other words, in the recipient anonymous revelation game, the agents have to commit themselves to net trades before the random choice is known, when such a commitment cannot be obtained with taxation schemes.

3 Let us summarize briefly the lessons of this (quick) investigation.

[32] Unless the social welfare functional is linear in the sense made precise in next assumption *SWF*. For a discussion of the usefulness of random contracts – that can be transposed to taxation – the reader should refer to Arnott–Stiglitz (1988).

When the IMP considers using mechanisms that only retain one kind of anonymity (recipient anonymity or anonymity in influence), then his superiority over the TSP is not overwhelming: either it is partly definitional (AIRG versus NAATS) or relies on the ability to force *ex ante* commitments that can be viewed as unrealistic (as well as they obtain to the cost of a weakening of strategic robustness) (RARG versus randomized ATS).

This provisional conclusion suggests that we focus attention now on synergies between the two types of anonymity. We shall argue that indeed the combination of both kinds of anonymity allows the IMP to exploit the correlations between the characteristics of agents in a potentially efficient way that the TSP cannot mimick. The argument is better illustrated by an example.

Take the polar case where it is known a priori that the trajectories of the stochastic process are (almost surely) continuous. Then the knowledge of $\underset{\sim}{\omega}$, the equivalence class of the trajectory, implies (almost surely) knowledge of $\theta(a)$. Hence the planner knowing the truth for everybody but $a$, also knows the true characteristics of $a$, and he can impose the allocation he likes. In this case a first-best solution is certainly attainable through mechanisms when it may be outside the reach of tax systems. **More generally, if there are correlations between the $\theta$ of others and $a$'s $\theta$, they can be exploited in the design of mechanisms when they cannot be in the design of tax systems.** And, in the exploitation of such a correlation, non-anonymity is clearly crucial.

### 1.6.3 On a class of situations where non-anonymous tax systems are 'as good' as general mechanisms

In this subsection, we exhibit a class of problems where tax systems are as 'good' as mechnisms. Two conditions seem to be needed.

First, the last remark of the previous subsection suggests that one can expect similar performances of tax systems and mechanisms only in the case where there is some kind of independence between the (random) trajectory $\theta(\cdot)$ restricted to $A/\{a\}$ and the (random) variable $\theta(a)$. Besides the independence requirement just mentioned, it is necessary to define tax systems on a domain large enough in order to make them comparable to mechanisms. In other words, the fact that we cannot incorporate in the design of tax systems any information on the precise trajectory has to be counterbalanced by the fact that we are sure of strong compensations along the trajectory. Both requirements are satisfied when we consider the following set of environments.

(i) For each $a \in [0,1]$, $\theta(a)$ is a random vector drawn from $\Theta$ according to the law given by the probability measure $\mu$.
(ii) Any sequence $(\theta(a_1),\ldots,\theta(a_n))$ is a sequence of independent random variables.

Such a process can be viewed as a process of a 'continuum of independent random variables'.

A standard argument based on the Kolmogorov theorem[33] shows that there actually exists such a stochastic process. Hence, in our setting it can be associated with some measure $\nu$ on $\Omega$, the set of states of nature.

However, generally the profile $\theta(\cdot)$ as a function of $a$ is badly behaved. It even has no reason to be measurable and hence $f(\theta(a))$ may not be measurable even if $f$ is and the Lebesgue integral $\int_{\Theta} f(\theta(a))d\alpha$ does not exist.

It makes sense to posit here a **definition** of the integral such that if the mapping $f$: $(A \times \Theta) \rightarrow \mathscr{R}^n$ is measurable; then $\forall \omega = \prod_a \theta(a)$

$$\int_A f(a,\theta(a))d\alpha \overset{\text{def}}{=} \int_A \left( \int_\Theta f(a,\theta)d\mu \right) d\alpha.^{34}$$

This is a definition the intuitive justification of which has to be found in the fact that in any interval $I(a)$ around $a$, as small as it may be, the empirical distribution of $\theta$ found by taking a large sample $\theta(a_1),\ldots\theta(a_n), a_1,\ldots,a_n \in I(a)$ tends according to the law of large numbers towards $\mu$.

When the uncertainty is of this form, in order to check whether a tax system or mechanism is admissible, it is enough to know $\mu$.

So in the above definition of general revelation games (GRG), condition (2) becomes

$$\int_A \psi(a,\theta(a),\underset{\sim}{\omega})da = \int_A \left[ \int_\Theta \psi(a,\theta,\underset{\sim}{\omega})d\mu \right] \in Fr\,Y \tag{2'}$$

Similarly in the above definition of a non-anonymous admissible tax system (NAATS), (1) changes in (1′)

$$\int_A z(a,\theta(a))d\alpha = \int_A \left[ \int_\Theta z(a,\theta)d\mu \right] d\alpha \in Fr\,Y \tag{1'}$$

We have now to be more precise on the social welfare function.

If agent $a$ of characteristic $\theta$ has a utility $V(a,\theta)$ (corresponding to some final transactions), social welfare associated with a profile of characteristics $\theta(\cdot)$ will be $\int_A \lambda(a,\theta(a))V(a,\theta(a))d\alpha$ (with the concept of the integral defined above). This can be expressed as assumption SWF.

[33] That the reader will find in Bewley (1980), see also Haller (1984).
[34] According to Fubini's theorem, the right-hand side also equals $\int_\Theta(\int_A f(a,\theta)d\alpha)d\mu$.

**SWF (Social welfare functional)**
*The social welfare function associates to every trajectory of characteristics and to every function of individual welfare $V(a, \theta)$, measurable in $a$, $\theta$, the number $W = \int_A \lambda(a, \theta(a)) V(a, \theta(a)) d\alpha$ where in the integral $\lambda$ is a given (measurable in $a, \theta$) numerical function with strictly positive values.*

We are now in a position to state and prove theorem 4.

**Theorem 4**
*Assume that the profile of characteristics is the realization of some stochastic process of a 'continuum of independent and identically distributed random variables' in the sense defined above. Then:*

1 *A transaction outcome*

$$Z: A \times \Omega \rightarrow \mathcal{R}^n$$

*is a truthful outcome of some AIRG $\psi$ on $\Omega$ if and only if it is the outcome of some NAATS with domain $\Omega$.*

2 *For any social welfare function satisfying SWF, given any (random) outcome of any general revelation game, there is an AIRG an outcome of which gives a higher social welfare level.*

*Proof*

*Part 1*

1 Suppose that $\psi$: $A \times \Theta \times \underset{\sim}{\Omega} \rightarrow \mathcal{R}^n$ is some AIRG. As the mechanism is anonymous in influence and as the set of environments is such that the distribution of characteristics $\theta$ is the same on every trajectory of $\Omega$, $Z$ only depends on $a$ and $\theta$. As we have:

$$\theta \text{ is a solution of } \max_{\hat{\theta}} U(z, \theta),\ z = \psi(a, \hat{\theta})$$

then:

$$\psi(a, \theta) \text{ is a solution of } \max_{z} U(z, \theta),\ z \in Z_a \overset{\text{def}}{=} \bigcup_{\hat{\theta}} \psi(a, \hat{\theta})$$

We derive then straightforwardly the existence of a non-linear function $\phi$ depending upon $a$, such that $\psi(a, \theta)$ belongs to $D(a, \phi, \theta)$. To complete the description of the tax system, we consider the price vector normal to the supporting hyperplane of $Y$ in $y = \int \psi(a, \theta(a)) d\alpha$ ($y$ equals by definition $\int_A (\int_\Theta \psi(a, \theta) d\mu) d\alpha$ and is actually constant over the set of trajectories).

2 Let $Z: A \times \Theta \rightarrow \mathscr{R}^n$ be an outcome of some NAATS $\phi$. To show that $Z(a, \theta)$ is an AIRG, it is enough to note that:

(a) $\theta$ is a solution of $\max_{\hat{\theta}} U(z, \theta)$, $z = Z(a, \hat{\theta})$, $\forall a, \theta$

(b) $\int_A Z(a, \theta(a)) da \in Fr\, Y$

These two properties are immediately implied by:

(a) the fact that $Z(a, \theta)$ is a solution of max $U(z, \theta)$, $\phi(z, a) \leq 0$, $\forall a, \theta$
(b) the definition of NAATS.

*Part 2 Let* $Z(a, \theta, \underset{\sim}{\omega})$ be the outcome of a GRG on the set of environments $\Omega$ under consideration.

Associate to every trajectory $\omega$

$$W(\omega) = \int_A \lambda(a, \theta(a))\ U(Z(a, \theta(a), \underset{\sim}{\omega}),\ \theta(a)) da$$

(As $Z$ and $\lambda$ are measurable (in $a, \theta$), this 'generalized' integral exists.) Social welfare associated with the GRG under consideration equals: $\int_\Omega W(\omega) d\nu(\omega)$ (which also exists). If $\bar{W}$ the supremum of $W(\omega)$ is reached in $\bar{\omega}$, then we consider $Z(a, \theta, \underset{\sim}{\bar{\omega}})$ which straightforwardly defines an AIRG. If it is not the case, $\int_\Omega V(\omega) d\nu(\omega)$ is strictly smaller than $\bar{W}$ and then for some $\epsilon > 0$ strictly smaller than $\bar{W} - \epsilon$. Taking now a trajectory $\omega(\epsilon)$ such that $W(\omega(\epsilon)) = \bar{W} - \epsilon$, it is clear that $Z(a, \theta, \underset{\sim}{\omega}(\epsilon))$ can be associated with an AIRG.

In both cases the AIRG just defined meets the conclusion of the theorem. □

Again, theorem 4 and its proof reflect different intuitions. First, the small difference between AIRG and NAATS that had been previously stressed disappears here: because of the law of large numbers, the increased flexibility of AIRG – in varying the aggregate production plan across a set of environments that have the same distribution of characteristics or in adapting to different sets with different distribution of characteristics – either cannot be used or serves no purpose. This is part 1 of the theorem. Part 2 reflects the fact that there are no correlations between the agents' characteristics that can be usefully exploited by the planner as well as the fact that the social welfare function is linear in individual welfare. Then GRG can be no more efficient than AIRG. Note that with a non-linear SWF, more randomization than what is allowed by AIRG might be desirable; the discussion at the end of the previous subsection on the relative performance of GRG and NAATS can then be applied here.

### 1.6.4 Economies with a large but finite number of agents

In this last subsection, we touch on a last important point for our comparison of mechanisms with tax systems. We refer the reader to the bibliographical note for going beyond this sketchy presentation.

The results on the 'welfare equivalence' of tax systems and mechanisms which hold in a continuum economy are interesting only if we can find corresponding results in large but finite economies and point out how they relate asymptotically with the continuum economy results.

This is in itself a programme of research which deserves to be treated independently. However, keeping the basic information assumptions of the preceding section (which make general mechanisms and non-anonymous mechanisms equivalent), one can sketch a framework for the asymptotic comparison of mechanisms and tax systems.

In the $E^{(r)}$ economy, there are $r$ agents whose numbers $a$ are $\left[\frac{1}{r}, \frac{2}{r}, \ldots, \frac{r-1}{r}, 1\right]$. The characteristics $\theta$ of agent $a$ are drawn at random from $\Theta$ with the probability distribution $\mu$.

If we assume that the tax designer only knows the underlying distribution $\mu$, he cannot know exactly the actual distribution in the economy $E^{(r)}$.

For that reason, for the definition of admissible tax systems, feasibility should not be required; instead a tax system would be called admissible when the probability that the norm of excess demand exceeds some small number $\epsilon$, is small enough (smaller than $\epsilon'$). This would be called a $\epsilon - \epsilon'$ tax system.

One should also define $\epsilon - \epsilon'$ mechanisms where the feasibility constraint would be similarly relaxed. Within this setting, the finite economy version of the previous analysis can be analysed. A brief assessment of the present development of this programme will be presented in the bibliographical note that follows.

## 1.7 Conclusion (*)

In conclusion, the early literature on incentives of the seventies conveyed very optimistic prospects: clever design of mechanisms allows the extraction of much information and solves (at least in theory) problems which had been for a long time considered as unsolvable (as the free-rider problem). To some extent, the results obtained here (in a different context) go the other way: the usual taxation schemes do as well as the more sophisticated incentives devices, at least when a minimal amount of information (here the distribution) is available to the centre. However, this conclusion is relativized by the analysis of section 1.6 where mechanisms become again more powerful when they are allowed to be at least non-anonymous and when stochastic properties of the unknown environments do not fall into the particular class studied in subsection 1.6.2.

Let us be reminded of some lessons of the analysis.

Tax systems (as usually defined) are incentive compatible but their implementation requires a priori information which is not needed (since it could be in theory extracted) for the implementation of abstract direct mechanisms.

In rather similar words, a given tax system can feasibly allocate resources in a rather restricted set of environments when the adaptation to a larger set of environments is incorporated into the definition of a mechanism. However, some desirable properties of the outcome – such as uniqueness – may be lost through an extension.

Even when some taxation schemes are implicit in incentives mechanisms these schemes are more flexible than what is allowed for by tax systems. This is a point made clear in section 1.6 where AIRG may imply variable wedges between consumer and producer prices within a class of environments where tax systems introduced, by definition, invariable wedges. But, as argued later, the problem may be semantic.

Also, the theory of mechanisms assume *ex ante* commitments of the player (as to what they will do when the actual environment will be later revealed) that have no counterpart in tax theory. But, on this matter, the latter may be more realistic than the former.

Mechanisms can incorporate information about the trajectories of characteristics and take them into account whenever it is relevant to the knowledge of individual characteristics. Tax systems cannot. In fact it would be possible to introduce a more general notion of tax systems where **the individual budget set would depend** not only possibly on the name of the agent but also on the **profile of transactions of all others individuals in the society**. This would allow at least in some cases to equalize the performances of general mechanisms and non-anonymous tax systems, but the definition would lead us away from standard terminology (not to speak of implementation possibilities).

Finally, it may be thought that the assumptions of section 1.6.3 on the structure of the stochastic process governing trajectories are reasonable and consequently that optimal (non-anonymous) tax schemes mark the limits to redistribution in the context of our problem.

It should however be kept in mind that, on the one hand, the literature on Bayesian–Nash implementation has argued that very small correlations could be forcefully exploited and that, on the other hand, the introduction of observability in the context of section 1.6 does not lead to an immediate generalization of the results (as in section 1.5) since then the absence of correlation of the global characteristics does not imply the absence of correlation of hidden characteristics with some of the observable characteristics. This correlation issue might not hence be easily avoided. Also, the study of the relationship between the incentive compatibility problems in the type of large economies considered here and in large but finite economies – that received attention in the recent past – remains, to the best of my understanding, partly unsettled.

Finally, the intricate mix of different issues raised by the comparison – multiplicity, commitment, information, social objectives – is reminiscent of the lessons of general incentives theory but gives them a significantly distinct flavour (more on that in the bibliographical note).

## 1.8 Bibliographical note

Although optimal taxation (Mirrlees (1971)) had been justified with the informal incentive compatibility argument in the early seventies, an explicit confrontation of taxation and incentives issues was undertaken only at the end of the seventies. The analysis developed by Hurwicz, that was concerned with Nash implementation, made it clear that individual allocations associated with incentive compatible procedures could be viewed as the outcomes of utility maximization over pseudo-budget sets (see particularly Hurwicz (1979) and the early versions of this paper). However, the relationship between incentives theory and taxation issues was systematically stressed first in the context of dominant strategy implementation in Hammond's work (1979), then in a mixed context in the early (and final) stages of my own work, Guesnerie (1981a). The role of pseudo-budget sets in the theory of incentives as it appears in the quoted contributions, reflects what J.C. Rochet (1986) proposed calling the 'taxation principle'.

The so called 'taxation principle' is indeed at the heart of Hammond's (1979) article that establishes the equivalence of taxation systems and dominant strategy incentive mechanisms in the absence of retrading (these are corollaries 1 and 2 of section 1.4 that would be rewritten in the spirit of section 1.5). Other sections of Hammond's article concern, for example, the implementation of the Walrasian equilibrium; the analysis of this latter question has been pursued by Champsaur–Laroque (1981) who stressed the connectedness issue, that has been alluded to in the text.

The present chapter originates from my own work at this period (Guesnerie 1981a). Voluntarily, the present text attempts to stick to the last discussion paper that was circulated (Bonn D.P 89). Although I have been tempted to rewrite it in a way that reflects more recent trends in incentive theory, I felt that the basic message is not obsolete and I refrained from making too many changes: only a few modifications have been made in section 1.6 that either correct some inaccuracies or, and mainly, limit the scope of the argument (and simplify it) by ruling out the second-step trades. The initial ambition of the analysis – an attempt to apply Hurwicz's methodology to the problem under study in this chapter – was significantly enlarged after the publication of Hammond's work. It finally included: (i) mixed linear and non-linear taxation; (ii) relaxation of the anonymity assumption; (iii) emphasis on the correlation issue; (iv) brief suggestions for consideration of the case of large but finite economies.

Aspect (i) has been later analysed more fully by Hammond (1987) who has explored tracks that relate to the more basic view of the retrading process suggested in the text (section 1.3). This line of investigation has been pursued by Hammond–Kaneko–Wooders (1989).

Questions relating to (ii) and (iii) have come more to the surface of the recent incentives literature. An overview of this literature, which may also be useful to the reader as an introduction to this chapter, can be found in the surveys of Maskin (1985) and Moore (1992). Apart from progress in Bayesian implementation, to which I come back later and which has put the correlation issue at the forefront of the analysis, the main breakthroughs have been made in the field of implementation with symmetric information (Nash and perfect Nash) and are of no direct relevance for the issues of this chapter; also the taxation principle seems to have been rediscovered recently (Sojström 1992).

My brief suggestions on (iv) – a part of which have been deleted in the present version, even if some (not all) turned out right – have been made obsolete by a recent contribution of Dierker–Haller (1990) to which the reader is invited to refer.

Other work on the basic relationship of taxation and incentives issues include Roberts (1984), who refers to the taxation principle in contexts where the feasibility constraint only is taken into account on average; he also considers the intertemporal version of the incentives problem, a question out of the scope of the present analysis and pursued by Harris (1987). A selected survey of some of the issues evoked above, putting more emphasis on public goods, can be found in Champsaur (1989).

In the conclusion of the book, a broader discussion of the informational problems of income redistribution attempts to put the present chapter in a broader perspective. Sticking to the adverse selection framework that has been favoured here, let me stress some directions of present and/or recent research that deal with problems that have been unsatisfactorily resolved here.

The first one concerns the correlation issue that became a significant concern of the research on incentives only during the eighties, particularly in the literature on Bayesian implementation (d'Aspremont, Cremer and Gerard Varet (1993)). On the one hand, the findings of this literature seem to question the robustness of the results of section 1.6.3 since it suggests a discontinuity when one reaches the limit case of no correlation. On the other hand, this fact reinforces the argument for considering not only individual but also collective manipulations through coalitions. The advantage of mechanisms for exploiting correlation may turn out to be illusory in view of the increased possibilities of manipulations, that seem to be offered to coalitions by correlated information.

The second one concerns the uniqueness issue: in the present chapter, the revelation game has a unique (truthful) solution only in the framework of section 1.3 (at least in the case of absence of retrading, and because of the commitment hypothesis that is implicit in the analysis). Uniqueness is clearly an important theoretical question; it is at the heart of the contribution of Mas Colell–Vives (1993). They address in a slightly different framework, a question similar to the one considered here – implementation within a large group – but their analysis reflects the peculiarities of their initial motivation (collusion between firms) and puts the emphasis on the uniqueness of the solution of the revelation game – a question that certainly arises in our framework in sections 4 and 5, and that has not been treated here. One may, however, wonder whether uniqueness is the right requirement in our setting and if for example some strategic robustness of the revealing equilibrium – in the spirit of what Piketty (1992) looks for in the context of a one-dimensional taxation problem à la Mirrlees – would not be equally (or even more) desirable.

The third problem concerns the relationship between the limit results that obtain in the continuum economy and the results that obtain in large but finite economies. As already mentioned, Dierker–Haller have analysed the problem in the framework suggested in subsection 1.6.4.; a similar modelling option is adopted, in their setting, by Mas Colell–Vives (1993) where the issue at stake, in connection with the uniqueness problem, is the continuity of the implemented outcome when the economy's size increases.

2

# Positive economics: the structure of tax equilibria

In the previous chapter, the taxation of transactions has been justified by incentive compatibility arguments. These arguments can be briefly recalled as follows: as the agents' characteristics upon which transfers should be based are private information, a central authority is bound to the use of mechanisms whose enforceable outcomes are verifiable variables. Assuming that the (observable) variables were the net trades between the production and the consumption sector, we have shown conditions under which the outcomes which can finally be achieved are the same as those which would prevail in the presence of tax systems mixing linear and non-linear taxes.

As noted earlier, the basic argument of the preceding chapter holds true with a fixed bundle of public consumption. The model we consider in the following actually incorporates public goods, but their level is possibly variable. We leave it to the reader to see how and under which conditions – concerning the nature of conditional information on the taste parameters for public goods – the conclusions of the previous chapter extend to the case of this chapter.[1]

In this chapter, we shall *only consider linear taxation* and shall rule out non-linear taxes associated in the previous chapter with commodities $L_2$. This modelling option is first justified by its simplicity. Non-linear schedules are difficult to handle in a general context: understanding fully what is going on in the simple case of linear taxes is a natural first step towards an in-depth investigation (sketched in chapter 4) of the more difficult non-linear problem. Linearization, here as in many other scientific fields, is a useful simplifying device. Also, simplicity is not here so much at odds with realism. Non-linearities in real tax systems are generally concentrated in income tax schedules that display a limited number of marginal tax rates. Real tax schedules may then lie half way between the linear tax system

[1] For more on this, see Champsaur (1989). Everything would go right if preferences for public goods were uncorrelated with private characteristics and were public information.

considered here – indeed an affine system that for income taxation mixes a 'negative income tax' together with a single marginal tax rate – and the fully non-linear tax schedules envisaged in theoretical models. A more complete assessment of the limitations and significance of the basic modelling option of linearity will be attempted in the conclusion of this book.

The chapter proceeds as follows:

Section 2.1 is devoted to the description of the basic model, the feasible states of which are tax equilibria. A discussion of its assumptions precedes an introductory assessment of questions related to the structure of tax equilibria.

Section 2.2 analyses in full generality the structure of tax equilibria from a local point of view. It displays a parametrization of all tax equilibria that are in a close neighbourhood of an a priori given equilibrium, providing then all relevant local information on the feasible states of our model.

Section 2.3 takes the more demanding global viewpoint. First, it shows that, at least generically, the set of tax equilibria will have minimum regularity properties. Second, it establishes that under some circumstances the set of tax equilibria can be globally and not only locally parametrized along the lines explored in section 2.2. In this latter case, at least, we arrive at a good and rather comprehensive understanding of the structure of the set of feasible states of our model. Such an understanding will turn out to be helpful for normative and positive studies as well.

Section 2.4 illustrates indeed how the global knowledge of the set of tax equilibria allows us to answer – although possibly in conjunction with more standard methods – traditional questions of positive economics: considering some fixed tax system, instead of the freely variable taxes that generate the whole set of tax equilibria under consideration before, one asks in particular whether there exists an equilibrium with respect to the exogenously given tax system. Answers to such a question are shown to have peculiar features when compared to the purely Walrasian answers.

## 2.1 The basic model (*)

This section has three subsections. Subsection 2.1.1 is devoted to the presentation of the linear model we are considering here. With respect to the previous chapter, particular attention is given to the description of the production of the public goods. Also, two different institutional assumptions concerning the degree of control of the government on the production of such public goods lead to two variants of the model. The discussion of policy tools started in subsection 2.1.1, pursued in subsection 2.1.2, puts particular emphasis on the analysis of the government budget in connection with the price normalization problem. Finally, subsection 2.1.3 presents a series of low-dimensional versions of the model that are amenable to explicit computation. These examples illustrate a series of properties of the local and global structure of the set of tax equilibria, properties whose generality will be ascertained in the remainder of this chapter.

### 2.1.1 Presentation of the model[2]

We are first going to describe the constraints faced by consumers. Commodities are both private (in number $n$) and public (in number $n'$). A transaction bundle in private commodities is denoted $z \in \mathscr{R}^n$. A public consumption bundle is denoted $y'_0 \in \mathscr{R}^{n'}_+$. A couple transaction bundle, public consumption bundle is $(z, y'_0) \in \mathscr{R}^{n+n'}$. Consumers have preferences defined on some subset of $\mathscr{R}^{n+n'}$.

If taxes are linear, consumers are faced with the same prices for all private goods. The corresponding *price system* is denoted $\pi$: $\pi \in \mathscr{R}^n_+$. It is the *consumption price system*.

Different types of linearization could be considered. We take the one suggested above, considering that the budget set (the same for all consumers) is limited by a hyperplane which does not necessarily go through the origin.[3]

$$\text{so } B(\pi, R) = \{z | \pi.z \leq R\}$$

$R$ is here a uniform lump-sum transfer.

The maximization programme of the typical consumer can be written as

$$\max U(z, y'_0),\ z \in B(\pi, R) \cap Z$$

where $Z$ is the set of admissible transactions.

In the remainder of the book, we shall assume that the solution of this programme is always unique and exactly meets the budget constraint in the relevant range of $\pi$ and $R$. This fact would follow from the strict quasi-concavity and the strict monotonicity in $z$ of the utility function. This solution depends on the parameters of the programme $\pi, y'_0, R$, and is denoted $d(\pi, R, y'_0)$. It is the *competitive demand* for transactions.

Let us now come to the production sector. First, we have to incorporate public goods: $Y_0 \subset \mathscr{R}^{n+n'}$ is the production set associated with the production of public goods.

[2] Vectors are abstract objects. However, the usual convention of this book is that in formulas vectors to the (extreme) left are row vectors and vectors to the (extreme) right are column vectors. Hence $\pi.z$ designates the inner product of the row vector $\pi$ and the column vector $z$. In $pA\pi$ where $A$ is a matrix $pA$ is the product of the row vector $p$ and of matrix $A$ and $\pi$ is a column vector.

[3] More complex linearizations have been considered in a previous version of the manuscript of this book. The complication cost seems however to exceed the gain in new insights.

Second, the production of private goods is described through a set $Y_1(\cdot) \subset \mathscr{R}^n$ – that can be considered as the sum of individual production sets for private goods – but this set may depend upon the actual production of public goods – the vector $y'_0$.

Note that our presentation is (voluntarily) asymmetric: the public good production set is in $\mathscr{R}^{n+n'}$ when the private goods production set depends upon the public good vector in $\mathscr{R}^{n'}$ but is in $\mathscr{R}^n$. This notational asymmetry attempts to reflect an economic asymmetry: with the production set $Y_0$, we can use private goods as inputs (labour) or produce them as outputs (electricity) but, with the second production set, the public goods enter only as parameters that affect the technology (infrastructure).

Symmetry can be reintroduced at the aggregate level by defining a global production set in the space of public and private goods as

$$Y = \{(y'_0, y'') \mid y'' = y''_0 + y''_1,\ (y'_0, y''_0) \in Y_0, y''_1 \in Y_1(y'_0)\}$$

In the following, unless an explicitly contrary statement, we shall suppose that $Y_0$ and $Y_1(\cdot)$ are convex sets. We shall also refer to sectors 0 and 1 for the sector of production of public goods and for the sector of production of private goods respectively. For short, although this interpretation does not always hold, we will talk of public sector (0) and private sector (1).

Assume that sector 0 is given the exogeneous objective of producing $\bar{y}'_0$. We can envisage the cost minimization problem with respect to the (production) price vector $p$:[4]

$$\max p \cdot y''_0,\ (\bar{y}'_0, y''_0) \in Y_0$$

The (set of) solution(s) of this programme is denoted $\eta_0(\bar{y}'_0, p)$. The correspondence $\eta_0$ from (a subset of) $\mathscr{R}^{n'} \times \mathscr{R}^n_+$ to $\mathscr{R}^n$ is the *public cost minimizing correspondence*. Now $C(y'_0, p) \stackrel{\text{def}}{=} -p \cdot \eta_0(y'_0, p)$, minus the value of the above programme is the minimum cost associated with the objective $y'_0$, when the price vector is $p$.

The competitive profit-maximizing behaviour of the private sector can now be formalized. Given $p$ the production price system for private goods (an element of $\mathscr{R}^n_+$), the production plan of sector 1 is determined through the solution of the following programme

$$\text{Max } p \cdot y_1,\ y_1 \in Y_1(\cdot)$$

The set of solutions of this programme is denoted $\eta_1(y'_0, p)$. The correspondence $\eta_1$ from (a subset of) $\mathscr{R}^{n+n'}_+$ to $\mathscr{R}^n$ is the competitive supply correspondence.

[4] At this stage, the choice of the price vector from which cost is measured is rather arbitrary.

We shall use two different reference models for describing the control of production: in the first one, production decisions concerning private goods, either in sector 0 or in sector 1, are made on the basis of profit maximization (or cost minimization) with respect to the same set of production prices. It follows in this case that the aggregate production plan is on the frontier of the section, for given levels of public goods, of the global production set (in the space of private goods). (Note that mechanisms considered in the previous chapter were constrained to have this property.) We shall refer to this case as (of private goods) *production efficiency*. On the contrary, we can suppose, this will be our second assumption, that the whole production plan of sector 0 can be exogenously chosen. We will refer to this case where production efficiency is not assumed as *controlled public production*.

We introduce now the two corresponding models. As in the previous chapter, each model is defined through a set of feasible states, the attainment of which reflects assumptions on available policy tools. These definitions refer to the functions $d_i$ and the correspondences $\eta_0$ and $\eta_1$ just introduced. More precise information on the properties of these latter mappings (including their domain of definitions, the various assumptions that they are supposed to meet) is introduced later.

***Model A** Production efficiency*

*A feasible state is associated with transactions bundles $z_i$ $(z_i \in \mathscr{R}^n)$, $(i = 1,\ldots,m)$, a private sector production plan $y_1''(y_1'' \in \mathscr{R}^n)$, a public sector production plan $(y_0', y_0'')$ $y_0' \in \mathscr{R}^{n'}, y_0'' \in \mathscr{R}^n$, a uniform lump-sum transfer $R$, production and consumption price systems $p$ and $\pi$, $(p, \pi \in \mathscr{R}^n_+)$, such that the following hold*

$$z_i = d_i(\pi, R, y_0') \qquad i = 1,\ldots,m \tag{2.1}$$

$$y_1'' \in \eta_1(y_0', p) \tag{2.2}$$

$$y_0'' \in \eta_0(y_0', p) \tag{2.3}$$

$$\sum_{i=1}^{m} z_i \leq y_0'' + y_1'' \tag{2.4}$$

Note that (2.2) and (2.3) can be aggregated in

$$y'' \in \eta(y_0', p) \tag{2.2$'$}$$

where $y''$ is a straightforward compact notation for $y_1'' + y_0''$ and $\eta \overset{\text{def}}{=} \eta_0 + \eta_1$.

Later, the behavioural rule (2.2′) has a key role in the introduction of model C.

***Model B*** *Controlled public production*

*A feasible state is associated with transactions bundles $z_i$, two production plans $(y_0', y_0'')$, $y_1''$, two price vectors of $\mathscr{R}^n_+$, $p$, $\pi$, one transfer $R$ such that*

$$z_i = d_i(\pi, R, y_0'),\ i = 1, \ldots, m \tag{2.1}$$

$$y_1'' \in \eta_1(y_0', p) \tag{2.2}$$

$$y_0 = (y_0', y_0'') \in Y_0 \tag{2.3'}$$

$$\sum_{i=1}^{m} z_i \leq y_0'' + y_1'' \tag{2.4}$$

Note that (2.2) and (2.3'), by themselves, do not put much restriction on the choice of the private good global production plan $y''$ in $Y \cap \{y_0' = \bar{y}_0'\}$, i.e., in the (restriction of the) global production set (to a fixed level of public goods).[5]

We shall also use as a synonym for a *feasible state* of model A, B the expresssion of a *tax equilibrium* of model A, B. When the inequality (2.4) between uses and resources becomes an equality, we say that the corresponding tax equilibrium is *tight* (or *strict*).

These definitions call for a certain number of joint comments.

Our justification of taxation in the previous chapter relied on the assumption of 'many' traders (a continuum in fact). The formulation adopted here satisfactorily reflects incentives constraints, up to linearization, only if we consider demand functions $d$ as *aggregate demand for a continuum of infinitesimally small consumers of the same type i.* We shall keep in mind this interpretation; however, for the sake of simplicity, comments on results will be carried out by referring to agent $i$, or consumer $i$, rather than to agents of group $i$. Most of the time, the comments are easily transposed to the case where $i$ is explicitly considered as an aggregate.

The above definitions of tax equilibria reflect the power of the sophisticated planner of the previous chapter and, up to the simplification of linearization, the taxation power which we have shown to be equivalent. This 'taxation power' includes what the usual terminology refers to under the heading of commodity taxation, income taxation and profit taxation.

[5] If $y$ is any production plan in $Y = Y_\alpha + Y_\beta$ where $Y_\alpha$ and $Y_\beta$ satisfy the free disposal assumption then $y$ can be written down

$$y = y_\alpha + y_\beta,\ y_\alpha \in Y_\alpha \text{ and } y_\beta \in \eta_\beta(p)$$

It is even the case under additional assumptions (convexity of $Y_\alpha$, $Y_\beta$ possibility of inaction, irreversibility) that any $y$ of $Y$ can be written down as (see Weymark (1981b))

$$y = y_\alpha + y_\beta,\ y_\alpha \in \eta_\alpha(p_\alpha) \text{ for some } p_\alpha, y_\beta \in \eta_\beta(p_\beta) \text{ for some } p_\beta$$

Commodity taxation[6] is reflected in the difference between the consumption price $\pi_h$ and the production price $p_h$ of commodity $h$. As taxation is linear, the difference (positive or negative) $T_h = \pi_h - p_h$ is a per unit tax.[7]

Income taxation relates to the difference between the consumption price and the production price of any commodity of which the consumer is endowed (labour of some particular type, capital goods). In the simple case where one type of labour exists, model A describes a system which combines a uniform lump-sum transfer with a unit tax or subsidy on labour income. This is the 'linear income tax' of the literature. The terminology of affine income tax (to which we most often refer here) seems more adequate.

Profit taxation is implicit in the fact that the pure profit of the private sector $p \cdot \eta_1(\cdot, p)$, which appears in each model, and which is different from zero unless the production set is constant returns to scale, does not appear in consumers' incomes. It is taxed away at a rate of 100 per cent. Note again that this 100 per cent profit taxation only applies to pure profit. Other factors owned by consumers are taxed at varying rates.

Finally, in all models, the government has full control on the level of public goods. In model B, the choice of techniques for the production of public goods is also under government control, when in model A this choice is made on the basis of production prices.

The assumption of 100 per cent taxation of profit deserves some discussion. It can be justified on several grounds.

First, since rents accruing to final agents give rise to transactions and are taxable, pure profits can be viewed as rents associated with 'hidden' factors of production which are owned by nobody. It is makes sense to assume that such rents accrue to the government.

Second, and more importantly, the assumption of 100 per cent taxation of profits is well in line with the basic justification of the model given in the previous chapter. It was then assumed that the sophisticated planner had full information and had (direct or indirect) control of the production sector. Clearly, one can argue that this is an unreasonable hypothesis. One could, as Mirrlees[8] did, refer to an entrepreneurial theory of the firm

[6] Note also that pricing and taxation are not in these models different issues. Particularly, there are no sectoral budget constraints for the public sector as in the Boiteux tradition. (On this literature, see Guesnerie (1980b).)

[7] Calling $T_h$ a tax when $h$ is a factor is a somewhat debatable (terminology) option. In this latter case $\pi_h > p_h$ means that factor $h$ is subsidized (it is on the contrary when $h$ is a consumption commodity). (The terminology is unambiguous only in a world with a single untaxed factor.)

[8] Mirrlees (1972). (See also Munk (1978).)

attempting to take into account the disincentive effects of profit taxation. However, a realistic approach to this latter question requires a specific study which is itself complex. In particular, the implicit informational problems behind the management and control of firms are likely to be better analysed using a different framework. Any theory isolates questions. Even if no frontier is perfectly satisfactory, a clear line separates fiscal problems relating, on the one hand, to the absence of government control and information on the household sector, and, on the other hand, to the absence of control and information on the production sector. The first field resorts to the taxation of transactions between the production sector and the consumption sector in which (static) redistribution issues are important; the second one resorts to the study of corrective taxation of firms, profit taxation and investment taxation (in which intertemporal efficiency aspects are crucial). Such a separation is both convenient for analytical purposes and well grounded on informational considerations. Although there are necessarily some interactions between the results obtained in the two fields, on each side of the separation line which has been suggested, the study of these interactions is premature here. We will content ourselves with a coherent – although partial, on grounds of realism – view of the world.

In fact if the ultimate references of our analysis are indeed models A and B, most of the technical work in the book will refer to model C. Here, the public and private sectors are aggregated as suggested after the introduction of model A.

***Model C*** *Production efficiency and aggregation of production*

*A feasible state is associated now with transactions bundles* $z_i$, *an aggregate production plan of private goods* $y''$ *and a production vector for public goods* $y_0'$ *such that*

$$z_i = d_i(\pi, R, y_0') \; i = 1, \ldots, m \tag{2.1}$$

$$y'' \in \eta(y_0', p) \tag{2.2'}$$

$$\sum_{i=1}^{m} z_i \leq y'' \tag{2.4'}$$

where as defined above

$$\eta(y_0', p) = \eta_1(y_0', p) + \eta_0(y_0', p)$$

denotes the aggregate supply of private goods when the production of public goods is $y_0'$ and when both sectors 0 and 1 make production decisions – concerning the use of private goods – on the basis of the production prices vector $p$.

Although, we are a priori more interested in models A and B we will mainly study model C in the following. The reasons for that will become clearer later. Let us however say some words here. On the one hand, in the positive study of model A undertaken in this chapter, only the properties of the aggregate supply function $\eta$ will matter; on the other hand, the normative study undertaken in the next chapter leads us to refer to a simplified version of model B (without public goods) which, thanks to a trick that will be explained later, can be obtained from model C.

Throughout this book, the standard convexity assumptions that allow the definition of the individual excess demand *function* $d_i$ (i.e., strict convexity of preferences) and of competitive supply *correspondences* (convexity of the relevant production sets of sectors 0 and 1) will always be made (unless explicit notice to the contrary).

A number of other technical assumptions will be repeatedly used and can be presented now.

(CS) is a technical assumption that implies in particular that the aggregate supply correspondence $\eta$, just defined, is single valued. More precisely, we have:

**(CS)** *Convexity property of sections*

*The global production set, restricted to a fixed level of public goods is strictly convex, satisfies free disposal. Also it has a unique supporting hyperplane at each point of its boundary.*

The first part of the assumption implies that the correspondence $\eta(y'_0,\cdot)$ is a function defined on a subset of $\mathscr{R}^n_+$. The second part that rules out kinks at the frontier of the production set, is mainly quoted for memory since it is redundant to the smoothness assumptions that will be most often made later, starting from section 2.3.

A stronger assumption on the properties of sections is (BP):

**(BP)** *Boundary conditions for production prices*

$\forall y'_0$, $\eta(y'_0,p)$ *is defined for every* $p\in\mathring{\mathscr{R}}^n_+$
$\forall y'_0$, $p_h/\|p\|\to 0$ *for some* $h\Rightarrow\exists k|\eta_k(y'_0,p)\to -\infty$
*(where* $\|p\|$ *designates the – Euclidean – norm of* $p$*).*

BP says that if the price vector goes to the boundary of its domain of definition which is assumed here to be $\mathring{\mathscr{R}}^n_+$ (but might be the simplex with another normalization) then there is some commodity that becomes an input, the demand of which tends to $-\infty$. When BP is verified the section under consideration has the negative orthant of $\mathscr{R}^n$ as asymptotic cone.[9]

The next assumption still concerns the fixed public goods section of the production set. It concerns the positivity of aggregate marginal cost and is stated under the assumption that $\eta$ has a derivative with respect to $y'_0$.

**(PAMC)** *Positivity of aggregate marginal cost*

$$\forall y'_0,\ \forall p \in \mathscr{R}^{0_n}_{+},\ -p \cdot \partial_{y_0'} \eta(y'_0, p) > 0$$

*where* $\partial_{y_0'}\eta$ *is the matrix of derivatives (with* $k^{th}$ *column* $\partial_{y'_{0k}}\eta$*).*

Noting that $-p \cdot \partial_{y'_0}\eta(y'_0, p) = -p \cdot \partial_{y'_0}\eta_0(y'_0, p) - p \cdot \partial_{y'_0}\eta_1(y'_0, p)$, we see that the positivity of the first term – the marginal cost of production of public goods – is a rather innocuous assumption but that the second term should be expected to be negative; in the interpretation suggested above, it is minus the marginal benefit of the public good for the private sector. Hence PAMC is a rather strong assumption that asserts that for every public good level its marginal cost exceeds its marginal benefit for production (a fact, however, that certainly occurs when $Y_1(y'_0)$ is independent of $y'_0$).

In order to be exhaustive on the properties of the fixed public goods section of the production set, let us mention for memory that, later on, we will refer to a property stronger than CS and BP – property EBPG1 – that implies that the sections under consideration are bounded from above.

Assumptions on demand – like differentiability – will be stated when needed – since our differentiability assumptions differ across chapters. Let us however state one boundary assumption for demand.

**(LBD) (1)** *Limit behaviour for demand*

*Let* $(\pi_n, R_n, y'_{0n})$ *be an infinite sequence of consumption prices, income and public goods vector such that* $(\pi_n/\|\pi\|, y'_{0n}) \to (\bar{\pi}, \bar{y}'_0)$ *(where* $\|x\|$ *designates the – Euclidean – norm of* $x$*).*

$$\text{If } R_n \to +\infty, \text{ then } \exists\, k \,|\, \lim d_k(\pi_n, R_n, y'_{0n}) = +\infty$$

LBD1 has been quoted for memory only since it follows from consumer theory – with strictly monotonic and convex preferences (an assumption maintained throughout the book) – and aggregation of individual demand.

LBD2 and LBD3 will be introduced later, but in the 'extended' economy.

[9] See Artzner–Neuefeiend (1978).

### 2.1.2 The government budget and the normalization of prices

Feasible states or tax equilibria defined in the previous sections are associated with the set of policy tools that we have just made explicit after the introduction of models A and B. The use of these fiscal policy tools is associated with expenditures and receipts of the government and raises the question of the government budget. This is a question that public finance analysis rightly emphasizes. We are providing here a discussion of the government budget before putting at the front stage the problem of price normalization. Discussions of notions of 'more taxed' or 'more distorted' that are compatible with the normalization freedom are then provided.

Receipts and expenditures can be identified as follows (we do it for model B, leaving to the reader the transposition of the argument to model C).

*Receipts from linear commodity and income taxation* $\Delta_1$

When the vector of transactions of household $i$ is $z_i$, then these receipts (which may be negative) are $\sum_h T_h \sum_i z_{ih}$, where $T_h = \pi_h - p_h$. If we call $\Delta_1$, the total receipts in this category, then

$$\Delta_1 = (\pi - p)\cdot\sum_i z_i$$

*Receipts associated with fixed fees* $\Delta_2$

In this model they only consist of the uniform lump-sum transfer, which generates a negative receipt per capita $-R$, so that (recalling that $m$ is the number of consumer types)

$$\Delta_2 = -mR$$

*Receipts from profit taxation* $\Delta_3$

When the aggregate production plan of the private sector is $y_1''$, the pure profits are $p\cdot y_1''$, so that

$$\Delta_3 = p\cdot y_1''$$

*Expenditures on public goods*

Assuming that inputs for the production of public goods are obtained at production prices from the private sector, the cost of these inputs is[10]

$$\Delta_4 = -p\cdot y_0''$$

[10] The formulation does not rule out that the public sector actually produces private goods. We assume then that they are sold by public firms at production prices. Any alternative assumption only implies intra budget movements of funds, and the conclusion of proposition 1 is robust to such changes in the treatment of the public sector.

*The excess budget* is then $\Delta$

$$\Delta \overset{\text{def}}{=} \Delta_1 + \Delta_2 + \Delta_3 - \Delta_4$$

The following proposition thus easily obtains.

*Proposition 1*

*Consider a tax equilibrium and assume that preferences are such that budget constraints are tight for every household.*

*Then, the excess budget is positive.*

*If the tax equilibrium is tight, the excess budget is zero.*

*Proof*

From the definition we have

$$\Delta = (\pi - p)\sum_i z_i - mR + p \cdot y_1'' + p \cdot y_0''$$

Equivalently

$$\Delta = \sum_i (\pi \cdot z_i - R) + p \cdot \left[ y_1'' + y_0'' - \sum_i z_i \right]$$

The individual budget constraint being tight, $\pi \cdot z_i - R = 0$; and the market clearing conditions imply $y_1'' + y_0'' - \sum_i z_i \geq 0$. Hence $\Delta \geq 0$; and $\Delta = 0$ when all markets clear. □

Production of public goods requires that commodities used as inputs are taken out from the market. To make market clearing again possible the purchasing power of the consumption sector has to be sufficiently reduced. Such is the purpose of the financing of public expenditures. The fact that markets clear indeed signals that enough purchasing power has been confiscated; in other words the government budget is necessarily balanced. This is proposition 1. The argument also relates with Walras' law. In the standard general equilibrium model, Walras' law implies that if all markets clear and if the budget of all households but one is balanced then the budget of the last one is also necessarily balanced. Proposition 1 says the same thing, the last agent now being the government.

As we said, the result proved here for model B applies with slight modifications to model A. It is in fact extremely general and would apply in particular to more complex variants of models A and B or C.

Going back to model A, a striking property of normalization appears: if $z_i, y_0', y_1''$ is a feasible state associated with the price system $\pi, p$ and the poll subsidy $R$, then it can also be associated with the price systems $\lambda\pi, \mu p$ and the poll tax $\lambda R$ when $\lambda$ and $\mu$ are strictly positive parameters $\lambda > 0$, $\mu > 0$. Consequently, we can associate with a given feasible state as many tax vectors as there are vectors $T_{\lambda\mu} = \lambda\pi - \mu p$, $\pi, p$, fixed, $\lambda, \mu > 0$. Similarly the amount of uniform lump-sum transfers has in itself no significance. Although this latter fact is not surprising – one would expect that only the purchasing power of the lump sum, i.e., the ratio of $R$ over the price of some commodity bundle, is relevant – the former is more disturbing: one would like to give meaning to sentences like: some commodity is more taxed than another, some tax vectors introduce more distortions than others. However, from the above remark, the hierarchy of taxes associated with a given normalization is meaningless. For example take

$$p = \begin{bmatrix} 1 \\ 4 \end{bmatrix} \pi = \begin{bmatrix} 3 \\ 5 \end{bmatrix} T = \begin{bmatrix} 2 \\ 1 \end{bmatrix}$$

Tax $T_1$, on commodity 1 is 'higher' than tax $T_2$ on commodity 2. But with $\pi = \begin{bmatrix} 300 \\ 500 \end{bmatrix}$, $T = \begin{bmatrix} 299 \\ 496 \end{bmatrix}$ and $T_2 > T_1$.

However, a hierarchy can be defined which is invariant through changes in normalization. Consider for example $\rho_h = \dfrac{\pi_h}{p_h}$ the consumption price over production price ratio on commodity $h$, multiplying $\pi$ by $\lambda$ and $p$ by $\mu$, $\rho_h$ is transformed into $(\lambda/\mu)\rho_h$: the ratio is affected but *not the ranking of ratios.* This suggests that the ranking might be adequate for reflecting the idea of 'more taxed'.

Note also that given $\bar{h}$ we can choose $\lambda$ and $\mu$ such that $\lambda\pi_{\bar{h}} = \mu p_{\bar{h}} = 1$, i.e., such that the consumption and the production prices of commodity $\bar{h}$ are equal. In this case $\bar{h}$ is the *numeraire*. It would be rather natural to say that $h'$ is more taxed than $\bar{h}$ if it is positively taxed when $\bar{h}$ is the numeraire.

Two candidate definitions of more taxed commodity have obtained

*Definition 1*

*Commodity h is* ***more taxed*** *than commodity k, if the ratio $\rho_h$ is greater than or equal to the ratio $\rho_k$.*

*Definition 2*

*Commodity h is* ***more taxed*** *than commodity k, if and only if the tax on commodity h is positive when commodity k is the numeraire.*

The following 'proposition' shows that the definitions are equivalent.

*Proposition 2*

*Consider a couple of price systems* $\pi$ and $p(\in \mathring{\mathscr{R}}^n_+)$. *Both definitions 1 and 2 of 'more taxed' are equivalent and define a complete preordering on the set of commodities.*

*Proof*

We have already argued that definition 1 is meaningful, the ranking of tax rates being invariant through changes in normalization. Clearly this ranking defines a complete preordering (which is an ordering unless $\rho_h = \rho_k$ for two distinct commodities $h, k$) on the set of commodities.

Suppose now $h$ more taxed than $k$ in the sense of definition 2. Normalize such that $k$ is the numeraire. By definition then $\pi_h > p_h$. So that $\rho_h = \dfrac{\pi_h}{p_h} \geq 1$ when $\rho_k = 1$; $h$ is more taxed than $k$ in the sense of definition 1. It follows that the binary relationship defined on all couples $(h,k)$ of commodities by definition 2 is identical to the (pre)ordering induced by definition 1. (Note by the way that this proof shows that definition 2 is 'consistent': if $h$ is strictly more taxed than $k$ in the sense of this definition, it is not the case that $k$ is strictly more taxed than $h$.) □

One would like to give meaning to sentences such as the following ones: Situation 1, associated with $(\pi_1, p_1)$ is 'more distorted' than situation 2 associated with $(\pi_2, p_2)$. Some notions of increased distortions come immediately to the mind: one could say for example that situation A $(\pi_A, p_A, T_A)$ is more distorted than situation B $(\pi_B, p_B, T_B)$ whenever $(\alpha) T_A > T_B$ (inequality between tax vectors), $(\beta)$ $T_{Ah}/p_{Ah} > T_{Bh}/p_{Bh}$ (inequality between tax rates) or $(\gamma)$ $T_A = kT_B$, $k > 1$ (inequality between the norms of collinear tax vectors). Such definitions are significant only if they are numeraire free. This is not the case in general.[11] However, it can be shown that $(\gamma)$ is invariant to a change of numeraire when production prices are kept constant $(p^A = p^B = \bar{p})$. It remains difficult in general to compare distortions in a satisfactory way.

[11] Considering $\pi_A = (1, 1{,}5, 3)$, $p_A = (1,1,1)$, $\pi_B = (1, 1{,}1, 2{,}3)$. $p_B = (1,1,1)$, the reader will realize that if $T_A > T_B$ when commodity 1 is the numeraire, the inequality does no longer hold when commodity 2 is the numeraire. So neither $\alpha$ nor $\beta$ are invariant through normalization changes. To show the inadequacy of $\gamma$ one can, for example, consider the following situation:

$$\pi_A = (1, 1{,}5, 3), p_A = (1,1,1) \text{ and } \pi_B = (1, 9{,}25, 9001), p_B = (1,9,9000).$$

In situation B commodity 2 is more taxed than 3 in the sense of our previous definition when the reverse holds in situation A. The equality $T_A = 2\,T_B$ cannot be numeraire free since when commodity 2 is the numeraire, 3 is subsidized in situation B and is taxed in A.

The degree of freedom left by normalization has striking consequences (at least, if one assumes, in the spirit of the definitions of model A and B, that changing norms is a costless operation). For example:

Any commodity can a priori be chosen as a numeraire.
All taxes can be positive: it is enough to choose as numeraire (one of) the least taxed commodity. (Note however that the term 'taxes are positive' has to be taken in the sense defined above – see footnote 7.)
All taxes are negative as soon as the chosen numeraire is the 'most taxed' commodity.

It has to be understood that when starting from a given tax equilibrium, a normalization change does not affect the balance of the government budget, although *it may considerably modify all the components of the government budget*. As an example, let us consider the rather extreme change from the case where all taxes are negative (situation A) to the case where they all are positive (situation B). Suppose that production prices are unchanged so that consumption prices (as well as lump-sum fees) necessarily increase when passing from A to B. We note that indirect taxes on consumption commodities resulted in government expenditures (since taxes are actually subsidies) in situation A when they give positive budget receipts in situation B; the converse holding for factors. Similarly if lump-sum fees were positive, they induced small expenditures in situation A when they require high spendings in situation B. As the other terms of the government budget are unaffected, these moves in opposite directions of the terms $\Delta_1$ and $\Delta_2$ of the budget (as defined above) exactly compensate.[12]

In order to improve his intuition along the same lines, the reader is invited to analyse compensations occurring within the central budget when the norm of production prices is changed (all other things being equal).

### 2.1.3 Questions and introductory examples

The initial questions investigated in this chapter concern the structure of the set of feasible states or tax equilibria of the basic models defined in section 2.1.1. We should discuss first the reasons why we are interested in a detailed knowledge of the mathematical structure of tax equilibria.

These reasons are straightforward if we believe that the 'society' or the planner has enough degrees of freedom in the choice of tax systems to implement any tax equilibrium defined for example by (2.1) to (2.4). Such

[12] We are implicitly in a world in which transactions are costlessly observable, i.e., without either administrative costs or tax evasion problems. Both administrative costs and tax evasion could indeed be affected by normalization changes.

an assumption is generally adopted in the literature on optimal taxation where the subset of feasible states is nothing other than the basic set where optimization takes place. Tax reform theory, when it assumes the possibility of unrestricted small changes of taxes, consists in a systematic exploration of the neighbourhood of an initial tax equilibrium. Also with the preoccupations and terminology of social choice theory, the subset of feasible states is the set of 'alternatives'. Hence, a full understanding of the issues of optimal taxation, of tax reform, of the political process of the determination of taxes, is hardly conceivable if we ignore the mathematical structure or more intuitively the 'geometry' of the set of tax equilibria.

Even if we believe that, given the actual limitations of taxation power due for example to administrative costs, many feasible states of our definition are not in fact attainable, it remains that the knowledge of the full set of tax equilibria of our definition is extremely helpful for the analysis of a more restricted set of actual tax equilibria. This assertion will be illustrated in the second part of this chapter where extreme limitations of the taxation power will be considered. For example, it will be shown that the solution of the existence problem: does an equilibrium exist with respect to a given tax system? – i.e., a tax system which rigidly relates production prices and consumption prices – greatly benefits from the understanding of the structure of tax equilibria. Also comparative statics questions have solutions which can be derived from the knowledge of the general structure of tax equilibria.

We shall first give some examples, which are intended to motivate the reader by giving him some flavour of the type of questions which appear and the nature of difficulties which will be encountered. We shall start from a very simple example, of a two private commodity world in which the set of tax equilibria is extremely well behaved. We shall then complicate the example by introducing a third private commodity. Finally, coming back to lower dimensional examples, we shall point out that 'strange' structures of the set of tax equilibria may occur, inducing paradoxical phenomena that obtains without pathological features neither of production sets nor of preferences.

*Example 1 A well-behaved set of tax equilibria*

Let us consider an economy with two private goods: the first one is labour, the second one is some consumption good. There is also one public good. Consumers are indexed by $i=1,\ldots,m$. They are endowed with one unit of leisure and have utility functions of the form $U_i = \alpha_i \log x_{i1} + \beta_i \log x_{i2} + \gamma_i \log y_0'$ where $x_{i1}, x_{i2}, y_0'$ are the consumption respectively of leisure, consumption good and public good and where $\alpha_i + \beta_i = 1$. The consumption good (as well as the public good) are produced according to constant returns to scale

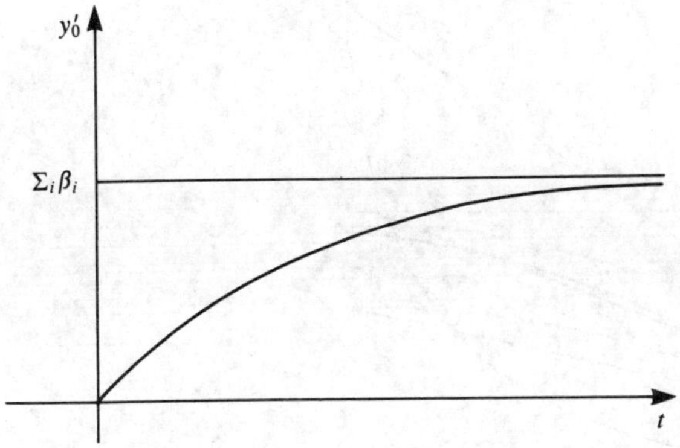


Figure 2.1

technologies which transform one unit of labour into one unit of consumption good (resp. public good). Labour (or leisure) being taken as numeraire, the competitive production prices of public good and commodity 2 are necessarily equal to one. The consumption price of commodity 2 is $\pi = 1 + t$ where $t$ is the tax on this commodity. We have then a specific crude version of model A where any tax equilibrium can be associated with a couple $(\pi, y_0')$ or equivalently with a couple $(t, y_0')$. The set of tax equilibria identifies then with a subset of $\mathscr{R}_+^2$ which can be easily characterized as follows.

Total demand for commodity 2 equals $\left[\frac{\Sigma\beta_i}{1+t}\right]$, so that total receipts of the government equal $\frac{t}{1+t}(\Sigma\beta_i)$; from the equilibrium of the budget (proposition 1 above) $y_0' = (\Sigma\beta_i)\frac{t}{1+t}$. This is the equation of the set of tax equilibria, which is visualized in figure 2.1.

Note that the utility of an agent is indirectly determined when $t$ and $y_0'$ are fixed. Indirect indifference curves are given by the equation

$$\frac{y_0'^{\gamma_i}}{(1+t)^{\beta_i}} = K.$$

The shape of these indifference curves is sketched in figure 2.2 when $\gamma_i = \beta_i$ (full line), $\gamma_i < \beta_i$ (dotted line), $\gamma_i > \beta_i$ (alternated line).

*Example 2 A well-behaved set of tax equilibria: continuation*

We complicate the preceding example by introducting one more commodity, commodity 3. This commodity, as the others, is produced from labour

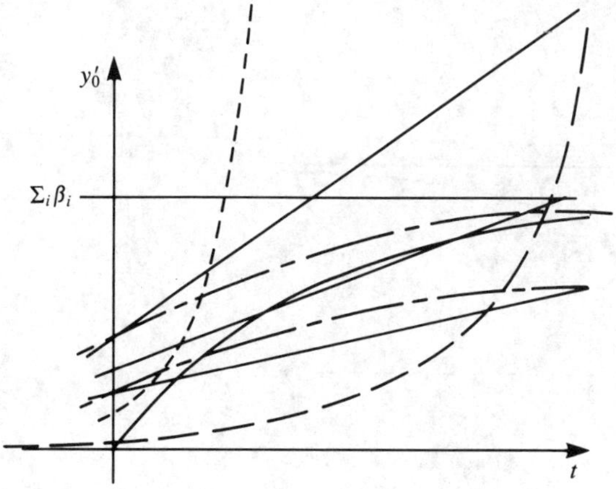


Figure 2.2

with a constant returns to scale technology (one unit for one unit). The individual utility functions are changed in

$$U_i = \alpha_i \log x_{i1} + \beta_i \log x_{i2} + \gamma_i \log x_{i3} + \delta_i \log y'_0 \qquad (\alpha_i + \beta_i + \gamma_i = 1)$$

A tax equilibrium identifies with a point in $\mathscr{R}^3$, of coordinates $(t_2, t_3, y'_0)$ or equivalently $(\pi_2, \pi_3, y'_0)$ when $t_2, t_3$ (resp. $\pi_2, \pi_3$) are the taxes (resp. prices) on commodities 2 and 3. Computations along the same lines as above show that the set of tax equilibria is a surface whose equation is

$$y'_0 = \left(\frac{t_2}{1+t_2}\right)(\Sigma\beta_i) + \left(\frac{t_3}{1+t_3}\right)(\Sigma\gamma_i)$$

The shape of this surface in $\mathscr{R}^3$ can be understood from the study of sections. For example, the section by any coordinate plane of equation $t_2 = c^{st}$ or $t_3 = c^{st}$ is a hyperbola, as visualized in figure 2.3 for the section $t_3 = 1$

The sections by planes $y'_0 = c^{st}$ are shown in figure 2.4; they are also hyperbolas with asymptots parallel to the axes. The horizontal asymptot of the iso public good level curve $y'_0$ is

$$t_3 = \frac{-(\Sigma\beta_i - y'_0)}{\Sigma\beta_i + \Sigma\gamma_i}$$

Note that these curves are nothing other than the set of 'equal yield tax alternatives' of the literature on theoretical public finance.

This simple economy provides an example when both the set of tax equilibria and the set of equal yield tax alternatives are well behaved.

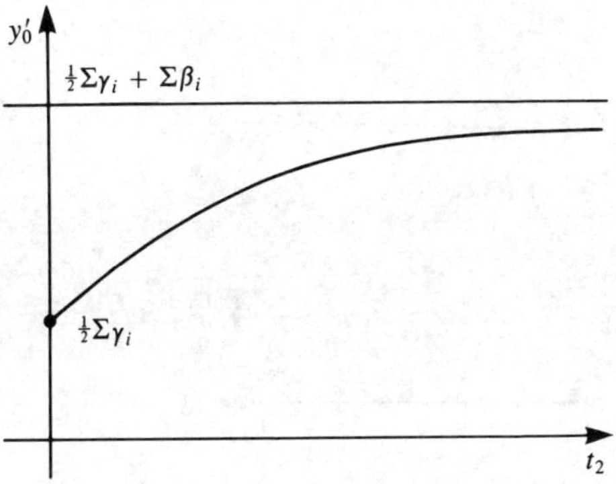


Figure 2.3

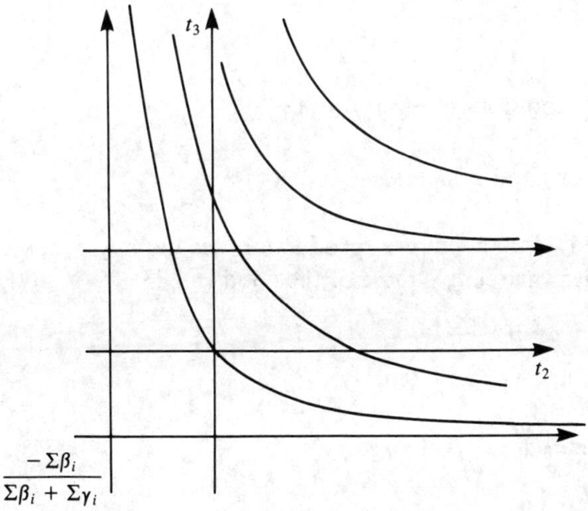


Figure 2.4

*Example 3 A strange set of tax equilibria*
Let us come back to an economy with two commodities. Suppose that we have two classes of consumers. For each class there is a representative consumer. The first one has a utility function $U_1 = x_1 x_2^{\alpha(y_0')}$ when the second one has a utility function $U_2 = x_1 x_2 y_0'$. The fraction of the population of the first class is $\gamma$ (hence $1-\gamma$ for the second class). The total endowment in leisure in the economy is normalized at 1 and equally shared between all consumers.

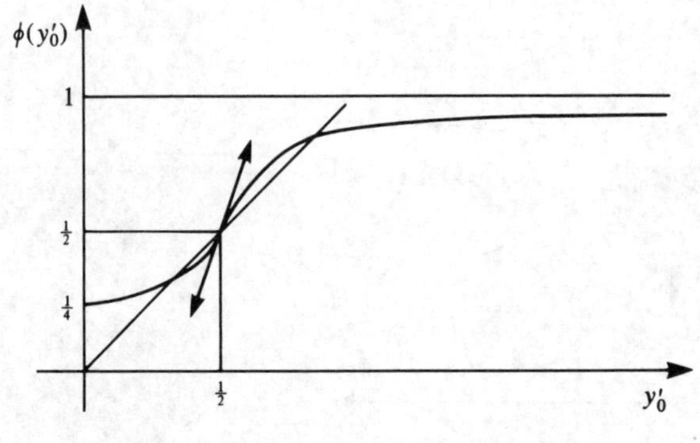

Figure 2.5

Putting $g(y_0') = \dfrac{1}{1+\alpha(y_0')}$, it is easy to see that when the relative price of the consumption good is $\pi$:

total supply of labour is $\gamma(1-g(y_0'))+(1-\gamma)\frac{1}{2}$

total demand for good 2 is $\frac{1}{\pi}(\gamma(1-g(y_0'))+(1-\gamma)\frac{1}{2})$

Good 2 is produced with a convex production technology whose competitive supply, when the relative price of the good is $p$, is

$$\eta_1(p) = 1-\sqrt{p} \qquad \eta_2(p) = 1-(\sqrt{p})^{-1} \tag{2.5}$$

Market clearing on markets 1 and 2 imply

$$\gamma(g(y_0')-1)+(1-\gamma)\left(-\frac{1}{2}\right) = 1-\sqrt{p}-y_0' \tag{2.6}$$

$$\gamma(1-g(y_0'))+(1-\gamma)\frac{1}{2} = \pi\left(1-\frac{1}{\sqrt{p}}\right) \tag{2.7}$$

Replacing $\sqrt{p}$ in equation 2.7 by the value drawn from equation 2.6 leads to

$$\pi = \gamma\left(\phi(y_0')-\frac{1}{2}\right)+\frac{3}{2}+\frac{1}{\frac{1}{2}-y_0'+\gamma\left(\phi(y_0')-\frac{1}{2}\right)} \quad \text{with} \quad \phi(y_0') = 1-g(y_0') \tag{2.8}$$

Now take $\phi(y_0') = \frac{1}{2}+\frac{1}{\Pi}\operatorname{Arctg}\left(k\left(y_0'-\frac{1}{2}\right)\right)$ a function which is visualized on figure 2.5 (with $k=2$, $\Pi = 3{,}14159\ldots$). Note that $\alpha(y_0')$ then equals

$$\frac{\frac{1}{2}+\frac{1}{\Pi}\,\mathrm{Arctg}\left(k\left(y_0'-\frac{1}{2}\right)\right)}{\frac{1}{2}-\frac{1}{\Pi}\,\mathrm{Arctg}\left(k\left(y_0'-\frac{1}{2}\right)\right)}$$

This is an increasing function of $y_0'$ which is reasonable on economic grounds.

It is easy from equation (2.8) to draw the graph of $\pi$ as a function of $y_0'$. An important role is played by the zeros of denominator of the last term of (2.8) which for $\gamma=1$ are given by the intersection of $\phi(y_0')$ with the first bissectrix on figure 2.5 and for $\gamma=\frac{1}{2}$ are given by the intersection of the graph of $\frac{1}{2}\phi(y_0')$ by the line of equation $y=y_0'-\frac{1}{4}$.

Taking into account the fact that equation (2.8) describes economically meaningful tax equilibria only when $\pi$ is positive and $y_0'$ small enough (and certainly smaller than 2) can we visualize the set of $(\pi, y_0')$ associated with tax equilibria in the following cases

$$\gamma=0 \text{ (Figure 2.6)} \qquad \gamma=\frac{1}{2} \text{ (Figure 2.7)} \qquad \gamma=1 \text{ (Figure 2.8)}$$

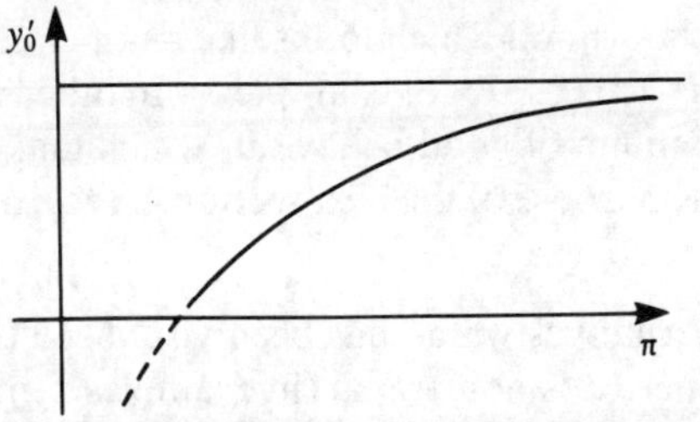


Figure 2.6

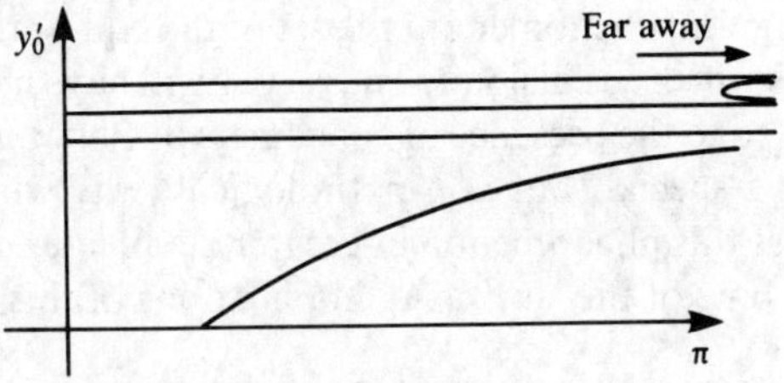


Figure 2.7

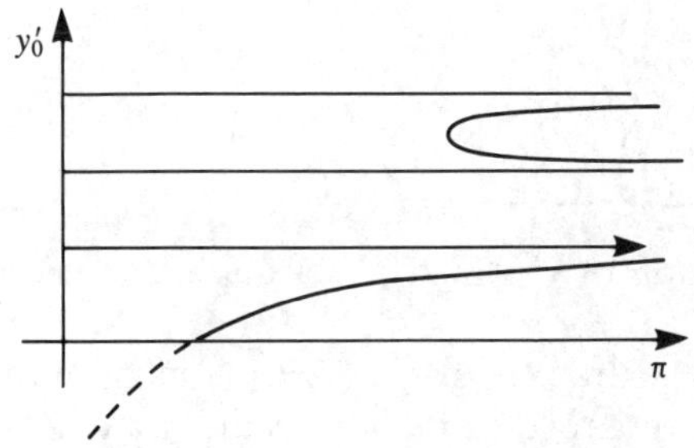


Figure 2.8

Note that, in this model, we can give some meaning to equilibria with a negative $y_0'$ (with a reversible technology producing labour from the public good) which are associated with the dotted part of the graph. However, if we drop this negative part of the graph, and if we take the *convention of descriptive geometry* (i.e., by representing in a related way on the page both the projection of the set of equilibria on the plane $(\pi, y_0')$ and its projection on the plane $(p, y_0')$), we can visualize on the same figure $(\pi, p, y_0')$. Figures 2.9 and 2.10 incorporate this new dimension from figures 2.6 and 2.8.

These examples[13] suggest the following remarks:

$\alpha$ We have never found pictures with self intersections. More precisely, the following minimal regularity has always been observed: each point in the set of tax equilibria has a neighbourhood which looks like an open set of a Euclidean space ($\mathscr{R}$ for examples $1, 3, \ldots, \mathscr{R}^2$ for example 2). In other words the set of equilibria has the minimum of good behaviour which makes it a (smooth) manifold. It will be the purpose of the next section 2.3 to examine whether this property is a general one.

$\beta$ The set of equal yield tax alternatives which has been visualized (figure 2.4) in the case of example 2 where it is non-trivial (in examples 1 and 3 it reduces to a single point) had also the minimum regularity property of having, for each point, neighbourhoods similar to open sets of $\mathscr{R}$. It is also a smooth manifold. The extension of this property will be considered in section 2.3.

$\gamma$ Example 3 shows an intriguing phenomenon: the set of tax equilibria has two connected components which are disjoint. The reader will have noticed that this phenomenon related to the presence of consumers of class 1 whose labour supply interacts in a special (but non-pathological) way with the public good. We will discuss this phenomenon in greater detail later on: let us however examine now some of the surprising implications of this fact:

[13] The help of H. Boussouf for the computation of these examples is acknowledged.

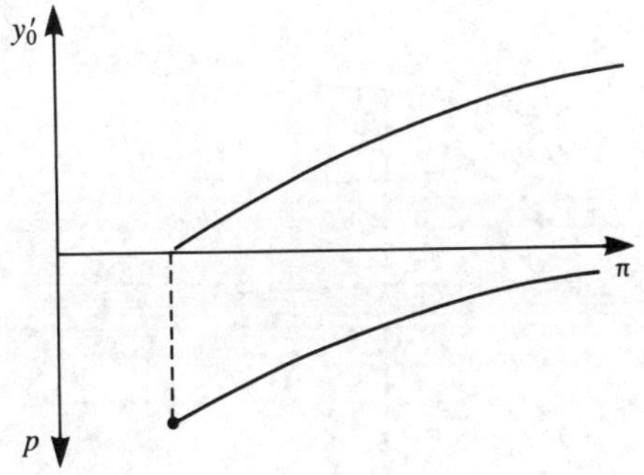


Figure 2.9

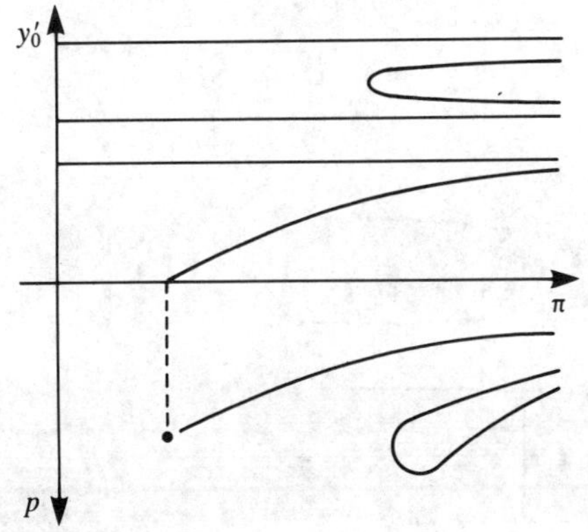


Figure 2.10

$\gamma_1$ Consider an algorithm computing small moves of the system which for example are desirable according to some welfare criterion: if the trajectory defined by the algorithm is continuous – as is typically the case for algorithms relying on local information as does the tax reform algorithms that we will design later on – it will not leave the connected component where it starts from. Hence, an algorithm of tax reform designed to improve some welfare criterion, can hope at best to reach the welfare optimum relative to the connected component where it starts from; hence if the indifference curves to the social welfare function are the dotted curves of figure 2.11, a continuous tax reform algorithm starting from C will reach A, but not B the full optimum. There are other reasons why *tax reforms algorithms may be trapped far from the full optimum*, but the limitations described above seem to be very basic.

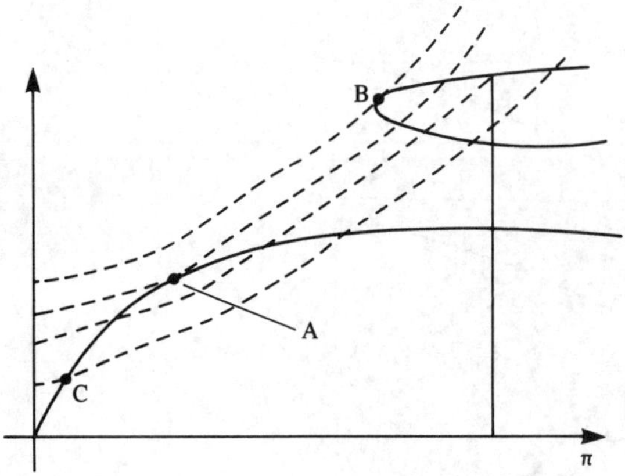


Figure 2.11

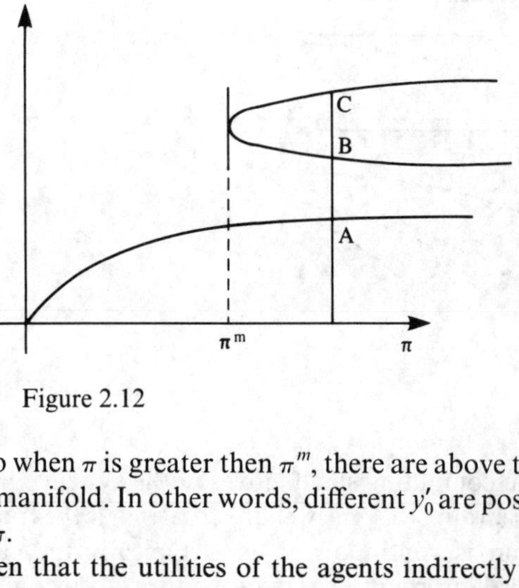


Figure 2.12

$\gamma_2$ Also when $\pi$ is greater then $\pi'''$, there are above the same $\pi$ several points of the manifold. In other words, different $y'_0$ are possible associated with the same $\pi$.

Given that the utilities of the agents indirectly depend upon $\pi$ and $y'_0$, there will be an immediate normative ranking of points like A, B, C in figure 2.12: C Pareto dominates B which Pareto dominates A. Hence in some weak sense, and at least for a restricted region of $\pi$, the *two connected components can be ranked according to the Pareto criterion.*

$\gamma_3$ Looking at the projection of the manifold on the plane $\pi,p$, and considering its intersection with the line $\pi = p + \bar{T}$, we see that non-connectedness of the manifold translates here into non-uniqueness of equilibria when a specific tax equals $\bar{T}$. Although *non-uniqueness* of equilibrium, with respect to what we will call in the following a given tax

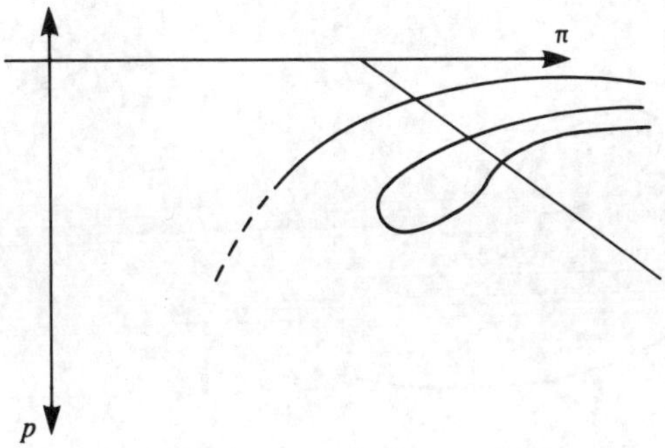


Figure 2.13

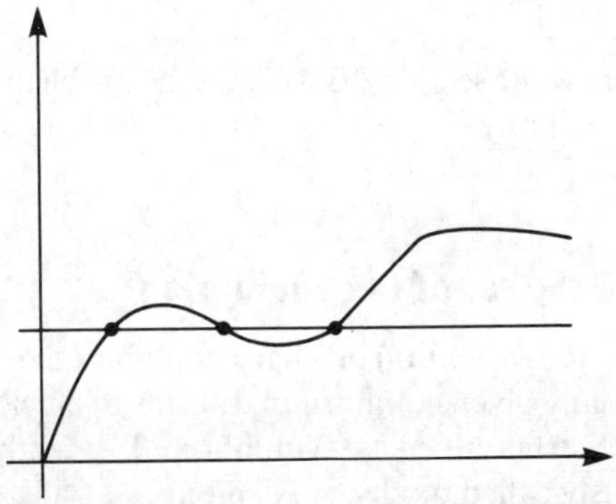

Figure 2.14

system, can occur with a perfectly connected manifold of tax equilibria, it becomes unavoidable at least for 'many' tax systems when connectedness fails to hold.

δ In example 2, as in fact in other examples, the set of equal tax yield equilibria is connected (as it is trivially in the other examples). It is easy to see that this property related to the fact that there is some kind of monotonicity of 'fiscal receipts' with respect to taxes. For example, in figure 2.14 the set of equal tax yield equilibria corresponding to $\bar{y}'_0$ is disconnected. Such a non-monotonicity property would induce in the case of a three goods economy as in example 2 a set of equal tax yield alternatives which would have the qualitative features of figure 2.15.

The question of the properties of the set of tax equilibria – hence the test of the generality of the properties appearing in the just described specific examples – is indeed the subject of this chapter. The next section focuses

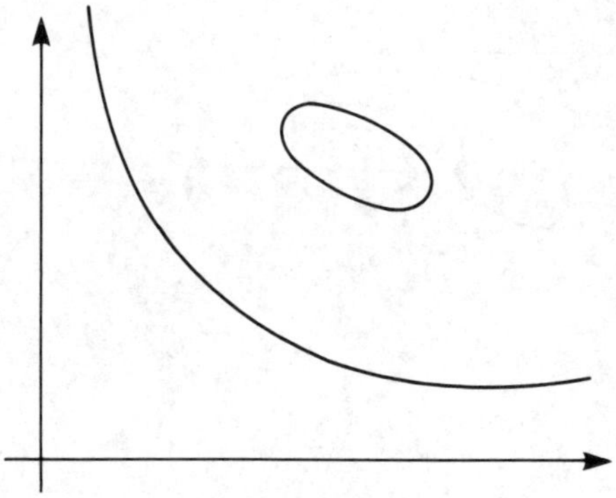

Figure 2.15

attention on the local structure while section 2.3 will face the problem of the global structure. Section 2.4 will rely on previous results in order to solve standard existence problems.

## 2.2 The local structure of the set of tax equilibria (*)(**)

The analysis of this section focuses attention on all tax equilibria that are in the neighbourhood of an initially given equilibrium. It leads to elucidating what can be called the local structure of tax equilibria. The analysis is restricted to what we previously called model C. All along, we will assume that the aggregate supply correspondence $\eta$ (for fixed $y_0'$) is single valued (a fact that follows from previous assumption CS) and differentiable.

Subsection 2.2.1 proposes a first analysis of the problem, partly based on intuitive considerations. This analysis is pursued and made fully rigorous in subsection 2.2.2.

### 2.2.1 The local structure: an intuitive approach (*)

Let us start from an initial equilibrium which is strict, i.e.

$$\bar{z}_i = d_i(\bar{\pi}, \bar{R}, \bar{y}_0') \tag{2.9}$$

$$\bar{y}'' = \eta(\bar{y}_0', \bar{p}) \tag{2.10}$$

$$\Sigma \bar{z}_i = \bar{y}'' \tag{2.11}$$

All characteristics of the equilibrium are known as soon as the sequence $\bar{\pi}, \bar{p}, \bar{R}, \bar{y}_0'$, is known so that the equilibrium could legitimately be identified with such a sequence. Also counting equations and unknowns around the equilibrium state, one easily checks that the number of degrees of freedom is $n + n' + 1$. However, the above discussion on price normalization has shown that two degrees of freedom were only apparent since ineffective. Hence the relevant number of degrees of freedom is $n+n'-1$. Associated with these degrees of freedom, one expects to find a whole subset of tax equilibria. The purpose of that section is indeed to provide a comprehensive and intelligible description of these neighbourhood equilibria or in other words to analyse the local structure of tax equilibria.

Let us develop an heuristic analysis, which will be made rigorous later on. For that, let us consider an infinitesimal change of consumption prices, lump-sum transfers and public good production $d\pi, dR, dy'_0$. Assume differentiability and call $\partial_\pi d_i$, $\partial_{y'_0} d_i$ *the Jacobian matrices* of the derivatives of $i$'s demand with respect to $\pi$ and $y'_0$ and $\partial_R d_i$ the vector of derivatives with respect to $R$.

The infinitesimal change in $i$'s demand for transactions equals

$$dz_i = (\partial_\pi d_i)d\pi + (\partial_R d_i)dR + (\partial_{y'_0} d_i)dy'_0 \tag{2.12}$$

Recalling that $\eta \overset{\text{def}}{=} \eta_0 + \eta_1$ is the total supply of private goods when the production of public good is $y'_0$ and production prices are $p$, let us call $\partial\eta$ the Jacobian matrix of derivatives with respect to $p$.[14] The forthcoming analysis is based on a local regularity assumption concerning $\partial\eta$. This local regularity assumption (LR1) insures that, in some sense, the sketch of the analysis presented in the introductory part of this book – that assumes that the 'global production set' is locally a hyperplane – can be adapted to the more complex case under consideration here. Lemma 1 then makes precise the nature and conditions of the adaptation.

**(LR1)** *Local regularity of the Jacobian $\partial\eta$ of total supply*

*In $\bar{p}$, $\partial\eta$ is exactly of rank $(n-1)$.*

From LR1, it follows:

***Lemma 1***

*Under (LR1) the linear mapping $(\partial\eta)$ is a bijection of $V(\bar{p}) = \{\lambda | \bar{p}\cdot\lambda = 0\}$ into itself.*

*Proof*

$(\partial\eta)$ is a linear mapping. From standard results we know:

1 $(\partial\eta)\bar{p} = 0$ (homogeneity of supply)
2 $\bar{p}\cdot(\partial\eta) = 0$

[14] This is an abbreviation for $\partial_p\eta$: we shall also use $\partial_{y'_0}\eta$. Here, the matrix $\partial X$ has $\partial X/\partial y_k$ as the $k^{\text{th}}$ column vector. Also, $d\pi$, $dy'_0$ and hence $dZ$ are column vectors (see footnote 2).

1 implies that $\bar{p}$ belongs to the kernel of $\partial\eta$ so that $\partial\eta$ is at most of rank $n-1$.

2 implies that the image of $\mathscr{R}^n$ by $\partial\eta$ is included in $V(\bar{p})$, and, with (LR1), is of dimension $n-1$. Then it equals $V(\bar{p})$. Lemma 1 then follows from the fact that there is a one-to-one correspondence between the image of a linear mapping and the complement of its kernel. □

In more intuitive words, the lemma means that:

(a) Any small change $dp$ of production prices around $\bar{p}$ induces a change in net supply $dy=(\partial\eta)dp$ which is normal to $\bar{p}:\bar{p}\cdot(\partial\eta)=0$.

(b) Reciprocally, any small change $dy$ which satisfies $\bar{p}\cdot dy=0$ can be obtained through a production price change $dp$ satisfying $p\cdot dp=0$, i.e., $dy=(\partial\eta)\cdot dp$. (Note that $p\cdot dp=0$ corresponds to an implicit normalization rule $\|p\|=1$ when $\|p\|$ is the Euclidean norm of $p$).

We shall denote $(\partial\eta)^{-1}$ the inverse mapping of $\partial\eta$ which is restricted to $V(\bar{p})$.

Now consider the (infinitesimal) change $dZ$ in total excess demand induced by the (infinitesimal) change $d\pi$, $dR$, $dy_0'$

$$dZ=\sum_i dz_i-(\partial_{y_0'}\eta)dy_0'$$

From (2.12) and, if we call, with straightforward notation

$$\partial_\pi d=\sum_i \partial_\pi d_i,\ \partial_R d=\Sigma\partial_R d_i,\ \partial_{y_0'} d=\sum_i \partial_{y_0'} d_i$$

we have

$$dZ=(\partial_\pi d)d\pi+(\partial_R d)dR+(\partial_{y_0'}d-\partial_{y_0'}\eta)dy_0' \tag{2.13}$$

Now we suppose that $\bar{p}\cdot dZ=0$. Comming back to LR1 and reminding ourselves of its interpretation we are led to consider the following change

$$dp=(\partial\eta)^{-1}dZ \tag{2.14}$$

These two conditions ($\bar{p}\cdot dZ=0$ plus 2.14) express relationships between $d\pi, dR, dy_0', dp$ which are necessary and sufficient to make the neighbourhood state $\bar{\pi}+d\pi$, $\bar{R}+dR$, $\bar{y}_0'+dy_0'$, $\bar{p}+dp$, a *strict* equilibrium. For that reason, we will refer to these equations as *the local equations of the set of tax equilibria.*

We rewrite them

$$\bar{p}\cdot(\partial_\pi d)d\pi+\bar{p}\cdot(\partial_R d)dR+\bar{p}\cdot(\partial_{y_0'}d-\partial_{y_0'}\eta)dy_0'=0 \tag{2.15}$$

$$dp=(\partial\eta)^{-1}\{(\partial_\pi d)d\pi+(\partial_R d)dR+(\partial_{y_0'}d-\partial_{y_0'}\eta)dy_0'\} \tag{2.16}$$

where all derivatives are taken in the inital state.

Call $\Phi_\pi(\bar{u})=\bar{p}(\partial_\pi d)_{(\bar{u})}$ (a row vector of $\mathscr{R}^n$)

$\Phi_R(\bar{u})=\bar{p}\cdot(\partial_R d)_{(\bar{u})}$ (a real number)
and $\Phi_{y_0'}(\bar{u})=\bar{p}\cdot(\partial_{y_0'}d-\partial_{y_0'}\eta)_{(\bar{u})}$ (a row vector of $\mathscr{R}^{n'}$)
where $\bar{u}=(\bar{\pi},R,\bar{y}_0',\bar{p})$.

Let us comment on these definitions: $-\Phi_{\pi_l},\Phi_R$ are respectively proportional to the (algebraic) cost measured with production prices of the change in excess demand induced by a decrease of $\pi_l$ and an increase of $R$. We will refer to them as *the marginal production cost of a decrease in $\pi$ and the marginal production cost of an income increase.*

Two assumptions can now be stated.

**(LR2)** *Positivity of marginal (production) cost of (uniform) income transfer*[15]

$$\Phi_R(\bar{u})=\bar{p}\cdot(\partial_R d)_{\bar{u}}>0$$

(LR2) states that the marginal (production) cost of meeting the excess demand generated by a (small) increase of the uniform lump-sum transfer is positive
Note that:

(i) The marginal cost under consideration, if it were measured with consumption prices, is necessarily positive: $\pi(\partial_R d)=m$, where $m$ is the number of (classes of) consumers. So the problems with the validity of LR2, if any, can only originate in the distortions between production prices and consumption prices.
(ii) Also, when there are no inferior goods in the initial situation, LR2 is necessarily verified since then $\partial_R d_i>0$ and $\partial_R d>0$.

Now, consider $\Phi_{y_0'}=\bar{p}\cdot\partial_{y_0'}d-\bar{p}\cdot\partial_{y_0'}\eta$.

The second term $-\bar{p}\cdot\partial_{y_0'}\eta$ has an already stressed interpretation; it is the vector of what we called above the aggregate marginal costs for the different public goods. Again those costs are algebraic costs including benefits for the private sector and might not be positive (assumption PAMC, which asserts that they are is discussed above).

The first term is a vector the $l^{\text{th}}$ component of which $\bar{p}\cdot\partial_{y_{0l}'}d$ measures the cost, evaluated with production prices $\bar{p}$ of the change in households' total excess demand induced by an increase of the quantity of the $l$th public good available; it may be positive (increasing the number of TV stations – everything else being equal – increases the consumption of TV sets) or

[15] In the previous literature devoted to the analysis of the recalled distortion problem (and analysed in chapter 4, section 3) a similar condition was known as the Hatta conditions.

negative (public safety devices are substitutes for private safety devices) and can be viewed as the (indirectly induced) demand cost of the production of public good. It would be zero under separability assumptions (see later) that make the demand for the private goods independent of the public good consumption.

In summary, $\Phi_{y_0'}$ can be interpreted as a vector of 'generalized' marginal costs.

We can now state:

**(LR3)** *Positivity of generalized marginal costs of public goods*

$$\Phi_{y_0'}(\bar{u}) > 0$$

Let us repeat that generalized marginal costs differ from aggregate marginal costs so that LR3 is *not* a local version of the global PAMC (Positivity of Aggregate Marginal Cost) (unless $\bar{p} \cdot \partial_{y_0'} d = 0$).

Rewriting (2.15) as

$$\Phi_\pi(\bar{u}) d\pi + \Phi_R(\bar{u}) dR + \Phi_{y_0'}(\bar{u}) dy_0' = 0 \tag{2.17}$$

it is easy to see that, when LR2 and LR3 are true in the initial equilibrium, all elements of the neighbouring strict equilibrium are determined, once either (with LR2) $d\pi$ and $dy_0'$ are fixed, – since thanks to LR2, the coefficient of $dR$ is positive, so that $dR$ can be computed – or (with LR3) $d\pi$ and $dR$ and all components of $dy_0'$ but one are fixed – since this last component can then adjust.

In other words, $\pi, y_0'$ or $\pi$, $R$ and a truncated $y_0'$ provide good parameters to describe locally the neighbourhood of the equilibrium. In terms which will be made more precise later on, these variables can serve for the *parametrization* of the neighbourhood.

### 2.2.2 The local structure of the set of tax equilibria: the formal analysis (**)

In this subsection we will give a more rigorous statement of the facts analysed in subsection 2.2.1. These facts pointed out what we called the local equations and lead us to discuss – under additional assumptions LR – possible local parametrizations. In the first part of this section we give a more rigorous and correct formulation of the local equations; in the second part, the intuitive analysis of local parametrization just given is fully formalized.

*Local equations as describing feasible directions of changes*

Let us consider a tight tax equilibrium $\bar{u}$ defined by

$$\sum_i d_i(\bar{\pi}, \bar{R}, \bar{y}_0') = \eta(\bar{y}_0', \bar{p})$$

In $\bar{u}$, all functions are assumed to be differentiable. Differentials have been used in a loose way in section 2.2.1. A more satisfactory treatment can be obtained by defining a notion of feasible directions of changes.

*Definition:* ***Equilibrium preserving*** *direction of change*

*A sequence of vectors $\dot{\pi}$, $\dot{R}$, $\dot{y}_0'$, $\dot{p}$, that we also denote with reference to some variable time as* $\frac{d\pi}{dt}, \frac{dR}{dt}, \frac{dy_0'}{dt}, \frac{dp}{dt}$ *is said to be equilibrium preserving (in $\bar{u}$) if the following holds*

$$(\partial_\pi d)\dot{\pi} + (\partial_R d)\dot{R} + (\partial_{y_0'} d)\dot{y}_0' \leq (\partial_{y_0'}\eta)\dot{y}_0' + (\partial\eta)\dot{p} \tag{2.18}$$

The sequence is said to be *tight equilibrium preserving* if (2.18) holds with equality.

We have then:

**Theorem 1: Characterization of equilibrium preserving directions of changes**

*Suppose that in the initial tight tax equilibrium $\bar{u}$, demand and supply functions are differentiable, that the local regularity assumption LR1 (rank of the matrix $\partial\eta$) is satisfied.*
*Then, given any direction of consumption prices, income transfer and public good changes $\dot{\pi}, \dot{R}, \dot{y}_0'$, which satisfies*

$$\bar{p}\cdot(\partial_\pi d)\dot{\pi} + \bar{p}\cdot(\partial_R d)\dot{R} + \bar{p}\cdot(\partial_{y_0'} d - \partial_{y_0'}\eta)\dot{y}_0' \leq 0 \tag{2.19}$$

*there exists a direction of production prices change $\dot{p}$ such that $\dot{\pi}, \dot{R}, \dot{y}_0', \dot{p}$ is (tight) equilibrium preserving.*

*Proof*

Suppose first that (2.19) holds with equality; the proof is a step by step rigorous rearrangement of the argument of the previous section, 2.2.1. Equation (2.16) is rewritten as:

$$\dot{p} = (\partial\eta)^{-1}\{(\partial_\pi d)\dot{\pi} + (\partial_R d)\dot{R} + (\partial_{y_0'} d - \partial_{y_0'}\eta_0)\dot{y}_0'\} \tag{2.20}$$

Then

$$(\partial\eta)\dot{p} = (\partial_\pi d)\dot{\pi} + (\partial_\pi d)\dot{R} + (\partial_{y_0'} d - \partial_{y_0'}\eta_0)\dot{y}_0'$$

This latter equality is nothing else other than (2.18) (with equality).

The case where (2.19) holds with inequality is easily dealt with, using free disposal. □

Theorem 1 does not call for new comments since it is only a rigourous reformulation of the analysis of section 2.2.1 which has been lengthily discussed.[16]

*Local parametrization of the set of tax equilibria*

The heuristic analysis of section 2.2.1 turns out in the following precise statement

**Theorem 2: Local parametrization of tax equilibria**

*Take an initial tight tax equilibrium in which all functions are $C^2$ in a neighbourhood and in which LR1 (rank of the matrix $\partial\eta$) holds.*
*Then, under LR2 – positivity of marginal cost of transfer – the following holds:*
*There is a neighbourhood of $\bar{u}$ in which the set of tax equilibria is defined by*

$$R = \mathcal{R}(\pi, y_0'),\ p = \mathcal{P}(\pi, y_0')$$

*where $\mathcal{R}$, $\mathcal{P}$, are $C^2$ functions (which have $\bar{R}$, $\bar{p}$, as values in $\bar{\pi}, \bar{y}_0'$).*
*Under LR3 – positivity of generalized marginal costs – the following holds:*
*There is a neighbourhood of $\bar{u}$ in which the set of tax equilibria is defined by*

$$y_{0h}' = \tilde{\mathcal{Y}}_{0h}'(\pi, R, \tilde{y}_0');\ p = \tilde{\mathcal{P}}(\pi, R, \tilde{y}_0')$$

*where $h$ is some public good and $\tilde{y}_0'$ designates the vector of public goods truncated of its $h^{\text{th}}$ coordinate and where $\tilde{\mathcal{Y}}_{0h}'$, $\tilde{\mathcal{P}}$ are $C^2$ functions.*

*Proof*

In a tight equilibrium

$$\sum_i d_i(\bar{\pi}, \bar{R}, \bar{y}_0') - \eta(\bar{y}_0', \bar{p}) = 0$$

The Jacobian matrix associated with these equations is

$$(\partial_\pi d, \partial_R d, \partial_{y_0'} d - \partial_{y_0'}\eta, \partial\eta)$$

16 In the case where the production sector is constant returns to scale, Theorem 1 remains true when a convenient variant of LR1 is assumed (see, e.g., an earlier version of this chapter, available upon request from the author).

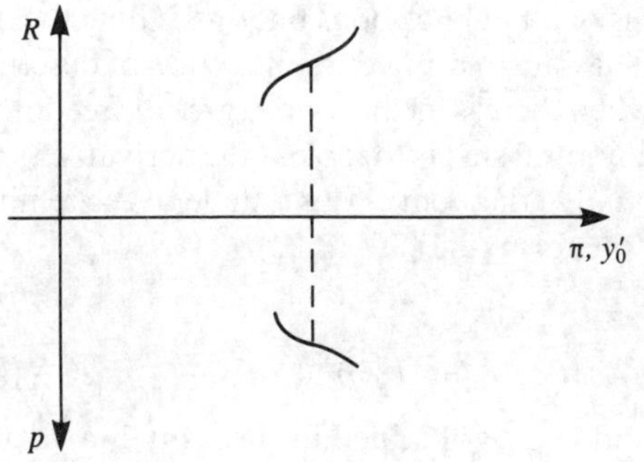


Figure 2.16a

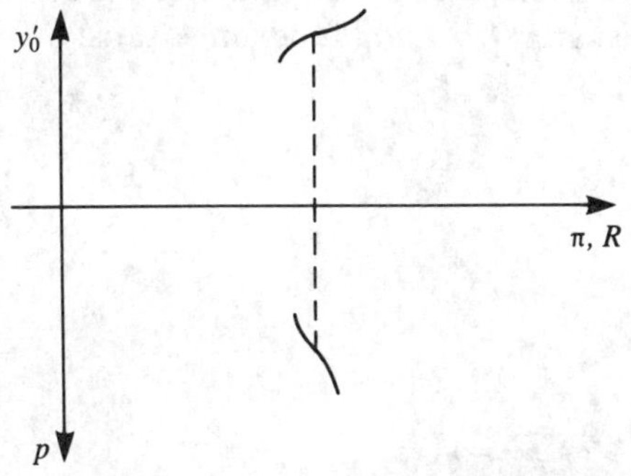


Figure 2.16b

Now it is easy to see that:

if LR2 holds at $\bar{u}$ the submatrix $(\partial_R d, \partial\eta)$ is of rank $n$. Because $\bar{p}\cdot\partial_R d \neq 0, \bar{p}\cdot\partial\eta = 0$, and $\partial\eta$ is of rank $(n-1)$, $\partial_R d$ and $n-1$ independent vectors of $\partial\eta$ are linearly independent.

If LR3 holds at $\bar{u}$ the submatrix $(\partial_{y'_{0h}} d - \partial_{y'_{0h}}\eta, \partial\eta)$ is of full rank (for similar reasons).

Theorem 2 follows then from the application of the implicit function theorem (see Mathematical appendix). □

Theorem 2[17] indicates two different possible local parametrizations of the set of tax equilibria, the first one depending upon the consumption prices and the public goods levels, when the second uses the consumption prices,

[17] Again, in the case of constant returns to scale, a variant of theorem 2 holds true. The proof is similar: it is easy to check that the Jacobian associated with the market clearing equations is analogous to the one exhibited above with the only difference that some new matrix $\partial\Lambda$ replaces $\partial\eta$. The rest of the argument is unchanged.

the transfer level and the levels of all public goods but one. These two local parametrizations are illustrated – again using the convention of descriptive geometry, described above, when there is locally one degree of freedom – in figures 16a and 16b. The next natural step is to look at the derivatives of the parametrization functions found in theorem 2. For that, let us be reminded of the local equations under the form (2.21) to (2.22).

$$\Phi_{\pi}(u)\dot{\pi}+\Phi_{R}(u)\dot{R}+\Phi_{y_0'}(u)\dot{y}_0'=0 \tag{2.21}$$

$$\dot{p}=(\partial\eta)^{-1}\{(\partial_{\pi}d)\dot{\pi}+(\partial_{R}d)\dot{R}+(\partial_{y_0'}d-\partial_{y_0'}\eta)\dot{y}_0'\} \tag{2.22}$$

Using the function $\mathscr{R},\mathscr{P}$ and $\tilde{\mathscr{Y}}'_{0h},\tilde{\mathscr{P}}$ obtained in theorem 2, a rigorous rearrangement of the argument of section 2.2.1. leads to the following:

α/ For the first parametrization (under LR2) the parameters are $\pi$ and $y_0'$ and the derivatives of the parametrization function $\mathscr{R}$ satisfy

$$\Phi_{R}(\bar{u})\frac{\partial\mathscr{R}}{d\pi}+\Phi_{\pi}(\bar{u})=0$$

$$\Phi_{R}(\bar{u})\frac{\partial\mathscr{R}}{\partial y_0'}+\Phi_{y_0'}(\bar{u})=0$$

It follows that

$$\frac{\partial\mathscr{P}}{\partial\pi}=(\partial\eta)^{-1}\left\{\partial_{\pi}d+(\partial_{R}d)\frac{\partial\mathscr{R}}{\partial\pi}\right\}$$

$$\frac{\partial\mathscr{P}}{\partial y_0'}=(\partial\eta)^{-1}\left\{(\partial_{R}d)\frac{\partial\mathscr{R}}{\partial y_0'}+(\partial_{y_0'}d-\partial_{y_0'}\eta)\right\}$$

β// For the case of the second parametrization (under LR3) the parameters are $\pi, y_{0h}'$, $k\neq h$, $R$ and the derivatives of the parametrization function $\tilde{\mathscr{Y}}'_{0h}$ satisfy

$$\Phi_{y_{0h}'}(\bar{u})\frac{\partial\tilde{\mathscr{Y}}'_{0h}}{\partial\pi}+\Phi_{\pi}(\bar{u})=0$$

$$\Phi_{y_{0h}'}(\bar{u})\frac{\partial\tilde{\mathscr{Y}}'_{0h}}{\partial R}+\Phi_{R}(\bar{u})=0$$

$$\Phi_{y_{0h}'}(\bar{u})\frac{\partial\tilde{\mathscr{Y}}'_{0h}}{\partial y_{0k}'}+\Phi_{y_{0k}'}(\bar{u})=0$$

It follows that the derivatives of the function $\mathscr{P}$ satisfy

$$\frac{\partial\mathscr{P}}{\partial\alpha}=(\partial\eta)^{-1}\left\{\partial_{\alpha}d+(\partial_{y_{0h}'}d-\partial_{y_{0h}'}\eta)\frac{\partial\tilde{\mathscr{Y}}'_{0h}}{\partial\alpha}\right\}$$

where $\alpha$ designates either $\pi$, $R$, or $y_{0k}'$ $k\neq h$

Finally, a more compact statement of the above formulas is given in Theorem 3.[18]

**Theorem 3: Derivatives with respect to local parameters**

*Assume that we are in the conditions of theorem 2*
*(1) Then the parametrization functions $\mathscr{R}$, $\mathscr{P}$, defined under LR2 have the following derivatives*

$$\frac{\partial \mathscr{R}}{\partial \alpha} = -\frac{\Phi_\alpha(\bar{u})}{\Phi_R(\bar{u})} \qquad \frac{\partial \mathscr{P}}{\partial \alpha} = (\partial \eta)^{-1}\left\{\partial_\alpha d + \partial_R d \frac{\partial \mathscr{R}}{\partial \alpha}\right\}$$

*where $\alpha$ is any variable $\pi_l$. The formula holds true whenever $\alpha$ is any $y'_{0h}$ and $\partial_\alpha d$ in the second formula is replaced by $\partial_\alpha d - \partial_\alpha \eta$.*
*(2) The parametrization functions $\tilde{\mathscr{Y}}'_{oh}$, $\tilde{\mathscr{P}}$ defined under the second parametrization have the following derivatives*

$$\frac{\partial \tilde{\mathscr{Y}}'_{0h}}{\partial \alpha} = -\frac{\Phi_\alpha(\bar{u})}{\Phi_{y'_0}(\bar{u})} \qquad \frac{\partial \tilde{\mathscr{P}}}{\partial \alpha} = \partial \eta^{-1}\left\{\partial_\alpha d + (\partial_{y'_{0h}} d - \partial_{y'_{0h}} \eta)\frac{\partial \tilde{\mathscr{Y}}'_{0h}}{\partial \alpha}\right\}$$

*where $\alpha$ is any variable $\pi_l$, $R$, $y'_{0k}$, $k \neq h$.*

As we will see in the following, the formulas provide a milestone for any comparative statics study.[19] The reader should convince himself that these formulas are not mysterious. Take for example part 1 of the theorem. The first formula gives the derivative of $R$ with respect to one local parameter $\alpha$. It says how the (infinitesimal) changes in $R$ and $\alpha$ must compensate in order to remain in the set of tax equilibria. The fact that such a compensation reflects the ratio of the marginal cost of the parameter to the marginal cost of increasing income, both measured with production prices, is in direct line with the intuitive analysis of section 1. The second formula indicates how the production price change must match the total change in demand induced by a change of one parameter: the expression on the right-hand side is only a total – rather than a partial – derivative with respect to the parameter.

Theorem 2 gives a valid parametrization and theorem 3 gives all the derivatives with respect to this parametrization, i.e., all the directions of state variable changes with respect to the parameter changes, and we have thus achieved our goal of providing a comprehensive and economically relevant description of the neighbourhood of our tax equilibrium. The passage from the local viewpoint to a global viewpoint is the subject of the next section.

[18] Note again that under the conditions of a constant returns to scale production, the argument of theorem 3 can be repeated.

## 2.3 The global structure of the set of tax equilibria (**)(T***)

In this section, we attempt to understand, starting from the local properties of the set of tax equilibria which have been exhibited in section 2.2, the global structure of tax equilibria. We will first focus on minimal regularity properties (2.3.1) showing that the set of tax equilibria is 'generically' a smooth manifold. We will then exhibit conditions assuring that this set is extremely regular (2.3.2), the first local parametrization of section 2.2 being extended to a global one so that the manifold of tax equilibria in particular is simply connected. A technical lemma will rule out under additional assumptions some kinds of points at infinity on the manifold. This lemma which is of independent interest for the study of the manifold is also useful as an introduction to an argument of the next subsection. In subsection 2.3.4., we focus attention on some of the sections of the set of tax equilibria – particularly the set of 'equal yield linear tax equilibria' – that may not be connected and we provide additional conditions that do assure connectedness. Lastly, in section 2.3.5, we examine conditions that assure the global validity of the second local parametrization of section 2.2. In the whole section, the economy is identified with the functions $d_i$, $\eta$; and all assumptions concern these functions.

### 2.3.1 The global structure of tax equilibria: generic regularity properties (**)

Counting the number of equations and unknowns in the previous section suggested that the system had a certain number of degrees of freedom; these degrees of freedom were made explicit in subsequent analysis. In this perspective, the question of the present subsection is roughly the question of the constancy of the number of degrees of freedom across the set of tax equilibria. When this number is indeed constant, then the corresponding set is said to be a smooth manifold: each point has a neighbourhood that looks like – is homeomorphic, diffeomorphic to – an open set of a Euclidean space of constant dimension. Remember that regularity properties of this kind had been noted in all the specific examples presented at the end of section 2.1.

In fact we do show that, for our model, the number of 'local' degrees of freedom is indeed constant, the set of tax equilibria being a smooth *manifold*, either under specific circumstances (theorem 4) or for the 'generic' case (theorem 5).

[19] See section 2.4.4.

Before doing that we need first to strengthen the differentiability assumption in the following way:[20]

**(DI)** *Differentiability*

*The functions $d_i$, $\eta$ that are homogeneous of degree zero respectively in $\pi$, R and p are $C^\infty$ on the interior of their domain.*

Under (DI), a tax equilibrium identifies with a sequence $(p, \pi, R, y'_0)$ which satisfies

$$\sum_i d_i(\pi, R, y'_0) - \eta(y'_0, p) = 0$$

We will rule out complications due to boundary problems (for example, if the uniform lump sum transfer is much too negative – a fact depending upon $\pi$ – the consumer will be bankrupt) by focusing attention on tax equilibria associated with the points interior to the domain of definition of the functions $d_i, \eta$. We call such equilibria interior tax equilibria.

*Definition*

*The set of* **interior tax** *equilibria* $\epsilon$ *is:*

$$\epsilon = \{(p, \pi R, y'_0) \in A' \text{ where } \sum_i d_i(\pi, R, y'_0) - \eta(y'_0, p) = 0\}$$

where $A'$ is an open set in $\mathscr{R}^{2n+n'+1}$, the interior of the domain of definition of the functions $d_i, \eta$ (or $\eta_1$ and $\eta_0$). However, as $d_i$ and $\eta$ are homogeneous of degree zero, two degrees of freedom are irrelevant. From now on, *prices will be normalized by the rule* $\pi_1 = p_1 = 1$. The interior of the domain which is then a set in $\mathscr{R}^{2n+n'-1}$ is denoted A. Unless there are explicit contrary statements, the set of interior tax equilibria is now taken in A.[21]

Also, from now on, we will always suppose without explicit mention that the set of interior tax equilibria is non-empty.

**(NE)** *(Non-emptiness)*

*The set of interior tax equilibria is non empty.*

Property NE is not guaranteed at the very general level that we adopt here (take, for example, $d_i = K$, $\eta = K'$ where $K$ and $K'$ are different constants).

[20] As the reader may notice later, most statements in the following hold with weaker differentiability assumptions. However, this assumption avoids cumulating too many technical difficulties.

[21] Note that no assumption is made on its structure, at this stage.

However it is not restrictive on economic grounds: many weak assumptions imply it. For example it will become true later when economic flesh is introduced into the model and in particular under the conditions that are sufficient for the validity of theorem 6.

More substantive assumptions can now be introduced.

**(AP)** *Additivity of preferences between private and public goods*

*Whatever i, the utility function of household i is of the form*

$$U_i(W_i(z_i) + \Gamma_i(y_0'))$$

This is a standard hypothesis of additivity of preferences. There are many examples of non-separable interactions between public and private goods (TV broadcasts and TV sets, etc.). The hypothesis is often viewed as a useful benchmark.

Assume also that the local regularity assumption LR1 holds at every point where supply is defined, a fact that we restate as FRJS.

**(FRJS)** *Full rank of the Jacobian of supply*

*At every $(p, y_0') \in$ Proj A, the $n \times n$ Jacobian matrix of total supply (with respect to p) is of rank $n-1$.*

Let us also assume that there are no inferior goods in the aggregate, i.e.,

**(NIW)** *Non-inferiority weak form*[22]

$$\forall(\pi, R, y_0') \in \text{Proj A}, \ \partial_R d(\pi, R, y_0') > 0$$

NIW is a standard non-inferiority assumption that does not require long comment. Note however that it implies the global validity of the local assumption LR2.

Under these assumptions, an unambiguous statement obtains:

**Theorem 4[23]: The manifold of tax equilibria**

*Let us assume (DI)(Differentiability) and FRJS (Full rank of Jacobian of supply). Let us also assume*

[22] Again $>0$ means that all coordinates are strictly positive.

[23] To some extent, this statement can be viewed as belonging to the previous section. As the final part of the proof shows, the global property described is nothing else other than the 'union' of the local properties analysed above.

*either NIW (Non-inferiority weak form)*
*or AP (Additivity between private and public good) and PAMC (Positivity of aggregate marginal costs)*

*Then* $\epsilon$*, the set of interior tax equilibria, is a smooth manifold of dimension* $n+n'-1$.

*When the latter property holds true, the* economy *is said to be* regular

*Proof*

Consider first the case where NIW holds true: it implies that condition LR2 of the previous section is true in every tax equilibrium. A first proof obtains then as follows: according to theorem 2, section 2.2, each interior tax equilibrium has a neighbourhood $\mathscr{V}(\cdot)$ which can be parametrized by functions of $\pi, y_0'$; this neighbourhood $\mathscr{V}(\cdot)$ being then diffeomorphic to an open set of $\mathscr{R}^{n+n'-1}$. It follows that $\epsilon$ is a smooth manifold of dimension $n+n'-1$. An alternative proof can be obtained by considering the mapping

$$f: (p, \pi, R, y_0') \in A \rightarrow \sum_i d_i(\pi, R, y_0') - \eta(y_0', p) \in \mathscr{R}^n$$

If we compute the Jacobian derivative $df$, an argument exactly similar to the one of the proof of theorem 2, section 2.2.2, shows that the rank of $df$ is $n$. From the inverse image theorem (Mathematical appendix), it follows that $f^{-1}(0)$ is a smooth manifold of dimension $2n+n'-1-n=n+n'-1$.

Considering now the second set of assumptions AP, PAMC, we remember that assumption LR3 of the previous section (positivity of the generalized marginal cost) holds

$$C(\pi, p, R, y_0') = -p \cdot \partial_{y_0'} \eta + p \cdot \partial_{y_0'} d = -p \cdot \partial_{y_0'} \eta > 0$$

The previous argument can be transposed, using either the second parametrization of theorem 2 or again the inverse image theorem. □

The reader will realize that no assumption is superfluous for the argument. For example when AP and PAMC do not hold, there is nothing that assures that the generalized marginal cost is positive in any tax equilibrium. In that case the second local parametrization of theorem 2 does not necessarily hold true at every point of the set of tax equilibria.

Then, theorem 4 requires significantly strong assumptions. Does that mean that, outside the domain of validity of the theorem, regular economies do not exist or even are exceptional? The answer is negative, as we shall see. The coexistence of these two facts is not paradoxical. It must be understood that unless assumptions like those of theorem 4 are met, it is difficult to be sure that a given economy is regular. However, outside the field of the theorem, regularity remains, in a sense to be made more precise, 'very likely' or 'most often' true.

To give content to the latter assertion, we imbed the considered economy in a 'space of economies'. An economy $\epsilon$ is there associated with an ($n$-dimensional) vector $\omega$ of exogenous endowments, that can be interpreted as an exogenous manna.

We then define:

*Definition: The set of interior tax* ***equilibria for the economy ω****, $\omega \in \mathscr{R}^n$, is*

$$\epsilon(\omega) = \{(p, \pi R, y_0') \in A, \text{ s.t. } d(\pi, R, y_0') - \eta(y_0', p) = \omega\}$$

The initial economy corresponds then to $\omega = 0$, the case where there is no exogenous manna.

We can now state:

**Theorem 5: The Manifold Structure**

*Assume DI (Differentiability) and suppose that there exists a neighbourhood $\mathscr{V}$ of 0 such that for every economy $\omega$ in $\mathscr{V}$, NE (Non Emptiness) holds true.*

*Then, for every $\omega$ in $\mathscr{V} \backslash N$, where N is of Lebesque measure zero, the set of interior tax equilibria $\epsilon(\omega)$ is a smooth manifold of dimension $n + n' - 1$.*

*Proof*

Consider the mapping

$$f\colon (p, \pi, R, y_0', \omega) \in (A \times \mathscr{V}) \rightarrow d(\pi, R, y_0') - \eta(y_0', p) - \omega \in \mathscr{R}^n$$

We argue first that 0 (in $\mathscr{R}^n$) is a regular value of $f$; considering the Jacobian matrix of $f$, we see that the submatrix associated with the derivatives with respect to $\omega$ define an identity matrix, which is clearly of rank $n$.

The inverse image theorem (Mathematical appendix) shows that $f^{-1}(0)$ is a smooth manifold whose dimension is $3n + n' - 1$ minus $n$, i.e., $2n + n' - 1$.

Consider now $\psi$: $(p, \pi, R, y_0', \omega) \rightarrow \omega \in \mathscr{R}^n$, the projection operator, and consider the restriction of $\psi$ to $f^{-1}(0)$.

According to (a variant of) Sard's theorem (Appendix), the set $N$ of critical values of that mapping is of measure zero. At every $\omega$ in the complement set, the inverse image theorem can be again invoked: As from (NE), $\psi^{-1}(\omega)$ is non-empty (for $\omega$ in $v$), it is a smooth manifold of dimension $n + n' - 1$ (withdraw $n$ from $2n + n' - 1$). □

A number of comments on theorem 5 are called for.

On the one hand, theorem 5 says that the set of regular economies – in the 'space of economies' considered above – is dense since its complement is of measure zero – but not open and dense. With an open dense set of regular economies, a small neighbourhood of a regular economy would only consist of regular economies. Regularity could be truly called 'generic'.

On the other hand, theorem 5 could indeed be modified in order to conclude at genericity in the just evoked sense. There are two (not mutually exclusive) ways for doing that.

The first one relates to the fact that in theorem 5 the mappings $d$ and $\eta$ are fixed and might be 'badly' chosen. This suggests that one should enlarge the space of economies; an economy close to the initial economy not only differs by the vector of endowments $\omega$ but also by the demand and supply functions. Indeed, if the topology on the new space of economies is well chosen (it is the Withney topology for the functions $d$ and $\eta$), then regularity is an open dense property. The interested reader will find elsewhere a proof of this fact,[24] which, although applying to a slightly different model, could be transposed here. Hence it is true that *there is an open dense set of data for which the economy is regular*. It should be clear however that the proof appeals to more sophisticated tools (infinite dimensional spaces and corresponding topologies, Thom transversality theorem) the use of which has been ruled out in this book.

A second way to obtain a more satisfactory version of theorem 5, would be to enlarge the space of economies by making demand and supply dependent on finite dimensional parameters and/or introducing appropriate boundary behaviour for the demand and supply functions.[25]

In conclusion, although theorem 5 is not entirely conclusive, the reader should keep in mind that it is only for exceptional values of parameters that the set of tax equilibria may display irregularities. Again although exceptional, this situation is extremely difficult to rule out on the basis of particular assumptions on preferences and technologies (but those of theorem 5).

### 2.3.2 The global structure of tax equilibria: the connectedness issue (**)

The preceding subsection focused attention on the minimal regularity properties of the set of tax equilibria. The present section attempts to take another step in the direction of the understanding of the structure of this set. In fact, attention will be focused on an economy which will be more broadly defined than the initial economy we are considering: particularly levels of

[24] Fuchs–Guesnerie (1983).

[25] We have finally ruled out such an option here, both because the assumptions that have to be made on the way the economy depends on the finite-dimensional parameters are somewhat *ad hoc*, and because the conditions that are required (in view of the conclusions obtained in the more abstract setting alluded to above) are superfluous.

public goods will be allowed to be positive or negative and the consumption sets will not be bounded from below. This economy can be viewed as an *extension* of the initial economy; the consideration of this extended economy being justified by the simplicity of its structure. The original economy then inherits of this simple structure but for some 'accidents' which can be identified and classified: accidents coming from the restriction of the extended economy for example to the positive levels of public goods, also accidents relating to the procedure of extension.

We will exhibit assumptions under which the extended manifold of tax equilibria is extremely regular; it is diffeomorphic to a Euclidean space. This is a particularly remarkable structure: the set is globally parametrized, it is made of one piece, there is no 'hole' in it, and two tax equilibria can be linked with a continuous path (it is connected). Many interesting subsets of tax equilibria will be obtained as sections of the extremely well-behaved manifold. The knowledge of the general manifold will provide helpful information on its sections, although obviously they will not necessarily inherit its extreme regularity and in particular its connectedness.[26]

From now on, we will state a certain number of assumptions. These assumptions have to be considered as applying to an *extended economy*. The extent to which a given economy can be so extended will be briefly discussed. The first assumption ECS extends the regularity properties of sections whereas the second one makes explicit the extended domain of definition.

**(ECS)** *(Extended) Convexity of sections*

*Assumption CS holds true* $\forall y'_0 \in \mathscr{R}^{n'}$.

**(EDD)** *(Extended) domain of definition*

$$d_i \text{ is defined for every } \pi, R, y'_0 \in \dot{\mathscr{R}}_+^{n-1} \times \mathscr{R} \times \mathscr{R}^{n'},$$
$$\eta \text{ is defined on } AC^+ \times \mathscr{R}^{n'}, \text{ where } \mathrm{AC}^+ \subset \mathscr{R}_+^{n-1}.$$[27]

[26] A general point should be made here: because the section of a connected manifold is not in general connected, it is true in some sense that a property like connectedness is more likely to hold when the set of tax equilibria we consider is 'bigger'. Consider for a limit example the set of tax equilibria associated with all economies when preferences, endowments, production sets are allowed to vary: it is rather intuitively straightforward that any $\pi, p, y'_0$ can be rationalized as an equilibrium and belongs to this big set, which is hence connected. However, this property is almost useless for the understanding of the questions we have in mind (and which are treated in this book). On the contrary, the analysis of this chapter which exhibits the minimal assumptions assuring the strong regularity of the set of tax equilibria is of direct relevance for the examination of the questions which are at the heart of the economic analysis.

[27] The fact that AC does not depend upon $y'_0$ simplifies notation and sometimes the argument without affecting substantially the conclusions of this section.

Two main remarks: First, EDD says that the demand for transactions of consumer $i$ is defined for normalized prices and more importantly every $R$; preferences underlying such a demand function have to be defined on a 'transaction space' which is $\mathscr{R}^n$, a fact which would be incompatible with a consumption set bounded from below. Note that a similar assumption on the domain of the demand function is not unusual in the classical studies of the Walras model.[28] Second, the vector $y_0'$ can be any vector of $\mathscr{R}^{n'}$. Implicit to that assumption is the fact that the production set $Y_0$ allows any (positive or negative) production of any public good to any extent, at least when adequate inputs of private goods are brought in (or withdrawn).

From now on, when we refer to the extended economy we will always suppose that ECS and EDD hold true. Finally we assume EDI *Extended Differentiability*[29] and EFRJS *Extended Full Rank of Jacobian of Supply* that states that DI and FRJS hold true in the extended economy.

The next assumption consists of a global non-inferiority property (ENIS) stronger than previous (NIW).

**(ENIS)** *(Extended non-inferiority (strong form))*

*$\forall(\pi, R, y_0'), (\partial_R d_i) > \mu(\pi, y_0')$ where $\mu$ is a vector of minimal income effects which is allowed to depend upon $\pi, y_0'$, but which has all its components strictly positive.*

ENIS says that for given $(\pi, y_0')$, all income effects have a strictly positive lower bound that may however vary with $(\pi, y_0')$. It does not seem a very restrictive[30] addition to NIW (which itself can be viewed as a global version of LR2). It implies that the expansion path through a given point is contained in a cone, that is itself included in the translation of the cone formed by the positive and negative orthants.

We have shown (theorem 2) that as a consequence of the local assumptions LR1, LR2, the set of tax equilibria around any tax equilibrium $\bar{u}$ was locally defined by

[28] See for example Balasko (1976). In fact the underlying question is to know whether the demand and supply functions which are naturally associated with a 'sufficiently smooth' economy can be extended to the domain above in as smooth a way. Standard results in mathematics suggest that this is reasonable.

[29] Note here that, even very weak, the definition EDI is not, strictly speaking, compatible with the fact that the global production set is a cone (although it can be as close as desired to a cone, in a certain sense). In the case of a cone, the section $y_0'=0$ is itself necessarily a cone which cannot be strictly convex, so that for this isolated value of $y_0'$, $\eta$ would not be a function. Although this is disturbing if one wants to assume constant returns to scale in the aggregate, this remark cannot be taken as too restrictive since it only concerns the section $y_0'=0$; informal approximations arguments suggest that there are no basic changes in the structure of the manifold when the production set is an exact cone.

[30] Even if one takes into account the extension procedure generating the preferences of the extended economy.

$$R = \mathscr{R}(\pi, y_0'),\ p = \mathscr{P}(\pi, y_0')$$

Next theorem 6 asserts that this parametrization is indeed global.

**Theorem 6: Structure and connectedness of the set of tax equilibria**

*Consider an extended economy (i.e., satisfying EDD (Extended domain of definition) ECS (Properties of sections)) and suppose EDI (Differentiability), EFRJS (Full rank assumption for supply), ENIS (Non-inferior goods (strong form)).*

*Then $\epsilon$ the manifold of equilibria is diffeomorphic to $\mathring{\mathscr{R}}_+^{n-1} \times \mathscr{R}^{n'}$ and thus simply connected; it admits a global parametrization $\mathscr{R}$, $\mathscr{P}$*

$$R = \mathscr{R}(\pi, y_0'),\ p = \mathscr{P}(\pi, y_0')$$

*Proof*

Consider a given $(\pi, y_0')$ and consider the position of $\sum_i d_i\ (\pi, R, y_0')$ with respect to $\mathrm{ES}(y_0') = \bigcup_p \eta(y_0', p)$ the frontier of the section of the global production set in $y_0'$. Take $\bar{y} \in \mathrm{ES}(y_0')$ and $\bar{B} = \bar{y} + \mathring{\mathscr{R}}_+^n$, $\underline{B} = \bar{y} - \mathring{\mathscr{R}}_+^n$. ENIS implies that when $R \to -\infty$, $\sum_i d_i(\pi, R, y_0')$ enters $\underline{B}$ and when $R \to +\infty$ enters $\bar{B}$. But from free disposal (ECS), $\bar{B}$ is 'above' $\mathrm{ES}(y_0')$ and $\underline{B}$ is 'below'. As $\mathrm{ES}(\bar{y}_0')$ is the frontier of the convex set $\mathrm{ES}(y_0') - \mathscr{R}_+^n$, it follows that there exists at least one $R$ and one $p$ such that

$$\sum_i d_i(\pi, R, y_0') = d(\pi, R, y_0') = \eta(y_0', p)$$

Again, ENIS and free disposal rule out different $R$ and ECS and EDI rule out different $p$.

This part of the proof shows that there is a bijection between the space of $(\pi, y_0')$ and $\epsilon$.

Now EFRJS and ENIS (that imply LR1 and LR2) allow the application of theorem 2 (at every tax equilibrium), showing that locally $\epsilon$ is parametrizable in $\pi, y_0'$.

The bijection between $\epsilon$ and the space of $\mathring{\mathscr{R}}_+^{n-1} \times \mathscr{R}^{n'}$, being a local diffeomorphism, is a global diffeomorphism. □

The set of tax equilibria of the extended economy meeting our regularity assumptions is a very simple and well-behaved mathematical object. In particular, its simple topological structure provides an interesting reference point for the study of subsets of the set of tax equilibria which are of economic interest. We first consider sections of the manifold corresponding to given levels of public goods. Theorem 6 has an obvious consequence: the parametrization functions $\mathcal{R},\mathcal{P}$ define parametrizations of the global manifold as well as of any of its sections associated with a given level of public good. Corollaries 1 and 2 stress this remark.

**Corollary 1: Connectedness of sections**

*For any $\bar{y}'_{0h}$, the section $\epsilon \cap \{y'_{0h}=\bar{y}'_{0h}\}$, the set of tax equilibria associated with a fixed level of one public good, is diffeomorphic to $\mathring{\mathcal{R}}^{n-1}_{+} \times \mathcal{R}^{n'-1}$ (and hence simply connected).*

**Corollary 2: Connectedness of the set of equal yield tax equilibria**

*The section $\{\epsilon \cap \{y'_0=\bar{y}'_0)\}$ the set of tax equilibria, associated with fixed levels of all public goods, is diffeomorphic to $\mathring{\mathcal{R}}^{n-1}_{+}$ and is globally parametrizable with $\pi$, $R=\mathcal{R}(\pi,\cdot)$, $p=\mathcal{P}(\pi,\cdot)$.*

The section $\{\epsilon \cap (y'_0=\bar{y}'_0)\}$ describes tax equilibria which correspond to the same public good levels. It evokes, for readers familiar with specialized terminology, the set of 'equal yield tax alternatives' of public finance textbooks. In fact, different tax equilibria in the section under consideration involve different tax receipts and, strictly speaking, different fiscal yields. If one excepts very specific models where equal fiscal yield does imply equal public good consumption, the 'equal public good tax alternatives' are not strictly speaking 'equal yield tax alternatives'. Sticking to the spirit of the terminology rather than to its letter, we will however refer to $\{\epsilon \cap (y'_0=\bar{y}'_0)\}$ as the set of equal yield tax equilibria. *Corollary 2 then asserts that the set of equal yield tax equilibria is connected and diffeomorphic to the orthant of a Euclidean space.* Figure 2.17 illustrates Corollary 1 and also to some extent theorem 6.

Up to now, we have provided a powerful global parametrization result. This result implies in particular that the set of tax equilibria, but also a number of its sections of economic interest – as the so-called set of 'equal yield tax alternatives' – is connected. However, other sections of economic interest are not necessarily – even under our assumptions – connected. We examine next in subsection 2.3.4 a set called the set of 'equal yield linear tax alternatives'. Beforehand we choose to focus attention on a 'technical' property of the set of tax equilibria.

### 2.3.3 A technical lemma on points at infinity on the manifold of equilibria and a variant of theorem 6 (T***)

First, we choose to introduce a new set of assumptions concerning the extended economy. These assumptions are much stronger than the previous ones but are ingredients of the next two theorems.

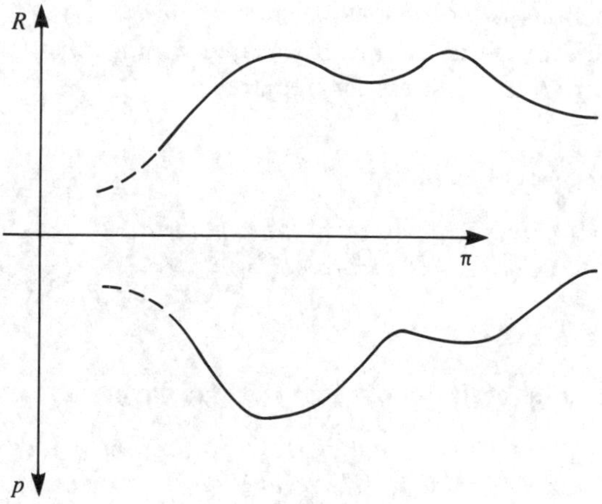


Figure 2.17

The first one (EBP) is the boundary condition for production prices (BP), stated in the extended economy. The second is a boundary assumption involving public good production (EBPG). The third one concerns the limit behaviour of demand in the extended economy (ELBD).

**(EBP)** *Boundary condition for production prices*

$\forall y_0', \eta(y_0', p)$ *is defined* $\forall p \in \mathring{\mathscr{R}}_+^{n-1}$

$\forall y_0', p_h/\|p\| \to 0$ *for some* $h \Rightarrow \exists k | \eta_k(y_0', p) \to -\infty$

Note that the BP that has been introduced (in the non-extended economy) and discussed in section 2.1 has the following consequence: if the vector of consumers' excess demand is finite, then the production price vector cannot be on the boundary of its domain of definition.

**(EBPG)** *(Extended) boundary assumption for public good production*

(1) $y_h = \lim_n \eta_h(y_{0n}', p_n) = +\infty \Rightarrow \exists k$ *such that* $y_{0kn}' \to -\infty$

(2) $\lim \eta_h(y_{0n}', p_n) = -\infty \quad \forall h \Rightarrow \exists k | \lim y_{0kn}' = +\infty$

(3) *If* $\|y_{0n}'\| \to \mp\infty$, *then* $\|\eta(y_{0n}', p_n)\|$ *becomes unbounded.*

Note first that EBPG1 says that an infinite production of a private good is possible only when the production of public good is minus infinity, i.e., when an infinite quantity of public input is provided. This property requires that all sections of the production set are bounded from above. Although such a boundedness property can easily be extended, its validity in the initial (non-extended) economy is a strong assumption (in fact it is stronger and even much stronger than what we actually need). Also, EBGP2 asserts that if an infinite amount of all private goods is provided to the production sector, then at least one public good can be produced in infinite amount. This property (normally) concerns the initial economy and requires that returns do not decrease too much with the level of public goods. Finally EBPG3 asserts that the quantity of a public good cannot increase or decrease infinitely without making some private good level infinitely high or low. It will be much used in the case where there is only one public good.

Note also, for the sake of illustration, an example of a three-good economy (one consumption good, one factor, one public good) meeting EBPG: the global production set, the sections of which for given levels of public good are represented on figure 2.18a, and whose asymptotic level of good one as a function of the public good level is represented on figure 2.18b meets the desired properties. (The dotted lines of figure 2.18b suggest what is forbidden by EBPG1, 2, 3.) Clearly the production sets under consideration, have features that can be replicated in $\mathscr{R}^n$. Note however that the following statements only refer to one or two of the properties EBPG.

The extended limit behaviour of demand is the following:

**(ELBD)** *(Extended) limit behaviour of demand*

*Let an infinite sequence* $\pi_n, R_n, y'_{0n}$ *be such that* $\pi_n/\|\pi_n\| \to \bar{\pi}, y'_{0n} \to \bar{y}'_0$

(1) *If* $R_n \to +\infty, \exists k | d_{ik}(\cdot) \to +\infty$
(2) *If* $R_n \to \bar{R}$ *and* $\bar{\pi} \in \mathscr{R}^{n-1}_+ | \mathring{\mathscr{R}}^{n-1}_+$
*then* $\exists h$ *such that* $d_{ih}(\cdot) \to +\infty$
(3) *If* $R_n \to -\infty$, *and* $\bar{\pi} \in \mathring{\mathscr{R}}^{n-1}_+$, $d_{ih}(\cdot) \to -\infty, \forall h$

Note that ELBD1 is nothing other than the extension of LBD1 introduced in section 2.1. ELBD1 is a classical property of the initial economy – we have already argued that it was redundant given our general assumptions on preferences. ELBD2 concerns the limit of demand when some prices of consumption goods but also of factors tend to zero. Although in line with the spirit of the extension procedure it is not innocuous: for low prices, not only the demand for commodities but also possibly the demand for others' labour time increases indefinitely. ELBD3 when $R<0$ is a property of the extended economy that holds for most procedures of extension (of indifference maps) that one can think of.

In view of the next proofs the reader is also invited to note that (ELBD1,3) together with EBPG prevents the occurrence of a tax equilibrium with an 'infinite' $R$ and finite $y'_0$. We have already noticed that with EBP (Boundary condition for production prices), a finite vector of excess

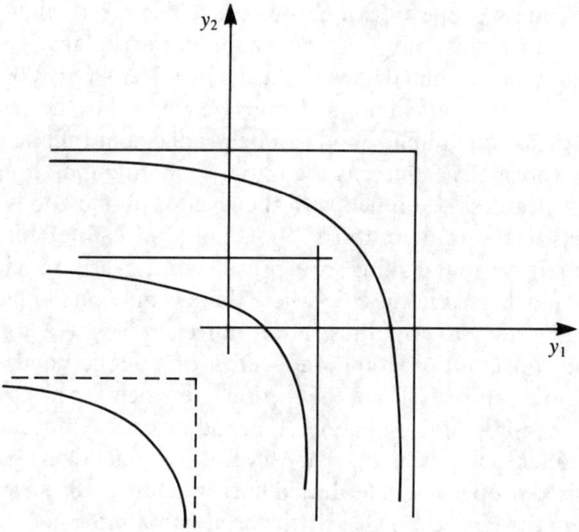


Figure 2.18a

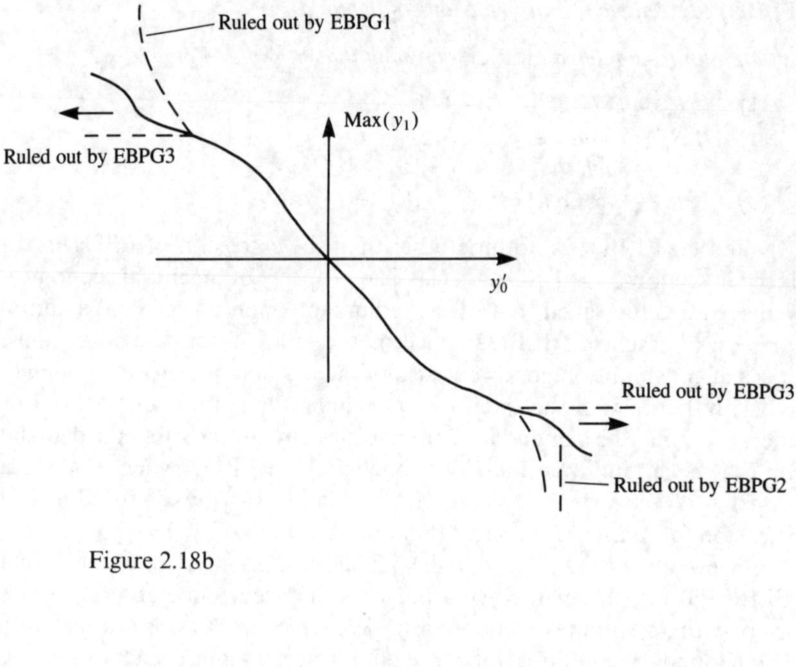


Figure 2.18b

demand was not compatible with production prices being at the boundary of their domain of definition. The combination of these two facts is at the heart of the next statement: Lemma 2.

**Lemma 2**

*Consider an economy satisfying EDD: Extended domain of definition, EDI: Differentiability, EBPG 1,2: Boundary assumption for Public Goods EBP: Boundary condition for production prices, ELBD 1,3: Limit behaviour of demand.*

*Consider a sequence* $(\pi_n, y'_{0n}, p_n, R_n)$ *of tax equilibria such that* $(\pi_n, y'_{0n}) \rightarrow (\bar{\pi}, \bar{y}'_0)$, $\bar{\pi} \in \mathring{\mathscr{R}}^{n-1}_+$.
*Then*

*(i)* $(p_n/\|p\|, R_n)$ *have no accumulation points on the boundary of their domain.*

*(ii) there exists a subsequence such that* $\bar{p}_n \rightarrow \bar{p} \in \mathring{\mathscr{R}}^{n-1}_+$, $R_n \rightarrow \bar{R}$.
*(and* $(\bar{\pi}, \bar{p}, \bar{R}, \bar{y}_0)$ *is a tax equilibrium).*

Lemma 2 implies that above some $(\pi, y'_0)$ belonging to the (projection of) set of tax equilibria there exists no point going to infinity so that the projection of the set of tax equilibria over $\mathring{\mathscr{R}}^{n-1}_+ \times \mathscr{R}^{n'}$ is closed.[31]

*Proof*
Consider such a subsequence $(\pi_n, y'_{0n}, p_n, R_n)$. Consider now the equation

$$\sum_i d_i(\pi_n, R_n, y'_{0n}) = \eta(y'_{0n}, p_n).$$

If $R_n \rightarrow +\infty$, $\exists h | d_{ih}(\ ) \rightarrow \infty$ (LBD1), then $\eta_h(p_n, y'_{0n}) \rightarrow +\infty$. But EBPG1 contradicts the fact that $y'_{0n} \rightarrow \bar{y}'_0$.

Now if $R_n \rightarrow -\infty$, $d_{ih} \rightarrow -\infty \forall h$(ELBD3). But the convergence of $y'_{0n}$ contradicts EBPG2. Finally, in the cases where $\|p_n\| \rightarrow +\infty$ or $p_{hn} \rightarrow 0$, when $R_n$ remains bounded, the convergence of a well chosen subsequence of $\sum_i d_i(\pi_n, R_n, y'_{0n})$ would contradict EBP.

This proves part (i) of this lemma. Part (ii) is a direct consequence. □

Lemma 2 is illustrated in figure 2.19: figures 2.19a and 2.19b show two situations that are excluded by lemma 2; figure 2.19c shows a situation that is *not* excluded by lemma 2.

There are three reasons for bringing attention to lemma 2. First, the properties that it emphasizes, although technical, provide useful indica-

[31] In technical terms, lemma 2 asserts that the projection is proper.

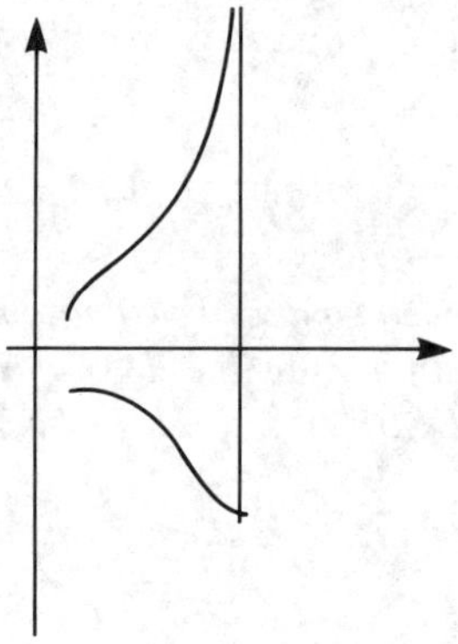

Figure 2.19a

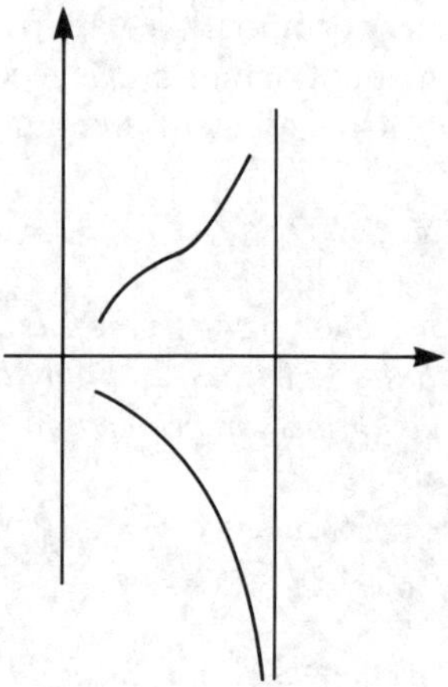

Figure 2.19b

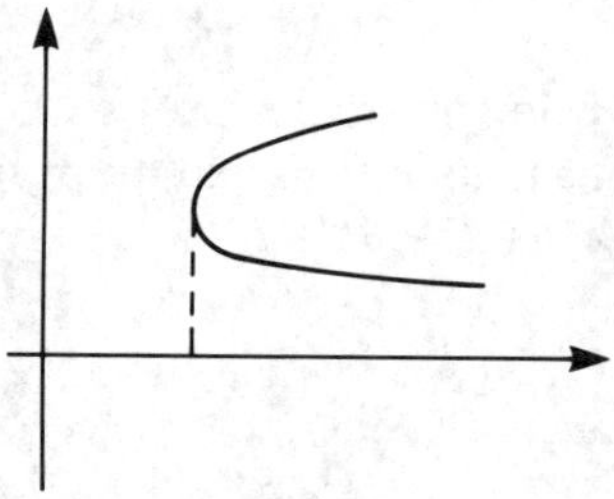

Figure 2.19c

tions on the projection of the set of tax equilibria. Second, it allows proof of a variant of theorem 6′ that replaces the strong form of non-inferiority with its weak form. Third, it introduces the same prototype argument that is used in the next theorems, 7 and 8.

Let us first come to the fact that from lemma 2, a variant of theorem 6 can be obtained. Again theorem 6 allows the weakening of the inferiority assumption of theorem 6, but at the rather high cost of introducing EBP EBPG and ELBD1,2.[32]

[32] It is somewhat troublesome that a slight weakening of assumption ENIS to NIW requires such strong compensations as those allowing the move from theorem 6 to theorem 6′. The reader should however convince himself (by looking at counter examples) that indeed such compensations are needed.

**Theorem 6′**

*Let us suppose that the assumptions of lemma 2 hold true. In addition let us assume ECS (convexity of sections) EFRJS (full rank assumption for supply) and ENIW (non-inferiority weak version).*

*Then the conclusions of theorem 6 hold true.*

*Proof*

With EFRJS and ENIW, the local parametrization of theorem 2 is valid around any $(\pi, y_0')$ belonging to the projection of $\epsilon$ on $\mathring{\mathscr{R}}_+^{n-1} \times \mathscr{R}^{n'} \stackrel{\text{def}}{=} Q$. Then $Q$ is an open set. But from lemma 2, it is a closed set. Then, it is the whole space $\mathring{\mathscr{R}}_+^{n-1} \times \mathscr{R}^{n'}$.

But then NIW and free disposal (CS) rule out two different $R$ 'above' one $\pi, y_0'$.

The conclusion follows as in theorem 6. □

### 2.3.4 The global structure of tax equilibria: connectedness of the set of equal yield linear tax alternatives (T***)

Let us now fix the uniform lump sum transfer $R$ to a given value $\bar{R}$. The set $\{\epsilon \cap (y_0' = \bar{y}_0') \cap (R = \bar{R})\}$ can be viewed as another set of equal yield tax equilibria, the taxes which are allowed to vary being indirect (commodity) taxes and direct linear taxes (factor taxes). We propose to term it the *set of equal yield linear tax equilibria*.

The set $\epsilon \cap \{y_0' = \bar{y}_0'\} \cap \{R = \bar{R}\}$ should be 'generally' well behaved. In fact, from a straightforward application of Sard's theorem it is most often a smooth manifold. The question arises of whether it is connected. In economic terms, connectedness of this set implies that there cannot be two disjoint areas of consumption price vectors where the yield from linear taxes are the same. As discussed in section 2.1 in a world with only one tax distortion (two private goods), Laffer's law can be viewed as a contradiction to connectedness. Building on that intuition, one will introduce an assumption which states that there is a direction of increase of taxes, in the tax space, which ensures an increase of tax receipts, i.e., that there is a direction of tax increases where Laffer's 'law' is violated.

Formally, let us assume:

**(ITR)** *Existence of an increasing tax receipts direction* (for public good production $\bar{y}_0'$ and lump-sum income $\bar{R}$)

$$\exists \text{ a vector } \lambda \text{ such that } \forall p, \pi, \ -(p \cdot \partial_\pi d(\pi, \bar{y}_0', \bar{R})) \cdot \lambda > 0$$

Note first in order to validate the terminology that a tax increase in the direction $\lambda$ with fixed $\bar{R}$ implies a change in tax receipts proportional to $(\pi-p)(\partial_\pi d)\cdot\lambda+d\cdot\lambda$, i.e., to $-(p\cdot\partial_\pi d)\lambda$. Note second that the assumption is stated with reference to some $\bar{y}'_0, \bar{R}$. It means that a change of taxes in the direction $\lambda$ around the set of equal yield tax equilibria implies an increase in tax receipts. It does not imply that the increase in tax receipts or in public good levels will be moving monotonically along a line of direction $\lambda$. However, if one starts from one equal yield linear tax equilibrium $(\bar{y}'_0, \bar{R})$ in the direction $\lambda$, one will never cross it again.

Note finally that a good candidate for $\lambda$ is a vector of the form $(0,0,0,\lambda_{l+1},\dots,\lambda_n)$ where the zero components correspond to the factors supplied by households, the non-zero components corresponding to consumption goods.

Thanks to ITR, it is intuitively clear that the set of equal yield linear tax alternatives is 'pierced' only once by a vector of direction $\lambda$. Theorem 7 builds upon this remark but uses boundary assumptions – and in particular ELBD2 that was not needed previously – to obtain a stronger conclusion, i.e., the fact that the set is diffeomorphic to some subspace of the price space (and hence connected).

One can assert:

**Theorem 7: Connectedness of the set of equal yield linear tax equilibria**

*Consider an economy meeting the assumptions of theorem 6. Assume in addition the existence of an increasing tax receipts direction (ITR) for $\bar{y}'_0, \bar{R}$ and suppose that ELBD2, EBP and EBPG1 hold true. Then $\epsilon \cap \{y'_0 = \bar{y}'_0\} \cap \{R=\bar{R}\}$ if non-empty, is diffeomorphic to the projection of the price space $\mathscr{R}^{n-2}$ (along $\lambda$) and simply connected.*

*Proof*[33] (sketch)

We take as a new system of coordinates in the price space the direction $\lambda$ and the space $\mathscr{R}^{n-2}$ orthogonal to this direction where $l^\lambda$ is a set of coordinates. We denote $\pi=(\pi^\lambda, a^\lambda)$ where $\pi^\lambda$ is the coordinate in the direction $\lambda$ and $a^\lambda$ the coordinate on $l^\lambda$.

Consider now the directional derivative of the parametrization $\mathscr{R}$ of theorem 2 with respect to $\lambda$. It is denoted $\dfrac{\partial \mathscr{R}}{\partial \pi_\lambda}$ and equals (theorem 3) $\dfrac{-p\cdot\partial_\pi d\cdot\lambda}{p\cdot\partial_R d}$. From ITR it is a strictly positive number when evaluated on $\epsilon \cap \{y'_0 = \bar{y}'_0\} \cap \{R=\bar{R}\}$. The latter set is in fact defined through the relation-

[33] The proof is closely similar to the proof of theorem 6 in Fuchs–Guesnerie (1983) to which the reader is invited to refer for more details.

ship $\mathscr{R}(\pi, \bar{y}'_0) = \bar{R}$; it follows from the implicit function theorem that this equation can locally be solved as $\pi^\lambda = \phi(a^\lambda)$.

Noting that above one $a^\lambda$ there can exist from ITR at most one $\pi^\lambda$, the above local parametrization, can be extended to the set $Q \overset{\text{def}}{=} \text{Proj}\ \{\epsilon \cap \{y'_0 = \bar{y}'_0\} \cap \{R = \bar{R}\}\}$ (Proj being the projection along $\lambda$ on the space generated by $l^\lambda$).

The above argument has shown that $Q$ is open. In order to prove that it equals the space generated by $l^\lambda$ (which is of dimension $n-2$), it remains to show that $Q$ is closed.

Consider then a sequence of equal yield tax equilibria $\pi_n = (\pi^\lambda_n, a^\lambda_n), p_n, \bar{y}'_0, \bar{R}$ and assume that there is a subsequence such that $a^\lambda_n \to \bar{a}^\lambda$. $Q$ is closed if and only if there exists a tax equilibrium 'above' $\bar{a}^\lambda$. If (a subsequence) $\pi^\lambda_n \to \bar{\pi}^\lambda$, $p_n \to \bar{p}$, then $\bar{\pi} = (\bar{a}^\lambda, \bar{\pi}^\lambda)$, $\bar{p}$, $\bar{y}'_0, \bar{R}$ is by continuity an equal yield tax equilibrium with projection $\bar{a}^\lambda$. It is then enough to show that there is no diverging subsequence $\pi^\lambda_n, p^\lambda_n$.

In the case where $\|p_n\| \to +\infty$ or $p_{hn} \to 0$, when $\pi_n$ remains bounded, the convergence of (a subsequence of) $\sum_i d_i(\pi_n, \bar{R}, \bar{y}'_0)$ contradicts (EBP). The case when $\pi^n_\lambda \to +\infty$ or $+0$ is ruled out by ELBD2 and EBPG1.

It follows that there is a bijection between $Q$ and the space generated by $l^\lambda$. Furthermore, the bijection is a local diffeomorphism and again one concludes that it is a global diffeormorphism. □

### 2.3.5 Global structure of tax equilibria: global validity of the second parametrization (T***)

At this stage we have provided conditions assuring that the first local parametrization of section 2.2 has a global extension (and we have relied on this result to explore the connectedness properties of various sets). But we have said nothing on the extension of the second parametrization emphasized in section 2.2. We will do it here in the case where, for the sake of notational simplicity, there is only one public good so that the number $y'_{0h}$ identifies with the vector $y'_0$. In that case, the second parametrization of theorem 2, valid under LR3, is of the form $y'_0 = \mathscr{Y}(\pi, R), p = \mathscr{P}(\pi, R)$. Theorem 8 below, using an argument reminiscent of that of theorems 6′ and 7, gives conditions that assure that this second parametrization indeed extends to a global parametrization.

**Theorem 8: Global extension of the second parametrization**

*Suppose that the assumption of theorem 6 holds true.*
*Assume that there is one public good and that in addition the boundary*

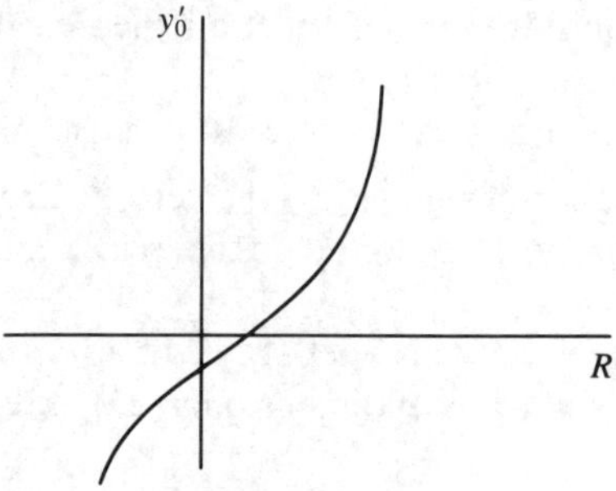


Figure 2.20

*assumptions for production prices (EBP) and for public goods (EBPG3) and the (extended) assumption of positivity of aggregate marginal costs (PAMC) and the (extended) additivity assumption (AP) hold true, then the manifold of tax equilibria can be globally parametrized by functions* $\tilde{\mathscr{Y}}, \tilde{P}$, *such that*

$$y_0' = \tilde{\mathscr{Y}}(\pi, R), \; p = \tilde{\mathscr{P}}(\pi, R).$$

*Proof*
Since theorem 6 holds true, let us consider the parametrization $R = \mathscr{R}(\pi, y_0')$, $p = \mathscr{P}(\pi, y_0')$.

From theorem 3, this chapter, we have

$$\frac{\partial \mathscr{R}}{\partial y_0'} = -\frac{\Phi_{y_0'}}{\Phi_R}$$

From the assumption AP and PAMC, it follows that LR3 (generalized positive marginal cost) holds so that $\Phi_{y_0'} > 0$, in any tax equilibrium.

From the implicit function theorem, the parametrization function of theorem 6, $\mathscr{R}$ is locally invertible in $y_0'$, for given $\bar{\pi}$. Hence locally around any tax equilibrium

$$y_0' = \mathscr{R}^{-1}(R, \bar{\pi}) \text{ and } \frac{\partial \mathscr{R}^{-1}}{\partial R} = -\frac{\Phi_R}{\Phi_{y_0'}} \neq 0$$

Let us call $Q(\bar{\pi})$, the setof $R$ that are associated with tax equilibria, for $\pi = \bar{\pi}$.

The above argument has shown that $Q(\bar{\pi})$ is an open set. Let us show now that it is closed (see figure 2.20)

Let us consider a sequence $(p_n, R_n, y_{0n}')$ such that $R_n \to \bar{R}$. We have to show that 'above' $\bar{R}$ there is some $\bar{y}_0', \bar{p}$ such that $(\bar{\pi}, \bar{p}, \bar{R}, \bar{y}_0')$ is a tax equilibrium.

We first show that $y_{0n}'$ is bounded: invoking additivity, $d(\bar{\pi}, R_n, y_{0n}')$ remains bounded; but from EBPG3 if $y_{0n}'$ were unbounded the norm of $\eta(p_n, y_{0n}')$ would be unbounded – hence a contradiction.

Considering then a subsequence $y'_{0n}$ converging to some $\bar{y}_0$, we then show using EBP that $p_n$ does not go to the boundary of its domain of definition; hence there is a converging subsequence $p_n \to \bar{p}$. And finally $\bar{\pi}, \bar{p}, \bar{R}, \bar{y}'_0$ is indeed a tax equilibrium.

We finally note that $Q(\bar{\pi})$ being both open and closed is the whole real axis and that the argument holds true whatever $\bar{\pi}$. □

The following observations may be made:

(i) Note the modification which has to be brought to the above statement when there are several public goods: the parametrization functions should depend upon the other coordinates of the public good vector.

(ii) Note that additivity of preferences between public and private goods is needed: example 3, section 2.1 which has provided us with a counter-example to connectedness, strongly relied on the non-separability assumption. Note also that theorem 6 did not require separability. However, many studies of tax equilibria are only concerned with linear tax equilibria and implicitly assume a fixed $R$ so that they implicitly operate in a framework which is in line with theorem 8.

At this stage, we have gone as far as we can in the study of the global structure. Besides minimal general regularity properties that often obtain (theorem 5), or 'generically', we have exhibited conditions that assure that either the set of tax equilibria (theorems 6 and 8) or some of its sections (corollaries to theorems 6 and 7) has a well understood mathematical structure. As we shall see later, and as the preliminary discussion of subsection 2.1.3 indicated, such 'good behaviour' has implications for both normative and positive studies. Here we switch to a typical 'positive' study – maybe the prototype of 'positive' studies, i.e., the analysis of existence and of tax incidence. The relevance of the investigation of the present section for a renewed approach to these classical problems will become progressively clearer throughout section 2.4.

## 2.4 Positive economics: tax equilibrium and tax incidence (**)(***)(T***)

In the preceding section, the indirect taxes implicit to an equilibrium are known once the bundle, production and consumption prices, $(p, \pi)$ is known. A tax equilibrium could conceivably be implemented through the announcement of $p$ and $\pi$ and implicity of the tax vector $T = \pi - p$.

In fact, the detailed computation of a tax equilibrium, as well as the (detailed) computation of any market equilibrium requires computational means which are not accessible to a central government.[34] Tax intervention hence does not consist of deciding about $p$ and $\pi$ (that would immediately clear the markets), but *operates through tax systems which establish a rigid connection between $p$ and $\pi$*, the determination of equilibrium being left to market forces.

The connection operated by actual tax systems between production and consumption prices is exemplified by *ad valorem* taxes: the tax $T_h$ on commodity $h$ is an a priori fixed percentage $\alpha_h$ of the production price $p_h$; the consumption price $\pi_h$ equals then $p_h(1+\alpha_h)$. Contrary to this, *specific* taxes introduce wedges between consumption and production prices which are independent of the production prices of commodities; for commodity, $h, \pi_h = p_h + \bar{T}_h$ where $\bar{T}_h$ is a priori fixed (say in dollars).

*Tax systems*, as defining rigid connections between production and consumption prices, are objects of study of the standard public finance literature; in particular, tax incidence theory is concerned with the effects of small changes in tax systems on tax equilibria. This section is devoted to the study of tax incidence in the general equilibrium framework which has been designed. We proceed as follows:

First, a formal definition of (direct or indirect) tax systems will be provided and discussed. This is the purpose of subsection 2.4.1.

Second, continuity properties of tax equilibria with respect to tax systems will be given. This is the purpose of subsection 2.4.2.

Third, the existence question will be considered in subsection 2.4.3.

Fourth, the standard tax incidence problem of the public finance literature – How does the equilibrium vary when the exogenous tax system varies? – is the subject of subsection 2.4.4.

Fifth, a particular emphasis will be put on the uniqueness question in subsection 2.4.5.

Note that part of the development of this subchapter is conducted under the assumption that there is *only one public good* ($y_0'$ is a one-dimensional vector). This does not much affect the argument, but simplifies the exposition.

### 2.4.1 Definition of tax systems (**)

The indirect tax systems we have discussed above (*ad valorem* and specific) associate consumption prices to production prices through a given relationship. It is natural to define general tax systems as mappings from production prices to consumption prices. By extension, tax systems which are not

[34] Note, however, that the justification given in chapter 1 assumes that global demand is known to the centre, although individual demand (and preferences) are unknown.

exclusively indirect, can be described through a mapping which associates to a given production price vector a consumption price(s) vector and a uniform lump-sum transfer $R$. This is the approach taken here.

However, before going to the formal definition we have to be reminded of the normalization problem lengthily discussed at the beginning of this chapter. Multiplying $p$ by some positive constant $\lambda$ and $\pi, R$ by some positive constant $\mu$ does not change the economic state; similarly an abstract tax system should define the same relationship between $p$, $\pi$, $R$, whatever the normalization rule. This justifies the following definition.

*Definition:* ***Abstract tax systems***

*An abstract tax system is a mapping from the equivalence classes of $\mathscr{R}^n_+$ to the equivalence classes of $\mathscr{R}^n_+ \times \mathscr{R}$, equivalent classes being taken in both cases with respect to the proportionality relationship. We will denote $\psi$ the mapping so defined.*

$$\psi: \mathscr{C}(\mathscr{R}^n_+) \rightarrow \mathscr{C}(\mathscr{R}^n_+ \times \mathscr{R})$$

*when $\mathscr{C}$ designates the equivalence classes associated with the proportionality relationship.*

Although this is somewhat incorrect, we will not give a different name to the restriction of the mapping $\psi$ when some normalization rule is specified, and we will write down

$$(\pi, R) = \psi(p)$$
$$\text{or } \pi = \psi_1(p),\ R = \psi_2(p).^{35}$$

Also, from now on and absent explicit contrary statement, we shall identify the equivalence classes $\mathscr{C}(\mathscr{R}^n_+ \times \mathscr{R})$ with $\mathscr{R}^{n-1}_+ \times \mathscr{R}$, in line with the numeraire normalization adopted above.

Note that the definition given here does not take into account any public good production objectives. It puts the burden of adjustment precisely on public good levels. One should realize that, through the definition of tax systems, one dimension of adjustment has necessarily to be left free; given that fact, the above definition looks a reasonable formalization of the questions under scrutiny. However, adjustments through the uniform lump-sum transfer (choose $y_0'$ as a function of $p$ and let $R$ adjust), through one commodity tax (let the price of this commodity adjust) or through some taxation rate (let the taxation rate of a bundle of commodities adjust) are also conceivable. The analysis of these other adjustment procedures raises problems which are not too different from the ones we will consider here.

[35] Note that there is no loss in generality in assuming $R = \psi_2(p)$ rather than $R = g_2(p, \pi)$.

Tax systems themselves can belong to some a priori given subset. For the sake of simplicity we will consider only subclasses which are finite dimensional and indexed by some vector of parameters $\beta$, as defined below.

*Definition: An (open)* ***family of tax systems*** *is a family of mappings $\psi(\cdot,\beta)$ meeting the conditions of the preceding definition and indexed by $\beta$, an element of an open set $\mathcal{O}$ of a finite dimensional space.*

To illustrate the above definition, consider a value added tax system which places commodities in, let us say, three different groups; the same VAT rate applies to commodities of a given group so that the special type of *ad valorem* taxation obtains: $\pi_h = (1+\alpha_h)p_h$ with $\alpha_h = \alpha_{h'}$ for $h, h' \in H_i$, $i = 1,2,3$. The subset of tax systems obtained when the three different rates are allowed to vary between zero and one is an example of a simple family of tax systems of the above definition: it is then a three dimensional family. (It will be rather two dimensional once normalization is taken into account.)

For a given economy $\epsilon$, we call $E(\epsilon,\beta)$ the set of interior tax equilibria associated with the given tax system $\beta$ and $E(\epsilon)$ the set of tax equilibria associated with *some* tax system $\beta$.

From now on, we will restrict attention to families of tax systems which are associated with mappings $\psi$ continuous both in $p$ and $\beta$. There are two reasons for that: on the one hand, the examples just given satisfy such an assumption; on the other hand, the reader guesses that existence of a tax equilibrium cannot be assured for a discontinuous $\psi$. As we are working in a differentiable framework, we have to assure differentiability of $\psi$. To avoid technicalities we will assume $C^\infty$ differentiability. The precise assumption (DTS) is stated now.

**(DTS)** *Differentiability of tax systems*

*The mapping* $\psi: \mathcal{R}^{n-1}_+ \times \mathcal{O} \to \mathcal{R}^{n-1}_+ \times \mathcal{R}$ is $C^\infty$ *on the interior of its domain.*

### 2.4.2 Continuity properties of equilibria with respect to a given tax system (T***)

The next theorem concerns the continuity properties of tax equilibria with respect to tax systems of an open family. In fact, the properties that will be stated can only be expected to be in a sense 'generic': they may fail to hold for exceptional economies, or they may fail for exceptional tax systems. To deal simply with this problem, while obtaining a statement of significant interest, we will assume that the family of tax systems satisfies a so-called 'Richness Assumption'.

**(RF)** *Richness of the family of tax systems*

*$\forall(p,\beta)$ (belonging to the interior of their domain of definition) $\partial_\beta\psi$ is of rank n.*

In other words, consider the family and some value $\beta_0$ of the parameter; take any production price vector $p$. Then any $(\pi', R')$ close to $(\pi, R) = \psi(p, \beta_0)$ is reached – as $\psi(p,\beta)$ – for some $\beta$ close to $\beta_0$.

The assumption of richness of the family could not be true if the dimension of the space of parameters $\beta$ were not itself greater than (or equal to) $n$. RF is clearly a strong assumption. However, one may note that a given family of tax systems can be imbedded – and generally in many ways – in a family meeting RF.

The next assumption can now be stated.

**(CR)** *Compactness of the range*

*$\exists$ a compact set K such that $\psi(p,\beta) \subset K$, $\forall p, \beta$, where K is included in the interior of the domain of definition of $\pi$, R, i.e., $K \subset \mathring{\mathscr{R}}_+^{n-1} \times \mathring{\mathscr{R}}$ with our normalization.*

CR says that (non-normalized) consumption prices cannot tend either to zero or plus infinity and that income cannot tend to infinity.

One may be of two minds with respect to CR: on the one hand, simple tax systems, as the specific tax system evoked above, do not meet the assumption; on the other hand, on 'operational' grounds the fact that consumption prices and transfers may not be infinitely high does not seem too restrictive, so that these specific tax systems might be appropriately modified (when prices become very large) in order to meet CR.

We can now state theorem 9.

**Theorem 9: Continuity properties of tax equilibria**

*Consider an economy where the assumptions D1 (differentiability) FRJS (full rank of Jacobian of supply) and NIW (non-inferiority weak form) and AP (additivity between private and public goods) hold true.*

*Assume that in addition the (non-extended version of) assumption (E)BPG3 and the assumption BP (boundary conditions for production prices) are met.*

*Consider a family of tax systems that is rich in the sense of RF and has a compact range CR. Consider $E(\beta)$ the set of tax equilibria with respect to the tax system $\beta$. Then 'generically', i.e., for an open dense subset of $\beta$ in $\mathcal{O}$.*

*(i) $E(\beta)$ is either empty or is a finite set*

(ii) *Around β, the points in E(β) are locally constant in number and depend in a $C^1$ way on β.*
(iii) *Card E(β) (Cardinal of) is a constant modulo 2*

*Proof*

The first three assumptions allow us to refer to theorem 4: the set of tax equilibria $\epsilon$ of the economy is a smooth manifold of dimension $n$ (remember $n'=1$).

Consider then

$$f: (\pi, p, R, y'_0, \beta) \in \epsilon \times \mathcal{O} \rightarrow \mathcal{R}^n$$
$$f(\pi, p, R, y'_0, \beta) = \{\pi - \psi_1(p, \beta), R - \psi_2(p, \beta)\}$$

Consider now the tangent mapping $df$ (on any point of $\epsilon \times \mathcal{O}$). Because of RF, this mapping is surjective (from the Jacobian $df$ one can extract a matrix of rank $n$).

Hence, in particular 0 is a regular value of this mapping. The pre-image theorem applies: $f^{-1}(0)$ is then a smooth manifold whose dimension is the dimension of β (in $\mathcal{O}$).

Now consider $P$, the projection from $f^{-1}(0)$ to $\mathcal{O}$

$$P: (\pi, p, R, y'_0, \beta) \in f^{-1}(0) \rightarrow \beta \in \mathcal{O}$$

$P$ is a differentiable mapping between manifolds of the same dimension. Let us show that it is proper. It is equivalent to show that, from a sequence $(\pi_n, p_n, R_n, y'_{0n}, \beta_n) \in f^{-1}(0)$ where $\beta_n \rightarrow \bar{\beta}$, one can extract a converging subsequence.

Because of CR, there exists a subsequence $\pi_n \rightarrow \bar{\pi} \in \mathring{\mathcal{R}}^{n-1}_+$ $R_n \rightarrow \bar{R}$, and because of AP (and DI), there exists a converging subsequence $d(\pi_n, R_n, y'_{0n})$. But then, the equality $d(\pi_n, R_n, y'_{0n}) = \eta(p_n, y'_{0n})$ together with BPG3 rules out the subsequence $y'_{0n}$ being unbounded. BP then ensures that there exists no subsequence $p_n$ going to the boundary of its domain. One can finally extract a subsequence that converges to $(\bar{\pi}, \bar{p}, \bar{R}, \bar{y}'_0, \bar{\beta})$, that is a tax equilibrium.

We then refer to the fact that for a smooth map $g$ between compact manifolds of the same dimension, $\# g^{-1}(y)$ is generically a constant modulo 2, the properness of the projection map accounting here for the fact that the manifolds are not compact (Mathematical appendix, pp. 278, 279). □

The following comments concern first the proof of the theorem, and its scope.

The *proof* calls for two comments. On the one hand, one could have immediately assumed that the set of tax equilibria was a smooth manifold, instead of referring to theorem 4 thanks to NIW. Then, the statement can be viewed as applying to 'generic' economies – in the weaker sense of theorem 5 – that satisfy in addition AP, BPG3, BP.

On the other hand, regarding AP, one will easily check that it was much too strong for our purposes: it is left to the reader to show how it can be weakened (in order to allow only for bounded spillover effects of public consumption on private consumption). Note also that improvements in theorem 9, that would drop RF, seem rather costly – in terms of alternative assumptions and/or tools.

The *scope* of theorem 9 can be appreciated by noting three facts: the conclusion is strong and obtains for a truly 'generic' set of $\beta$; the assumptions on the economy as just noted are rather weak; the assumption on the family of tax systems and particularly RF are restrictive. However a family of tax systems that does not meet the Richness assumption RF, may generally be imbedded in a broader family that meets RF and for which theorem 9 applies. For example, the *ad valorem* tax systems that have as many rates as there are commodities,[36] if they were appropriately modified for high values of consumption prices (in order to meet CR) and extended in order to include the dimension of income redistribution (in such a way that RF is met), would satisfy the requirements of theorem 9.

Hence, theorem 9, as a generic statement, is not fully conclusive, but conveys, at reasonable cost, some understanding of the continuity question.

An attempt at visualization is made in figure 2.21, where the one dimensional set of tax equilibria is represented with the convention of descriptive geometry and where the graph of the function $\psi$ is visualized in the orthant $(p, \pi)$ and where the following are successively represented

tax systems with an even number of equilibria for generic $\beta$, (figure 2.21a)

tax systems with a number of equilibria that is not generically constant modulo 2, (figure 2.21b).

### 2.4.3 Existence of equilibria with respect to a given tax system (**)

If continuity is the subject of the first part of theorem 9, the second part of the theorem indicates that the number of equilibria is a constant modulo 2. The number of equilibria for some or all tax systems $\beta$ can still be zero. Existence of an equilibrium with respect to a given tax system might for

[36] This is an example of a family of specific tax systems of 'full dimension' of Fuchs–Guesnerie (1983).

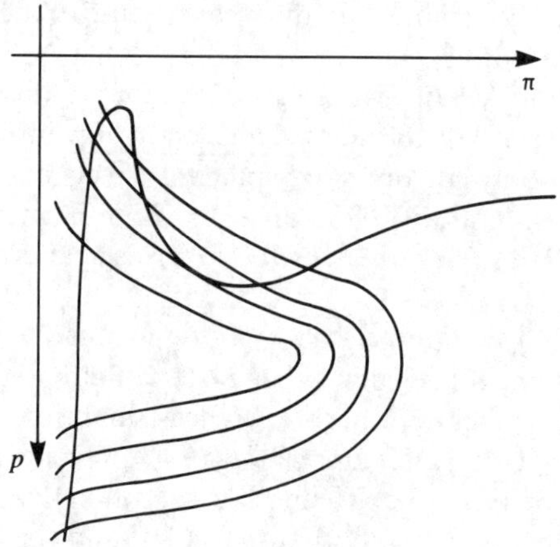


Figure 2.21a

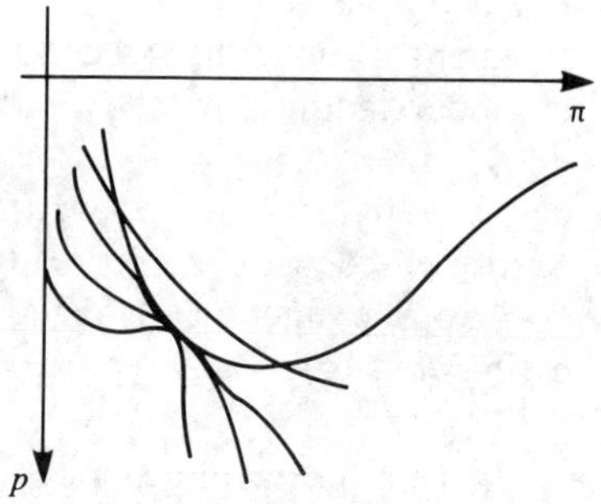


Figure 2.21b

example be established if, within the family of tax systems to which it belongs, one can show that there is at least one which has an *odd* number of equilibria.[37] Here, we will come back to a more standard viewpoint. The next theorem will provide conditions on $\psi$, a given tax system, that assure existence.

The theorem will be proved for an economy which satisfies the conclusion of theorem 8, i.e., whose set of tax equilibria is diffeomorphic to a Euclidean space, and 'globally parametrizable' in $(\pi, R)$. Conditions for existence bear upon the function $\psi$ and are rather strong since again we

[37] Note that this result immediately obtains from Walrasian theory for families of tax systems including 'no taxation' when all production sets are constant returns to scale.

assume that the image of $\psi$ – i.e., the set of all consumption prices, income transfer than can be obtained when $p$ varies – lies in a compact set.[38]

**Theorem 10: Existence**

*Consider an extended economy which is globally parametrizable in the sense of theorem 8, tax equilibria being described by functions $\tilde{\mathscr{P}}, \tilde{\mathscr{Y}}$ with $y_0' = \tilde{\mathscr{Y}}(\pi, R), p = \tilde{\mathscr{P}}(\pi, R)$*
*Consider some tax system $\psi$ with a compact range (CR). Then, there exists tax equilibria with respect to $\psi$.*

*Proof* (sketch)
Consider a 'big rectangle' $K = \times_h(\underline{\pi}_h, \bar{\pi}_h) \times (\underline{R}, \bar{R})$ of the product space $(\pi, R)$ containing the compact set in which the image of $\psi$ lies. Then, a standard fixed point argument (in the rectangle $K$) applies and leads to the conclusion. □

Consider also the following vector field on $K$

$$-\pi + \psi_1(\tilde{\mathscr{P}}(\pi, R))$$
$$-R + \psi_2(\tilde{\mathscr{P}}(\pi, R))$$

Note that tax equilibria with respect to $\psi$ are zeros of the vector field and that the assumption implies that at the boundary B the vector field 'points inwards'. Indeed $\pi_h = \bar{\pi}_h$ implies $\psi_{1h}(\pi, R) - \pi_h < 0$, $R = \bar{R}$ implies $\psi_2(\pi, R) - R < 0$, $\pi_h = \underline{\pi}_h$ implies $\psi_{1h}(\pi, R) - \pi_h > 0$, $R = \underline{R}$ implies $\psi_2(\pi, R) - R > 0$. This fact will be used later in the proof of Theorem 11.

Note that the essence of the argument of Theorem 10 when the manifold of tax equilibria is one dimensional is well conveyed by our standard diagram. Figure 2.22 indeed provides a graphical proof in this case.

The diagram also shows that assumptions on $\psi$ adopted in this theorem that directly imply that the vector field points inwards are stronger than needed. For example, they do not exploit the properties of the set of tax equilibria involved by the boundary assumptions presented above (properties suggested by the dotted line of figure 2.22). Indeed the boundary conditions on $\psi_1$ are more restrictive than the ones needed for the existence theorems found in contributions[39] where the asymptotic properties of

[38] As argued below, theorem 10 illustrates the power of the parametrization result of section 2.3 although it does not fully exploit its possibilities.

[39] Guesnerie (1979a) or Fuchs–Guesnerie (1983) have results along these lines. Also, in order to compare the statement with other existence results of tax equilibria found in the literature, three more points should be recalled. First, the set of globally parametrizable economies is larger than the set of economies satisfying the sufficient conditions of theorem 8. Second, tax systems considered here have a 'non linear' part when the existing literature focuses, more often, on 'indirect linear' tax systems. Third, some equilibria of the extended economy may not be equilibria of the original one.

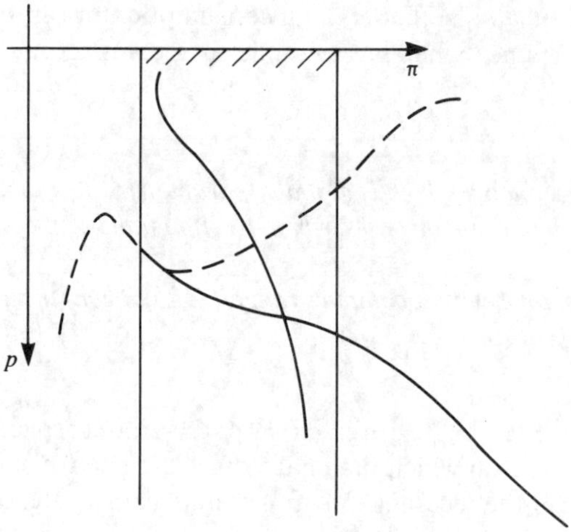


Figure 2.22

demand and supply functions are used. We leave it to the reader to find along the lines just suggested other existence statements. Note, however, that in the absence of a strong assumption on the asymptotic properties of $\psi_2$, existence might not be assured.

Two additional remarks are in order:

(i) The above argument makes it clear that with a fixed tax system the adjustment is left to changes in public goods levels. Here, the equilibrium public good level obtains as $\tilde{\mathscr{Y}}(\pi, R), \pi, R$ being at their equilibrium values.

(ii) In fact, the number of equilibria found in theorem 10 is 'generically' odd – as it is well known that vector fields pointing inwards have generically an odd number of zeros. The reader will easily find a formulation of this property for example by considering, for the genericity argument, a rich family introduced in section 2.4.2.

Finally, theorem 10 considers tax equilibria in an extended economy in the sense of section 3. When this extension is built from an original economy, the analysis of tax equilibria should come back to the original economy. In particular, in the original economy, public good levels are expected to be positive.

We will formulate an assumption on tax systems, which assures that tax equilibria with respect to such tax systems exhibit a positive level of public good.

*Definition* ***Effective financial source***[40]

*A tax system $\psi$ is an effective financial source if*

$$-p\cdot d(\psi_1(p), \psi_2(p), y_0') > 0, \forall p, y_0'$$

Note that the terminology is justified by the consideration of tax receipts associated with the tax system which are $(\pi - p)\cdot d - mR$, which reduce to the above expression since $\pi\cdot d = m\cdot R$.

**Lemma 3** *Assume that 0 belongs to the intersection of the global production set $Y$ with $y_0' = 0$ $(0 \in Y \cap \{y_0' = 0\})$ and that $Y \cap \{y_0' = K\} \subseteq Y \cap \{y_0' = K'\}$ when $K \geq K'$.*
*A tax equilibrium (of the extended economy) with respect to a tax system which is an effective financial source has a positive level of production of public goods,*

*Proof*
The above assumption imply $p\cdot\eta(p, y_0') \geq 0$, for $y_0' < 0$.
Then if $p\cdot\eta(p, y_0') \leq 0$, necessarily $y_0' \geq 0$
As $d(\ ) - \eta = 0$, $p\cdot d = p\cdot\eta$. The effective financial source assumption now implies $p\cdot d < 0$. Then $p\cdot\eta < 0$ and $y_0' \geq 0$. □

Consider now a purely linear tax system (such that $R = \psi_2(p) = 0$)·, which is an effective financial source in the sense of the above definition. According to lemma 3, an equilibrium with respect to this tax system will be associated with $R = 0$, some $\pi$ and some positive $y_0'$. Then it will be an equilibrium of the initial economy and not only of the extended one. This is stated in corollary 3.

**Corollary 3** *Assume that the tax system is linear, in the sense just mentioned, and that it is an effective financial source. Then, any equilibrium of the extended economy – as those found in theorem 10 – is an equilibrium of the original economy.*

### 2.4.4 Tax incidence (**)

Tax incidence theory is concerned with the following question: How does a tax equilibrium vary when the tax system varies? Within the formalization adopted above, the question takes the more precise form: how does a tax

[40] The terminology of effective financial source is that of Guesnerie (1979a).

equilibrium vary when the parameter $\beta$, indexing the tax system in some family of tax systems, varies? The above analysis makes it clear that under the conditions of theorem 9 this question is meaningful but for a subset of $\beta$ of measure zero. In most cases for almost all $\beta$ one can compute the derivative of tax equilibrium with respect to $\beta$.

We will make these computations in the framework of an extended economy which is globally parametrizable in the sense of theorem 6 by $\pi$, $R$.

$$p=\tilde{\mathscr{P}}(\pi, R),\ \tilde{y}_0'=\tilde{\mathscr{Y}}(\pi, R)$$

In such an economy a tax equilibrium $(p, \pi, R, y_0')$ with respect to a tax system $\psi(p, \beta)$ satisfies (the notation 0 denotes the composition of mappings)

$$\pi=\psi_1 0\tilde{\mathscr{P}}(\pi, R) \tag{2.23}$$

$$R=\psi_2 0\tilde{\mathscr{P}}(\pi, R) \tag{2.24}$$

$$y_0'=\tilde{\mathscr{Y}}(\pi, R) \tag{2.25}$$

Differentiating the above relations (2.23), (2.24) gives

$$[I-(\partial_p\psi_2)(\partial_R\tilde{\mathscr{P}})]dR=(\partial_p\psi_2)(\partial_\pi\tilde{\mathscr{P}})d\pi+\partial_\beta\psi_2 d\beta$$

$$[I-(\partial_p\psi_1)(\partial_\pi\tilde{\mathscr{P}})]d\pi=(\partial_p\psi_1)(\partial_R\tilde{\mathscr{P}})dR+\partial_\beta\psi_1 d\beta$$

$$\left[I-(\partial_p\psi_1)(\partial_\pi\tilde{\mathscr{P}})-\frac{(\partial_p\psi_1)(\partial_R\tilde{\mathscr{P}})(\partial_p\psi_2)(\partial_\pi\tilde{\mathscr{P}})}{1-(\partial_p\psi_2)(\partial_R\tilde{\mathscr{P}})}\right]d\pi$$

$$=\left[\partial_\beta\psi_1+\frac{(\partial_p\psi_1)(\partial_R\tilde{\mathscr{P}})(\partial_\beta\psi_2)}{1-\partial_p\psi_2(\partial_R\tilde{\mathscr{P}})}\right]d\beta$$

or calling $A$ the matrix on the left-hand side and $b$ the vector on the right-hand side, the above equality writes down

$$A d\pi=b d\beta \tag{2.26}$$

for 'regular' $\beta$ the matrix is invertible and

$$d\pi=A^{-1}b d\beta \tag{2.27}$$

Note that the derivatives $\partial\tilde{P}$ that have been computed in section 2 can be reported in the above expression. That makes it undoubtedly complex.

A better understanding of 2.26, 2.27 can, however, be obtained by looking at the case of a purely linear tax system. Then $R$ remains constant

$$\partial_p\psi_2=0,\ \partial_\beta\psi_2=0,\ A=(I-(\partial_p\psi_1)(\partial_\pi\tilde{\mathscr{P}})),\ b=(\partial_\beta\psi_1)$$

We can now rely upon part 2 of theorem 3, section 2.2.2, in order to compute $\partial_\pi\tilde{P}$

$$\partial_{\pi_k}\tilde{\mathscr{P}} = (\partial\tilde{\eta})^{-1}\left[\partial_{\pi_k}d - (\partial_{y_0'}d - \partial_{y_0'}\eta)\frac{p\cdot\partial_{\pi_k}d}{p\cdot(\partial_{y_0'}d - \partial_{y_0'}\eta)}\right]$$

and calling $\Theta$ the matrix whose term in the $h^{\text{th}}$ row, $k^{\text{th}}$ column is

$$\theta_{hk} = (\partial_{y_0'}d_h - \partial_{y_0'}\eta_h)\frac{p\cdot\partial_{\pi_k}d}{p\cdot(\partial_{y_0'}d - \partial_{y_0'}\eta)}$$

we obtain

$$\partial_\pi\tilde{\mathscr{P}} = (\partial\tilde{\eta})^{-1}[\partial_\pi d - \Theta] \tag{2.28}$$

Consider the matrix $B$

$$B \stackrel{\text{def}}{=} (\partial_p\psi_1)(\partial_\pi\tilde{\mathscr{P}}) = (\partial_p\psi_1)(\partial\tilde{\eta})^{-1}(\partial_\pi d - \Theta) \tag{2.29}$$

(2.27) becomes $d\pi = (I - B)^{-1}bd\beta$

Assume provisionally that the norm of the matrix $B$ is smaller than one so that

$$(I - B)^{-1} = I + B + B^2 + \ldots B^n + \ldots$$
$$d\pi = (I + B + B^2 + \ldots + B^n, \ldots)bd\beta$$

This formula has an intuitive interpretation as the *outcome of an infinite process of adaptative responses of the system to an initial shock*. The initial shock $b = (\partial_\beta\psi_1)$ on consumption prices is induced by the change in the parameter $\beta$; it corresponds to the first term $Ib$ of the series. This first shock, however, induces a change in demand $(\partial_\pi d)b$ which is, to be made feasible, accompanied by a change in public good production

$$-\left(\frac{p\cdot(\partial_\pi d)b}{p\cdot(\partial_{y_0'}d - \partial_{y_0'}\eta)}\right)$$

But, this change in public good generates itself a change in excess demand; which is seen to be $-\Theta b$. Then the total excess demand induced by the first shock $b$, i.e., $(\partial_\pi d - \Theta)b$ is itself matched by a change in production price $(\partial\tilde{\eta})^{-1}(\partial_\pi d - \Theta)b$, which generates, from the tax system adaptation rule, a change $(\partial_p\psi_1)(\partial\tilde{\eta})^{-1}(\partial_\pi d - \Theta)b = Bb$ in consumption prices; this corresponds to the second term of the series. A new wave of adaptations is then generated which leads to a new change in consumption prices $B^2b$ and so on.

However, this interpretation only holds when $\partial_p\psi_1$ has a small enough norm; by contracting changes in $\pi$ it stabilizes the process. When this is not the case $B$ may not be invertible and the adjustment process described above does not converge (and then does not describe the action of

$(I-B)^{-1}$). However, the ingredients of the above interpretation can still be applied to the equality $(I-B)d\pi = bd\beta$ which still holds and reads

$$d\pi = (\partial_\beta \psi_1)d\beta + [(\partial_p \psi_1)(\partial \tilde{\eta})^{-1}(\partial_\pi d - \Theta)]d\pi.$$

The change in consumption prices $d\pi$ induced by the change in $d\beta$ is the sum of three terms: $(\partial_\beta \psi_1)d\beta$ which measures the *direct incidence* of the change, $(\partial_p \psi_1)(\partial \tilde{\eta})^{-1}(\partial_\pi d)d\pi$ which measures the *indirect incidence* which results from changes in production prices which match the change in price-driven demand, $-(\partial_p \psi_1)(\partial \tilde{\eta})^{-1}\Theta$ which measures the *indirect incidence* due to changes in production prices designed to match the change in public production induced by the change in tax receipts.

Instead of considering the parametrization in $(\pi, R)$, we could have looked at the parametrization $(\pi, y'_0)$ (assuming that the set of tax equilibria is globally parametrizable, which is the case when the conditions of theorem 6, subsection 2.3.2 hold). Consider then an indirect tax system $\psi_1$ which is designed in such a way that it maintains fixed the public good level $\bar{y}'_0$. The burden of adjustment is then left to the uniform lump sum transfer $R$. For a given $\psi_1$, this can be done by choosing $\psi_2$ such that $R = \tilde{\mathscr{R}}(\pi, \bar{y}'_0) = \tilde{\mathscr{R}}(\psi_1(p), \bar{y}'_0) \overset{\text{def}}{=} \psi_2(p)$.

Since $p = \tilde{\mathscr{P}}(\pi, \bar{y}'_0)$,

equilibrium with respect to $\psi$ is determined by

$$\pi = \psi_1 \circ \tilde{\mathscr{P}}(\pi, \cdot) \quad R = \tilde{\mathscr{R}}(\pi, \cdot)$$

The above argument can be reproduced and we obtain $(I-B')d\pi = b'd\beta$ with $B' = (\partial_p \psi_1)(\partial \tilde{\eta})^{-1}(\partial_\pi d) - (\partial_p \psi_1)(\partial \tilde{\eta})^{-1}\Theta'$, with $\Theta'_{hk} = (\partial_R d_h)\dfrac{p \cdot \partial_{\pi_k} d}{(p \cdot \partial_R d)}$

$$b' = \partial_\beta \psi_1$$

All the above comments can be transposed to this new setting and as above different readings of the formula obtain according to whether the norm of $B'$ is smaller or greater than one. This exercise is left to the reader.

### 2.4.5 Uniqueness (***)

Existence of a tax equilibrium with respect to a given tax system obtains in the conditions of theorem 10. When is such an equilibrium unique?

Uniqueness is a classical subject of study of the Walrasian model for which a lot of results are available (see for example Arrow–Hahn).[41] Our

[41] Arrow–Hahn (1971).

first task in this subsection is to compare the present problem with the standard Walrasian problem in the absence of taxation. This is done in the first part of the subsection. A quick assessment of the similarities and differences suggests pessimistic prospects concerning straightforward transposition of the Walrasian approach to uniqueness. In the second part of the section, we deliberately switch to an approach that exploits the potential of the knowledge of the structure of tax equilibrium that we have developed until now. Theorem 11 is an example of the findings that can be obtained adopting this path.

First let us attempt to attack the problem by transposing the standard practice which relies on the study of zeros of an excess demand function. Such a transposition of Walrasian methods can actually be performed when preferences are additive between public and private goods (assumption AP) and when the production possibilities of the private sector are not affected by the public good production. For seeing that, consider for simplicity a purely indirect tax system, and consider $-p\cdot d(\psi(p))+p\cdot\eta_1(p) = R(p)$ the amount of fiscal receipts associated with $p\cdot$; consider now the cost function of the public good $p\cdot\eta_0(p,y_0')$ and the equation $p\cdot\eta_0(p,y_0') - R(p)=0$. Call $\beta_0(p)$ the implicit function defined by this equation. From the implicit function theorem (that applies with PAMC)

$$\frac{d\beta_0}{dp}=\frac{1}{\mathrm{MC}(p,\beta_0(p))}[-p\cdot(\partial_\pi d)(\partial_p\psi)-d+\eta_1]$$

where $\mathrm{MC}(p,\beta_0(p))$ is the marginal cost of production of the public good.

Consider now

$$Z(p)\overset{\mathrm{def}}{=}d(\psi(p))-\eta_1(p)-\eta_0(p,\beta_0(p)) \tag{2.30}$$

This can be viewed as a *generalized excess demand function*; it coincides with the Walrasian excess demand function in an economy without pure profit and where $\psi$ is the identity (then $\beta_0(p)\equiv 0$, and $p\cdot\eta_1(p)=R(p)=0$).

Such an excess demand function can also be viewed as describing excess demand registered by a kind of Walrasian auctioneer which would control production prices, announce consumption prices after taking into account the fiscal law, and take into account government's demand resulting from the spending of fiscal receipts.

The Jacobian of $Z$ can be written

$$\partial Z=(\partial_\pi d)(\partial_p\psi)-\partial\eta_1-\partial\eta_0-\partial_{y_0'}\eta_0\frac{\partial\beta_0}{dp}$$

For simplicity, consider the case of a specific tax system; $\psi(p)=p+\bar{T}$, so that $\partial_p\psi=I$. At an equilibrium point, we have

$$\partial Z = \partial_\pi d(\psi(p)) - \partial \eta_1 - (\partial_{y_0'} \eta_0) \frac{(-p \cdot \partial_\pi d - \eta_0)}{\mathrm{MC}(p)} \tag{2.31}$$

the derivatives being taken in $\psi(p)$, $p$, $\beta_0(p)$.

The expressions (2.30) and (2.31) make clear that there are significant differences between the pseudo excess demand we are considering and the Walrasian excess demand: no simple transposition of the standards results of Walrasian theory concerning uniqueness obtains. Also, a tatonnement process working along the lines sketched above would not necessarily converge under assumptions sufficient to ensure the convergence of the Walrasian tatonnement. To illustrate these assertions, the reader will convince himself that:

The weak axiom of revealed preference for the consumption sector may not guarantee uniqueness, even when $\psi$ is associated with a specific tax system (consider formula (2.30)).

Gross substituability of Walrasian excess demand in an economy does not guarantee gross substitutability of the excess demand function associated with a given tax system in the same economy (formula (2.31)).

The dynamics of the 'tatonnement' process may differ considerably when some tax law is introduced in a given economy (formula (2.31)).

After noting the difficulties of this approach, we will not go further in that direction. Another line approach to uniqueness is suggested by the tax incidence analysis.

Come back to formulas (2.23), (2.24), which define a tax equilibrium w.r.t. $\psi$ by

$$\pi - \psi_1 \circ \mathscr{P}(\pi, R) = 0, \; R - \psi_2 \circ \mathscr{P}(\pi, R) = 0$$

Consider the matrix

$$M_\psi(\pi, R) = \begin{bmatrix} I - (\partial_p \psi_1)(\partial_\pi \mathscr{P}) & -(\partial_p \psi_1)(\partial_R \mathscr{P}) \\ -(\partial_p \psi_2)(\partial_\pi \mathscr{P}) & 1 - (\partial_p \psi_2)(\partial_R \mathscr{P}) \end{bmatrix}$$

Referring to the case where the normalization has been solved through the choice of a numeraire, we are in a position to make the following assumption:

*Assumption* **NS** *Non-singularity of the matrix* $M_\psi$

$\forall(\pi, R)$, $\mathrm{M}_\psi(\pi, R)$ *has a non-zero determinant.*

Assumption NS can be enforced by the following property.

*Assumption* ***NR*** *Non-reversal of sign patterns*

*$\forall(\pi, R)$, there does not exist a direction of consumption price changes $\tilde{\lambda}$ ($\tilde{\lambda}=(\lambda_1,\ldots,\lambda_{n-1})\in\mathscr{R}^{n-1}$) and of income change $\lambda_n(\lambda_n\in\mathscr{R})$ such that*

$$\lambda^h(M_\psi(\pi, R)\lambda)^h \leq 0 \qquad \forall h=1,\ldots,n$$

If assumption NR holds, $M$ is a $P$-matrix in the sense of Nikaido, its determinant is positive so that NS holds.

Assumption NR has an economic content which is easy to understand. A price and income change of direction $\lambda$ on the manifold of equilibria induces a change in production prices which turns into, through the tax system $\psi$, in a price and income change of direction $-M_\psi\lambda+I\lambda$ ($I$ is the identity matrix of $\mathscr{R}^n$). The difference between both changes, the initial change and the induced change is $M_\psi\lambda$. Assumption NR states that the sign pattern of the initial change cannot be completely reversed when one looks at the difference between the initial change and the induced change. This assumption would be true if, for example, the norm of $\partial\psi$ were small enough.

Assumption NR has a more intuitive content when applied to an indirect tax system which is a specific tax system $\bar{T}$. Then $M_\psi=I-\partial_\pi P$ and $M_\psi\lambda$ is nothing other than the change in the vector $T=\pi-p$ of specific taxes (computed over the manifold of equilibria) associated with a change in consumption prices in the direction $\lambda$. Assumption NR then means that the sign pattern of consumption price changes cannot be completely reversed through general equilibrium effects when compared to the sign pattern of tax changes. Equivalently, the sign pattern of tax changes cannot be reversed when compared to the sign pattern of consumption prices that it induces through general equilibrium effects. Assumption NR expresses then a local comparative statics property. In the case of the one-dimensional manifold of figure 2.23 when the graph of the fixed tax system is the dotted line, Assumption NR allows positions, 1, 2 and 3 for the manifold (full lines).

We can now state:

**Theorem 11: Uniqueness**

*Consider an economy which is globally parametrizable in the sense of Theorem 8. Suppose that assumption NR holds for some tax system $\psi$ that satisfies the compactness assumption CR. Then there exists a unique tax equilibrium with respect to $\psi$.*

The *proof* is simply sketched as follows:

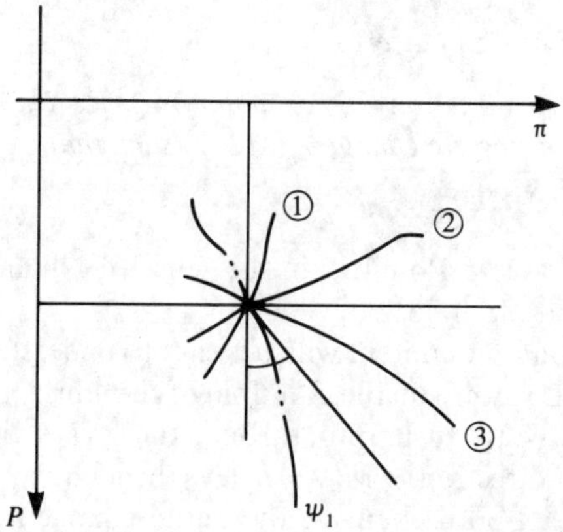


Figure 2.23

Consider the vector field $\pi-\psi_1 \circ \mathscr{P}(\pi, R)$, $R-\psi_2 \circ \mathscr{P}(\pi, R)$ on the space $\pi, R$. Assumption NS implies that the vector field has a Jacobian with positive determinant in any of its zeros. As after the proof of theorem 10, we introduce a 'big rectangle' on which the vector field 'points outwards' (as shown above the opposite vector field 'points inwards'). The Poincare–Hopf theorem can thus be applied, implying that the vector field has a unique zero.[42] □

In proving theorem 11, we supposed that assumption NS or NR held for every $(\pi, R)$, serving to parametrize $\epsilon$. If these assumptions were supposed to hold only in the economically relevant part of the manifold ($y_0' > 0$), and if $\psi$ were an effective financial source, then the theorem would remain true with the unique tax equilibrium lying in the relevant part of the manifold. (see bibliographical note).

The study of uniqueness just sketched probably deserves to be pursued further, along the lines which have been mentioned. Up to now, the results are somewhat disappointing. Condition NS is not extremely intuitive but may be in the special case of specific tax systems.

## Conclusion

The chapter has performed an exploration of the positive economics of taxation. This exploration has primarily aimed at being broad and synthetic while meeting some reasonable standards of rigour. A number of other legitimate objectives have been sacrificed. On the one hand, the statements do not aim at maximal generality and many extensions with different levels

[42] See Mathematical appendix. For a similar argument see Varian (1977).

of difficulty have been suggested within the text – let us mention again the example of BP that could be relaxed in many statements. On the other hand, if the extension procedure illuminates many issues, the present analysis leaves some shadow over both its validity and all its implications for the initial non-extended economy.

From the hopefully coherent and broad view of the subject presented here, many theoretical research tracks are still open. Also, a number of connections between the theoretical analysis and models used in specific studies – and evoked in the bibliographical note – remain to be ascertained.

## 2.5 Bibliographical note

The general equilibrium model considered in this section relates to different literatures. It is the model considered by the literature on redistributive taxation, the normative study of which was initiated by Diamond–Mirrlees (1971). A larger set of references on this literature is provided at the end of the next chapter. Note, however, that a low dimensional version of the present model coincides with the model used for the study of linear income tax (see Sheshinsky (1972), or more recently Hellwig (1986)).

The present model can also be rather easily modified in order to coincide with the two factors, two commodity model used for the study of incidence of the tax on corporate profit (A sample of contributions, reviewed by Atkinson and Stiglitz (1980), includes Harberger (1962), Mieskowsky (1967), (1969), (1972), McLure (1975).) The modifications that allow the introduction of a constant returns to scale production sector in the present model were fully assessed in a previous version of this text, alluded to in footnotes.

The views presented at the beginning of the chapter on budget balance and price normalization are standard. The discussion of the concept of 'more taxed', which draws on a similar discussion in Guesnerie–Roberts (1984), and of 'more distorted' attempts a systematic presentation of the main ideas. The examples of section 2.1.3 are either borrowed or derived from examples contained in Fuchs–Guesnerie (1983).

The analysis of the local structure of tax equilibria follows Guesnerie (1977) (1979a) and also Fuchs–Guesnerie (1983).

The remaining of the chapter finds part of its inspiration in studies of the Walrasian model using differential topology (Dierker, 1976).

The arguments and genericity statements of section 2.3.1 are variants of those presented in Guesnerie (1979a), and Fuchs–Guesnerie (1983). However, as has been mentioned in the text, Fuchs–Guesnerie (1983) use more powerful techniques (transversality Theorem) by viewing the economy as an infinite-dimensional object.

The connectedness issue of section 2.3.2 has also been analysed in Fuchs–Guesnerie (1983). However, Fuchs–Guesnerie considered a world without uniform lump-sum transfers and with only one public good. The statement of theorem 8 here has close connections with theorem 5 in Fuchs–Guesnerie. Again, the analysis of the connectedness of the set of equal yield tax equilibria is closely related with that of Fuchs–Guesnerie (1983). Theorem 7 is close to theorem 6 in Fuchs–Guesnerie, and is proved along similar lines.

The differences in assumptions of theorems 7 and 8 here and in the corresponding theorems, 6 and 5, of Fuchs–Guesnerie essentially reflect the differences in the 'extension' procedures for the extended economy (however, theorem 8 here may require too much). The extension procedure of the present book is more economically appealing but probably less satisfactory on other grounds than that of Fuchs–Guesnerie.

Section 4 on tax equilibria and tax incidence also relies on earlier literature.

The fact that some rule of government budget balance was required for obtaining equilibrium is clear in the work of Sontheimer (1971), and particularly in Mantel (1975). Such an idea is reflected in the concept of effective financial source of Guesnerie (1979a). Other work on general equilibrium and taxes includes Shafer–Sonnenschein (1976).

The existence and continuity properties found in theorem 9 are similar in spirit, but slightly different in content, to Fuchs–Guesnerie's (1983) theorems 8–9. The boundary conditions used in theorem 10 are stronger than needed, and more restrictive than the ones considered in the existence theorem of Guesnerie (1979a) and theorem 9 of Fuchs–Guesnerie (1983) where CR can be dispensed with. The analysis of tax incidence and uniqueness of section 2.4.3 relies heavily on the parametrization of the manifold of equilibria and hence significantly differs from standard analysis, again with the exception of Fuchs–Guesnerie (1983) who derive a theorem close to theorem 11, but that applies to specific tax systems that are effective financial sources. However there is no discussion of tax incidence in Fuchs–Guesnerie. On the contrary, these are results on the bounds of the number of equilibria that have no counterpart here.

Finally, the connections between the theoretical model and applied computable general equilibrium models would require a specific assessment that should start from Shoven–Whalley (1973) and Shoven (1974).

# 3

# Normative economics of taxation: reform and optimization

Normative economics is generally opposed to positive economics. Positive studies aim at understanding the properties of economic systems, thus elucidating here the structure of the set of tax equilibria. Normative studies are concerned with the welfare effects of economic choices, here with the consequences, for the agents' welfare of different tax policies. Normative studies are not opposite but complementary and in fact logically consecutive to positive studies: the results of positive analysis are normally a prerequisite to a comprehensive welfare assessment. This logical order is the one adopted here. The study of the normative economics of taxation will utilize our understanding of the positive economics of taxation gained in the previous chapter.

The present chapter proceeds as follows:

Sections 3.1 and 3.2 are devoted to the welfare analysis of tax equilibria when at first only small changes are considered. The title 'tax reform' reflects both the normative emphasis of the analysis and the fact that small tatonnement changes – rather than the large once and for all changes suggested by optimal taxation – are a priori considered. These first two sections can indeed be viewed as extensions in the normative direction of the positive study of section 2.2, chapter 2; they provide a comprehensive welfare analysis of a neighbourhood of a given tax equilibrium whose structure has been ascertained in the just recalled 'positive' investigation. The third section, 3.3, gives up the purely local viewpoint by examining how the infinitesimal changes suggested in the previous subsections can be linked along a finite path of tax reform. This subsection is more technical and can be, at first, skipped by the reader.

Section 3.4 continues the discussion of tax reform in two directions. First, it transposes the analysis of tax reform of sections 3.1 and 3.2 to the case where the welfare of individual agents can be aggregated into a social welfare function. In subsection 3.4.1, a more specific algorithm of tax reform – of the gradient projection type – is suggested; a 'Musgravian'-like interpretation of its instructions is proposed in subsection 3.4.2.

Section 3.5 entitled Second-best Pareto optima switches from the tax reform viewpoint to the standard optimal taxation viewpoint. Indeed, the characterization results concerning second-best Pareto optima obtain here as direct consequences of the tax reform analysis of sections 3.1 and 3.2. These characterization results are lengthily commented on in subsection 3.5.2. Subsection 3.5.3 goes further into the discussion of optimal taxes in special cases.

## 3.1 Tax reform, the canonical argument (**)

Consider an a priori given tax equilibrium. Finding a neighbouring tax equilibrium which is better on welfare grounds constitutes in our terminology a desirable (small) tax reform.

This section examines in full generality the geometry of (local) tax reform and develops the canonical argument. A number of special cases, including a case of particular relevance for the study of cost–benefit analysis in the context of the present model, will be discussed next in section 3.2. Section 3.3 will switch from a local to a global viewpoint. The present section has two parts: in subsection 3.1.1 a brief reminder is given and appropriate concepts are introduced. Subsection 3.1.2 gives the central argument.

### 3.1.1 Brief reminder and new concept

Let us consider an initial (strict) tax equilibrium. It is associated with the commodity bundles $z_i, y_1'', y_0', y_0''$, the price vectors $\pi, p$ and the uniform lump-sum transfer $R$ satisfying

$$z_i = d_i(\pi, R, y_0') \tag{3.1}$$

$$y_1'' = \eta_1(y_0', p) \tag{3.2}$$

$$y_0'' = \eta_0(y_0', p) \tag{3.3}$$

$$\sum_i z_i \leq y_0'' + y_1'' \overset{\text{def}}{=} \eta(y_0', p) \tag{3.4}$$

It is tight (strict) if:

$$\sum_i z_i = y_0'' + y_1'' \tag{3.5}$$

Equations (3.1) to (3.5) only repeat the definition of a tax equilibrium of what we called model A in chapter 2. Note however that the expression of 3.2 and 3.3 given here assumes that the profit-maximizing plan of the private firm and the cost minimizing plan of the controlled firm are uniquely determined. This assumption is made for notational simplicity.

But the reader will convince himself that the argument below applies as well to the case of constant returns to scale.[1]

From now and throughout this section, we assume:

(DI) Differentiability

(FRJS) Full Rank of the Jacobian of Supply.

(FRJS has been defined in chapter 2 as the global extension of the local rank assumption LR1).

The tax reform approach explores, with normative emphasis, the neighbourhood of the strict tax equilibrium under consideration. The 'positive' dimension has been explored in chapter 2. Without reexplaining notation, let us briefly be reminded of some significant definitions and results. Again such definitions and results refer to the aggregate supply function, i.e., what we called model C, where constraints 3.2 and 3.3 are replaced by 3.4.

**Equilibrium Preserving Directions of Changes** $(\dot{\pi}, \dot{R}, \dot{y}_0', \dot{p})$ are those which satisfy equations (2.18), i.e.

$$(\partial_\pi d)\dot{\pi} + (\partial_R d)\dot{R} + (\partial_{y_0'} d)\dot{y}_0' \leq (\partial_{y_0'}\eta)\dot{y}_0' + (\partial\eta)\dot{p}$$

The direction is said to be strict equilibrium preserving if the equality holds in the previous expression.

From theorem 1 (which assumes differentiability and the local validity of (FRJS) on the rank of the matrix $\partial\eta$), we know that equilibrium-preserving directions of changes, are those meeting conditions (2.20)

$$(p\cdot\partial_\pi d)\dot{\pi} + (p\cdot\partial_R d)\dot{R} + p\cdot(\partial_{y_0'} d - \partial_{y_0'}\eta)\dot{y}_0' \leq 0 \qquad (2.20)$$

If we note as in chapter 2

$$\Phi_\pi = p\cdot\partial_\pi d,\ \Phi_{y_0'} = p\cdot(\partial_{y_0'} d - \partial_{y_0'}\eta),\ \Phi_R = p\cdot\partial_R d$$

the above inequality writes down

$$\Phi_\pi\dot{\pi} + \Phi_R\dot{R} + \Phi_{y_0'}\dot{y}_0' \leq 0$$

Note here that $(p\cdot\partial_\pi d)\pi + (p\cdot\partial_R d)\ R = 0$ (since $(\partial_\pi d)\pi + (\partial_R d)R = 0$ by homogeneity of degree zero of the function $d$), i.e., that $\Phi_\pi\pi + \Phi_R R = 0$.

Remember also that, as stated in theorem 1 chapter 2, to any direction $(\dot{\pi}, \dot{R}, \dot{y}_0')$ meeting condition (2.20) with equality, one uniquely associates one direction $\dot{p}$ so that $(\dot{\pi}, \dot{R}, \dot{y}_0', \dot{p})$ is 'strict equilibrium preserving'.

The local analysis of the set of tax equilibria undertaken in section 2.2 constitutes indeed the basis of a welfare exploration of the neighbourhood tax equilibria. What remains to be done for performing the local tax reform

[1] The only part of the argument which might rely on specific returns assumptions is based on theorem 1 of chapter 2; we know from various footnotes of the previous chapter that this theorem also holds in the case of constant returns to scale.

analysis is to make explicit the individual welfare changes involved by local tax equilibria changes. To keep in line with the previous analysis that considers 'directions of changes', we will define for this purpose 'welfare improving directions of changes'.

Elementary results in consumer theory, that fit economic intuition, indicate that consumer $i$'s **welfare-improving directions of changes** $(\dot{\pi}, \dot{R}, y_0')$ are as those satisfying:[2]

$$-z_i \cdot \dot{\pi} + \dot{R} + C_i \cdot \dot{y}_0' > 0 \tag{3.6}$$

where $z_i = d_i(\pi, R, y_0')$ and

$$C_i(\pi, R, y_0') = \left[\frac{\partial}{\partial y_0'}[U_i(d_i(\pi, R, y_0'), y_0')]\right] \left[\frac{\partial}{\partial R}[U_i(d_i(\pi, R, y_0'), y_0')]\right]^{-1}$$

$C_i$ denotes the vector the components of which are the standard marginal willingness to pay for public goods.

**Pareto-improving directions of change** are then naturally defined as those which are welfare improving for every individual agent, i.e., that satisfy

$$-z_i \cdot \dot{\pi} + \dot{R} + C_i \cdot \dot{y}_0' > 0, \ \forall i$$

To achieve compact notation, let us write:

$$\Phi = (\Phi_\pi, \Phi_R, \Phi_{y_0'}), \ \Gamma_i = (-z_i, 1, C_i)$$

A direction $\delta = (\dot{\pi}, \dot{R}, \dot{y}_0')$ is equilibrium preserving and Pareto improving if it satisfies

$$\Phi \cdot \delta \leq 0 \tag{3.7}$$

$$\Gamma_i \cdot \delta > 0, \ \forall i \tag{3.8}$$

If we restrict the direction of changes only to some set A of coordinates of $(\pi, R, y_0')$ (the number of which is $|A|$), we denote the corresponding direction $\delta^A$. With straightforward notation, **a direction of change** $\delta^A$ **restricted to the set A of coordinates is equilibrium preserving and Pareto improving if it satisfies**:

$$\Phi^A \cdot \delta^A \leq 0 \tag{3.9}$$

$$\Gamma_i^A \cdot \delta^A > 0, \ \forall i \tag{3.10}$$

where all vectors $\Phi^A, \Gamma_i^A, \delta^A$ are restrictions of $\Phi$, $\Gamma$, $\delta$ to $\mathscr{R}^{|A|}$.

[2] Formally, the argument follows from the derivation of the indirect utility function, the use of Roy identities and of the definition of $C_i$. Note that $C_i$ is generally later a row vector.

### 3.1.2 The central statement

We are now in a position to answer a central question of the tax reform problem: do there exist equilibrium-preserving and Pareto-improving directions of change? The question amounts to knowing whether the set of directions associated with (3.7), (3.8) (or (3.9), (3.10)) is or is not empty. The answer given by the next theorem 1 relies on the careful analysis of the simple geometry of the problem. Although we shall elaborate on this later, it should be noted that the assumptions (i) and (ii) underlying the theorem are weak.

**Theorem 1: Equilibrium-preserving and Pareto-improving directions of change**

*Consider a subset A of coordinates of* $(\pi, R, y_0')$

*Consider a strict tax equilibrium in which: (i)* $\Phi^A \neq 0$*, (ii) The set of Pareto-improving directions of change (relative to A) is non-empty.*[3]

*Then, one of the three following situations occurs:*

*(1)* **The vector $\Phi^A$ belongs to the cone generated by the vectors $\Gamma_i^A$** *if and only if there exists no equilibrium-preserving and Pareto-improving direction of changes (restricted to the subset A).*

*(2)* **The vector $\Phi^A$ belongs to the cone generated by the vector $-\Gamma_i^A$** *if and only if there exist* **necessarily non-strict** *equilibrium-preserving and Pareto-improving directions of changes (restricted to the subset A).*

*(3)* **The vector $\Phi^A$ belongs to the complement of the above cones** *if and only if there exist (again in subset A) strict equilibrium-preserving and Pareto-improving directions of tax changes.*

*Proof*

(i) The fact that there exist no equilibrium preserving and Pareto improving changes is equivalent to the fact that the inequalities $\Phi^A \cdot \delta^A \leq 0$ $\Gamma_i^A \cdot \delta^A > 0$, $i = 1, \ldots, m$ are not compatible. In other words, the $m$ open convex cones (hyperplanes) $\Gamma_i^A \cdot \delta^A > 0$ and the closed convex cone (hyperplane) $\Phi^A \cdot \delta \leq 0$ have an empty intersection. A known theorem asserts[4] that this latter property is equiva-

[3] I.e. there exists a vector $\delta^A$ that satisfies (3.10) (*not* a priori (3.9)!).

[4] This is the separation theorem for convex cones given in the Mathematical appendix. 'Let $K_0, \ldots K_{p-1}$ be $p-1$ open convex cones and $K_p$ a convex cone.

$$\bigcap_0^p K_i = \phi <=> \exists\, q_0, \ldots q_p \text{ (not all zero) such that } \sum_0^p q_i = 0,\ q_i \cdot x \leq 0,\ \forall x \in K_i$$

This statement provides a rather general expression of an idea that is central to the mathematical literature as optimization.

lent to: $\exists\lambda_i \geq 0$, $\lambda \geq 0$, some of them non-zero, such that $-\sum_i \lambda_i \Gamma_i^A + \lambda\Phi^A = 0$. But $\lambda = 0$ is impossible since from the same theorem $\sum_i \lambda_i \Gamma_i^A = 0$ is equivalent to the emptiness of the set of Pareto-improving changes (relative to A), a fact which contradicts the initial assumption (ii).

Then $\Phi^A = \frac{1}{\lambda}\sum \lambda_i \Gamma_i^A$. Conclusion (1) follows.

(ii) Now from the same separation theorem (footnote 4), the fact that $\Phi^A$ belongs to the cone generated by the vectors $-\Gamma_i^A$ is equivalent to the fact that the inequalities $\Phi^A \cdot \delta^A \geq 0$, $\Gamma_i^A \cdot \delta^A > 0$, $\forall i$, are not compatible. But in that case, the Pareto-improving directions of changes (those that satisfy $\Gamma_i^A \cdot \delta^A > 0$, $\forall i$), that exist from assumption (iii) necessarily satisfy $\Phi^A \cdot \delta^A < 0$.

Assertion (2) follows.

(iii) Assertion (3) follows from the two preceding ones. □

Theorem 1 classifies situations according to normative criteria in a neighbourhood of a strict equilibrium. This classification rests on the analysis of the relative position of the vector $\Phi^A$ *vis-à-vis* a partition of the space in the three cones built from the vectors $\Gamma_i^A$.

The equivalence of the existence of equilibrium-preserving and Pareto-improving changes with the fact that $\Phi^A$ belongs to the complement of the cone generated by the vectors $\Gamma_i^A$ and $-\Gamma_i^A$ determines a basic two-partition.

However, assertion (2) in the theorem introduces another partition within the set of 'favourable' cases: in the circumstances described in (2), although there exist equilibrium-preserving and Pareto-improving directions of change, none of them is strict equilibrium preserving. In other words, the requirement of Pareto improvement tends to induce some waste in the use of resources because the direction of change which is taken tends to lead to an inefficient production (starting from an efficient one). This phenomenon may look strange. Later, one will argue that it may be ruled out in certain circumstances. It will also be shown that when it appears such a phenomenon can only remain temporarily in effect in a process of tax reform leading to second-best Pareto optimality. This latter remark justifies the terminology of **temporary inefficiencies**.

The lessons of theorem 1 are summarized in the stylized figure 3.1 (when the shaded area visualizes the (non-empty) Pareto-improving direction of change).

In the case suggested by figure 3.1c, there do exist strict equilibrium-preserving and Pareto-improving directions of change; they do not exist in

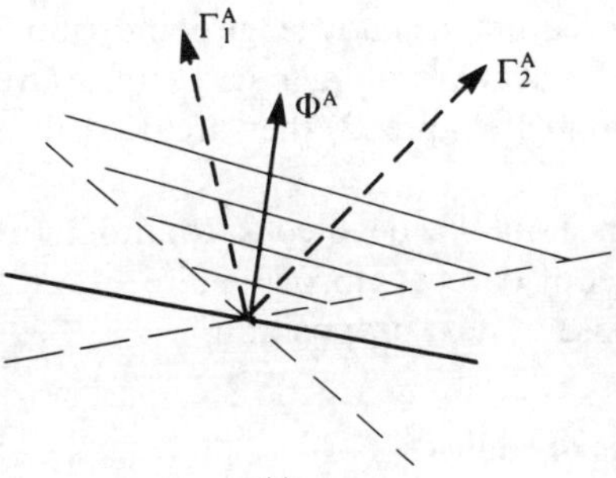


Figure 3.1a

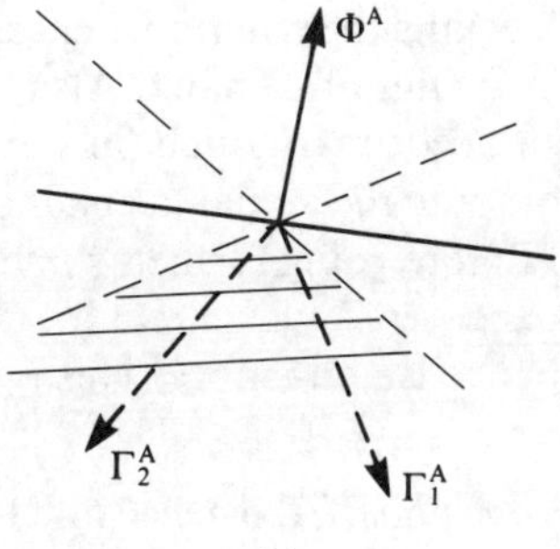


Figure 3.1b

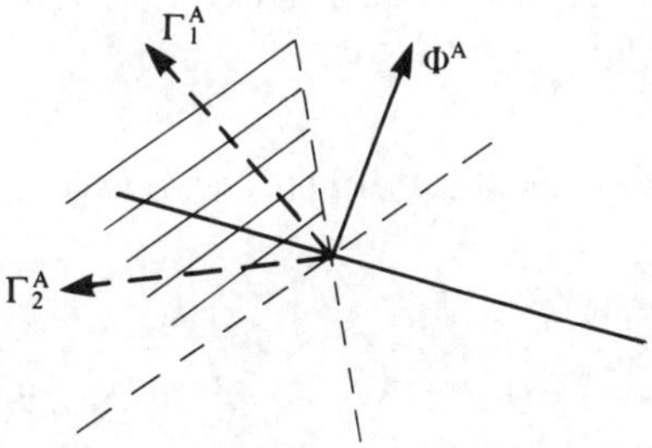


Figure 3.1c

the case of figure 3.1a when figure 3.1b corresponds to the (somewhat) strange case of temporary inefficiencies. (While reflecting on figure 3.1, the reader will note that more explicit versions of the figure, corresponding to explicit coordinate subsets will be discussed in subsection 3.1.2; also one will come back to the case of temporary inefficiencies.)

At this stage it is worth emphasizing the information needed to check (for example with a computer) the criteria of theorem 1.

The vector $\Phi^A$ can be computed whenever one knows:

the production prices vector $p$
the derivatives $\partial_\pi d$, $\partial_R d$, $\partial_{y_0'} d$ of **aggregate demand** with respect to $\pi$, $R$, $y_0'$ and the derivatives $\partial_{y_0'}\eta$ of aggregate supply with respect to $y_0'$. In fact, only the derivatives with respect to the subset A of coordinates are required.

The vector $\Gamma_i^A$ is known when the $m$ vectors of **individual transactions** $z_i$ and the $m$ vectors of **individual marginal willingnesses to pay** are known. (Still the A coordinates are sufficient.)

Checking the criterion, hence, does not require the knowledge of individual elasticities of demand. Also, the price derivatives of aggregate supply are not needed, although (in view of theorem 1 chapter 2) they are needed to compute the actual tax change.[5]

Before going further, some attention should be devoted to condition (ii) of theorem 1 which requires that the set of Pareto-improving directions of change is non-empty. This is the purpose of next proposition 1.

*Proposition 1* **Existence of PI directions of changes**

*Condition (ii) of theorem 1 on the existence of Pareto-improving directions of change is satisfied whenever either (α) or (β) holds:*

> (α) *The set A of coordinates under consideration includes either R or one coordinate of $y_0'$, say $y_{0k}'$, for which $C_{ik}>0\ \forall i$.*
> (β) $\Sigma\lambda_i z_i^A=0$ *with* $\lambda_i\geq 0$ *implies* $\lambda_i=0\ \forall i$.

*In particular, (β) is satisfied whenever there exists in A some commodity $h_0$ such that $z_{ih_0}z_{jh_0}>0\ \forall i,j$.*

*Proof*

The set of Pareto-improving changes is defined by: $\Gamma_i^A\cdot\delta^A>0$. (α) is immediate when checking the above inequality with

$$\delta^A=(0,\ldots,0,\dot{R},00),\ \dot{R}>0$$
$$\text{or } \delta^A=(0,\ldots,0,0,0,\ldots\dot{y}_{0k},0),\ \dot{y}_{0k}>0.$$

(β) again obtains as a consequence of the theorem (on the intersection of convex cones) used in the proof of theorem 1. The last assertion is a straightforward consequence of (β). □

Proposition 1 formally expresses a particularly straightforward intuition: increasing a uniform lump-sum subsidy, the level of a unanimously desired public good (α) or decreasing the price of some unanimously demanded commodity (β) are Pareto-improving moves.

Note that although condition (α) may or may not be satisfied in specific versions of the model, the condition of existence of one commodity $h_0$ for which every consumer is a demander (resp. a supplier) is a weak require-

[5] It is useful to compare the informational requirements of computation of directions of tax reform with the more basic informational requirements of chapter 1. The knowledge of aggregate demand (and supply) transactions (and also prices) is indeed well in line with these requirements. The knowledge of willingness to pay suggests that preferences for public goods are public knowledge (compare however with the remarks at the beginning of chapter 2 concerning public goods).

ment in all versions of the model. Then proposition 1 supports previous comments on the weakness of condition (ii).

## 3.2 Tax reform: a closer examination of specific situations (**)

To get a better understanding of the above statements, it is worth considering a number of specific situations. We will consider cases of particular interest.

First, we look at the case where the set A of indices of admissible changes consists in the whole set of coordinates of $\pi, R, y_0'$. Then we consider cases in which a given subset of such coordinates is allowed to change (all coordinates of $\pi$ and $R$, all coordinates of $\pi$). In order to focus on cost–benefit analysis issues, we finally focus attention on a case where public goods are not desired (or do not exist) $C_i=0$.

Three statements that will obtain (corollaries 1–3) are rather straightforward adaptations of theorem 1. The reader is however invited to make a careful reading of these statements which will help him to become familiar not only with the specific messages of the corollaries but also with the basic message of theorem 1. Particular emphasis should be put on corollary 4 which proposes a first incursion into the important topics of cost–benefit analysis in the framework of the present model.

### 3.2.1 First corollaries

Let us come to corollary 1.1 which corresponds to the case where the set of coordinates A is the whole set of coordinates under consideration. Let us call this case the comprehensive case.

**Corollary 1: The comprehensive case**

*Consider a strict tax equilibrium in which the vector* $\Phi = [(p\cdot\partial_\pi d, p\cdot\partial_R d, p\cdot(\partial_{y_0'} d - \partial_{y_0'}\eta))]$ *is different from zero. Then, three situations may occur:*

*1* **No equilibrium-preserving and Pareto-improving move** $\Leftrightarrow$ *$\Phi$ belongs to the cone $\Gamma$ generated by the vectors $(-z_i, +1, C_i)$, $\forall i$.*

*2* **Temporary inefficiencies**
$\Leftrightarrow$ *$\Phi$ belongs to the cone $-\Gamma$.*

*3* **Existence of strict equilibrium-preserving and Pareto-improving moves**
$\Leftrightarrow$ *$\Phi$ belongs to $C(\Gamma U - \Gamma)$ (where $C(\ )$ designates the complementary of $(\ )$).*

*Furthermore if LR2 (positivity of marginal cost of income transfer) holds then situation (2) of temporary inefficiencies cannot occur. The same is true if LR3 (positivity of generalized marginal cost of public goods) holds and if* $C_i > 0, \forall i$.

*Proof*

Note first that with $R$ being an admissible coordinate of change, the set of Pareto-improving directions of changes is necessarily non-empty (proposition 1) so that condition (ii) of theorem 1 holds.

Now, it remains to prove that LR2 forbids (2). But LR2 is nothing else than $p \cdot \partial_R d > 0$. Looking at the conditions of situation 2, the reader will check that its occurrence implies $p \cdot \partial_R d = -\Sigma \lambda_i$, all $\lambda_i \geq 0$, some $\lambda_i > 0$; the contradiction immediately obtains.

A similar argument rules out (2) if LR3 holds: $p \cdot (\partial_{y_0'} d - \partial_{y_0'} \eta) > 0$ cannot be equal to $-\sum_i \lambda_i C_i$ □

Corollary 2 considers the case where the 'forbidden' directions of changes respectively concern the public good levels and the uniform lump-sum transfers (either because we are in specifications of the model where they do not exist or because they are temporarily forbidden).

**Corollary 2** *If there are no admissible directions of change in public goods, the above corollary remains true with* $\Phi$ *being* $(p \cdot \partial_\pi d, p \cdot \partial_R d)$ *and* $\Gamma$ *being the cone generated by* $(-z_i, +1)$*; and LR2 rules out temporary inefficiencies.*

*If the change in uniform lump-sum transfers is not admissible but changes in public goods are, then the above corollary remains true with* $\Phi$ *being* $p \cdot \partial_\pi d, p \cdot (\partial_{y_0'} d - \partial_{y_0'} \eta)$ *and* $\Gamma$ *being the cone generated by* $(-z_i, +C_i)$*; and LR3 together with* $C_i > 0$ *rules out temporary inefficiencies.*

*Proof*

It is an immediate variant of the proof of corollary 1. □

Corollary 3 restricts attention to price changes only.

**Corollary 3** *If the only admissible coordinates of changes are price coordinates, if* $p \cdot \partial_\pi d \neq 0$ *and if there exists some commodity* $h_0$ *such that* $z_{ih_0} > 0$ *(or* $< 0$*)* $\forall i$*, then the basic 3 partition of theorem 1 is as follows:*

*1* **No equilibrium-preserving and Pareto-improving move**
$\Leftrightarrow$ *$(p \cdot \partial_\pi d)$ belongs to the cone $\Gamma^\pi$ generated by the vectors* $(-z_i)$

*2* **Temporary inefficiencies**
$\Leftrightarrow$ *$(p \cdot \partial_\pi d)$ belongs to the cone* $-\Gamma^\pi$

*3* **Existence of equilibrium-preserving and Pareto-improving moves**
$\Leftrightarrow$ *$(p \cdot \partial_\pi d)$ belongs to* $C(\Gamma^\pi U - \Gamma^\pi)$.

*Proof*

The fact that $z_{ih_0} > 0$ (or $< 0$), $\forall i$ implies that the set of Pareto-improving directions of price changes is not empty (cf. proposition 1). Corollary 3 is then only a restatement of theorem 1 (the A coordinates being the $\pi$ coordinates). □

We can visualize the different situations depicted in corollary 3 in the following economy: There are three commodities and two consumers; in the initial strict equilibrium $R=0$. Then the vector $\Phi_\pi = p \cdot \partial_\pi d$ is normal to the vector $\pi$ so that we can get a two-dimensional diagram in the budget hyperplane. Figure 3.2 then appears as a more concrete specification of the symbolic features of figure 3.1.

Figure 3.2a visualizes case 1: the set of equilibrium-preserving moves on the one hand and Pareto-improving moves on the other hand are disjoint; $\Phi_\pi$ belongs to $\Gamma^\pi$. Equivalently, $-\Phi_\pi$ belongs to the cone generated by $z_1$ and $z_2$.

Figure 3.2c, visualizes situation 3 in which equilibrium preserving and Pareto optimal changes do exist: $\Phi_\pi$ (as well as $-\Phi_\pi$) belongs to the complement of $\Gamma^\pi U - \Gamma^\pi$.

Figure 3.2b visualizes the case of temporary inefficiencies. Some comments are now in order concerning the case of temporary inefficiencies. Above, in the so-called comprehensive case – corollary 1 – as well in corollary 2, temporary inefficiencies are ruled out when either LR2 and/or LR3 holds. The intuitive reason is the following: when the uniform lump-sum $R$ can be varied, any positive surplus can be transferred to consumers by increasing $R$ (when LR2 holds). The same is true with an increase in (desired) $y'_0$ (when LR3 holds true).

One may wonder then whether, in the present case, lowering the consumption goods prices or increasing the prices of factors (which are obviously Pareto-improving moves) cannot be made equilibrium preserving in the conditions of corollary 3. The answer to this question is negative. In fact, the difficulty originates in the distortion between production and consumption prices: when $\pi = p, p \cdot \partial_\pi d = -\Sigma_i z_i$ so that we are necessarily in (1) of theorem 1 but this is no longer necessarily the case when $\pi$ differs from

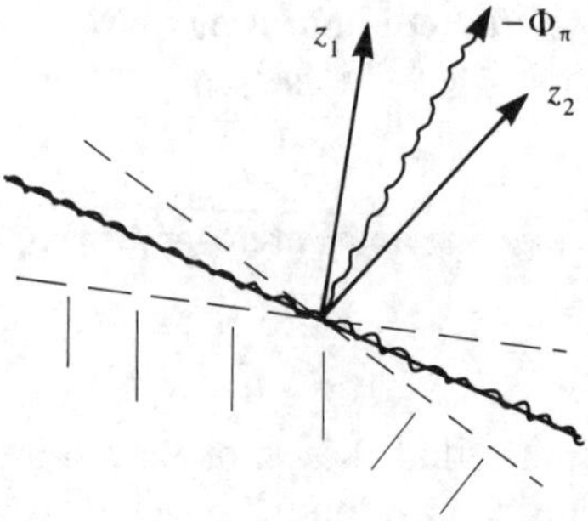


(a)

Figure 3.2a

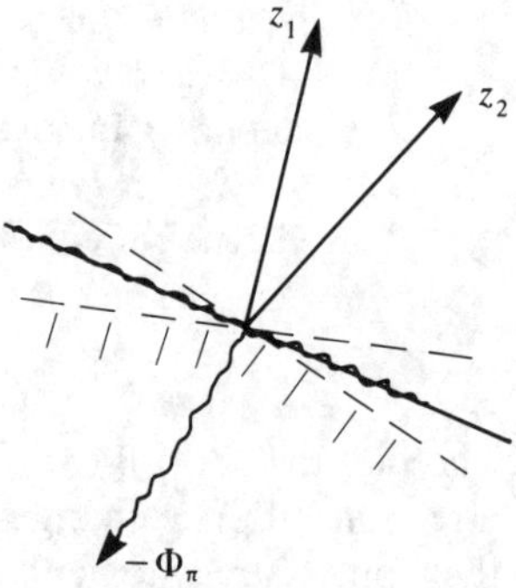


(b)

Figure 3.2b

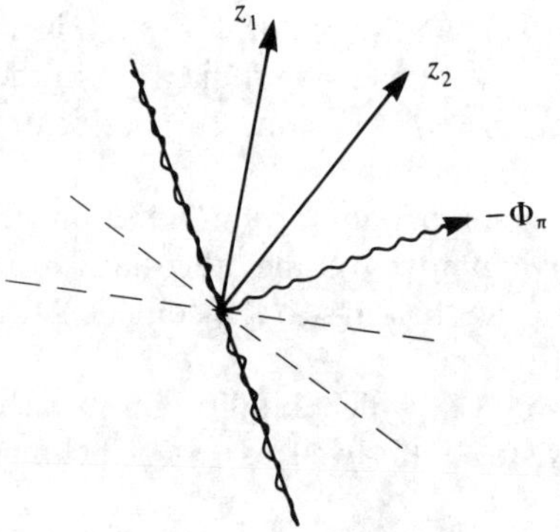


(c)

Figure 3.2c

$p$ and particularly the more it differs from $p$. A numerical example given elsewhere[6] illustrates the role played by a 'large' distortion between production and consumption prices in the occurrence of temporary inefficiencies. The reader is referred to it for a more in-depth understanding of temporary inefficiencies in the present context.

It is helpful to rewrite condition (1) with compensated derivatives rather than with uncompensated ones. Then[7]

[6] See Guesnerie (1977) where a much more detailed discussion of the phenomenon is provided. See also the bibliographical note for indication of further studies and applications.

[7] Here, contrarily to our standard convention, $(\partial_R d_i)(d_i)$ is the product of the column vector $\partial_R d_i$ with the row vector $d_i$, i.e. a $n \times n$ matrix; and $(\partial_\pi d)^c$ (in line with the convention for $(\partial_\pi d)$) is the set of columns $(\partial_{\pi_1} d)^c, \ldots, (\partial_{\pi_n} d)^c$.

$$p\cdot\partial_\pi d = p(\Sigma\partial_\pi d_i) = p\cdot\left[\sum_i (\partial_\pi d_i)^c - (\partial_R d_i)(d_i)\right]$$
$$= (p\cdot\partial_\pi d)^c - \sum_i (p\cdot\partial_{R_i} d)d_i$$

where $(\partial_\pi d_i)^c$(resp. $(\partial_\pi d)^c$) is the matrix of compensated derivatives of consumer $i$ (resp. of total demand).

The condition: $p\cdot\partial_\pi d$ belongs to the cone $\Gamma^\pi$, writes down

$$p\cdot(\partial_\pi d)^c - \sum_i (p\cdot\partial_{R_i} d)z_i = -\sum_i \lambda_i z_i \qquad \lambda_i \geq 0 \text{ some } \lambda_i \neq 0$$

or

$$p(\partial_\pi d)^c = \sum_i (-\lambda_i + p\cdot\partial_{R_i} d)z_i \tag{3.11}$$

We leave it to the reader to restate corollary 1.3 using the above formulas.

### 3.2.2 An incursion into the reform viewpoint for cost–benefit analysis

We are now going to concentrate on a specification of the model which allows us to discuss the question of cost–benefit analysis in the public sector. Such a specification relates to what has been called model B in chapter 2. It obtains from the complete model 3.1 to 3.4 presented at the outset of this chapter as follows:

1 $y_0'$ does not enter any longer the preferences of consumers. The consequences of such an assumption for local analysis are

$$\partial_{y_0'} d = 0,\ C_i = 0 \qquad \forall i = 1\ldots m \tag{3.12a}$$

Similarly, $y_0'$ does not enter the supply function of the private sector, i.e.

$$y_1'' = \eta_1(p) \tag{3.12b}$$

2 The interpretation of vector $y_0'$ does not relate any longer to public goods. It is supposed to have $n-1$ components (the number of private goods minus one) which are the first $(n-1)$ components of a production plan of the public firm: the $n^{\text{th}}$ component of the considered production plan is constrained by feasibility considerations. This interpretation translates into

$$y_{0h}'' = y_{0h}' \qquad h = 1,\ldots,n-1$$
$$y_{0n}'' + f(y_0') = 0$$

Note that, once the production set under consideration has a smooth frontier, the latter formulation of feasibility does not imply any loss of generality.

Formally, the initial equations of model A, recalled at the beginning of this chapter, are modified as follows

$$\eta_0(y_0', p) = (y_0', -f(y_0')), f \text{ differentiable} \tag{3.13}$$

In other words, $y_0'$ is an $n-1$ dimensional vector, the first $n-1$ coordinates of an $n$-dimensional supply vector of private goods, which is independant of $p$ and is interpreted as the public production vector of private goods.

With our assumptions (3.12) and (3.13), a tax equilibrium[8] consists of $(z_i, y_1'', y_0', y_0'', \pi, p, R)$ that satisfy constraints (3.1) to (3.4), rewritten as follows

$$z_i = d_i(\pi, R) \tag{3.1}$$
$$y_1'' = \eta_1(p) \tag{3.2}$$
$$y_0'' = {}^t(y_0', -f(y_0')) \tag{3.3}$$
$$\sum_i z_i \leq y_0'' + y_1'' \tag{3.4}$$

Again (3.2) and (3.3) can be aggregated and $y_0'' + y_1''$ can be defined as $\eta(y_0', p)$. The reduced form of the model – which now makes it a version of what we called model $C$ – is then

$$\sum_i d_i(\pi, R, y_0') - \eta_1(p) - (y_0', -f(y_0')) = 0$$

Economically, however, it is a model in which the public sector produces private goods while being controlled by the government. Hence, if rewritten as suggested in footnote 8 it can be viewed as a special case of model B of the previous section.

Corollary 5 presents a tax reform analysis that proceeds from theorem 1: it says that the discrepancy between the shadow prices of the 'public sector' and the real prices faced by the private sector signals the availability of potential 'social surplus' that has to be 'freed'.

**Corollary 4: Tax reform with a controlled public sector producing private goods**

*Assume that the model is modified as described by (3.12), (3.13).*

[8] Our presentation has started from model A, but the reader can check that the present model can be viewed as a specification of model B where the constraint $y_0 \in Y_0$ is as specified by (3.3).

*Consider an initial strict tax equilibrium* $(\cdot)=(\pi,p,R,y_0')$ *and define* $\rho=(\partial_1 f,\ldots,\partial_{n-1}f,1)$, *all derivatives being taken in the initial tax equilibrium.*

1. *If* $\rho$ *and* $p$ *are not proportional, then there exists strict equilibrium-preserving and Pareto-improving moves.*
2. *If* $\rho$ *and* $p$ *are not proportional and if:*

   2a *either LR2 holds:* $p\cdot\partial_R d>0$

   2b *or* $\exists$ *a commodity* $h_0$ *such that* $z_{ih0}>0\ \forall i$ *and we are not in a situation of temporary inefficiencies with respect to the price coordinates (i.e., there exist Pareto-improving moves restricted to price coordinates that are either strict equilibrium-preserving or non-feasible).*

*then, associated with any public production change* $\dot{y}_0''$ *such that* $p\cdot\dot{y}_0''>0$, *there exist strict equilibrium-preserving and Pareto-improving directions of change.*

*Proof*

The proof will obtain from the specification of corollary 1 to the present model.

Recall

$$\Phi=(p\cdot\partial_\pi d, p\cdot\partial_R d, -p\cdot\partial_{y_0'}\eta);$$

and that feasibility of a direction of change $\delta$ writes down $\Phi\cdot\delta\leq 0$.

The last element of $\Phi$ now equals $(-\tilde{p},-p_n)\begin{pmatrix}1\ldots 0\\ \ldots\ldots\ldots\\ 0\ldots 1\\ -\tilde{\rho}\end{pmatrix}$

where $\sim$ designates the truncation of a vector to its $n-1$ first coordinates and where the sketched matrix is an $(n-1)\times n$ matrix, the last row of which consists of the $(n-1)$ first coordinates of $-\rho$.

It comes: $-p\cdot\partial_{y_0'}\eta=-p_n[p_1/p_n-\rho_1,\ldots,p_{n-1}/p_n-\rho_{n-1}]=-p_n\left(\dfrac{\tilde{p}}{p_n}-\tilde{\rho}\right)$.

However, in this model, we have $C_i=0$, $\forall i$, so that $\Gamma$ is here the cone generated by the vectors $(-z_i,+1,0)$.

Then:

If $p$ and $\rho$ are not proportional $-p\cdot\partial_{y_0'}\eta\neq 0$ and $\Phi$ cannot belong either to $\Gamma$ or $-\Gamma$. Corollary 1 implies the conclusion 1.

In order to prove 2, note first that $\dot{y}_0''=(\dot{y}_0',-\partial f\cdot\dot{y}_0')=(\dot{y}_0',-\tilde{\rho}\cdot\dot{y}_0')$

Then, $p\cdot\dot{y}_0''>0\Leftrightarrow p_n[\tilde{p}/p_n-\tilde{\rho}]\cdot\dot{y}_0'>0$.

From the above computation, this latter fact is equivalent to $p\cdot\partial_{y_0'}\eta\cdot\dot{y}_0'>0$. Considering the conditions of theorem 1, chapter 2 it follows that any $\dot{y}_0''$ such that $p\cdot\dot{y}_0''>0$, one can associate some $\dot{R}$ ($>0$ if LR2 holds) such that

$(p \cdot \partial_R d)\dot{R} - (p \cdot \partial_{y_0'} \eta_0)\dot{y}_0' = 0$. The corresponding move is a strict equilibrium-preserving and Pareto-improving move. This proves conclusion 2a.

Coming to 2b, the negation of the assertion 'we are in a situation of temporary inefficiencies with respect to price coordinates' together with the existence of $h_0$ imply: 'there exist Pareto-improving changes $\dot{\pi}$ such that $(p \cdot \partial_\pi d)\dot{\pi} \geq 0$'. Any $\dot{\pi}$ such that $(p \cdot \partial_\pi d)\dot{\pi} = 0$ obeys the conclusion of the corollary. If, contrarily, $(p \cdot \partial_\pi d)\dot{\pi} > 0$, take $\lambda$ such that

$$\lambda(p \cdot \partial_\pi d)\dot{\pi} - (p \cdot \partial_{y_0'} \eta_0)\dot{y}_0' = 0$$

$(\lambda\dot{\pi}, \dot{y}_0')$ defines (with $\dot{R} = 0$) a strict equilibrium-preserving and Pareto-improving move. □

In contrast with the previous statements relative to public good production and tax 'reform', with corollary 5 we touch upon the field of tax reform and **cost–benefit analysis**.

In particular, corollary 5 shows us the role played by $p$ in cost–benefit analysis even from a local perspective: every discrepancy between the public shadow prices and the real production prices signals an inefficiency (part 1). Also, from part 2 of this corollary, it is meaningful to view $p \cdot \dot{y}_0''$ as the (direction of) benefit, measured with production prices $p$, associated with the production change $\dot{y}_0''$; this benefit would be a surplus which could actually be 'freed' or 'liberated'.[9] There are two ways of 'liberating' benefit (or surplus); first, through a uniform lump-sum transfer increase when LR2 holds, second, through an adequate change of consumer prices when we are not in a situation of temporary inefficiencies with respect to the price coordinates.

As well as the positive part of corollary 5, its negative part – i.e. the restriction it brings to the possibility of 'freeing positive surplus' – can be emphasized. In a situation of temporary inefficiencies with respect to price coordinates, a surplus might not be liberated.

Finally we should note that this first brief incursion in the domain of cost–benefit analysis will be followed by several further analyses of the problem in this chapter.

## 3.3 Tax reform: from infinitesimal to finite changes – algorithms of tax reform (T***)

### 3.3.1 The problem: formal statement, informal discussion (**)

The analysis we have developed until now considers directions of change, i.e., infinitesimals. Its relevance for small but finite changes must now be

[9] All these terms are taken in the sense used by Allais (1977b). The terminology is intuitive but may not exactly fit more standard uses of the word surplus.

scrutinized. This is the purpose of this subsection. The exposition of the problematic within the next two pages precedes the technical analysis that the less technically oriented reader may skip.

The infinitesimal analysis identifies 'directions of changes'. Intuitively, these directions of changes suggest small finite changes that can be linked together to generate a path of reform. Formally, these directions of change determine differential equations which have to be integrated in order to generate actual finite changes.

Indeed, let us consider the set of strict equilibrium-preserving and Pareto-improving directions of change (in an initial situation $(\cdot)$). This set has been defined as the intersection of strict equilibrium-preserving directions of change (equation 3.9 with equality that defines a hyperplane) and of Pareto-improving directions of change (equation 3.10 that defines an open cone). When this set is non-empty – a fact that has been characterized under various assumptions in the two preceding subsections – it contains 'many' directions – in the sense of having a non-empty relative interior. Let us call this set SEPPI$(\cdot)$ (strict equilibrium-preserving Pareto-improving directions of change). Here SEPPI has been defined over the set of welfare relevant directions of change $\dot{\pi}$, $\dot{R}$, $\dot{y}'_0$. Remembering that a change $\dot{\pi}$, $\dot{R}$, $\dot{y}'_0$ has to be matched by a change $\dot{p}$, along the lines that have been carefully discussed in the preparation of theorem 1, chapter 2, we can write that finite equilibrium-preserving and Pareto-improving changes are generated as solutions of the following system of differential equations.

$$\left(\frac{d\pi}{dt}, \frac{dR}{dt}, \frac{dy'_0}{dt}\right) \in SEPPI\,(\pi, R, y'_0) \cap \{\delta \in \mathscr{R}^{n+n'+1} \mid \|\delta\| \leq 1\} \tag{3.14}$$

$$\frac{dp}{dt} = \partial\eta^{-1}(p)\left[(\partial_\pi d)_{(\cdot)}\frac{d\pi}{dt} + (\partial_R d)_{(\cdot)}\frac{dR}{dt} + (\partial_{y'_0} d - \partial_{y'_0}\eta)_{(\cdot)}\frac{dy'_0}{dt}\right] \tag{3.15}$$

Because SEPPI is a set, not a vector, the differential equation (3.14) necessarily has a multivalued right-hand side; note that, without loss of generality, the second part of the right-hand side of (3.14) restricts directions in SEPPI to be of (Euclidean) norm smaller than one.

A first straightforward proposition is in order: it says in particular that if the system has a solution, then, along this solution, the path of reform is satisfactory in the sense that everybody's welfare is monotonically increasing.

*Proposition 2*

*Let $\pi(t)$, $R(t)$, $y'_0(t)$, $p(t)$ be a solution of the differential equations (3.14), (3.15) starting from a tight tax equilibrium $p(0)$ $\pi(0)$, $R(0)$, $y'_0(0)$, and defined on $(0, T)$. Then,*

*Each point of the solution defines a tight tax equilibrium.*
*The utility of every household* $V_i(t) = U_i(d_i(\pi(t),\ R(t),\ y_0'(t)))$ *is strictly increasing along the trajectory,* $\forall i$.

The reader will establish proposition 2 as a rather straightforward application of previous analysis and definitions. (Write the derivatives of individual welfare and excess demand in every point of this solution and show that the former are strictly positive and the latter are zero.)

Another preliminary remark is in order: as written, the system (3.14), (3.15) may cease to be defined after some finite time, for example, when it reaches a point where SEPPI $= \phi$. In the latter case, the point reached is, in some sense that will be discussed later, 'satisfactory' and it is natural to assume that the system remains immobile afterwards. This suggests to introduce the modified equation

$$\left(\frac{d\pi}{dt}, \frac{dR}{dt}, \frac{dy_0'}{dt}\right) \in \text{SEPPI } (p, \pi, R, y_0') \cap \{\delta \in \mathcal{R}^{n+n'+1} \mid \|\delta\| \leq 1\}$$

if SEPPI $(\cdot) \neq \phi$

$$\left(\frac{d\pi}{dt}, \frac{dR}{dt}, \frac{dy_0'}{dt}\right) = 0 \text{ if SEPPI } (\cdot) = \phi \tag{3.16}$$

At this stage, we have a satisfactory formal definition of the tax reform algorithm suggested by the analysis of the two previous subsections.

Four questions are now in order.

1. Consider a tight tax equilibrium where SEPPI $\neq \phi$. Has the system of multivalued right-hand side differential equations a solution on some finite interval $[0, T]$?
2. Can the solution be extended to $[0 + \infty]$?
3. Assuming a positive answer to the preceding questions, what is the limit behaviour of the solution? Does it converge?
4. Does it converge towards second-best Pareto optima?

Let us realize that a positive answer to all the questions would mean that our tax reform algorithm performs very well: it has a solution always defined and which converges towards a second-best Pareto optimum. We immediately understand that this ideal situation is unlikely. According to (3.16) the algorithm stops when it reaches a point where SEPPI is empty; such a point may not be a second-best Pareto optimum, it may only be a local optimum or even only some kind of 'extremum'. We cannot expect that whatever the starting point the algorithm reaches is for sure a full optimum. We shall discuss this point more precisely later in this section. Now, we have to ascertain that a positive answer can be given to questions 1 and 3. The non-technical reader might think that such a positive answer is intuitive – 1 and 2 being perhaps dismissed as mathematical sophistication and the positive answer to 3 being 'intuitively obvious' from proposition 2 above. He would be both right and wrong. Right because we do give a positive answer to the three questions. Wrong because such a positive answer does not hold true for the most general version of the model; it requires a number of specific conditions of economic relevance. Whether these specific conditions are imbedded in some 'economic intuition' (which would suggest the positive conclusion) is much debatable. Also, actual difficulties in the computations of tax reforms will be avoided whenever they take place in models in which the conditions sketched in the following – sufficient for a positive answer to questions 1–3 – hold true.

The formal analyses of questions 1–3 which follow may however be skipped at first reading.

### 3.3.2 Existence and convergence theorems (T***)

We present in this sub-section three statements theorem 2, corollary 1, theorem 3, together with a sketched proof, that gives answers respectively to questions 1, 2 and 3. A discussion of economic desiderata underlying these statements follows in 3.3.3. The analysis here assumes that the following is true.

> (AR) The set of interior tight tax equilibria (in the sense defined in chapter 2) is a smooth manifold.

From chapter 2, we know conditions which imply AR (cf. theorem 4). Also we know that such a property is 'generically' true in the sense discussed after the statement of theorem 5.

Condition AR is indeed sufficient for providing a positive answer to question 1 (existence of solutions on some finite interval for the system 3.14, 3.15).

**Theorem 2: Existence of solutions to the differential equations**

*Assume AR. Then starting from any* $(p, \pi, R, y_0')$ *where* $SEPPI(p, \pi, R, y_0') \neq \phi$ *the system (3.14) (3.15) of differential equations with a multivalued right-hand side has a solution on some finite interval.*

*Proof*

First, consider a local parametrization of the manifold and look at the right-hand side of equation (3.14). Then consider, as a 'function' of the local parameters of the manifold, the set which is the intersection of the tangent space to the manifold, of the hyperplanes $(\Gamma_i)_{(\cdot)} \cdot \delta \geq 0$ (defined in section 1) and of the sphere $\|\delta\| \leq 1$. The corresponding correspondence is upper hemi-continuous: it is the intersection of upper hemi-continuous correspondences, the correspondence which associates to every point the part of the tangent space inside the sphere and the correspondences which associate the intersection of the hyperplanes with the unit sphere. A specific argument shows it is lower hemi-continuous.[10] Furthermore, each value of the correspondence has a non-empty interior (relative to the tangent space). Then, one can pick up a continuously differentiable selection in the correspondence with norm $\epsilon, 0 < \epsilon < 1$. To conclude, it is enough to apply the standard existence theorem of differential equations (see Mathematical appendix) to the system (3.14), (3.15) where the right-hand side of (3.14) is replaced by the continuous selection. □

How far can the local solution so defined be extended?

The following result, which reflects classical considerations on the extension of solutions of differential equations, obtains:

**Corollary 5** *Consider an initial equilibrium (0).*

*Assume (C):*
*there exists some compact subset C(0) of the manifold of tax equilibria such that the following holds:*

> *For every tax equilibrium* $e = (p, \pi, R, y_0')$ *outside* $C(0)$, $V_i(e) < V(0)$ *where* $V_i(e)$ *is the (indirect) utility of agent i in e and* $V_i(0)$ *his utility at the starting point.*
>
> *Then, the differential equation (3.16), (3.15) has a solution (starting from (0), defined on* $[0, +\infty]$*) and called a trajectory.*

*Proof*

Coming back to the argument of theorem 2, one sees that the continuous selection argument holds for every $e$ where SEPPI $(e) \neq \phi$. Consider an associated solution starting from (0). From proposition 2, it will remain in the compact set $C(0)$.

If after successive extensions there is a limit time $\bar{t}$ after which the extension is impossible, consider $t_n \to \bar{t}$ and $e(t_n)$ a point on the solution at time $t_n$. The sequence $e(t_n)$ has a converging point; call it $e(\bar{t})$. There are two cases: either, SEPPI $(e(\bar{t})) = \phi$, or SEPPI $(e(\bar{t})) \neq \phi$. In the first case, the

[10] See Fogelman–Guesnerie–Quinzii (1978), Castaing (1966).

system remains immobile after $t$, but the solution remains well defined; in the second case, the system can still move after $t$. Both cases contradict the starting point of the argument.[11] □

We shall come back later to comment on the assumption of corollary 2.1. Now, we immediately turn to the third question raised above: what is the limit behaviour of a trajectory, i.e., the behaviour of a trajectory when time indefinitely increases? Formally, this refers us to the concept of a limit point.

Let us recall the definition of a **limit point**: $\bar{e}$ is a limit point of a trajectory $e(t)$ if there exists a sequence $t_n \to +\infty$, $n \to \infty$, such that $e(t_n) \to \bar{e}$.

Also the 'immobile points' considered later fit the standard concept of *equilibrium* of a system of differential equations. Formally, for the system (3.16), (3.15)

$$\bar{e} \text{ is an equilibrium} \Leftrightarrow \text{SEPPI}\ (\bar{e}) = \phi$$

Let us associate now to every tight tax equilibrium the following

$$f(e) = \max_{\delta} \min_{i} \{\Gamma_i(e) \cdot \delta \mid \delta \in \text{SEP}\ (e) \cap S\}$$

where SEP ($e$) designates the set of strict equilibrium-preserving directions of changes and $S$ is the sphere of unit radius (in $\mathscr{R}^{n+n'+1}$) and $\Gamma_i(e)$ is the specification in $e$ of the vector $\Gamma_i$ defined at the beginning of section 1 of this chapter.

Note that $f(e)$ is the maximal speed of increase of utility of the less-favoured agent (a Rawlsian type index for evaluating tax reform). As discussed below, this index acts as a technical device: we are only concerned with the speed of increase of utility of the less favoured agents because, when making this speed large enough, we are sure that all speeds (of utility increases) are large enough. It is straightforward that:

in every $e$ where SEPPI $(e) \neq \phi, f(e) > 0$
$e$ where SEPPI $(e) = \phi, f(e) = 0$

$f$ is a continuous function: ($SEP \cap S$) is a continuous correspondence and $\min_i \Gamma_i \cdot \delta$ is a continuous function (concave in $\delta$) and then the maximum theorem applies.[12]

We are now ready to state:

[11] This is a classical argument in this sort of problem (see for example Hirsch–Smale (1974)).
[12] For a statement of the maximum theorem, see Berge (1959).

**Theorem 3: Convergence**
*Assume AR and C*[13]
*Consider a trajectory of system (3.16) (3.15) where in each point* $\min_i (\Gamma_i(e)\cdot\delta) \geq \nu f(e),\ 1 \geq \nu > 0$

*Then every tax equilibrium e* which is a limit point of the trajectory satisfies SEPPI* $(e^*) = \varnothing$ *(i.e., is an equilibrium of the system of differential equations).*

*Proof* (sketch)
Let $e^*$ be a limit point, and let $t_n \to +\infty$ be a sequence such that $e(t_n) \to e^*$.
The conclusion of the theorem is equivalent to $f(e^*) = 0$.

Assume $f(e) = \epsilon > 0$ and consider a local parametrization of the manifold around $e^*$. Consider a compact sphere (of radius $2\eta$), denoted $S(2\eta)$, in which the local parametrization holds and in which $f(e) > \frac{\epsilon}{2}$. Call $S(\eta)$ the compact sphere of radius $\eta$. For $n \geq n_0$, $n_0$ large enough, $e(t_n) \in S(\eta)$. The key point is then that the time length $\Delta t$ in which $e(t_n + \Delta t)$ remains in $S(2\eta)$ is greater than some $\mu > 0$. As this occurs an infinity of times, the utility of some agent $i$ can then be shown to increase above $V_i^* = V_i(e^*)$, a contradiction. □

Before going further, let us comment on theorem 3: it asserts that any trajectory of the algorithm (whose existence is guaranteed by (C) from corollary 5) converges to points $e^*$ where SEPPI $(e^*) = \phi$. However, a condition has to be met which requires that some part of the potential gain for Pareto improvement, as measured with the Rawlsian type index $f(e)$, is exploited. The logic of this condition is easy to understand: imagine that we pick up in SEPPI a vector whose norm decreases exponentially with time; the algorithm may then be trapped in points where SEPPI $\neq \phi$. Here the Rawlsian index is a technical device which assures that everybody's welfare increases at some minimum pace (necessarily higher than the worse off's pace).

It is important to come back to points where SEPPI $= \phi$: they are points in which a Pareto improvement which is strict equilibrium preserving is impossible. It may however be the case that there exists non-strict equilibrium-preserving directions of change which are Pareto improving. Points where SEPPI $= \phi$ then fall into two categories:

[13] C is not formally needed for theorem 3, but in the absence of C the trajectories (with limit points being tax equilibria) envisaged in theorem 3 might not exist.

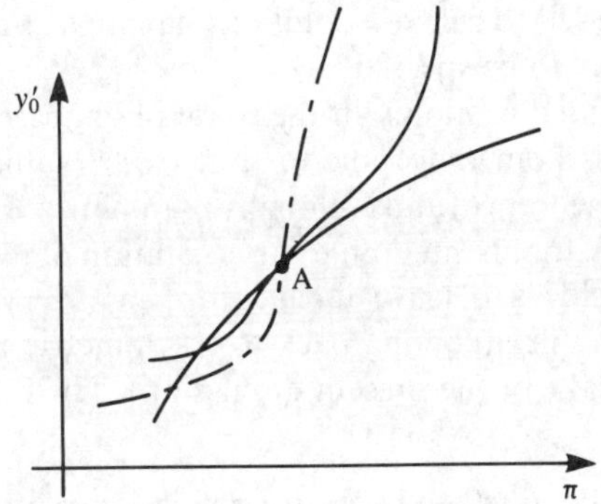


Figure 3.3

Equilibria in which the phenomenon of temporary inefficiencies is observed (type 2 of theorem 1); Note that such equilibria may exist in general, but also that they are ruled out under some assumptions, as made clear by the corollaries to theorem 1.
Equilibria which are local optima in the sense associated with type 3 situations of theorem 1.

These latter equilibria are themselves of two types, they are either local Pareto optima (in their neighbourhood they are not Pareto dominated), or they are of the type suggested by figure 3.3 which sketches indirect utility curves on the manifold of equilibria: although SEPPI $=\phi$, there are Pareto better equilibria in every neighbourhood of the limit point A. The extremum so obtained has some of the features of an inflection point.

### 3.3.3 Discussion of results and extension (T***)

We are now in a position to gather and discuss the results.

First, the local existence of solutions to the system (3.14), (3.15) holds very generally, and for example is guaranteed if the set of tax equilibria is a smooth manifold. (This global condition is unnecessarily strong, since we only need to have a local manifold structure.)

However, the extension of a local solution to a trajectory faces two difficulties. Either the solution may have a tendency to 'leave' the manifold (by going to the boundary of its closure), or it may go to infinity in some direction. Taking into account proposition 1 according to which the utility increases monotonically along a solution, assumption C of corollary 5 rules out difficulties in a way which is somewhat *ad hoc*. Its discussion is the main subject of the remainder of the subsection.

Essentially, the argument needed to rule out solutions having a 'wrong' behaviour in finite time are likely to be specific.

Consider the case of an extended economy in the sense of chapter 2 in which the set of tax equilibria is homeomorphic to $\mathring{\mathscr{R}}_+^{n-1} \times \mathscr{R}_+^{n'}$ (sufficient conditions for that are given in theorem 6) and is globally parametrized by $\pi$ and $y_0'$. In that case, the only way for an integrable curve solution of (3.16), (3.15) on the manifold to go outside is to 'leave' it *either* in $y_0' \mid \|y_0'\| = +\infty$ *or* on the boundary of the price simplex (coming back to a symmetric price normalization is better for the sake of the present discussion). The reader will check that:

The first possibility can be ruled out by the following assumptions:

($\alpha$) (1) $U_i(z_i, y_0') = W_i(z_i) + \Lambda_i(y_0')$
(2) $W_i$ and $\Lambda_i$ are bounded from above and tend to $-\infty$ when one component of $z_i$ or $y_0'$ tends to $-\infty$.

($\beta$) If $y_{on}'$ is a sequence of public production and $p_n$ a sequence of production prices such that $y_{onh}' \to +\infty$ then either $\exists k \mid y_{onk}' \to -\infty$ or $\exists j \mid y_{nj}'' = \eta_j(p_n, y_{on}') \to -\infty$

Assumption ($\alpha$) is a reinforced version of AP of chapter 2 (Additivity of Preferences between public and private goods), that strongly penalizes the consumption of highly negative quantities while limiting the reward of highly positive consumption. Assumption ($\beta$) is a (weaker) assumption[14] on the production of public goods.

Together these assumptions prevent a trajectory – along which everybody's welfare increases – to reach a point where $\|y_0'\| = +\infty$.

The second possibility is ruled out when the two following additional assumptions hold:

($\gamma$) is nothing else other than ELBD2 of the previous chapter, i.e., which says that if a consumption price sequence has an accumulation point that belongs to the boundary of the price simplex, then $\exists h \mid d_{ih}(\pi_n, \cdot) \to +\infty$

($\delta$) is nothing else other than EBPG1 of the previous chapter, i.e.

$$y_h = \lim_n \eta_h(p_n, y_{0n}') = +\infty \Rightarrow \exists\, k \text{ such that } y_{0kn}' \to -\infty$$

Assumption ($\delta$) is a rather strong assumption – the section of the production set is bounded from above – that has been discussed above. We may

[14] It has the same spirit although it is less strong than (E)BPG3 used above in chapter 2. Again, the production set of figure 2.19 (chapter 2), meets it.

argue that assumption ($\gamma$) is reasonable for an extended economy.[15] Together ($\delta$) and ($\gamma$) (given $\alpha$, $\beta$) make it impossible to have a trajectory reaching the boundary of the price simplex.

Note, however, that assumption ($\gamma$) would not hold in an economy where the consumption sets are bounded from below, and where initial endowments are on the boundary of the consumption sets. Then ($\gamma$) has to be replaced by ($\epsilon$):[16]

($\epsilon$) If $(\pi_n, R_n, y'_{on})$ is a sequence such that $\pi_n$ converges to $\bar{\pi}$ belonging to the boundary of the price simplex, then:

$$\text{either } \exists h | d_{ih}(\pi_n, \cdot) \to +\infty$$
$$\text{or } \lim_n V_i(\pi_n, \cdot) < V_i(\pi_0, R_0, y_0'^0)$$

Finally, let us note that in the equations under consideration, all feasible directions of change could until now be used for local improvement. The equations and the algorithm modify straightforwardly when one or several coordinates of $\pi, y'_0, R$ are supposed to be fixed. For example, tax reform can be viewed as concerning only some coordinates of $\pi$, with a fixed level of public goods, or without uniform lump-sum transfers. The whole analysis conducted above is immediately transposed as soon as the subset of tax equilibria associated with the fixed coordinates is itself a smooth manifold. This is stated as theorem 4 which the reader is invited to check:

**Theorem 4**

*Consider the system (3.16), (3.15) with the additional restrictions:* $\frac{d\delta'}{dt} = 0$ *where* $\delta'$ *is a subset of components of* $\delta = (\pi, R, y'_0)$. *Assume that the set of tax equilibria such that* $\delta' = \delta'(0)$ *is a smooth manifold. Then, theorem 2, corollary 5, theorem 3 remain true for the new system.*

[15] In the sense that under separability, it would follow from the more basic assumption that the asymptotic cone of the upper contour set of preferences (over private goods) is $\mathscr{R}^n_+$.

[16] ($\epsilon$) is reasonable in a non-extended economy with one factor of production (taken as numeraire): at the boundary of the price simplex one consumption price is either 0 or $+\infty$; in the latter case, consumption has to tend to zero, putting utility below any prespecified level. Now, in such an economy, the only way to 'leave' the manifold of equilibria for a solution to (3.16), (3.15) is either to go to the boundaries where $\|y'_0\| = +\infty$ (this can be ruled out by the assumption, natural in that context, that the set of physical feasible states is compact), or to go to the lower boundary (for example, with one public good $y'_0 = 0$). This latter possibility has in general to be ruled out by an *ad hoc* argument (in order for C to hold). Consider for instance example 2 of the beginning of chapter 2. Assumption $\epsilon$ holds as well as the compactness property alluded to above. However, it is easy to modify preferences (change the utility of $y'_0$) to obtain tax reform solutions converging to $y'_0 = 0$. Note that they are not 'bad' solutions since then $y'_0$ is a (possibly local) optimum. However, they do not converge to a point when SEPPI $= \phi$. Such solutions can be ruled out by adequate assumptions such that for instance, in example 2 $y'_0 \to 0$ implies $\Lambda_i(y'_0) \to -\infty$.

*Also the assumptions guaranteeing that C holds in the complete economy guarantee that it holds in the section.*

As we know, the fact that the section $\delta' = \delta'(0)$ is a smooth manifold is generically true (conditionally) to AR which is itself generic. Theorem 4 has hence a wide applicability. The general discussion on the limit points which are attained by trajectories of our algorithms is also immediately transposed to these cases. Note however that, depending on which coordinates are constrained, the likelihood of reaching a point displaying temporary inefficiencies will differ, since this situation has been ruled out in a certain number of cases above.

## 3.4 Tax reform – further discussions (**)

This section provides further discussions on tax reform when instead of looking at Pareto improvements, the social planner refers to some (exogenously given) social welfare function. Subsection 3.4.1 successively considers the characterization of welfare-improving tax reform, the design of an algorithm (of the gradient projection kind) whose application to cost–benefit analysis is particularly emphasized. Subsection 3.4.2 introduces further considerations, i.e., a Musgravian interpretation of the tax reform algorithm and a discussion of existence and convergence questions.

### 3.4.1 Tax reform: the social welfare function approach (**)

*General characterization of a welfare-improving tax reform*

Until now attention in tax reform has focused on Pareto-improving changes. Pareto improvement can be viewed both as a much too demanding and/or an unsufficiently discriminating criterion. As it is usual in public economics, it can be replaced by a social welfare criterion. For the purpose of local analysis, an individualistic social welfare criterion is entirely specified through a set of positive weights $\lambda_i$, where $\lambda_i$ has the interpretation of the social value of agent $i$'s income. In conformance with such an interpretation, a $\lambda$ **welfare-improving directions of changes** $(\dot{\pi}, \dot{R}, \dot{y}_0')$ **is defined** as meeting the condition

$$-(\Sigma_i \lambda_i z_i)\dot{\pi} + (\Sigma_i \lambda_i)\dot{R} + (\Sigma_i \lambda_i C_i)\dot{y}_0' > 0 \qquad (3.17)$$

Note that multiplying all the $\lambda_i$ by the same positive number does not affect the set of welfare-improving directions of changes. Only the ratios $\lambda_i/\lambda_j$ matter or equivalently (change of) social welfare can be normalized in terms of the (change of) income of some prespecified agent.

The transposition of the previous analysis of Pareto-improving tax reform to the analysis of welfare-improving tax reform obtains straightforwardly by replacing the previous $m$ individual welfare indices by a unique social welfare index that appears as the first term of the definition (3.17) of welfare-improving directions of change.

All the previous results obtained for Pareto-improving changes have counterparts for social welfare changes. They are formally summarized in the next two statements, that we present as further corollaries of theorem 1 in this chapter.

**Corollary 6: Equilibrium-preserving and welfare-improving directions of change**

*Call $\Gamma(\lambda)$ the vector in $\mathscr{R}^{n+n'+1}$ $(-(\Sigma_i\lambda_i z_i),\ \Sigma_i\lambda_i,\ (\Sigma_i\lambda_i C_i))$ and $\Gamma^A(\lambda)$ its restriction (projection) in $\mathscr{R}^{|A|}$ to the set of coordinates A. Consider a strict tax equilibrium in which $\Phi^A \neq 0$.*
*Then, three situations can occur:*

1. $\Phi^A = \mu\Gamma^A(\lambda)$, $\mu > 0 \Leftrightarrow$ *There exists no equilibrium-preserving and λ-welfare-improving (given the set of weights λ) directions of change.*
2. $\Phi^A = \mu\Gamma^A(\lambda)$, $\mu < 0 \Leftrightarrow$ *There exists a (necessarily) non-strict equilibrium-preserving and λ-welfare-improving direction of change.*
3. $\Phi^A \neq \mu\Gamma^A(\lambda)$, $\forall\mu \Leftrightarrow$ *There exist strict equilibrium-preserving and welfare-improving directions of change.*

**Corollary 7: Equilibrium-preserving and welfare-improving directions of change**

*Corollaries 1, 2, 3, 4 are true with straightforward modifications (analogous to the ones brought in previously in corollary 6) when Pareto improving is replaced by λ-welfare improving. In particular, temporary inefficiencies are ruled out either by LR2 or LR3 together with $C_i > 0$.*

Hence, the pure theory of tax reform when reform is evaluated with respect to a social welfare criterion appears as an immediate application of tax reform theory built with the Pareto criterion. It identifies in case 3 a set of strict equilibrium-preserving and welfare-improving directions. Note that the cone of equilibrium-preserving and Pareto-improving directions, associated with what was called case 3 in previous sections, was there a (relatively) open cone (in $\mathscr{R}^{|A|}$) and is now a (relatively) open half space (in the same space). As neatly argued by Dixit (1975) the problem is not 'that there are few policies leading to partial welfare improvements . . . nor . . .

that partial welfare improvements are particularly difficult to characterize . . .' but 'that some particular rules that were thought to be intuitively plausible by some economists turned out to be wrong'. Rules that were thought to be intuitively plausible by economists were often based on the analysis of the one-consumer case, discussed in more detail later. Before reflecting more on that case, the reader may already appreciate the considerable simplification that the replacement of the aggregate weighted bundle $\Sigma\lambda_i z_i$ by a single bundle $z$ would introduce in previous statements.

*The gradient projection algorithm*

Comparing the social welfare and the Pareto viewpoints, one may think that in case 3, selection from among the set of strict equilibrium-preserving and welfare-improving (SEPWI) directions is easier than selection from among the set of strict equilibrium-preserving and Pareto-improving (SEPPI) directions. Indeed among all SEPWI directions, some seem particularly appealing (in terms of the social welfare criterion under consideration). This intuition can be formalized in two ways.

First, one can look at the direction of steepest ascent in the sense defined by the **gradient projection algorithms**. Roughly speaking such a direction obtains as the projection of the gradient of social welfare on the linear local approximation to the feasible set. Let us briefly recall the principles of the gradient projection method, using the following case: the objective function is $\rho_0(x)$ where $x$ belongs to the Euclidean space $R^N$; the feasible set is defined by $M$ equality constraints $\rho_i(x)=0$, $i=1,\ldots,M (M<N)$. All functions are supposed to be differentiable and their gradient is denoted $\nabla\rho_i$. The vector $\nabla\rho_o(x)$ can be decomposed uniquely as the direct sum of a vector in the space spanned by $\nabla\rho_i(x)\ldots\nabla\rho_M(x)$ and of a vector in its orthogonal complement. The latter space is nothing else but the space of locally feasible moves at $x$ so that writing

$$\nabla\rho_0(x)=\nabla\rho_p(x)+\Sigma_i\mu_i\nabla\rho_i(x) \tag{3.18a}$$

we call $\nabla\rho_p(x)$ the gradient projection.

An operational computation of the $\mu_i$ obtains from the following equalities

$$\nabla\rho_p(x)\cdot\nabla\rho_i(x)=0,\ i=1\ldots M. \tag{3.18b}$$

which determine (when $\nabla\bar{\rho}_p(x)$ is drawn from equation (3.18a)) a number of equations equal to the number of unknowns.

Another idea consists in seeking to **optimize locally social welfare** among the set of feasible directions. In the framework just sketched, the local approximation of objectives is given by $(\nabla\rho_0)\dot{x}$ when the locally feasible

directions satisfy $(\nabla \rho_i)\cdot\dot{x}=0$. The optimization problem is not well defined since $(\nabla \rho_0)\dot{x}$ is a linear form of $\dot{x}$ and can be, along a direction where it is positive, increased as much as desired. Local optimization can be meaningful only if some bounds are placed on the magnitude of $\dot{x}$. A bound for the norm of $\dot{x}$ is a rather natural restriction. It leads to the following local optimisation programme.
(LOP) $\max(\nabla \rho_0)\cdot\dot{x}$

$$(\nabla \rho_i)\cdot\dot{x}=0,\ i=1,\ldots M. \tag{3.19}$$

$$\|\dot{x}\|\leq 1 \tag{3.20}$$

where $\|\,\|$ designates the norm under consideration. When $\|\,\|$ is for example the Euclidean norm (3.20) reads $\dot{x}^2\leq 1$.

Both procedures, gradient projection and local optimization, under norm constraints are closely related, as can be shown by solving the LOP with the Euclidean norm. The associated Lagrangian is $(\nabla \rho_0)\cdot\dot{x} - \Sigma_i\mu_i(\nabla \rho_i)\cdot\dot{x}-\nu(\dot{x}^2-1)$. First-order conditions obtain: $\nabla \rho_0-\Sigma_i\mu_i\nabla \rho_i - 2\nu\dot{x}=0$. Hence $2\nu\dot{x}=\nabla \rho_0-\Sigma_i\mu_i\nabla \rho_i$ with $\nabla \rho_i\cdot\dot{x}=0$. The conditions determining the optimal $\dot{x}$ are similar to those characterizing the gradient projection $\nabla \rho_p(x)$ just defined above. Both conditions define the **same** 'direction of change'.

We can now come back to the tax reform problem. The variables under consideration are $p$, $\pi$, $R$, $y_0'$ (the vector $x$ of the previous general formulation). The local approximation of social welfare writes down $\Gamma(\lambda)\cdot(\dot{\pi},\dot{R},\dot{y}_0')$ and the feasibility constraints are

$$\Phi\cdot(\dot{\pi},\dot{R},\dot{y}_0')\leq 0 \tag{3.21}$$

plus the equations (2.17) determining $\dot{p}$ as a function of $(\dot{\pi},\dot{R},\dot{y}_0')$.

We choose here to rule out $\dot{p}$ from the set of variables under consideration: in the local optimization problem, the constraint on the norm concerns the vector $(\dot{\pi},\dot{R},\dot{y}_0')$ and not $\dot{p}$ (or $\dot{p}$ with a zero weight); also in the gradient projection, we project the gradient only on the feasibility constraint (3.22) and not on the others. The elimination of the variables $\dot{p}$ can be justified by the fact that they do not affect social welfare directly. The procedure remains somewhat arbitrary and is mainly justified by the simplicity and economic appeal of its results.

The simplified gradient projection restricted to the variable $\dot{\pi}$, $\dot{R}$, $\dot{y}_0'$ can be expressed as

Project $\Gamma(\lambda)$ on the hyperplane $\Phi\cdot(\dot{\pi},\dot{R},\dot{y}_0')=0$.

Similarly the **Local optimization problem restricted to** $(\pi,R,y_0')$ and with the **Euclidean norm** is the following:
(LOP) max $\Gamma(\lambda)\cdot(\dot{\pi},\dot{R},\dot{y}_0')$ under

$$\Phi_{\pi}\cdot\dot{\pi}+\Phi_{R}\cdot\dot{R}+\Phi_{y_0'}\cdot\dot{y}_0'\leq 0 \tag{3.22}$$
$$\dot{\pi}^2+\dot{R}^2+\dot{y}_0'^2\leq 1 \tag{3.23}$$

Next theorem 5 provides an explicit expression of the simplified gradient projection. We argue, after the proof of the theorem that this expression nicely appeals to economic intuition.

**Theorem 5: The simplified gradient projection algorithm**

*Consider an initial tight equilibrium $p$, $\pi$, $R$, $y_0'$ denoted $(\cdot)$, and associated with $z_i\ (=d_i(\cdot))$, $y_0''=\eta(y_0', p)$.*

*(1) The simplified gradient projection algorithm, just defined above selects the following directions of change*

$$\dot{\pi}=-\Sigma_i\lambda_i z_i-\mu\Phi_{\pi}(\cdot), \tag{3.24}$$
$$\dot{R}=\Sigma_i\lambda_i-\mu\Phi_R(\cdot) \tag{3.25}$$
$$\dot{y}_0'=\Sigma_i\lambda_i C_i(\cdot)-\mu\Phi_{y_0'}(\cdot) \tag{3.26}$$

*with*

$$\mu=\frac{\Phi\cdot\Gamma(\lambda)}{\Phi^2}$$
$$=\frac{(\Phi_{\pi})(\cdot)(-\Sigma_i\lambda_i z_i)+\Phi_R(\cdot)(\Sigma_i\lambda_i)+\Phi_{y_0'}(\cdot)(\Sigma_i\lambda_i C_i(\cdot))}{\Phi_{\pi}^2(\cdot)+\Phi_R^2(\cdot)+\Phi_{y_0'}^2(\cdot)} \tag{3.27}$$
$$\dot{p}=(\partial\eta^{-1})_{(\cdot)}[(\partial_{\pi}d)_{(\cdot)}\dot{\pi}+(\partial_R d)_{(\cdot)}\cdot\dot{R}+(\partial_{y_0'}d-\partial_{y_0'}\eta)_{(\cdot)}\dot{y}_0'] \tag{3.28}$$

*(2) Furthermore when $\mu>0$ the directions of change so defined correspond to the directions of change which solve the restricted LOP associated with the Euclidean norm.*

*(3) In the case where some components of the vector $\dot{\pi}$, $\dot{R}$, $\dot{y}_0'$ are zero, the above formula, with the corresponding components of $\Phi$ being taken equal to zero still define the gradient projection.*

*Proof*

1 From the reminder of the preceding pages, if projection is made on the hyperplane, the gradient projection $\nabla_1$ equals $\Gamma(\lambda)-\mu\Phi$, $\mu$ being determined by $\Phi\cdot(\Gamma(\lambda)-\mu\Phi)=0$ – hence formula (3.27) and then (3.24) to (3.26).

2 The equivalence result between gradient projection and LOP has been shown above to hold more generally. However, our above argument assumed that both feasibility constraints were tight, when here we have referred to the general definition of the gradient

without assuming tightness of the feasibility constraint 3.22. The equivalence result then only holds when the constraint 3.22 is tight at the optimum. This occurs whenever $\mu > 0$. Hence the statement.

3 Conclusion follows from the reconsideration of the argument for 1 with a restricted set of coordinates. □

Let us first comment on formulas (3.24) to (3.27). For the sake of simplicity, let us limit ourselves to price changes $((\dot{R}, \dot{y}_0') = 0)$. The reader will easily extend the comment to the general situation.

The best direction $\dot{\pi}$ combines two (generally) opposite moves

The first one $(-\Sigma_i \lambda_i z_i)$ is in some sense the 'more socially' desirable. The consumption price of commodity $h$ is reduced proportionally to the sum of the quantities consumed by each consumer weighted by the social marginal utilities of incomes. The price of commodity $h$ is reduced more if this good is consumed more or if it is demanded by people who have a high social marginal utility of income.

Corrections should be made in a second step in order to ensure feasibility. The cheapest corrections (in some sense) consist in increasing the consumption price of commodity $h$ in proportion of $-\Phi_{\pi_h} = -p \cdot \partial_{\pi_h} d$, i.e., of the 'benefit', measured with production prices, generated by an increase of the consumption price of commodity $h$.

In line with the local analysis of chapter 2, the appropriate weights of the two changes have to be inversely correlated with their costs, measured with production prices, i.e., $\Phi_\pi \cdot (\Sigma_i \lambda_i z_i)$, on the one hand, and $\Phi_\pi \cdot (-\Phi_\pi)$, on the other hand. Hence the formula (3.26) which (in the case $\dot{R} = 0, \dot{y}_0' = 0$) reduces to

$$\mu = \frac{\Phi_\pi \cdot (-\Sigma \lambda_i z_i)}{\Phi_\pi^2}$$

Note that if $\mu$ were negative, the first step would release resources.[17] In that case, the formula we have stressed does not define any longer the solution of the LOP with the Euclidean norm; in other words, the best local direction is no longer production efficient, and then does not coincide with the gradient projection which we have computed. Indeed, in that latter case, the gradient projection, as defined here, is no longer interesting.

[17] Remember that the sign of $\mu$ depends upon the sign of $\Phi$. $\Gamma(\lambda)$; hence $\mu < 0$ obtains within case 3 of corollary 1, outside the temporary inefficiency case (although it necessarily obtains in this case). Then, the second step would not be any longer desirable (since it is costly and not socially desirable).

Finally we should stress another dimension of arbitrariness of the selection of directions of change of the theorems. The direction which is selected in both methods is sensitive to changes of units. This is clear from the local optimization version. With a multiplication of the price unit by a factor $1/k$ then $\pi$ is changed in $k\pi$ and $\pi^2$ in $k^2\pi^2$; with $k>1$ price changes become relatively more constrained than income changes; in the norm constraint (3.23) the change of units is equivalent to a change of norms.

We have discussed the gradient projection algorithm in full generality. Now, it is worthwhile to concentrate on the version of the model where we have a public sector producing only private goods. This case has been introduced, and carefully discussed from the Pareto viewpoint, in subsection 2.2. We know that this case obtains when we specify the model as made explicit in formulas (3.12), (3.13) above, i.e. the public good is not desired (as a public good) ($C_i=0$) and does not affect the aggregate consumer demand $\partial_{y_0'} d=0$. The reduced form of the model is then:

$$\left[\sum_i d_i(\pi, R) - \eta_1(p) - y_0''\right] = 0$$

where $y_0''=[y_0', -f(y_0')]$ and $y_0'$ is an $n-1$ dimensional vector.

In this case the first term $\sum \lambda_i C_i$ of the right-hand side of formula 3.26 is zero and the second term $\Phi_{y_0'} = -p\cdot\partial_{y_0'}\eta$ has been computed in section 2.1 and equals $-p_n\left[\frac{\tilde{p}}{p_n} - \tilde{\rho}\right]$, where $\tilde{p}$ is the production price vector truncated of its last coordinate and $\tilde{\rho}$ the truncated shadow price vector of the 'public' sector. Recalling that the direction of change of public production is $\dot{y}_0'' = \{\dot{y}_0', -\tilde{\rho}\cdot\dot{y}_0'\}$, it comes out:

**Corollary 8: Cost–benefit analysis in the public sector, first version**

*In the case of a public sector producing private goods as described in assumptions (3.12) (3.13), theorem 5 has to be read with (3.29) replacing (3.26)*

$$\dot{y}_0'' = \mu p_n\left[\frac{\tilde{p}}{p_n} - \tilde{\rho}, -\tilde{\rho}\cdot\left(\frac{\tilde{p}}{p_n} - \tilde{\rho}\right)\right] \tag{3.29a}$$

The reader will note that such a $\dot{y}_0''$ satisfies, as desired, $(\tilde{\rho}, 1)\cdot\dot{y}_0''=0$.

Also, he is invited to comment on the characteristics of the directions of change (3.29a). He will note in particular that

$$p\cdot\dot{y}_0'' = \mu p_n^2\left[\frac{\tilde{p}}{p_n} - \tilde{\rho}\right]^2 > 0 \tag{3.29b}$$

According to 3.29b, the direction which is chosen by our gradient projection algorithm is necessarily, with $\mu > 0$, a direction where profit measured with the production price system increases. The reader will fruitfully compare the present statement with corollary 4, in subsection 3.2.2, which argues that changes in public production which increase profit can be made Pareto improving.[18]

It is also worth comparing this version of the gradient projection algorithm with a slightly different version where the unique feasibility constraint $\Phi \cdot (\dot{\pi}, \dot{R}, \dot{y}'_0) = 0$ is replaced by two feasibility constraints

$$\Phi_\pi \cdot \dot{\pi} + \Phi_R \cdot \dot{R} - p \cdot \dot{y}''_0 = 0 \tag{3.30}$$

$$\rho \cdot \dot{y}''_0 = 0 \tag{3.31}$$

It should be noted that both formulation (2.21) (as modified to take into account (3.12), (3.13)) or formulation (3.30), (3.31) are equivalent.

Consider the projection $\nabla_2$ of $\Gamma(\lambda)$ on two constraints: it obtains as

$$\nabla_2 = \begin{pmatrix} \Gamma(\lambda) \\ 0 \\ 0 \end{pmatrix} - \mu' \begin{pmatrix} \Phi_\pi \\ \Phi_R \\ -p \end{pmatrix} - \nu' \begin{pmatrix} 0 \\ 0 \\ \rho \end{pmatrix}$$

From (3.18b) we have $\nabla_2 \cdot (\Phi, -p) = 0$, $\nabla_2 \cdot (0, \rho) = 0$, i.e.

$$\Phi \cdot \Gamma(\lambda) - \mu' \Phi^2 - \mu' p^2 + \nu' p \cdot \rho = 0$$

and

$$+\mu' p \cdot \rho - \nu' \rho^2 = 0$$

Solving in $\mu'$ and $\nu'$, we obtain theorem 6.

**Theorem 6: Cost–benefit analysis in the public sector from the gradient projection viewpoint: second version**

*The second version of the gradient projection selects the following directions of change*

$$\dot{\pi} = -\Sigma \lambda_i z_i - \mu' \Phi_\pi \tag{3.32}$$

$$\dot{R} = +\Sigma \lambda_i - \mu' \Phi_R \tag{3.33}$$

$$\dot{y}''_0 = \mu' \left[ p - \frac{p \cdot \rho}{\rho^2} \rho \right] \text{ with } \mu' = \frac{\Phi \cdot \Gamma(\lambda)}{\Phi^2 + p^2 - \dfrac{(p \cdot \rho)^2}{\rho^2}} \tag{3.34}$$

$$\dot{p} = \partial \eta^{-1} [(\partial_\pi d) \dot{\pi} + (\partial_R d) \cdot \dot{R} - \dot{y}''_0] \tag{3.35}$$

[18] This **does not** imply that the change selected by the gradient projection algorithm – which in some sense maximizes the speed of increase of social welfare – is Pareto improving!

Note that from Schwarz inequality the denominator of $\mu'$ is positive; but the numerator is not necessarily positive. Part (2) of theorem 5 as well as part (3) have here counterparts which the reader is left to check. Remember again that theorem 6 differs from theorem 5 in two respects:

It considers the more specific context of a public sector producing private goods.

It rests upon a different version of the gradient projection algorithm that reflects the rewriting of the feasibility constraints.

The comparison between the directions selected by theorem 5 and theorem 6 suggests several worthwhile remarks. First, it is easy to check that $\mu$ of theorem 5 and $\mu'$ in theorem 6 are different numbers. Second, it is also the case that the direction selected for $y_0''$ by (3.29) generally differs from the direction selected by (3.34) unless $\frac{\tilde{p}}{p_n}$ and $\tilde{\rho}$ are collinear). In fact, the latter direction $p - \frac{p \cdot \rho}{\rho^2}\rho$ is nothing other than the projection of the vector $p$ on the hyperplane normal to $\rho$ and tangent to the hypersurface of production in the public sector. The cost–benefit rule has then a particular economic appeal; it recommends *change of the public sector production plan in the direction which maximizes the speed of increase of profit measured with production prices (faced by the private sector).*

Corollary 4 in section 3.2 has already underlined the role of the relative position of $p$ and $\rho$ in cost–benefit analysis. Corollary 8 and theorem 6 put an additional and somewhat strong emphasis on the role of production prices in a cost–benefit evaluation of production changes in a reform context.

### 3.4.2 Tax reform: further considerations (**)

*A 'Musgravian' interpretation*

The rules defined by formulas (3.29) and (3.34) select a direction of change which, when combined with the associated directions of price and income change, is welfare improving. Such rules depict somewhat arbitrary selections in the set of welfare improving directions. In particular, as the above discussion on the role of units suggests, the sense in which they are 'optimal' cannot be viewed as particularly deep. But these revision rules are relatively simple, economically appealing, and rather elegant. They should be helpful in developing intuition of the tax reform mechanics.

We now suggest a 'Musgravian' interpretation of the corresponding reform process which we will sketch below. This interpretation distinguishes between three functions: distribution, allocation, and stabilization. In the light of the formulas given in theorems 5 and 6, the three functions can be attributed to three different 'offices': the distribution office, the allocation office, the stabilization office. To describe the task of each office, we distinguish between (1), what it observes (2) which information it transmits or receives, (3) what it computes. (We take here the specific formulas of theorem 6 that apply in a context where the public production sector produces private goods.)

*The distribution office*

(1) Observes the transaction vector $z_i$, and the aggregate elasticities $\partial_\pi d$, $\partial_R d$. Also it knows the $\lambda_i$ (which for the sake of simplicity are not assumed here to be subject to revision).

(2a) Receives the information concerning the production prices $p$ from the stabilization office and the information concerning the gradient of the public sector production set, $\rho$, from the allocation office.

(2b) Computes and transmits to the allocation office

$$\mu' = \frac{\Phi \cdot \Gamma(\lambda)}{\Phi^2 + p^2 - \dfrac{p \cdot \rho}{\rho^2}}$$

(3) Computes $\dot{\pi}$ and $\dot{R}$ in conformity with formulas (3.32) and (3.33).

*The allocation office*

(1) Observes the production plan $y_0''$ of the public sector and deduces from it the vector $\rho$.

(2) Transmits $\rho$ to the distribution office and learns $\mu'$ from the latter and $p$ from the stabilization office.

(3) Computes $\dot{y}_0''$ according to formula (3.34).

*The stabilization office*

(1) Observes the vector $p$ of production prices.

(2) Transmits $p$ to the allocation and distribution office, is informed of the policy decisions $\dot{\pi}$. $\dot{R}$, $\dot{y}_0''$ of the other offices.

(3) Computes $\dot{p}$ according to formula (3.35).

It should be noted that our continuous-time formulation forces us to view observations, computation, and decisions of the three offices as simultaneous and not truly successive stages. Some timing of decisions is however suggested by the above description; it could be made realistic and precise in a discontinuous time version of our story. But as the reader will check, some price would then have to be paid in terms of elegance and conciseness of the formulation of the adjustment process. Also the reader will notice that we have stuck to the Musgravian distinction of allocation, distribution, and stabilization. But the stabilization office considered here is given tasks, similar in spirit but different in scope of those attributed by Musgrave to his regulating body. Furthermore, a higher level 'coordination' office could have been added, being in charge of task (2b) of the distribution office, i.e., of computing $\mu'$ and transmitting it to the distribution and allocation offices.[19]

Let us draw some conclusions from the above exercise. The reform decisions based on gradient projection considerations are necessarily interdependent. They could not be implemented by isolated Musgravian offices. However, reform decisions can be viewed as proceeding from interdependent offices, each one having specific tasks to perform and receiving and transmitting adequate information from or to others. At least, what precedes is the best Musgravian interpretation of the present tax reform algorithm that I can imagine!

### *Finite time algorithms*

At this stage, we have to give up the infinitesimal point of view, on which our definition and comments are until now based, in order to analyse the local and global properties of the algorithm. The analysis conducted above for algorithms directed at Pareto improvement can easily be transposed here. The results are summarized in theorem 7, whose assumptions AR and C have been defined in section 3.3 before the statement of theorems 2 and 3.

### Theorem 7: Gradient projection algorithms in finite time

*Consider the system of differential equations defined in theorem 5 (resp. theorem 6).*

*(1) Take any solution on* $[0, T]$*: along it social welfare is a non-decreasing function of time.*

*(2) Assume AR: then the system has a unique local solution starting from any given tight tax equilibrium.*

[19] The computation of the weights $\lambda_i$, which should be variable, could also have been given to this higher-level office.

(3) *Assume AR and C: then the unique solution can be extended to a trajectory (defined on* $[0, +\infty]$).
(4) *Assume AR and C: Then any limit point* $(*)$ *meets* $\Gamma(*)(\lambda) = \Phi(*)$.

*Proof* (sketch)

(1) Generalizes proposition 2 and is immediate.
(2) Obtains if one notes that the gradient defined in both systems is a continuously differentiable function; the proof of theorem 2 based on a continuously differentiable selection in the set of Pareto-improving moves is immediately transposed. The argument for (3) is identical to the argument for corollary 5 of section 3.3.
(4) Follows from an argument paralleling the argument sketched for the proof of theorem 3. However, condition min $\Gamma_i \cdot \delta > \epsilon f(e)$ is no longer needed: the full potential of welfare improvement is necessarily used by the algorithm. Also, instead of following the proof of theorem 3 a Liapounov type of argument could have been directly used. □

In conclusion theorem 7 provides a relatively simple account of the existence and convergence properties of our gradient projection algorithm. The comments of section 3.3 concerning the validity of AR and in particular of C could be repeated word by word. Avoiding replication, let us only transpose the findings concerning convergence.

As the algorithms aimed at the search of Pareto optima considered in section 3.3, gradient projections algorithms converge either:

to equilibria of type 2 where temporary inefficiencies are present;
or to equilibria of type 3 which are **local welfare optima**;
or to equilibria of type 3 which are 'inflection points'.

Also the discussion on how to screen inflection points in the most appropriate way is left to the reader.

## 3.5 Second-best Pareto optima (**)

A second-best Pareto optimum is by definition a tax equilibrium such that there exists no other tax equilibrium which dominates it in the Pareto sense (i.e., that makes every household better off). More technically, second-best Pareto optima are maximal elements of the Pareto preordering over the set of (here strict) tax equilibria (which have been studied in chapter 2).

This section focuses attention on such second-best Pareto optima. As is intuitively obvious, such second-best Pareto optima are tax equilibria in which there are no equilibrium-preserving Pareto-improving directions of change, i.e., which are rest points of our tax reform algorithms. This remark provides the basis of our analysis.

The section proceeds as follows: Subsection 3.5.1 presents characterization results. Section 3.5.2 comments upon them lengthily.

### 3.5.1 Characterization results (**)

This section is devoted to characterizing second-best Pareto optima. Logically speaking, such a programme can be viewed as a subproduct of the analysis of tax reform. Actually, our first characterization results strictly follow from theorems 1 and 2 and their corollaries. In the remainder of the section, we discuss in the sharpest way the second-best optimal prescriptions concerning consecutively taxes, public goods production, public production of private goods.

Again in the whole section we assume AR

(AR) The set of interior tax equilibrium is a smooth manifold.

Next theorem 8 characterizes second-best Pareto optimum in the case where there are no constraints on state variables.

**Theorem 8: Characterization of second-best Pareto optima without constraints on state variables**

*Consider a second-best Pareto optimum $\pi^*, p^*, R^*, y_0'^*$ of the general model (3.1) (3.4).*

*Let* $z_i^* = d_i(\pi^*, R^*, y_0'^*)$, $C_i^* = C_i(\pi^*, R^*, y_0'^*)$

*Then necessarily there exist positive numbers $\lambda_i$ such that*

$$p^*\cdot(\partial_\pi d)_{(*)} = -\Sigma_i \lambda_i z_i^* \tag{3.36}$$

$$p^*\cdot(\partial_R d)_{(*)} = \Sigma_i \lambda_i \tag{3.37}$$

$$p^*\cdot[(\partial_{y_0'} d)_{(*)} - (\partial_{y_0'} \eta)_{(*)}] = \Sigma_i \lambda_i C_i^* \tag{3.38}$$

*Also, combining (3.36) and (3.37) one can assert:*
*$\exists$ numbers $\nu_i = \lambda_i - p^*\cdot(\partial_R d_i)$ $(\nu_i > -p^*\cdot(\partial_R d_i)_{(*)})$ such that*

$$p^*\cdot(\partial_\pi d)^c_{(*)} = -\Sigma_i \nu_i z_i^* \text{ with } \Sigma_i \nu_i = 0 \tag{3.39}$$

*Proof*

The formal proof of theorem 8, whose details are left to the reader, follows the following straightforward lines:
First note that, as intuitively argued above, a second-best Pareto optimum

is necessarily a tax equilibrium in which there exist no equilibrium-preserving and Pareto-improving changes: if there were some strict equilibrium-preserving and Pareto-improving directions of change, then with AR and from theorem 2, there would be some finite Pareto-improving change; if there were some (non-strict) equilibrium-preserving and Pareto-improving changes, then the existence of a finite Pareto improving move is immediate and leads to the same contradiction.

Then, we are in case 1 of corollary (1) (of section 3.2 of this chapter) the statement of which is reproduced in (3.36) to (3.38).

Finally, passing from the above formulas to (3.39) only requires repeating the computations that followed corollary 3 of section 2; this leads to formula (3.11). □

Also, corollaries 2, 3, 4 which in section 3.2 analyse the tax reform process when some policy variables are constrained have counterparts which are stated as corollary 9.

Roughly speaking corollary 9 says that when some variables are fixed, the conditions (3.36) to (3.38) hold true at the corresponding optimum, for all the variables which are 'free' (or not fixed). In fact the statement is slightly more complex because it has to take into account some tedious problems related to normalization.

**Corollary 9: Particular cases**

*(α) If $y'_0$ is fixed in the optimization process conditions (3.36) and (3.37) (of theorem 8) still obtain at a second-best Pareto optimum (conditional on the fixed $y'_0$).*

*(β) If R is* **fixed** *and* **equal to zero** *and if all remaining variables (but possibly $y'_0$) are free, condition (3.36) obtains in a second-best Pareto optimum. It can still be written under the form (3.39) but $\Sigma_i \nu_i$ is no longer necessarily equal to zero.*

*Also (3.36) in this case is equivalent to*

$$p^* \cdot (\partial_{\pi_h} d)_{(*)} = -\Sigma_i \lambda_i z^*_{ih},\ h \in H_{n-1} \qquad (3.36')$$

*where $H_{n-1}$ is any subset of $n-1$ commodities.*

*(In other words, one line can be omitted in the statement of the conditions (3.36).)*

*(γ) If R is fixed and different from zero and with the same sign as the sign of $R^*$ (the optimal level of uniform transfer in the unconstrained problem) and if all remaining variables (except possibly $y'_0$) are free, conditions (3.36) and (3.37) obtain in a second-best Pareto optimum. In fact, in this case (3.36) ⇒ (3.37).*

(δ) *If R is fixed and different from zero, and if all remaining variables (except possibly $y_0'$) are free, with the exception of the price of an untaxed numeraire, then condition (3.36′) above holds (but does not imply either (3.36) or (3.37)).*

*Proof*

The conclusions of (β), (γ), (δ) result from the following remarks:

When $R=0, \sum_h \pi_h z_{ih}=0$ and $\sum_h \pi_h(\partial_{\pi_h} d_i)=0$

Then (3.36′) ⇒ (3.36). (Multiply (3.36′) by $\pi_h$, sum over $H_{n-1}$ and use the above homogeneity identity – aggregated over households – with $R=0$.)

When $R\neq 0, \sum_h \pi_h z_{ih}=R$ and $\sum_h \pi_h \partial_{\pi_h} d_i + R\partial_R d_i = 0$

Multiplying both sides of (3.36) by $\pi$ leads to:

$R(p^*\cdot\partial_R d) = -\left(\sum_i \lambda_i\right)R$ which is equivalent to (3.37).

In fact when sign $R=$ sign $R^*$, it can be directly shown that the second-best optimum under the policy assumptions of (γ) is the same as the second-best optimum under the policy assumptions (β). The freedom in the normalization left by the unconstrained choice of $\pi$ allows one to equate the purchasing power of the fixed-income transfer to its optimal value. When the sign of $R$ is different from the sign of $R^*$, if there is a second-best optimum, then it is different from the optimum of theorem 8 but statement (γ) holds true. However, in these circumstances a second-best Pareto optimum may fail to exist. To avoid ambiguities we have stated (γ) with the restriction sign $R^*=$ sign $R$.

The above arguments break down when there is an untaxed numeraire. This proves (δ). □

The case treated above in corollary 4, which corresponds to the specification of the model described in section 1, where the public sector provides private goods (hence is a controlled sector providing private goods) deserves special emphasis. The most important conclusion is stated in the next corollary 10, whose proof is left to the reader (who can view it either as an application of theorem 8 to the specific context under consideration – model (3.12) and (3.13) or as an implication of corollary 4 when using the argument of the proof of theorem 8).

**Corollary 10** *With the controlled public sector producing private goods of corollary 4, then when all price variables are free (except possibly the price of a numeraire) at the optimum $p^*=\rho^*$ where $\rho^*=(\partial_1 f,\ldots,\partial_{n-1} f, 1)_{(*)}$ is the shadow price vector of the public sector.*

Corollary 10 is an important statement on cost–benefit analysis – in direct line with the reform statements of corollary 8 of theorem 5 or of theorem 6 – that will be commented upon later on.

Coming back to corollary 9 note that it expresses a form of separability between the optimality conditions. When for example one component of $(R, y_0')$ is constrained at the optimum, the relationship, involving the other state variables and demand derivatives, which obtains is the same as when $R$ and $y_0'$ are free. This fact, which reflects straightforward separability properties of first order conditions should not be misleading. The optimum, for example optimal taxes, does depend upon the set of policy tools which are available. However, this kind of separability makes possible a sequential investigation of the different groups of formulas under consideration. Such an investigation is the purpose of the next subsection.

### 3.5.2 Comments on optimal rules (**)

We shall successively consider: rules for public production, rules for the provision of public goods and optimal taxes.

*Rules for public production*

Again the central result is expressed in corollary 10: the shadow price vector for private commodities which supports an optimal production plan of the controlled public sector is (proportional to) the **production price vector** faced by the competitive private sector.

For the sake of simplicity, this result has been established in the case where the controlled firm only produces private goods. But, as the reader will check, it holds in the general way it has just been expressed (i.e., when pure public goods are actually produced by the controlled firms).

An important implication of the result is that the production sector as a whole (private firms + controlled firms) works in an efficient way.[20]

A somewhat straightforward reinterpretation of the result obtains in the case where the model is modified to allow for different firms in the private sector. The transposed conclusion implies that such different firms should face the same price system for their transactions. Hence differentiated taxation between firms is undesirable. Note that a value added tax system rules out in principle differentiated taxation among firms, and this is one of the advantages stressed by its advocates when compared to other systems. Our argument supports this aspect of the value added tax procedure.

The role of production prices in cost–benefit analysis has already been

[20] At least, if there is only one public good: the result is actually known as a condition of **production efficiency** (this is Diamond-Mirrlees' terminology).

emphasized in a reform context (sections 2 and 4) and the conclusion drawn here is in line with previous findings. It is in direct line with our first analysis of cost–benefit analysis – from the point of view of Pareto-improving reforms – i.e., corollary 4 but also with our results on welfare-improving production changes, i.e., for example theorem 6: if $p$ provides correct signals for local changes of public production (in the sense of corollary 4 or theorem 6) in any tax equilibrium, it also provides correct signals at a second-best (or welfare) optimum. More precisely, at such an optimum there should be no local (and hence global because of convexity) change of production plan of the controlled firm which increases profit measured with production prices. In other words, production prices provide the right signals. They correctly reflect the social values of commodities or equivalently their **social opportunity costs**. The identification of production prices, and the social values of commodities (which must be understood up to some proportionality coefficient here unspecified) plays a central role in our interpretation of tax formulas given below.

Production efficiency is an important conclusion for cost–benefit analysis. It should however be noticed that it is a conclusion which holds in a polar case. The argument we are giving **crucially** depends on the fact that $p$ and $\pi$ can be chosen freely in a disconnected way (so that all equalities in 3.36 are met). In other words there are no (around the optimum) constraint on taxes up to normalization. The property would in general cease to hold in the absence of such a strong assumption on taxation power.

*The provision of pure public goods*

Let us now come back to formula (3.38). Let us restrict ourselves to the case where $y_0'$ is one-dimensional. Dropping the notation (*) we can rewrite (3.38) as follows

$$-p\cdot(\partial_{y_0'}\eta)-\sum_i C_i=(\bar{\lambda}-1)\sum_i C_i+\sum_i(\lambda_i-\bar{\lambda})C_i-p\cdot\partial_{y_0'}d) \tag{3.40}$$

with $\bar{\lambda}=\dfrac{\Sigma_i\lambda_i}{m}$.

The left-hand side is the difference between the marginal cost of the public good and the sum of the marginal willingness to pay. This difference is zero in a first-best context. Here it is the sum of the three terms of the right-hand side of equation (3.40). Let us briefly discuss these three terms.

The last one $-p\cdot\partial_{y_0'}d$ can also be written $T\cdot\partial_{y_0'}d$ with $T=\pi-p$. It is zero when preferences are additively separable between public and private goods. A priori, it can have any sign.

The second one is the covariance across households between the coefficients $\lambda_i$ (which in line with the analysis of subsection 3.2.1, and our subsequent interpretation will be called the social values of agent $i$'s income) and the marginal willingnesses to pay $C_i$. Again this expression cannot be signed a priori.

In order to discuss the first term on the right-hand side of (3.40), some algebra is helpful: this term can be shown to be the sum of three terms, only one of which can be signed; a somewhat more informative rewriting of formula (3.40) obtains.[21]

**Corollary 11: Modifications of Samuelson's rules**

*Formula (3.40) can be rewritten as*

$$-p\cdot\partial_{y_0'}\eta_0=(1-k)\sum_i C_i+\varphi(C_i,\lambda_i,T,\partial_{R_i}d)$$

*where k is a positive number whenever the total tax receipts $T\cdot(\Sigma_i z_i)$ are positive and where none of the three terms of*

$$\varphi=-[\textstyle\sum_i(\lambda_i-\bar{\lambda}+T\cdot\partial_{R_i}d)(T\cdot z_i)]\left(T\cdot\sum_i z_i\right)^{-1}(\sum_i C_i)+\sum_i(\lambda_i-\bar{\lambda})C_i$$
$$+T\cdot\partial_{y_0'}d$$

*can a priori be signed.*

Hence the present second-best analysis suggests an argument for the existence of a systematic bias between the marginal cost of public good and the sum of marginal willingness to pay for the public good. Note however that this systematic bias can be more than counteracted by terms which are 'a priori' unsigned. Note also that the actual detection of such a negative bias in the characterization of the optimal provision of public good would not allow us to conclude that the second-best optimal level of public good is smaller than the first-best one.

21 We are first reminded that $\nu_i$ in formula (3.38) equals $(\lambda_i-p\cdot\partial_R d_i)$(we drop (*)). Introducing $T$ and rearranging the terms in (3.38) leads to:

$$T\cdot(\partial_\pi d)^c=(\bar{\lambda}-1)\Sigma_i z_i+\Sigma_i(\lambda_i-\bar{\lambda}+T\cdot\partial_R d_i)z_i$$

Multiplying (to the right) by $T$ gives:

$$(\bar{\lambda}-1)=(T\cdot\Sigma z_i)^{-1}[T\cdot(\partial_\pi d)^c\cdot T-\Sigma_i(\lambda_i-\bar{\lambda}+T\cdot\partial_R d_i)(T\cdot z_i)]$$

The term $\Sigma_i(\lambda_i-\bar{\lambda}+T\cdot\partial_{R_i}d)(T\cdot z_i)$ is the sum of $\Sigma_i(\lambda_i-\bar{\lambda})(T\cdot z_i)$, the covariance of social values of income and total taxes paid by individuals and $\Sigma_i(T\cdot\partial_R d_i)(T\cdot z_i)$. None of these expressions can a priori be signed. However $T\cdot(\partial_\pi d)^c\cdot T$ is necessarily negative, and $(T\cdot\Sigma_i z_i)$ is the total tax receipt.

Calling $k$ the number $-(T\cdot\Sigma z_i)^{-1}T\cdot(\partial_\pi d)^c T$, we obtain the corollary (see Besley–Jewitt (1992), Lau–Sheshinsky–Stiglitz (1978) for simplifying assumptions).

It should finally be acknowledged that our assertion that some terms 'cannot a priori be signed' is somewhat ambiguous. We leave to the reader to think how and to what extent it could be transformed into a rigorous statement.

*Optimal taxes: A first discussion*

We will start by proposing a verbal interpretation of formulas (3.36) and (3.39).

Relying on the interpretation of $p^*$ as the vector of **social opportunity costs of commodities**, the left-hand side of the $h^{\text{th}}$ component of (3.36) measures the social cost of the change in demand induced by an increase in the price of commodity $h$ or equivalently by an increase in the tax on commodity $h$ (everything being equal). On the right-hand side, the $\lambda_i$ are the implicit social values of income for consumer $i$ (this is in fact their explicit interpretation when the social welfare function approach is taken), then $-\Sigma\lambda_i z^*_{ih}$ is the social benefit induced by the increase in the price of commodity $h$. Considering price decrease rather than price increase, we can paraphrase (3.36) as follows.

> **The social cost of the change in demand induced by a decrease in the tax on commodity $h$ – everything being equal – equals the social value of the tax change to the consumers, i.e., the sum of commodity $h$'s individual consumptions weighted by the marginal social values of income.**

Now let us come back to (3.39): after replacing $p$ by $\pi - T$ and taking into account the symmetry of the Slutsky matrix, it gives the following equalities

$$T\cdot(\partial_\pi d_h)^c = \Sigma_i \nu_i z_{ih}$$

Dividing each side by $z_h = \Sigma_i z_{ih}$ (when it is different from zero) yields

$$\frac{T\cdot(\partial_\pi d_h)^c}{z_h} = \Sigma_i \nu_i \frac{z_{ih}}{z_h}$$

The numerator of the left-hand side can be interpreted as (proportional to) the effect on the compensated demand for commodity $h$ of an 'intensification' of taxes in the direction of actual taxes.[22] The ratio of the left-hand side relates this change in demand to total demand for commodity $h$. It is usually

[22] This intensification, i.e., a movement of taxes along the direction of the vector of actual taxes has to be understood everything being equal, i.e., in fact as a change in consumption prices along the direction of actual taxes.

called the (relative) index of discouragement of commodity $h$.[23] If we do not consider the ratio, the number $T\cdot(\partial_\pi d_h)^c$ will be called – in a consistent way – the absolute index of discouragement of commodity $h$.[24]

For a complementary justification of the terminology, consider the limit case where $(\partial_\pi d_h)^c$ is a vector with only two non-zero components (the first one and the $h^{\text{th}}$ one), i.e., the case where substitution effects with goods other than the numeraire are zero. We then say that the Slutsky matrix is quasi-diagonal.

Assume (without loss of generality as seen later) that $T_1 = 0$, then $T\cdot(\partial_\pi d_h)^c = T_h a_{hh}$ where $a_{hh}$ is the $h^{\text{th}}$ component of $(\partial_\pi d_h)^c$. Then the relative index of discouragement is $\frac{T_h a_{hh}}{z_h}$, i.e., the relative effect on the compensated consumption of commodity $h$ of an increase in its own tax in proportion to its actual value. It is negative when the good is taxed, and positive when it is subsidized, a fact which fits the intuitive connotation of the term index of discouragement (again we assume one factor untaxed).

Now let us come back to the formula. When $\Sigma \nu_i = 0$ the right-hand side is the covariance of the share ratios of households in the consumption of commodity $h$ and of individual coefficients $\nu_i$. But $\nu_i$ (cf. above definition) can be interpreted as the net social value of income for agent $i$, i.e., the difference between the (gross) social value $\lambda_i$ and the social cost of meeting the additional demand induced by a unit income transfer to agent $i$.

This will be summarized as corollary 8.3.

### Corollary 12: Ramsey many-person tax rule

*At a second best optimum when conditions (3.36) and (3.39) of theorem 8 hold we have*

$$\frac{T\cdot(\partial_\pi d_h)^c}{z_h} = \Sigma_i \nu_i \frac{z_{ih}}{z_h}, \ \forall h, \tag{3.41}$$

**i.e., the relative index of discouragement of commodity $h$ equals the covariance, across households, of consumption shares of commodity $h$ and of the net marginal social values of income.**

Supposing $\pi^*$, $z_i^*$, $\nu_i^*$ are known, formula (3.41) allows us in principle to compute (optimal taxes). In this sense, it summarizes everything that

[23] In fact the index is negative when the so-called intensification decreases demand (and positive on the contrary), as well as an increase in tax of a taxed good decreases demand. The discussion of the sign of the index is pursued here.

[24] Note however that the relative index is independent of this unit of measurement (it has no 'dimension') when the absolute one is not.

concerns 'optimal taxes'. The question is that the formula is rather opaque and does not seem to lead immediately to the kind of qualitative conclusions that economists would have a priori expected (for example conclusions of the kind: luxuries should be taxed, necessities should be subsidized, etc. . .).

We present later efforts towards a further understanding of the mechanics of tax determination based on formula (3.41). Here we will content ourselves with the brief exploration of two directions of reflections.

First, it is helpful to explain why the above formula is labelled a 'Ramsey' many-person tax formula. In fact the present model provides a (somewhat sophisticated) formalization of the problem originally considered by Ramsey when this model is specialized along the following lines: there is one consumer (so that distributional problems associated with taxation are ruled out), the public good level is fixed, and no uniform lump-sum transfer is available. In the model specialized along these lines, corollary 12 still holds and a variant of (3.41) holds at the optimum, i.e.

$$T\cdot(\partial_{\pi_h} d)^c = \nu z_h \qquad \nu \neq 0$$

With the quasi diagonal Slutsky matrix just discussed the formula would reduce to

$$a_{hh} T_h = \nu z_h$$

or dividing by $\pi_h$

$$\frac{T_h}{\pi_h} = (-\nu)\frac{z_h}{\pi_h(-a_{hh})}$$

The right-hand side is the product of $(-\nu)$ by a number which is nothing other than the inverse of the elasticity of compensated demand relative to its own price. These are the Ramsey inverse elasticity formulas: At the optimum, tax rates are inversely proportional to the price elasticities of the good.

Second, let us consider the above model in the case where there are only two consumers (in the general model $m=2$).

Also, let us consider the case where the uniform lump-sum subsidy is indeed optimal. In such a case, $\nu_1 + \nu_2 = 0$, i.e., $\nu_1 = -\nu_2$.

The many-person Ramsey tax formula (3.41) takes then a simplified form

$$T\cdot(\partial_{\pi_h} d)^c = \nu_1(z_{1h} - z_{2h}), \ \forall h \tag{3.42}$$

where again $\nu_1$ is the net social value of income for consumer 1 and $z_{ih}$ are the (optimal) consumptions of commodity $h$ by consumer $i$.

Multiplying (3.42) by $T_h$ and summing over $h$ shows that

$$T \cdot (\partial_\pi d)^c T = \nu_1 \cdot (T \cdot z_1 - T \cdot z_2)$$

W.l.o.g. one can assume $T \cdot z_1 > T \cdot z_2$; i.e., that the tax bill of consumer 1 is higher than the tax bill of consumer 2.

Ruling out the case of equality, we conclude that $\nu_1 < 0$.

Using this fact in equation (3.42), we can state the following formal result:

**Corollary 13: Optimal taxation in a two class economy**

*At the second-best optimum of a two-class economy with uniform lump-sum transfer the following holds for a commodity h which is positively consumed by both agents* ($z_{1h} > 0$ $z_{2h} > 0$) *(a symmetric property holds for factors):*
*The index of discouragement is negative whenever the highest consumption of the good comes from the consumer who pays the highest tax bill.*

It makes intuitive sense to associate the consumer with the highest tax bill with the one with the highest wealth. In the context of a redistributional social objective, this property holds true if $\lambda_2 > \lambda_1 \Rightarrow T \cdot x_1 > T \cdot x_2$. This property is not necessarily true at the optimum. In the case where it however holds, corollary 13 says that the index of discouragement is negative (resp. positive) when the poorest consumer consumes less (resp. more) of this good.

In view of our previous discussion of the concept of the index of discouragement, the latter statement may be invoked in support of the intuitive prescription that luxuries should be taxed and necessities should be subsidized: a negative (resp. positive) index of discouragement being associated with a 'tax' (resp. a 'subsidy').

Clearly, the support given by the analysis to the intuitive prescription is only weak (it relies on a somewhat sophisticated reinterpretation of the words tax and subsidy or equivalently – as seen in the next chapter – on a bold redefinition of the concept of commodity); also it has limited scope given the special conditions that allow the identification of 'highest tax bill' with 'highest wealth'.

## 3.6 Bibliographical note

The plan adopted in this chapter follows an order, hopefully logical as argued in the text, but contrary to the historical order of the pioneering contributions; indeed the study of optimal taxation (Diamond–Mirrlees (1971)) has preceded studies of tax reform in the context of the present model. The analysis of **tax reform** performed in this chapter as advocated by Feldstein (1975) relies much upon the work in which I have been previously involved, i.e. Guesnerie (1977), Fogelman–Guesnerie–Quinzii (1978), (1979), Guesnerie (1979a), and Tirole–Guesnerie (1981).

There is a significant segment of literature on gradual tax reform in the context of a one-consumer Ramsey-like model where tax changes are accompanied by offsetting lump-sum income changes. Allais (1977b), Bruno (1972), Dixit (1970), Foster–Sonnenschein (1970), Hatta (1977) and Kwan Koo Yun (1989) is a somewhat arbitrary sample of articles along these lines. The articles by Guesnerie (1977), and then Dixit (1979), Diewert (1979), Weymark (1979) initiated tax reform studies of redistributive taxation in a Diamond–Mirrlees type of setting. Later, a number of empirical studies adopted a similar setting using variants of the theoretical methodology and propositions reproduced in chapter 3; they have assessed small tax reform programmes for different countries (see Ahmad–Stern (1981), (1983), (1984) for India, King (1983) for the UK, Laisney–Baccouche (1986) for France, Wibaut (1986) for Belgium).

Theorem 1 on the characterization of equilibrium-preserving and Pareto-improving directions of change relies on a systematization of the argument provided in Guesnerie (1977) (see also Weymark (1979)). Corollary 2 (second part) is theorem 5 in Guesnerie (1979a), and corollary 3 is proposition 4 in Guesnerie (1977). Proposition 1 gives sufficient conditions for the existence of Pareto-improving directions of changes which are particular cases of the conditions found in Weymark (1979). The existence of the situation termed 'temporary inefficiencies' is recognized in Guesnerie (1977) for Pareto-improving moves, and Dixit (1979), Diewert (1979) for welfare-improving changes. (See also Smith (1983) and Roell (1985).) Previous work in the one-consumer framework had been faced with related difficulties and (the version of) condition LR2 is called in this setting the Hatta condition. The relevance of the phenomenon of temporary inefficiencies in a multi-consumer setting for cost–benefit analysis (Dixit (1987), or international trade, Kemp–Wan (1986)) has been noticed more recently.

The analysis of the algorithms of tax reforms of sections 3 closely follows Fogelman–Guesnerie–Quinzii (1978). Alternative methods for computing (local) optima are proposed in Harris–McKinnon (1979), Heady–Mitra (1977), (1982). The study of the gradient projection algorithm introduces the statements and argument of Tirole–Guesnerie (1981). The connections of the gradient projection algorithm with local maximization under a norm constraint (cf. Dixit (1979), Diewert (1979)) are also established in Tirole–Guesnerie (1981). A more detailed investigation of local directions of tax reform can be found in Weymark (1981(a)), (1984). Earlier work using gradient projection algorithms in a first best context include d'Aspremont–

Tulkens (1980) [see also the related work of Drèze de la Vallée Poussin (1971), Heal (1972), Malinvaud (1971].

There is a large literature on cost–benefit analysis in a second-best context. Studies in the spirit of what is presented here include Boadway (1975), Hammond (1986). (See also Hammond (1983), Harris (1978) for a complementary viewpoint.) A synthetical assessment of cost–benefit analysis in a second-best context is provided by Drèze–Stern (1987).

Section 5 starts with theorem 8, which is the analogue, for second-best Pareto optima, of Diamond–Mirrlees' (1971) main characterization result for second-best social welfare optima. Most of the properties quoted in the corollaries are well known, and the interpretations proposed are standard. Let us stress that the results on the modification of Samuelson rules (corollary 11) are borrowed from Atkinson–Stern (1974). Later work on public goods valuation in the presence of optimal taxes is referred to in the next chapter. (See also footnote 21 and Wildasin (1984).) The variant of optimal tax formulas called the Ramsey many-person tax rules has been emphasized by Diamond (1975). The terminology of the index of discouragement is due to Mirrlees (1976).

The study of the two-class economy was first made by Mirrlees (1975). For a discussion of the optimal taxes in the general case (that is more careful and detailed than the one presented in this book), as well as for specifications of demand conditions allowing analytical simplifications, the reader should consult the article by Deaton (1981) as well as the references contained in this article. A limited sample of additional readings, for the reader who wishes to understand more fully the logic and history of optimal taxation, may consist of Atkinson–Stiglitz (1972), (1980), Dasgupta–Stiglitz (1972), Drèze (1984), Dixit (1970), Kolm (1970), (1987), Guesnerie (1980b), Harris (1979), Sandmo (1974), Stern (1986), Stiglitz–Dasgupta (1971).

# 4

## Normative economics of taxation: further essays on optimization and reform

The previous chapter has led us to investigate in depth, from the complementary viewpoints of optimization and reform, the normative properties of our model. At the present stage we should however consider two opposite drawbacks of our study: on the one hand, we have assumed too many degrees of freedom for the planner's action; on the other hand we have assumed too few such degrees of freedom for the same planner's action.

We have assumed **too many degrees of freedom**. This objection can be seen as an objection which is external to our approach: our assumptions on the degrees of freedom of the planner's action are grounded in more basic informational and observational assumptions and, if correct, the objection should concern these more basic assumptions. Indeed, the assumption that all transactions between the production sector and the consumption sector can be observed at no cost is an extreme idealization of the conditions under which the taxation power of the government can be exercised. In fact, the complete disconnection between consumption and production prices, permitted by the no-cost assumption, is not accessible to actual tax systems. Administrative costs – or what are usually considered as such – lead to a definition of a small number of categories of commodities, which are treated similarly – in the sense of being (usually) taxed at the same *ad valorem* rate. On the grounds of realism, a further step to our analysis would be to take into account these additional constraints. Note also that the above objection makes sense even as an objection internal to our approach. The reason is the following: until now we have considered tax reform algorithms where all relevant variables are simultaneously modified. Other tax reform algorithms might be considered where some variables are temporarily held fixed when others would be subject to reform procedures; for example (some or all) taxes may be temporarily fixed when public production changes are considered in the reform algorithm. Note that such

[1] Even if they remain tatonnement algorithms for our purpose

algorithms in which the variables under control alternate,[1] would reflect the preoccupations of the literature on the search for piecemeal policies – such as piecemeal cost–benefit rules. We can conclude that whatever side – internal or external – the motivation is introduced, the consideration of additional constraints to the optimization process is a desirable further step to the present study.

We have assumed **too few degrees of freedom** for the planner's action. This remark is more complementary than contradictory to the previous one. In fact, at the outset of this book, we adopted a simplification – linearization – which restricts too much the taxation power of the planner. Actual tax systems have indeed more non-linearities than have been afforded here. An obvious complement to the present study is to ascertain the effects of the use of policy tools involving non-linearities in the normative analysis of taxation.

This chapter illustrates the double research programme that has been sketched through three (out of four) introductory essays. Section 1 relates with the first direction of analysis – introducing less policy tools. Sections 2 and 4 focus on the non linearity issues.

The first section is entitled 'The social values of commodities'. The rationale for this reflection is the following: when the set of policy tools is restricted, one crucial property of the Diamond–Mirrlees world is lost: production prices cease to play the central role that they previously had in the analysis either as a guidance to the reform process (as seen in section 2 of chapter 3) or as the reference shadow prices – or social values of commodities – at the second-best optimum (section 5). With additional constraints, the fact that discrepancies emerge between actual prices – here production prices – and what we termed the social values of commodities is a key difficulty of the normative analysis. More generally, it is a key difficulty to any second-best problem as soon as one leaves the polar worlds in which actual market prices also provide the 'socially' right social signals.[2] Section 1 tackles the problem through the analysis of a second-best model with much broader scope than the taxation model considered in previous chapters.

The second section focuses attention on policies, that introduce a non-linearity element in the tax system, i.e., quotas. Clearly the non-linearity introduced by quota policies is not of the most general type – it is even a very peculiar one but one of clear practical importance. The section gives conditions that justify the use of quotas in addition to linear taxes.

[2] I have argued elsewhere (for example in Guesnerie (1979b)) that this happens exceptionally outside two polar cases: the Diamond–Mirrlees case where production prices are the right shadow prices and the case of C-C efficiency where consumers' prices are the right shadow prices (see Guesnerie (1975)). See also Greenwald–Stiglitz (1986).

The third section comes back on a different subject, i.e., the reform and optimization problems of the last section of chapter 3. We turn attention to the simpler version of this general problem that occurs when there is a single consumer. In addition to providing insights that may be useful for the understanding of the more complex cases, the analysis puts at the forefront issues that were important for the development of the subject and that place it in a better historical perspective.

Finally, the fourth section provides a bird's eye view of a simplified version of our central model, when linear taxes coexist with a non linear income tax schedule.

We should here warn the reader that, in this chapter, we have voluntarily adopted a justification of the argument that is much looser (and sometimes clearly unrigorous) than in previous chapters. References to more rigorous pieces of work are provided in the bibliographical notes.

## 4.1 The social values of commodities (C***)

As argued above, our purpose in the present subsection, is to analyse the 'social values of commodities'[3] in a context which is broad enough to capture some general difficulties of second-best analysis.

For that we will first introduce a second-best model, the formulation of which is abstract and general enough to capture as special cases many economically relevant second-best models. Then, the so-called social values of commodities will appear – in the solution of the second-best optimization problem – as Lagrange multipliers associated with the scarcity constraints of the problem. In general the relationship between the vector of social values and the vector of actual prices – or more generally with the technological conditions prevailing in the economy – is difficult to assess. The remainder of the analysis is intended to provide key guidelines to such an assessment, showing in which way technological conditions are reflected in 'social values'. We will argue that the questions behind such an assessment may be reminiscent of the questions creeping into the nineteenth-century controversy on the relationship between prices and values.

We shall first introduce an abstract second-best model which has the following features (So far as preferences technologies and endowments are concerned, the economy is the same abstract economy considered in the previous chapters of this book.):

> Agents consist of consumers with convex preferences indexed as previously by $i=1,\ldots,m$ and of firms indexed by $j=1,\ldots,q$. For

[3] As above, the 'social values of commodities' is taken as a synonym of 'social opportunity costs of commodities' although the latter terminology may be better.

the sake of notational simplicity, all firms are uncontrolled in the terminology of chapter 2. The commodity space is $\mathscr{R}^n$.

The second-best aspects of the situation formally derive from 'behavioural' constraints. More precisely, agents face a vector of signals $s \in S$ and

**H1** *Associated with each consumer is a demand function $\chi_i(s)$ defined on $S$ and $C^1$ differentiable. The corresponding indirect utility function is $V_i(s) \overset{\text{def}}{=} U_i(\chi_i(s))$.*

**H2** *Associated with each uncontrolled firm is a supply correspondence $O_j(s)$ defined on $S$. The set $O_j(s)$ is a subset of $Y_j$ the production set of firm $j$.*

We shall sometimes assume:

**H2′** *$O_j$ is a $C^1$ differentiable (supply) function.*

A feasible state of the abstract normative model consists then of a sequence of consumption bundles $(x_i)$, production plans $(y_j)$, and signal vectors $s$ such that

$$x_i = \chi_i(s),\ y_j \in O_j(s) \qquad \forall i, \forall j. \tag{4.1}$$

$$s \in \bar{S} \subset S \tag{4.2}$$

$$\sum_i x_i \leq \sum_i y_j + w \tag{4.3a}$$

When constraints (4.2) are tight, we have

$$\sum_i x_i = \sum_j y_j + w, \tag{4.3b}$$

Equations (4.1) express the 'behavioural' constraints alluded to above. Agents, either final agents – households – or firms, react to the vector of signals they face. This reaction is described through the functions $\chi_i$ or correspondences $O_j$ which are exogenous and outside the planner's control; hence the terminology of uncontrolled that here applies to consumers as well as to firms.

Equation (4.2) describes possible constraints on the set of signals when equations (4.3) are the standard scarcity constraints: the vector of initial endowments $w$ will also be interpreted in the following as the initial public production plan.

The abstract model is a second-best model in the sense that, unless the signal vector and the functions $O_j$, $\chi_i$ are chosen in a very specific way, the first-best optima of the economy are not feasible states of the model. Note also that the prototype model considered in this book obtains when the abstract model is specified as follows (putting public goods aside)

$$s = (\pi, p, R),\ \chi_i(s) = d_i(\pi, R),\ O_j(s) = \eta_j(p),\ S = \bar{S} = \mathscr{R}^{2n-1}.$$

The model displays a minimal economic structure (scarcity constraints, agents' behaviour) but is flexible enough to contain, as particular cases, most existing second-best models.[4] It is remarkable that, in spite of the generality of the model, the analysis leads to significant results for the problem under scrutiny in this section.

At this stage, however, the economic structure of demand behaviour has to be made more precise. If $\chi_i(s)$ is a single-valued correspondence, one can write (without loss of generality when preferences are smooth)

$$\chi_i(s)=d_i(\psi_i(s),\, m_i(s))$$

where $\psi_i(s)=\nabla U_i(\chi_i(s))$ is the gradient in $\chi_i(s)$ of $i$'s utility function, where $m_i(s)=\psi_i(s)\cdot\chi_i(s)$ and where $d_i$ denotes, as usual, the (notional) demand functions.

Also we assume:

**H3** *$\psi_i(s)$ and $m_i(s)$ are differentiable functions of $s$.*

Hence $\psi_i(s)$ and $m_i(s)$ are respectively the shadow price vectors and the shadow income associated with the response of consumer $i$ to signal $s$: they are the price vectors and the income which would induce a 'competitive' consumer to choose $\chi_i(s)$. Note that this formulation is not intended to mean that consumers are not utility-maximizers; in second-best models, the 'deviant' behaviour associated with this formulation may reflect missing markets, constraints on policy tools (see again the relevant references in the bibliographical note). Note also that the prototype model associated with $s=(\pi,p,R)$ corresponds to the case where $\psi_i(s)=\pi$, $m_i(s)=R$, $\forall i$.

Let us consider one component of $s$ and, for the sake of notational simplicity, let us call it $\alpha$.

Let us define

$$E_i(\alpha,\cdot)=\frac{\partial m_i}{\partial \alpha}(\cdot)-\frac{\partial \psi_i(\cdot)}{\partial \alpha}\cdot\chi_i(\cdot)=\psi_i(\cdot)\frac{\partial \chi_i}{\partial \alpha}(\cdot) \tag{4.4}$$

The equality of the two expressions of $E_i(\alpha,\cdot)$ that are given in (4.4) straightforwardly results from the derivation of the definitional equality of shadow income. The second expression of $E_i$ makes it clear that it can be interpreted as $i$'s benefit associated with a small (unit) change of signal $\alpha$;

Considering $\beta$ another coordinate of the vector $s$, we can define

$$\left(\frac{\partial \chi_i}{\partial \alpha}\right)^{U=C/\beta}(\cdot)=\left(\frac{\partial \chi_i}{\partial \alpha}\right)(\cdot)-\frac{E_i(\alpha,\cdot)}{E_i(\beta,\cdot)}\left(\frac{\partial \chi_i}{\partial \beta}\right)(\cdot) \tag{4.5}$$

[4] Before making up his mind on this question, the reader is invited to consult the references on the present model that are given in the bibliographical note at the end of the chapter.

The notation $\left(\frac{\partial \chi_i}{\partial \alpha}\right)^{U=C/\beta}$ is intended to indicate that the move is at fixed utility; i.e., that $\psi_i \cdot \left(\frac{\partial \chi_i}{\partial \alpha}\right)^{U=C/\beta} = 0$ – a fact that is an immediate consequence of definition (4.4) – and that compensation is obtained through a move of $\beta$.

At this stage, the presentation of the abstract model has been completed. The next step of our programme consists of the characterization of the second-best optima of this model. This is the purpose of next theorem 1 where necessary conditions for a social optimum are exhibited. These necessary conditions give a central role to the so-called social value of commodities, a role that is better ascertained from an envelope theorem (theorem 2). A further analysis of social values of commodities in connection with technological possibilities of the economy – which is the main subject of this section – provides results that will be summarized in theorems 3–4.

Let us look first at the optimization problem. For the sake of facility of interpretation let us consider that the planner maximizes a (utilitarian) social welfare function.

$$W(s) = \sum_i \lambda_i V_i(s)$$

A second-best welfare optimum obtains as the solution of the following programme.

max $W(s)$ subject to (4.1), (4.2), (4.3).

The following theorem provides a rather general characterization of the second-best welfare optimum, i.e., social optima of our abstract normative model. The reader will notice that the statement sometimes refers to terms which will be defined later. Also the proof will not be complete. Before stating the theorem we should introduce excess demand $Z$, total demand $\chi$, and total supply $Q$

$$Z \stackrel{\text{def}}{=} \sum_i \chi_i - \sum_j O_j, \quad \chi \stackrel{\text{def}}{=} \sum_i \chi_i, \quad Q \stackrel{\text{def}}{=} \sum_j O_j, \quad Z = \chi - Q.$$

**Theorem 1: First order optimality conditions**

*Consider the abstract model (4.1) to (4.3) where assumptions H1, H2, H3 hold.*

*Let us consider a 'regular' second-best welfare optimum associated with* $s^*$ *and suppose H2′ is true. Then* $\exists$ *a vector* $\rho^* \in \mathscr{R}^n_+$, *numbers* $\delta^*_{1k}$, $\delta^*_{2k}$ *and positive numbers* $\mu_i$ *such that*

*(1)*

$$\rho^*\left(\frac{\partial Q}{\partial s_k}\right)_{(*)} - \delta^*_{1k} = 0 \tag{4.6}$$

$$\rho^*\left(\frac{\partial \chi}{\partial s_k}\right)_{(*)} - \Sigma_i \mu_i E_i(s_k, *) + \delta^*_{2k} = 0 \tag{4.7}$$

*where $\delta^*_{1k} + \delta^*_{2k}$ are the generalized 'dual' variables associated with the constraints $s \in \bar{S}$.*

*(2) If $s_k$ is free in $s^*$, i.e., if a small increase and decrease of $s_k$ around $s^*$, all other components of the signal vector being equal, leaves $s$ in $\bar{S}$, then calling $s_k$, $\alpha$ we have*

$$\rho^* \cdot \left(\frac{\partial Z}{\partial \alpha}\right)_{(*)} = \Sigma_i \mu_i E_i(\alpha, *) \tag{4.8}$$

*(3) If $\alpha$ and $\beta$ are two signals such that $\alpha$ is free around $s^*$ (in the sense just mentioned) and such that $\left(\frac{\partial \chi_i}{\partial \alpha}\right)^{U=C/\beta}$ is defined for every $i$, then*

$$\rho^*\left[\left(\frac{\partial \chi}{\partial \alpha}\right)^{U=C/\beta}_{(*)} - \left(\frac{\partial Q}{\partial \alpha}\right)_{(*)}\right] = \Sigma_i \gamma_i(\beta, *)\frac{E_i(\alpha|*)}{E_i(\beta|*)} \tag{4.9}$$

*where*

$$\gamma_i(\alpha, \cdot) = [\mu_i \psi_i(\cdot) - \rho]\frac{\partial \chi_i}{\partial \alpha}(\cdot) \tag{4.10}$$

*(4) If $\frac{\partial Q}{\partial \beta} = 0$ and if $\beta$ is a free variable, then*

$$\sum_i \gamma_i(\beta, *) = 0 \tag{4.11}$$

*Proof*

Rather than a rigorous proof, we provide here an idea of the proof. Let us write the Lagrangian in the case where the constraints $s \in \bar{S}$ defined by (4.2) are $s_k \leq 0$, $\forall k$. And let us assume that the derivatives of the Lagrangian of the problem are zero at the optimum (this is the definition of our regularity condition announced in the statement).

The Lagrangian is written (after compressing (4.1) and (4.2) into a single set of constraints)

$$\mathscr{L}(\ ) = \sum_i \lambda_i V_i(s) - \rho\left\{\sum_i \chi_i(s) - \sum_j O_j(s)\right\} - \sum_k \delta_k s_k$$

At the optimum

$$\sum_i \lambda_i\left(\frac{\partial V_i}{\partial s_k}\right) - \rho\sum_i\left(\frac{\partial \chi_i}{\partial s_k}\right) + \rho\sum_j \frac{\partial O_j}{\partial s_k} - \delta_k = 0$$

From the definition of $E_i(\alpha)$, it is clear that $\lambda_i \dfrac{\partial V_i}{\partial s_k}$ is proportional to $E_i(s_k)$.

If the coefficient of proportionality is called $\mu_i$ ($\mu_i > 0$), and if $\delta_k$ is split in $\delta_k = \delta_{1k} + \delta_{2k}$, we obtain (4.6) and (4.7).

Then $s_k$ being free implies $\delta_k = 0$, subtracting (4.6) from (4.7), we obtain (4.8).

After using definitions (4.4) and (4.5) and replacing in (4.8) straightforward algebra leads to (4.9).

Now if $\dfrac{\partial Q}{\partial \beta} = 0$, the corresponding $\delta_1$ is from (4.6) equal to zero. In addition, if $\beta$ is a free variable, the corresponding $\delta$ is zero and hence the corresponding $\delta_2$ is also zero. But then formula (4.7) can be rewritten as (4.11). □

We shall limit ourselves to a few remarks on the above formula.

First, the reader is invited to check how this statement leads to some of the optimization results obtained previously in chapter 3 for our prototype model. At the second-best optimum all production and consumption prices are free variables in the sense of the above theorem. Writing (4.6) for production prices leads to the production efficiency property stated in corollary 10 and discussed in section 5 of previous chapter. Also, writing (4.8) for consumption prices and noting that $E_i(\pi_l) = -z_{il}$ leads to formula (3.36) stated in theorem 8 and discussed later. Similarly it is easy to check that the many-person Ramsey tax formula obtains from (4.9) when $\alpha = \pi_l$, the consumption price of commodity $l$ and $\beta = R$, the uniform lump-sum transfer.

Second, the interpretation of the specific formulas stressed in chapter 3 for our prototype model can be extended to the more general formulas obtained here. Particularly, in line with the comments of formula (3.35) in theorem 8, one can comment on (4.8) as follows:

> The social cost of a change in excess demand induced by a small change around the optimum of a free signal $\alpha$ equals the weighted sum of individual benefits created by the change when the weights are the social values of benefits for each individual.

In line with the interpretation associated with corollary 12 of the previous chapter, one can view $\gamma_i(\beta,\cdot)$ as the **net social marginal efficiency of policy** $\beta$ for household $i$. We have, in view of (4.11):

> When $\alpha$ is a free variable which is not effective for the production sector, the sum across households of the net social marginal efficiency of policy $\alpha$ is zero.
>
> The social value of the change of total excess demand induced by a move of any free variable $\alpha$, compensated by the move of any other free variable which is not effective for the production sector (in the sense that $\frac{\partial Q}{\partial \beta}=0$), equals the covariance across households of the net social marginal efficiency of the second policy and of the efficiency of the first policy relative to the second one (relative efficiency being defined as the ratio $\frac{E_i(\alpha)}{E_i(\beta)}$).

If the characterization theorem of our abstract model (theorem 1) involves more complex considerations than the characterization theorem of the taxation model (theorem 8 and its corollaries), its interpretation refers to similar patterns of equalization of social costs and social benefits. A most noticeable difference is however that in the taxation model the social values of commodities are (proportional to) the production prices, when the vector $\rho^*$ of the social values of commodities (or social opportunity costs) of theorem 1 most generally differs from existing prices.[5] Furthermore, a quick reading of the statement seems to suggest that the technological patterns that play an essential role – together with the nature of competition – in the determination of 'real' prices, are somewhat irrelevant to the determination of shadow prices.

Before coming to this latter problem, one would like to go further into the analysis of the central role played by the so-called vector of the social value of commodities. Besides its role in the second-best optimality conditions, we want to ascertain its role in assessing small local changes of some variables which would have been left fixed in the optimization process.

For a precise formulation of this problem, let us consider a family of economies indexed by variables $v$, in such a way that the abstract normative model considered previously corresponds to $v=0$. Formally, there exist correspondences $O_j(s,v)$, functions $\chi_j(s,v)$, $V_i(s,v)$ such that $O_j(s,0)=O_j(s)$; $\chi_i(s,0)=\chi_i(s)$; $V_i(s,0)=V_i(s)$.

Consider the following programme

[5] In the abstract model, such real prices are not made explicit. They would be in most economically relevant specifications of the model. For example in the specification of the abstract model that coincides with the prototype model of this book, consumption and production prices are coordinates of the signal vector and the last sentence of the text applies whenever taxes cannot be freely chosen for every commodity so that the consumption and the production price vectors cannot be fully disconnected.

$$(P(v))\ \max \sum_i \lambda_i V_i(s,v)$$

$$s \in \bar{S} \tag{4.2}$$

$$\sum_i \chi_i(s,v) - \sum_j O_j(s,v) \leq w \tag{4.3'}$$

In line with previous differentiability assumptions we suppose that

**H4** *$O_j(s,v)$, $\chi_j(s,v)$, $V_i(s,v)$ are functions which are $C^1$ differentiable in s and in v, for v in a neighbourhood of zero.*

Also we call $W(v)$ the value of $P(v)$, i.e., the maximal value of social welfare $\sum_i \lambda_i V_i(s,v)$ under (4.2) and (4.3).

The next theorem is a standard envelope theorem that tells us how the maximal social welfare varies when the economy (identified here with the parameter $v$) varies.

**Theorem 2: Envelope theorem**

*Assume that H4 holds.*

*Assume that in the neighbourhood of $v=0$*

*(i) The solution of the programme is differentiable.*
*(ii) The programme is regular.*
*(iii) All scarcity constraints are binding.*

*Call $s^*(0)$ the optimal signals and $\rho^*(0)$ the vector of the Lagrange multipliers (the 'social values of commodities') which is associated with $v=0$.*

*Then if $\left(\frac{dW}{dv}\right)_{(0)}$ exists*

$$\left(\frac{dW}{dv}\right)_{(0)} = \sum_i \lambda_i \left(\frac{\partial V_i}{\partial v}\right)(s^*(0),0) - \rho^*(0)\left[\sum_i \frac{\partial \chi_i}{\partial v}(s^*(0),0) - \sum_j \frac{\partial O_j}{\partial v}(s^*(0),0)\right] \tag{4.12}$$

*Proof*

Again the proof is only sketched and in the case where there exist differentiable functions $\varphi_k$ such that $s \in \bar{S} \Leftrightarrow \varphi_k(s) \leq 0, k=1,\ldots,p$. The Lagrangian for the programme $P(v)$ writes down

$$\mathscr{L}(s,v) = \sum_i \lambda_i V_i(s,v) - \rho(v)\left[\sum_i \chi_i(s,v) - \sum_j O_j(s,v)\right] - \sum_k \delta_k \varphi_k(s)$$

In the conditions of the theorem the solution of the programme $s^*(v)$ is differentiable so that one can differentiate $\mathscr{L}(s^*(v), v)$

$$\frac{\partial \mathscr{L}}{\partial s}\frac{ds^*}{dv}+\frac{\partial \mathscr{L}}{\partial v}=\left\{\sum_i \lambda_i \frac{\partial V_i}{\partial s}-\rho(v)\left[\sum_i \frac{\partial \chi_i}{\partial s}-\sum_j \frac{\partial O_j}{\partial s}\right]-\sum_k \delta_k \frac{\partial \varphi_k}{\partial s}\right\}\frac{ds^*}{dv}$$
$$-\left\{\sum_i \chi_i-\sum_j O_j\right\}\frac{\partial \rho}{dv}+\sum_i \lambda_i \frac{\partial V_i}{\partial v}-\rho(v)\left[\sum_i \frac{\partial \chi_i}{\partial v}-\sum_j \frac{\partial O_j}{\partial v}\right] \tag{4.13}$$

But, because of the complementary slackness conditions, $\mathscr{L}(s^*(v), v) = \sum_i \lambda_i V_i(s^*(v), v) = W(v)$.

Then $\frac{dW}{dv}$ is nothing else other than the right-hand side of (4.13). But from theorem 1 the first group of terms is zero (optimality). Since scarcity constraints are binding, the second term also equals zero. We then have the conclusion. □

We evoked earlier reform algorithms mixing optimization and gradual reform. Clearly theorem 2 would be a key tool in the analysis of such algorithms. In the following we use it for evaluating the desirability of small quotas (section 4.2). An obvious consequence of theorem 2 is that a change in the initial endowment of the economy – the vector $w$ of formula (4.3) – is desirable if the value of the change computed with the vector $\rho^*$ is positive. (Take $O_j\,(s, v) = g(s) + v$) Hence, in line with its interpretation as the vector of social values, $\rho^*$ is the right *shadow price vector* for *assessing changes in public production.*

We can now turn to the main question raised in this section, i.e., the relationship between social values of commodities and prices.

This question is reminiscent of a debate in economics which has a long history since it takes its root in the nineteenth-century controversies on values and prices. Modern analysis offers rigorous statements connecting different notions of values with prices. For example, in the conditions where the 'main theorem of welfare economics' holds, production prices coincide with consumption prices and define in an unambiguous sense social values. In the polar model of this book, production prices are social values. Elsewhere a class of models has been identified in which consumption prices equal social values.[6] The optimality conditions exhibited for the abstract normative model of this section do not suggest close connections between prices (that are not made explicit here) and social values. Still more striking, if condition (4.6) suggests connections between the behavioural rules of the

[6] See Guesnerie (1975).

production sector and social values, it does not suggest any obvious relationship between the technological conditions prevailing in the production sector of the economy and 'values'. This is somewhat at variance with the intuition of economists.

One reason for such a discrepancy may be that the economists' intuition has been based on notions of values (nineteenth-century labour values) which are different from the modern notion of shadow values. However, the purpose of this section is to show that the discrepancy is less important than a superficial reading of formula (4.6) suggests. Theorem 3 will show that social values of commodities can be interpreted as fictitious market prices emerging from the competitive interaction of constant returns to scale firms whose production plans coincide with actual production plans, when some 'hidden' factors of production receive a remuneration equal to their social values.

Let us start from the abstract economy defined through (4.2), (4.3), and let us introduce an *extended* economy, by defining new supply correspondences

$$\tilde{O}_j(s,t) = t_j O_j(s), \ \forall s \in S, t_j \in \mathscr{R}, j \in J \tag{4.14}$$

In the extended setting parameter $t_j$ can vary; for a given $t_j$, the supply correspondence of firm $j$ is, in the sense made precise by formula 4.14, a 'homothetic' extension of the initial supply correspondence.

We now define a feasible state of the extended abstract economy consisting of $x_i, y_j, s, t = (t_1 \ldots t_q)$ that satisfies

$$\sum_i x_i(s) - \sum_j \tilde{O}_j(s,t) \leq w \tag{4.15}$$

$$O \leq t_j, \qquad s \in \bar{S} \tag{4.16}$$

When compared to the initial model (4.1), (4.2), (4.15), (4.16) introduce a new possibility i.e. to reduce or increase by some factors $t(0 \leq t \leq 1)$ the production scale of any uncontrolled firm.

Consider some given social welfare function and call $W(t)$ the maximal social welfare attainable when optimization is performed in the extended abstract economy at fixed $t = (\ldots t_j \ldots)$. Formally

$$W(t) = \max \Sigma \lambda_i V_i(s) \text{ such that (4.15) and (4.16) hold.}$$

Note that when $t = (1 \ldots 1)$, the $t$-economy of formulas (4.15), (4.16) coincides with the initial abstract economy; hence the maximum social welfare attainable over the abstract economy is $W(1, 1, \ldots, 1)$.

Next theorem 3 relies on the envelope theorem 2 in order to relate the social value of optimal production plans in the initial economy with the derivatives of the value function $W(t)$ in $t = (1 \ldots 1)$.

**Theorem 3: Shadow profit for second-best optimal production plans**

*Consider a regular social welfare optimum of the abstract economy (4.2), (4.3) around which the envelope theorem holds.*

*Then for any optimal production plan $y_j^*$, one has*

$$\rho^* \cdot y_j^* - a_j^* = 0$$

*where $\rho^*$ is the vector of social values of commodities and* $a_j^* = \left(\frac{\partial W}{\partial t_j}\right)_{(1)}$.

*Proof*

The assumptions allow us to rely upon theorems 1 and 2.

Identifying $t$ with $v$ in the envelope theorem 2 and applying it in $t=1$, we get with previous notation

$$\left(\frac{\partial W}{\partial t_j}\right)_{(1)} = \rho^* \cdot \frac{\partial \tilde{O}_j}{\partial t_j}.$$

Using 4.14, the computation of the left-hand side leads to

$$\left(\frac{\partial W}{\partial t_j}\right)_{(1)} = \rho^* \cdot O_j(s^*) = \rho^* \cdot y_j^* \qquad \square$$

Theorem 3 gives us interesting information on the second-best optimal production plans.

The profit measured with social values $\rho^* y_j^*$ is positive (resp. negative) when an increase (resp. a decrease) of the size parameter $t_j$ would be socially valuable. In other words firms would have a zero shadow profit if profit incorporated a shadow price of the size parameter (for use of each size 'unit').

The shadow value of the size parameter plays here the role played by rent in the explanation of real profit in a competitive environment. However, the shadow value is here more difficult to interpret. In particular, its sign is a priori ambiguous at least in the general version of the model. In order to obtain some intuition, we shall emphasize simple cases in which we can sign $a_j^*$.

α Suppose first $O_j(s) = \{Y_j\}$

Then one can assert that:

If $Y_j$ is star shaped and contains 0,

i.e. $y_j \in Y_j \Rightarrow t y_j \in Y_j$, $t \in [0, 1]$, then $a_j^* \geq 0$

If $Y_j$ displays increasing returns to scale and contains 0, i.e. $y_j \in Y_j \Rightarrow t y_j \in Y_j$, $t > 1$, then $a_j^* \leq 0$

The reason for these statements is straightforward: if $Y_j$ is star shaped (resp. displays increasing returns), then $tY_j$ for $t<1$ is included in $Y_j$ (resp. includes $Y_j$). Equivalently the set of feasible states of the extended economy for given $t>1$ (resp. $<$) is larger (resp. smaller) than for $t=1$. Then if $\frac{dW}{dt}$ exists, it is positive (resp. negative).

$\beta$ It is slightly more difficult to prove, and left to the reader, that when the abstract model coincides with our model of section 2 (forgetting about public goods for simplicity), i.e., when $O_j(s) = \eta(p)$ and $\chi_i(s) = d_i(\pi, R)$, then the fact that the production sets $Y_j$, from which $\eta_j(p)$ is computed, are star shaped still implies $a_j^* > 0$.

In fact, none of these results should be a surprise. The conclusions obtained in $\alpha$ would also result from the fact that $\rho^*$ are the adequate shadow prices for 'controlled' firms (although this fact has not been formally stated, it has been mentioned after the statement of theorem 2) and that the corresponding profit is positive (star shaped) or negative (increasing returns). The conclusions of $\beta$ are also consequences of the production efficiency conclusion obtained in section 2. Nevertheless, the previous analysis stresses in a different way, the role of purely technological factors (i.e., star shapedness or increasing returns to scale of the underlying production sets) in the determination of the sign of $a_j^*$.

Two corollaries of theorem 3 are easy to obtain:[7]

**Corollary 1** *If $O_j(s)$ is a correspondence such that $O_j(s) = tO_j(s)$ $\forall t \in [0, +\infty]$ then $\rho^* \cdot y_j^* = 0$.*

The proof is straightforward once one realizes that one can imbed the problem under consideration, in which the supply correspondence is a half line, in the previous setting 4.2, 4.3. For that, it is enough to increase the dimension of the signal vector in the initial problem (by including some new coordinates that duplicate the $t$ parameter). With this trick, under the conditions of the corollary the set of feasible states of the extended abstract economy for any fixed $t$ is the same. Then $\frac{dW}{dt} = 0$ and the conclusion. □

A consequence of corollary 1 is a well-known statement, first formulated by Diamond–Mirrlees (see bibliographical note).

[7] Although it should be recognized that the present formulation and proofs are rather loose.

**Corollary 2** *If the uncontrolled firm j is competitive and has constant returns to scale, then*

$$\rho^* \cdot y_j^* = 0$$

Clearly a competitive uncontrolled constant returns to scale firm satisfies the conditions of corollary 1. Hence the conclusion. □

At this stage, the programme of assessing the role of technological conditions in the determination of shadow prices has not been completed. But some key ingredients have been exhibited. To go further we would need more specific information on the structure of the economy and the behaviour of uncontrolled firms. The case of corollary 2 – competitive, constant returns to scale firms – is an interesting benchmark. In such a constant returns to scale economy where the non-substitution theorem holds, the Walrasian prices of goods can be uniquely derived from the (relative) prices of factors. Similarly here, the right shadow prices of goods can be determined from the 'social values' of factors only. Although the assessment of the distortion between the shadow values of factors and their real prices may be a difficult question, the just sketched argument sheds light on the sense and the extent to which the technological conditions of production will be reflected in the 'social values'.

Corollary 1 shows how the argument can be extended when firms are neither constant returns nor competitive: again social values of produced goods could be derived from social values of (visible and hidden) factors when using some adequately chosen, tangent, 'Leontieff-like' technology.

## 4.2 Non-linearities and quotas policies (***)

The present book focuses attention on policies which act on prices or incomes. Real life arrangements suggest that actual public policies sometimes use quantity restrictions such as quotas, rationing, etc. This section uses the results of the preceding section in order to analyse the desirability of a policy of personalized quotas at the margin of a second-best optimal situation. The results we shall obtain are immediately applicable at the margin of a situation of second-best optima of our taxation model, which have been characterized in section 1.

Let us consider the abstract normative model of the previous section. Let us identify one household $i_0$ on whom we concentrate attention. The signal vectors consist of consumption prices $\pi$ and other signals denoted $u$. We assume that household $i_0$ has standard competitive demand with respect to prices $\pi$ and income $R_{i_0}(u)$.

Formally, with the notation of the previous section as well as of the rest of the book, where $d$ designates competitive demand

$$\chi_{i_0}(s) = d_{i_0}(\pi, R_{i_0}(u))$$

In the interpretation that will be favoured later, the vector $\pi$ is a vector of consumption prices actually faced by consumer $i_0$ (and not a vector of shadow prices). On the contrary, $R_{i_0}$ may be a shadow income (possibly) depending upon all other elements of the signal vector.

Hence the abstract model 4.2, 4.3 is specified as follows

$$s = (\pi, u) \in \bar{S} \tag{4.17}$$

$$Z_{-i_0}(s) + d_{i_0}(\pi, R_{i_0}(u)) \leq w \tag{4.18}$$

where $Z_{-i_0}$ designates excess demand coming from all uncontrolled agents of the economy (firms and households) but household $i_0$; in previous notation, $Z_{-i_0} = \sum_{i \neq i_0} \chi_i - \sum_j O_j$.

The just described model does not incorporate any quota policy for consumer $i_0$. It will then be referred to as the model **without quota policy**.

Before considering a model with quotas, we have to introduce notation that allows us to describe rationing situations. For that, consider the following circumstances:

The consumption of commodity $n$ is not freely decided upon by household $i_0$, but is imposed upon him exogenously.

The **constrained demand function** for household $i_0$ is defined as follows:

$$\bar{D}_{i_0}(\pi, R, y) = \arg\max U_i(x),\ \pi.\ x \leq R,\ x_n = y \tag{4.19}$$

(Note that in (4.19) the consumption of commodity $n$ is fixed at $y$ but that consumer $i_0$ has to pay for this commodity.)

With this definition of constrained demand, it is natural to associate a quota policy with a real number $v$ measuring the discrepancy between the desired 'notional' consumption of commodity $n$ and the actual consumption. We accordingly define the following demand functions

$$\chi_{i_{0,n}}(\pi, u, v) = d_{i_{0,n}}(\pi, R_{i_0}(u)) + v \tag{4.20}$$

$$\chi_{i_{0,l}}(\pi, u, v) = \bar{D}_{i_{0,l}}(\pi, R_{i_0}(u), \chi_{i_{0,n}}(\pi, u, v)) \tag{4.21}$$

Equation (4.21) says that consumer $i_0$'s demand for commodities $l \neq n$ is the just-defined constrained demand with the same consumption price and shadow income (as in 4.19) and with the 'compulsory' consumption of commodity $n$ defined in (4.20). Hence the parameter $v$ that measures the discrepancy between commodity $n$'s notional and actual consumption is a pure rationing parameter that does not affect either the consumption prices faced by consumer $i_0$ or its shadow income. It is also a personal rationing parameter that only concerns consumer $i_0$ and has no effect on the signal vector $s$ that determines the others' behaviour. Note that when $v=0$, the demand of consumer $i_0$ coincides with his unconstrained demand of equation (4.18).

We are now in a position to define a new set of feasible states, corresponding to the case when a personalized quota policy, acting on household $i_0$ for commodity $n$, applies. This set of feasible states is associated with $s=(\pi, u)$ and $v$ such that

$$s=(\pi, u) \in \bar{S} \tag{4.17}$$

$$Z_{i_0}(s)+\chi_{i_0}(\pi, u, v) \leq w \tag{4.22}$$

Again when $v=0$, equation (4.22) coincides with equation (4.18) and the present model (**model with a personalized quota**) does coincide with the model without quota policy associated with (4.17), (4.18).

Let us consider now a social welfare function

$$W=\sum_i \lambda_i V_i$$

In the model with a personalized quota, individual utilities are given by

$$V_i=V_i(s)=U_i(\chi_i(s)) \; i \neq i_0$$

$$V_{i_0}=\bar{V}_{i_0}(s, v)=U_{i_0}(\chi_{i_0}(s, v))$$

and the social welfare function is

$$W(s, v)=\sum_{i \neq i_0} \lambda_i V_i(s)+\lambda_{i_0} \bar{V}_{i_0}(s, v)$$

The answer to the question: is a quota policy $v$ desirable? rests upon the comparison of the values of the programme $P(v)$ and $P(0)$ where
$P(v)$: max $W(s, v)$ subject to (4.17), (4.22).
$P(0)$: max $W(s)$ subject to (4.17), (4.18).

Before going further we should note that this comparison is likely to depend on the comparison of constrained and unconstrained demand. Actually, the next lemma gives useful information on the relationship between the derivatives of constrained and unconstrained demand.

**Lemma 1** *Consider the constrained demand function $\bar{D}$ defined in (4.19). Consider a situation $(\cdot)=(\pi, R, y)$ in which $y=d_n(\pi, R)$, i.e., an initially unconstrained situation. Call $d^c$, the compensated demand function associated with $d$ – the uncompensated one – then, under adequate differentiability assumptions*

$$\left(\frac{\partial \bar{D}_l}{\partial y}\right)_{(\cdot)} = \left(\frac{\partial d_l^c}{\partial \pi_n}\right)_{(\cdot)} \Big/ \left(\frac{\partial d_n^c}{\partial \pi_n}\right)_{(\cdot)} \quad l=1\ldots n. \tag{4.23a}$$

*If* $\bar{V}(\pi, R, y) = U(\bar{D}(\pi, R, y))$

$$\left(\frac{\partial \bar{V}}{\partial y}\right)_{(\cdot)} = 0 \tag{4.23b}$$

Let us have a brief look at formulas (4.23a), (4.23b). First note that the $n^{\text{th}}$ component of (4.23a) writes down $\frac{\partial \bar{D}_n}{\partial y} = 1$, a fact that (fortunately!) fits the definition of $\bar{D}$.

Now (4.23b) says that a small ration at the margin of an unconstrained situation has no first-order effect on the consumer welfare. This is an envelope property which economists are familiar with. With this latter condition in mind, (4.23b) is easier to explain: a small quota (at the margin of an unrationed situation) acts as a compensated price increase of commodity $n$. The fact that the quota acts as a price change of commodity $n$ is obvious; it is a compensated change because of the absence of first-order welfare effects as analysed in (4.23b). These considerations intuitively explain that the vector $\frac{\partial \bar{D}}{\partial y}$ is proportional to $\frac{\partial d^c}{\partial \pi_n}$; the fact that the commodity $n$'s price change under consideration should (by definition) increase the consumption of commodity $n$ by one unit explains that the proportionality coefficient of formula (4.23a) is $1/\frac{\partial d_n^c}{\partial \pi_n}$.

The formal proof of the lemma makes rigorous the intuitive line of argument just sketched. We only sketch this proof, referring the reader to the references mentioned in the bibliographical note.

Note first that with a quasi concave $U$, at the optimum of the rationed consumer's programme, marginal utilities for unrationed goods will be proportional to prices so that shadow prices supporting the optimum are of the form $\tilde{\pi}, \Phi_n$ where $\tilde{\pi}$ is the truncation in $\mathscr{R}^{n-1}$ of $\pi$ and $\Phi_n$ is some 'virtual' price. In other words

$$\bar{D}(\pi, \pi_n, R, y) = d(\tilde{\pi}, \Phi_n, R + (\Phi_n - \pi_n)y) \tag{4.24a}$$

In particular

$$y = d_n(\tilde{\pi}, \Phi_n, R + (\Phi_n - \pi_n)y) \tag{4.24b}$$

These equations define $\Phi_n$ as an implicit function of $(\pi, R, y)$. Writing (4.24) as identities, differentiating with respect to $R$ eliminating derivatives of $\Phi_n$ and rearranging leads to

$$\left(\frac{\partial \bar{D}_l}{\partial y}\right)_{(\cdot)} = \frac{(\partial d_l^c/\partial \pi_n)_{(*)}}{(\partial d_n^c/\partial \pi_n)_{(*)}} + (\partial_R \bar{D}_l)_{(\cdot)}(\Phi_n(\cdot) - \pi_n) \quad l=1,\ldots n-1 \quad (4.25a)$$

$$(\partial_R \bar{D})_{(\cdot)} = (\partial_R d)_{(*)} - \frac{(\partial_R d_n)_{(*)}}{(\partial d_n^c/\partial \pi_n)_{(*)}}\left(\frac{\partial d^c}{\partial \pi_n}\right)_{(*)} \quad (4.25b)$$

where $^c$ denotes Hicksian compensated derivatives and

$$(\cdot) = (\pi, R, y),\ (*) = (\tilde{\pi}, \Phi_n(\cdot),\ R + (\Phi_n(\cdot) - \pi_n)y)$$

Multiplying (4.25a) and (4.25b) by marginal utilities gives the derivatives of utility (with obvious notation)

$$\left(\frac{\partial \bar{V}}{\partial y}\right)_{(\cdot)} = \mu(\Phi_n(\cdot) - \pi_n), \qquad \mu = \left(\frac{\partial \bar{V}}{\partial R}\right) \quad (4.26)$$

When $(\cdot)$ is such that $y=0$, then $\Phi_n(\cdot) = \pi_n$ and the above lemma obtains. □

We are now in a position to come back to the question of the desirability of the quota policy, i.e., as argued above to the comparison of the values of $P(v)$ and $P(0)$. Theorem 4 provides a simple answer.

**Theorem 4: Desirable quotas**

*Under the regularity conditions (for the programme $P(0)$ and the programme $P(v)$) under which the envelope theorem 3 holds, a small positive quota $v>0$ (resp. negative) is socially desirable (with the social welfare function introduced above), if*

$$\delta_{i_0,n} = \sum_k (\pi_k - \rho_k)\left(\frac{\partial d^c_{i_0,k}}{\partial \pi_n}\right) < 0 \text{ (resp.} > 0)$$

*where $\rho = (\rho_1, \ldots \rho_n)$ are the social values of commodities associated with $P(0)$ and all data are taken in the solution of $P(0)$.*

*Proof*

The proof is a direct application of the envelope theorem 2 and of the above lemma.

From the envelope theorem, the derivative of social welfare with respect to $v$ is

$$\lambda_{i_0}\frac{\partial \bar{V}_{i_0}}{\partial v} - \rho\left(\frac{\partial \chi_{i_0}}{\partial v}\right)$$

From the above lemma and the definition of $\chi_i(s, v)$ and $\bar{V}_i$, $\dfrac{\partial \bar{V}_i}{\partial v} = 0$. From

(4.23) and the definition of $\chi_i$, $\rho \cdot \frac{\partial \chi_{i_0}}{\partial v} = \rho_n + \tilde{\rho} \frac{(\partial \tilde{d}^c_{i_0} / \partial \pi_n)}{(\partial d^c_{i_{0,n}} / \partial \pi_n)}$, where $\sim$ is a straightforward notation for truncation of a vector to its $(n-1)$ first coordinates.

Since $\partial d^c_n / \partial \pi_n < 0$, the derivative of social welfare is positive whenever $\rho \left( \frac{\partial d^c_{i_0}}{\partial \pi_n} \right) > 0$. The fact that this is equivalent to $(\pi - \rho) \left( \frac{\partial d^c_{i_0}}{\partial \pi_n} \right) < 0$ follows from a standard property of compensated demand. □

Note first that, as a consequence of theorem 4, it is '*almost always*' the case (since in general $\delta_{i_{0,n}}$ will not equal zero) that *corrections of the consumption decisions (of consumer $i_0$) are socially desirable*. These corrections may however go in either direction: consumption should be increased when the index is negative, but decreased when the index is positive.

Let us now comment in more detail on the formula that determines the desirability of quotas.

$\pi_k - \rho_k$ is a 'fictitious' tax on commodity $k$, so that one can label $\delta_{i_{0,n}}$ the fictitious absolute index of discouragement of commodity $n$ (for household $i_0$). The discussion of the intuitive meaning of an index of discouragement presented in chapter 3 can be transposed here (although it has to be qualified, because the considered index is personalized). A negative (resp. positive) fictitious index of discouragement can be associated with the idea that commodity $n$ is (fictitiously) taxed (resp. subsidized).

The flavour of the results is then the following:

> Impose a positive quota for consumption of commodities which are taxed.
>
> Impose a negative quota for commodities which are subsidized.

The intuition behind the results is the following: in a second-best situation, the price system provides incorrect signals to the households. (Fictitiously) taxed commodities are socially cheaper than what is indicated by prices; quotas should serve to promote their consumption. Fictitiously subsidized commodities are socially more expensive so that their consumption should be restricted through rationing.

The implications of this result for real world quota policies (which are anonymous and not personalized) is discussed elsewhere.[8] It is, however, useful to note the application of the above result to the case where the initial situation is the social optimum analysed in section 5 of chapter 3. Then,

[8] See Guesnerie (1981), Guesnerie–Roberts (1984). For motivation, see Weitzman (1977).

**Corollary 3** *At the margin of an optimal taxation scheme for the model of chapter 3, then given one consumer $i_0$, a positive (resp. negative) quota of some commodity n is socially desirable when the personalized absolute index of discouragement of this commodity is negative (resp. positive).*

*Proof*

The only difference with the previous statement is that the present index of discouragement is no longer fictitious but real. This comes from the fact that social values are proportional to production prices in the problem under consideration (see theorem 8, corollary 10 in chapter 3). □

We leave it to the reader to come back to situations in which some specific optimization results on indices of discouragement have been obtained (as for example the one-consumer economy or the two-class economy) and to discuss the implications of the results of this section in these situations.

## 4.3 Optimal taxes and tax reform in a one-consumer economy (****)

In this section the general model studied in this book is restricted to the case when there is only one consumer (or equivalently a certain number – or a large number of identical consumers). Also we assume that the level of public goods is fixed either at zero or at some positive level. Formally, dropping the fixed vector $y_0'$, a feasible state of the model is associated with $z$, the net trade of the unique consumer, $y_1$ the production vector of the private sector, $\pi, p$ the consumption and the production price vectors; $R$ the subsidy such that

$$z = d(\pi, R) \tag{4.27}$$

$$y_1 = \eta(p) \tag{4.28}$$

$$z \le y_1 + \gamma \tag{4.29}$$

where $\gamma$ is some vector of private goods that has to be interpreted for example as the input vector for the production of the public good.

This model can indeed be viewed as a specification of our general model (as the reader will check). Hence all previous results – either positive or normative – certainly hold true and some of their specifications may be of independent interest.

The purpose of this section is mainly to come back to the findings of the previous literature on taxation, particularly normative literature, that adopted this one-consumer framework rather than the $m$-consumers framework of this book.

Two pieces of literature come to mind.

The first one is associated with Ramsey's seminal contribution[9] and can be broadly put under the heading: **the Ramsey problem**. As already evoked, the Ramsey problem is to characterize optimal indirect taxes that allow the finance of public goods; in the present framework this means characterizing the social optimum over the set of feasible states (4.27), (4.28), (4.29) when $R$ is fixed at some a priori given level $\bar{R}$ (for example but not necessarily $\bar{R}=0$).

The second one is the literature on **the desirable reduction of distortions**: it analyses in the framework of a one-consumer economy the relationship between welfare improvement and the reduction of distortions between consumer and producer prices. This is in our terminology a tax reform question: starting from a tax equilibrium of the one-consumer economy, what are the (directions of) tax changes that increase the welfare of the unique consumer?[10]

The relationship of the approach of this monograph with the Ramsey problem, on the one hand, and the reduction of distortions problem, on the other hand, has to be ascertained.

If, on formal grounds, both the Ramsey and the distortion problems are particular cases of the general optimisation and reform problem respectively studied in sections 5 and 1 of the preceding chapter, neither of them particularly fits the spirit of the present investigation. The reason is the following: in a one-consumer economy, the basic justification of taxation that has been developed in chapter 1 does not support the use of distorting taxes; it is only because there are several different households of different unknown characteristics that one can justify the use of distorting commodity taxes in conjunction with (uniform) lump-sum transfers. In the perspective we have adopted, the Ramsey problem has not a well-defined theoretical status. The reduction of distortions problem faces similar although weaker drawbacks. The solution of the latter problem as an input to a tatonnement algorithm, the final outcome of which is clearly the no distortion point (when offsetting transfers are allowed), is meaningless. In that case the problem of reducing distortions only makes sense if within a process of reform, some (more or less *ad hoc*) constraints force the reduction in distortions to be gradual.[11]

The reader should not however conclude that it is only for the sake of historical interest that the present section proposes a more in depth investigation of the Ramsey problem and of the reduction of distortions

[9] Ramsey (1927).

[10] Note that this problem could itself have two versions according to whether tax changes can be accompanied by offsetting income transfers or not. The tax reform version of the Ramsey problem corresponds to the latter case and not to the former.

[11] The reader should note that such was **not** the viewpoint adopted in previous section.

problem. In fact, previous literature has provided us with an understanding of one-consumer problems that is much better than the understanding we have gained so far of optimal taxation and tax reform in a general $m$-consumers economy. Hence, in principle, we could expect to improve our knowledge of the general problem by relying on the specific insights gained in the one-consumer economy (even if this economy is somewhat meaningless in our view). One should say that this optimistic conjecture has not yet turned out to be proved. As the reader will see, there is no obvious route for exporting in the $m$-consumers case, the superior understanding of optimal taxes or of tax reform that we have in a one-consumer economy. But we cannot say that the last word has been said and that no such route exists.

Let us finish this introductory presentation by advising the reader who is not particularly interested by the history of the subject to skip this section at first reading.

We will consider the Ramsey problem (4.3.1) and the gradual reductions of distortions problem with offsetting lump-sum transfers (4.3.2).

### 4.3.1 The one-consumer Ramsey problem – further insights

We are going to focus attention on the one-consumer Ramsey model: let us repeat that the optimization of the unique consumer's welfare assumes that prices are choice variables but there is no choice of exogenous income which is assumed to be zero.

As argued as the end of section 5, chapter 3, what we called the many-person Ramsey tax rule now takes the following form

$$T\cdot(\partial_{\pi_h} d)^c = \nu z_h \tag{4.30}$$

Multiplying both sides by $T_h$ and summing over $h$ gives

$$T\cdot(\partial_{\pi_h} d)^c T = \nu(T\cdot z)$$

As the left-hand side is necessarily negative, the sign of $\nu$ is opposite to the sign of $T\cdot z$, which are fiscal receipts from indirect taxation.

The expression of $\nu$ given in the preceding chapter (theorem 8 in section 3.5) suggests that $\nu<0$ (resp. $\nu>0$), $T\cdot z>0$ (resp. $T\cdot z<0$) corresponds to the case where it is desirable, if possible, to decrease (resp. increase) the uniform transfer.[12] This is intuitively acceptable. $T\cdot z$ corresponds to a positive amount of receipts aimed at financing the public good and can be advantageously replaced by some negative transfer, both globally and at the margin.

[12] Also, this is indeed in line with our discussion of tax reform in section 4 and for example with the fact that in the gradient projection algorithm sign $\dot{R}=$ sign $\nu$.

Note that if $T$ is a solution of (4.30), $T+\lambda\pi$ is also one. Let us choose one numeraire, commodity 1;

Let us call $\partial\tilde{M}$ the matrix $(\partial_\pi d)^c$ truncated on its first line and first column and $\tilde{T}$ the tax vector in $\mathscr{R}^{n-1}$, which corresponds to $T_1=0$. The equation becomes

$$\tilde{T}\cdot\partial\tilde{M}=\nu\tilde{z} \tag{4.31}$$

with $\tilde{z}$ the vector consisting of the $n-1$ last lines of $z$.

Formula (4.31) is a reduced and compact form of what we called previously taxation formulas. Assuming that $\partial\tilde{M}$ is known and invertible and that $\nu$ and $\tilde{z}$ are known, the formula allows an explicit computation of the vector of taxes. A next obvious step for thought is to look at the inverse of $\partial\tilde{M}$. This is what we are doing now.

We will introduce the concept of an Antonelli matrix. For that, let us consider $U$ the utility function of the unique consumer.

Let $\nabla U(x)$ be the gradient of the utility function in $x$. Take a numeraire, commodity 1. Call $C_h(x)=\dfrac{(\nabla U)_h}{(\nabla U)_1}(x)$, the marginal willingness to pay for commodity $h$ in terms of the numeraire and $C(x)$ the vector of marginal willingnesses to pay ($C(x)\in\mathscr{R}^{n-1}$). We can define:

*Definition 1: The* ***Antonelli matrix*** $\partial\tilde{C}(x)$ *is the* $(n-1)(n-1)$ *matrix of coefficients* $\tilde{C}_{hk}=\dfrac{\partial C_h}{\partial x_k}-C_k\dfrac{\partial C_h}{\partial x_1}$, $h=2,\dots n;\ k=2,\dots n.$

Under the convexity and differentiability assumptions made throughout this book (see chapter 2), the following holds:

*Proposition 1*
*The Antonelli matrix is symmetric, negative definite. It is the inverse of the truncated Slutsky matrix* $\partial\tilde{M}$ *just defined above.*

The proof of this statement will not be given here.[13] However, I will make a number of comments which make the property intuitively plausible.

Note first that a column of the matrix $\partial\tilde{C}$ is some kind of compensated derivative of the vector $C$ with respect to $x_k$. Intuitively it describes the change in $C$ when $x_k$ is increased and $x_1$ is decreased of $C_k$, i.e., when the change in $x_k$ is accompanied by a change of $x_1$ which maintains utility at its initial level.

[13] The reader is for example invited to refer to the chapter 1 of Guesnerie (1980a).

Now consider the following diagram.

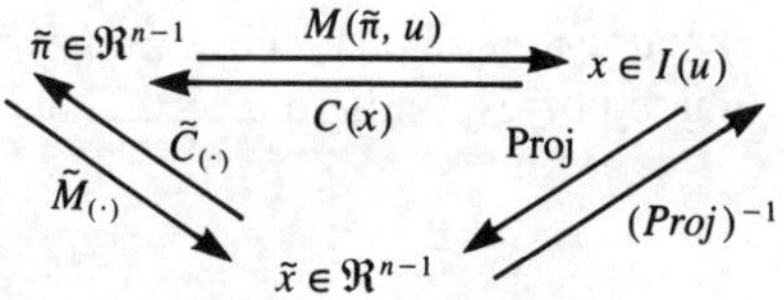


Let us choose commodity 1 as the numeraire so that $\pi = (1, \tilde{\pi})$ with $\tilde{\pi} \in \mathscr{R}^{n-1}$. Take $\tilde{\pi}$. Associate with it, and a utility level $u$, a vector of compensated demand $M(\tilde{\pi}, u)$ which is an element of $I(u)$ the indifference surface of level $u$. Take the operation of projection on $\mathscr{R}^{n-1}$ (denoted Proj); Proj $M = \tilde{M}$ when $\tilde{M}$ is the truncated compensated demand. Let us consider then the inverse mapping of $\tilde{M}$. It associates with $\tilde{x}$ one $x$ on the indifference surface $I(u)$ (by $\text{Proj}^{-1}$) and the vector $C(x)$ of marginal willingnesses to pay in $x$. Let us call this mapping $\tilde{C}$ so that $\tilde{M} \circ \tilde{C} = I$ ($I$ is the identity). Clearly the derivative of $\tilde{M}$ is $\partial \tilde{M}$. But the above intuitive interpretation of the Antonelli matrix $\partial \tilde{C}$ suggests that this matrix is the Jacobian derivative of $\tilde{C}$ just defined. If this is true $\tilde{M} \circ \tilde{C} = I \Rightarrow (\partial \tilde{M}) \partial \tilde{C} = I$ and the properties of $\partial \tilde{C}$ in the above proposition are easily derived from the known properties of $\partial \tilde{M}$.

Now (4.25) can be inverted as

$$\tilde{T} = \nu (\partial \tilde{C}) \tilde{z} \tag{4.32}$$ [14]

or if $\partial_k \tilde{C}$ is the $k^{\text{th}}$ column of $\partial \tilde{C}$

$$\tilde{T} = \nu \sum_{k=2}^{n} (\partial_k \tilde{C}) z_k \tag{4.33}$$

$\sum_{k=2}^{n} (\partial_k \tilde{C}) z_k$ can be viewed as the directional derivative in the direction of $\tilde{z} = \text{Proj}_{\mathscr{R}_{n-1}} z$ of the mapping $\tilde{C}$ defined above.

Accordingly we denote

$\sum_{k=2}^{n} (\partial_k C) z_k = D_{\tilde{z}} \tilde{C}$ where $D_{\tilde{z}}$ denotes the directional derivative along a vector $\tilde{z}$.

$$\text{Then } \frac{T_h}{\pi_h} = \frac{T_h}{C_h} = \frac{\nu}{C_h} D_{\tilde{z}} \tilde{C}_h \tag{4.34}$$

[14] In this section, our conventional notation has the inconvenience of making the same vector (for example $T$) a column or a row vector according to the formula where it enters. In spite of this weakness of the notation, we stick to it.

Then we can show the following, which is indeed a consequence of theorem 8 of the previous chapter:

**Corollary 4: Optimal taxes in the Ramsey problem: explicit formulas in the general case**

*In the one-consumer model with constraints on uniform lump-sum transfers, optimal taxes satisfy the following simple formulas (where all expressions are taken at the optimum).*

$$\tilde{T} = \nu \sum_{k=2}^{n} (\partial_k \tilde{C}) z_k \qquad (4.33)$$

$$\frac{T_h}{\pi_h} - \frac{T_k}{\pi_k} = \nu D_z \left( \log \frac{\tilde{C}_h}{\tilde{C}_k} \right) \qquad (4.35)$$

*Also if the preferences are separable between the numeraire and the other goods and if preferences are homothetic, then*

$$\frac{T_h}{\pi_h} = \frac{T_k}{\pi_k}, \ \forall h, k \neq 1 \qquad (4.36)$$

*i.e., proportional taxation is optimal.*

*Proof* (sketch)
(4.33) has been proved above. (4.35) obtains by subtraction of the formulas (4.34) for $h$ and $k$ and introduction of logarithms. In order to prove (4.36), we note that if preferences are separable, then $\frac{C_h}{C_k}$ does not depend upon commodity 1's consumption.

Then $D_z\left(\log \frac{\tilde{C}_h}{\tilde{C}_k}\right) = D_z\left(\log \frac{C_h}{C_k}\right)$ where $D_z$ is the directional derivative along $z$ in $\mathscr{R}^n$. But with homothetic preferences $D_z\left(\log \frac{C_h}{C_k}\right) = 0$ □

Now let us come back on (4.32) and (4.33).

Consider $\partial \tilde{C}$. It is a hermitian negative definite matrix in the sense of Gantmacher.[15] It has then $(n-1)$ real negative eigenvalues associated with $(n-1)$ orthogonal eigen vectors. Call $1/\lambda_i$ the eigenvalues and $N_i$ the eigen vectors (chosen with unit Euclidean norms). We have

[15] See Gantmacher (1986) for a statement more general than the one in the Mathematical appendix.

$$(\partial\tilde{C})N_i = 1/\lambda_i N_i \; i=2,\dots n \tag{4.37}$$

$$(\partial\tilde{M})N_i = \lambda_i N_i \; i=2,\dots n \tag{4.38}$$

Hence $N_i$ is a direction in $\mathscr{R}^{n-1}$ of price changes (for all goods but the numeraire) such that it induces a change of compensated demand of all goods but the numeraire collinear to the direction of price changes. Equivalently $N_i$ is a direction of quantity changes of all goods but the numeraire such that it induces a variation of the vector of marginal willingness to pay along an indifference surface which is proportional to the quantity changes.

Call $\underline{\tilde{z}}$ the coordinates of $\tilde{z}$ in the 'new' system of coordinates $\{N_i\}$. We have $\tilde{z} = B\underline{\tilde{z}}$ where $B = (N_2 \dots N_n)$ ($N_i$ is a column vector) and because of the hermitian structure $B^{-1} = B'$, when $B'$ is the transposition of $B$.

Considering $\underline{\pi}$ the coordinate of $\pi$ in the system, we have $\tilde{\pi} = \underline{\tilde{\pi}}\,B'$ ($\pi$ being a row vector). The change of coordinates preserves the inner product since $\pi\cdot\tilde{z} = R \Leftrightarrow \underline{\tilde{\pi}}\,B'B\underline{\tilde{z}} = \underline{\tilde{\pi}}\cdot\underline{\tilde{z}} = R$. In other words after the coordinate changes, the 'new' price system to take into account is the initial price vector written into the 'new' system.

If the new system of coordinates is viewed as defining $(n-1)$ composite goods, then $\underline{\tilde{z}}$ is the bundle of such composite goods. And $\underline{\pi}$ can be consistently interpreted as the price vector of composite goods: for example $\tilde{\pi} = \underline{\tilde{\pi}}\cdot B'$; we see that a price change of 1 of the $i^{\text{th}}$ composite good induces a price change along $N_i$ of the initial price vector. This justifies the following assertion: Take a numeraire. Then there exists $(n-1)$ composite commodities of $\mathscr{R}^{n-1}$ such that a price increase of one of these composite commodities induces a change of compensated demand affecting this composite commodity and the numeraire only.

Coming back to the equation

$$\tilde{T} = \nu(\partial\tilde{C})\tilde{z}$$

Putting $\underline{\tilde{T}} = B'\tilde{T}$ ($\underline{\tilde{T}}$ is a column vector)

$$\underline{\tilde{T}} = \nu B'(\partial\tilde{C})B\underline{\tilde{z}} \tag{4.39}$$

$$\text{i.e. } \underline{\tilde{T}} = \nu\begin{pmatrix} 1/\lambda_2 & & 0 \\ & \cdot & \\ 0 & & 1/\lambda_n \end{pmatrix}\begin{pmatrix} \underline{\tilde{z}}_2 \\ \cdot \\ \underline{\tilde{z}}_n \end{pmatrix}$$

$$\text{or } \underline{\tilde{T}}_h = \nu\frac{\underline{\tilde{z}}_h}{\lambda_h},\; h=2\dots n \tag{4.40}$$

When divided by the price $\underline{\pi}_h$, we obtain formulas formally similar to the inverse elasticity formulas derived in the previous subsection.

The next statement, that can be viewed as a corollary of theorem 8, chapter 3, summarizes our findings.

**Corollary 5: 'Intrinsic' inverse elasticity formulas**

*At the optimum of the Ramsey problem, there is an orthogonal basis of the commodity space consisting of* $(n-1)$ *composite commodities and of the numeraire such that the tax rates on these* $(n-1)$ *composite commodities are inversely proportional to their compensated demand elasticities.*

Besides the conciseness of the results a few restrictive remarks should be made:

The composite commodities are endogenous to the optimization problem.

Some of the composite commodities will have negative components, a fact which somewhat complicates their economic interpretation.

The question arises now of whether what we have learnt on optimal taxes in the Ramsey problem can be used to improve our understanding of optimal taxes in the $m$-consumers problems.

Consider now formula (3.39) of theorem 8 of the previous chapter as modified when introducing $T$. Let us repeat the truncation operation that led to formula (4.31). Instead of (4.31), but with the same notation (in particular $\partial\tilde{M}$ is the $n-1 \times n-1$ truncated $(\partial_\pi d)^c$ where $d$ is aggregate demand).

$$\tilde{T}\cdot\partial\tilde{M} = \sum_i \nu_i \tilde{z}_i$$

As above, $\partial\tilde{M}$ can be inverted and diagonalized, and in the new coordinate system

$$\underset{=}{T}_h = \frac{1}{\lambda_h}\sum_i \nu_i \, \underset{=}{\tilde{z}}_{ih} \tag{4.41}$$

i.e., after introducing $\underset{=}{\tilde{z}}_h = \sum_i \underset{=}{\tilde{z}}_{ih}$

$$\underset{=}{T}_h = \left(\frac{\Sigma_i \nu_i \underset{=}{\tilde{z}}_{ih}}{\underset{=}{\tilde{z}}_h}\right)\frac{\underset{=}{\tilde{z}}_h}{\lambda_h} \tag{4.42}$$

The above formula still suggests a relationship between tax rates of well-chosen composite commodities and inverse elasticities of compensated demand for those composite commodities.[16] However the proportionality coefficient differs across commodities depending on some kind of 'distributional characteristics' $\left(\sum_i v_i \frac{z_{ih}}{z_h}\right)$ of the composite commodity.

But even the sign of this 'distributional characteristics'[17] – the covariance between net social values of income and consumptions – is unclear so that the case for some of the composite commodities being taxed or subsidized – a weak qualitative information – is not settled. This somewhat disappointing remark helps us to understand that there is no obvious route for improving our analysis of optimal taxation formulas in the general case from the analysis of the Ramsey problem. More specific results that have been obtained in the literature rely upon specifications of demand functions, the discussion of which goes beyond the scope of the present study.

### 4.3.2 Gradual reduction of distortions with offsetting lump-sum transfer

Let us repeat the question considered here: how to characterize in an economy with one consumer, without public good – or with fixed public good – the tax changes which are welfare improving (for the unique consumer) when accompanied by adequate income compensation?

A segment of literature of significant size developed in the sixties in order to answer this question – which can be viewed as a special case of the tax reform analysis with a social welfare function presented in chapter 3.

The most significant answers to the question, known from existing literature, can be summarized in the next theorem. As we previously argued in section 3.1 of chapter 3, the theorem illustrates that there are many welfare-improving directions of tax changes. However, those selected by the next theorem are more intuitively appealing than those selected before in the $m$-consumer case.

**Theorem 5: Welfare improving tax changes**

*Consider an initial situation where* $(p \cdot \partial_R d)_{(0)} > 0$.

*The changes* $(\dot{\pi})$ *determined by the following rules and accompanied by adequate associated changes of* $(\dot{p}, \dot{R})$ *increase the unique consumer's welfare:*

(1) *All changes* $\dot{\pi}$ *such that* $(p \cdot (\partial_\pi d)^c)_{(0)} \dot{\pi} < 0$.
(2) *A change* $\dot{\pi}$ *in the direction of the vector of 'absolute indices of*

[16] Note also that the analysis of the spectrum of the matrix of aggregate compensated demand has no simple relationship with the analysis of the spectrum of individual matrices of compensated demand.

[17] See the references on this concept in the bibliographical note. The covariance interpretation only holds true when the uniform lump-sum income is optimized.

*discouragement' defined above. Furthermore, this change is the one selected by (the specification to this model of) the gradient projection algorithm ((3.24) to (3.27)).*

(3) *A change $\dot{\pi}$ in the direction of $-T(0)$, minus the vector of existing taxes.*

(4) *A change $\dot{\pi}$ which decreases, everything else being equal, the consumption price of one commodity which is less taxed than its complements and more taxed than its substitutes.*[18] *Particularly, decreasing the consumption price of the more taxed commodity is beneficial when all the other commodities are its substitutes.*

(5) *In the case where, in the initial situation, there is an untaxed numeraire and the taxation rate is the same for the other goods (equivalently $\tilde{T}=\mu\tilde{p}=\frac{\mu}{\mu+1}\tilde{\pi}$) any change $\dot{\pi}$ which increases the consumption prices of complements to the numeraire and decreases the consumption prices of substitutes.*

(6) *Finally, in the case when in the initial situation there is an untaxed numeraire, a change $\dot{\pi}$ which leads to a decrease of specific taxes proportional to their initial values $T(0)$.*

*Proof*

In the proof all data derivatives, prices, and quantities, are taken in an initial tight equilibrium (0). In all the proofs, we will use the precise findings of theorem 1 in chapter 3: in other words, we will show that all changes described above are (associated with) equilibrium-preserving and welfare-improving (directions of) changes. Indeed, equilibrium-preserving directions of change are defined by

$$p\cdot(\partial_\pi d)\dot{\pi}+(p\cdot\partial_R d)\dot{R}\leq 0$$

or, after a transformation already used, equivalently

$$p\cdot(\partial_\pi d)^c\dot{\pi}+(p\cdot\partial_R d)(\dot{R}-\dot{\pi}\cdot z)\leq 0 \tag{4.43}$$

However an increase in consumer welfare obtains if and only if $\dot{R}-\dot{\pi}z>0$ and hence obtains if and only if $p\cdot(\partial_\pi d)^c\cdot\dot{\pi}<0$, i.e., if the change $\dot{\pi}$ releases resources.

Using the findings of section 2.2, chapter 2 that tell us how equilibrium-preserving directions of change are matched by production price changes, one obtains conclusion (1). Then, we note that one can write

$$p\cdot(\partial_\pi d)^c\dot{\pi}<0 \Leftrightarrow T\cdot(\partial_\pi d)^c\dot{\pi}>0$$

[18] The definition of less taxed and more taxed that we are considering here is the one of chapter 2.

Remember that the definition in section 3 of $T{\cdot}(\partial_\pi d)^c$ as the vector of absolute indices of discouragement makes the proof of the first part of (2) a semantic matter. (Note that this terminology has been justified and commented on previously.) For the second part of assertion (3), it is left to the reader to show that a variant of the gradient projection algorithms of the previous chapter leads to select $\dot{\pi}$ proportional to $T{\cdot}(\partial_\pi d)^c$.

Coming to the proof of (3), the matrix $(\partial_\pi d)^c$ is negative semi-definite; then the latter inequality is satisfied for $\dot{\pi} = -kT$, $k > 0$, as soon as $T \neq 0$, $T \neq \lambda\pi$.

To prove (4) let us note that a decrease in the price of a commodity $h$ (everything being equal, but the lump-sum transfer) is beneficial if and only if $[T{\cdot}(\partial_\pi d)^c]_h < 0$.

This latter inequality can be written

$$\sum_{k \in K_1} T_k(\partial_{\pi_k} d_h)^c + \sum_{k \in K_2} T_k(\partial_{\pi_k} d_h)^c + T_h(\partial_{\pi_k} d_h)^c < 0$$

where $K_1$ (resp. $K_2$) is the set of complements (resp. substitutes) to commodity $h$.

Now, we can evaluate the above expression when commodity $h$ is less taxed than its complements and more taxed than its substitutes, and when it is chosen as a numeraire.

Remembering the two equivalent definitions of being 'more taxed' given in chapter 2, we note that $T_k > 0$(resp. $< 0$), $k \in K_1$(resp.$K_2$). As complements (resp. substitutes) are such that $\partial_{\pi_k} d_h < 0$(resp. $> 0$), conclusion follows.

To show (5), let us assume (w.l.o.g.) that commodity 1 is the numeraire: Again, let us compute $[T{\cdot}(\partial_\pi d)^c]_h$

From $\tilde{T} = \dfrac{\mu}{\mu+1}\tilde{\pi}$, this latter expression can be transformed

$$\frac{\mu}{\mu+1}\sum_{k \neq 1} \pi_k(\partial_{\pi_h} d_k)^c = \frac{\mu}{\mu+1}\sum_{k \neq 1} \pi_k(\partial_{\pi_k} d_h)^c = -\frac{\mu}{\mu+1}(\partial_{\pi_1} d_h)^c.$$

Again conclusion follows.

The proof of (6) requires that we consider the next formula

$$\tilde{T} = I - (\partial\tilde{\eta})^{-1}(\partial_\pi \tilde{d})^c \dot{\tilde{\pi}} \tag{4.44}$$

where $I$ is the $(n-1) \times (n-1)$ identity matrix and $\partial\tilde{\eta}^{-1}$, $(\partial^\pi \tilde{d})^c$ are the adequate truncated matrices associated with the mappings $\eta$ and $d^c$, and $\dot{\tilde{\pi}}$ is the $(n-1)$ dimensional truncation of $\dot{\pi}$.

(4.44) can be rewritten as

$$\dot{\tilde{T}} = [[(\partial_\pi \tilde{d})^c]^{-1} - (\partial\tilde{\eta})^{-1}](\partial_\pi \tilde{d})^c \dot{\tilde{\pi}} \tag{4.45}$$

Inverting (4.45), we get

$$\dot{\tilde{\pi}} = [(\partial_\pi \tilde{d})^c]^{-1}[[(\partial_\pi \tilde{d})^c]^{-1} - (\partial \tilde{\eta})^{-1}]^{-1} \dot{\tilde{T}}$$

It remains to show that $\dot{\tilde{T}} = -k\tilde{T},\ k > 0, \Rightarrow T \cdot (\partial_\pi d)^c \begin{pmatrix} 0 \\ \dot{\tilde{\pi}} \end{pmatrix} > 0$

This is equivalent to

$$\tilde{T}(\partial_\pi \tilde{d})^c [(\partial_\pi \tilde{d})^c]^{-1}[[(\partial_\pi \tilde{d})^c]^{-1} - (\partial \tilde{\eta})^{-1}]^{-1} \tilde{T} < 0$$

The latter inequality actually holds because the matrix $[\ ]^{-1}$ is negative definite (since $(\partial_\pi \tilde{d})^c$ and $-(\partial \tilde{\eta})$ are negative definite). □

## 4.4 Mixing linear and non-linear taxation: a bird's eye view (**)

This section provides a broad but quick overview of the problem of the introduction of non-linearities into the affine tax schedule considered in the present book.

For that, we do two things:

First, we restrict the model to the case where (i) we have only two households indexed by 1 and 2 and (ii) in which the global production set is limited by a hyperplane.

(i) the utility of consumer 1 (resp. 2) is $U_1(l_1, \tilde{z}_1, y_0')$ (resp. $U_2(l_2, \tilde{z}_2, y_0')$) where $l_1 \overset{\text{def}}{=} -z_{11}$ (resp. $l_2 = -z_{21}$) is the quantity of the numeraire commodity supplied to the market by consumer 1 (resp. 2) and $\tilde{z}_1$ (resp. $\tilde{z}_2$) is an $n-1$ dimensional vector.

(ii) A net trade plan $(l_1, \tilde{z}_1)$, $(l_2, \tilde{z}_2)$ together with a public good level $y_0'$ (here unidimensional) are technologically feasible if and only if

$$\bar{p} \cdot (\tilde{z}_1 + \tilde{z}_2) - l_1 - l_2 + y_0' \leq 0$$

where $\bar{p}$ is an $n-1$ dimensional vector.
With this simple formulation , $l_1$ and $l_2$ can be viewed as the quantities of labour supplied by households and $\bar{p}_l$ the 'labour value' of commodity $l$. Note that labour is better viewed here as 'efficient labour' in the sense of section 1 of the introduction, so that the differences in the utility function will reflect differences in abilities, as well as (or instead of) differences in tastes. Note that if efficient labour is a numeraire of price 1, $l_1$ and $l_2$ are also the (pre-tax) incomes of households 1 and 2.

Second, we introduce a non-linear tax schedule for commodity 1, i.e., in the interpretation just suggested a non-linear income tax.

Formally, we associate a non-linear income tax schedule with two couples $(l_1, R_1)$, $(l_2, R_2)$ where $l_i, R_i$ are respectively the pre- and post-income tax of household $i$.[19] Non-linear income taxation coexists with linear taxation of the other commodities for which the consumption price vector $\tilde{\pi} \in \mathscr{R}_+^{n-1}$ differs from $\bar{p}$ the production price vector.

We denote $d_1(\tilde{\pi}, R_1, l_1, y_0')$ (resp. $d_2(\tilde{\pi}, R_2, l_2, y_0')$) the $n-1$ dimensional vector of notional demand of household 1 (resp. 2) when he is forced to supply $l_1$ units of commodity 1 (labour) he gets $R_1$ of labour income, $y_0'$ of public good, and he faces the consumption price vector $\tilde{\pi}$. (For the sake of convenience, we depart slightly from previous notation that would have lead us to use $\tilde{d}_1$.)

We are now in a position to define a feasible state of the model mixing non-linear and linear taxation. It is associated with $(l_1, R_1)(l_2, R_2)$, $\tilde{\pi}$, $y_0'$ that satisfy

$$\bar{p} \cdot \{d_1(\tilde{\pi}, R_1, l_1, y_0') + d_2(\tilde{\pi}, R_2, l_2, y_0')\} + y_0' - l_1 - l_2 \leq 0 \tag{4.46}$$

$$U_2(l_2, d_2(\tilde{\pi}, R_2, l_2, y_0'), y_0') \geq U_2(l_1, d_2(\tilde{\pi}, R_1, l_1, y_0'), y_0') \tag{4.47}$$

$$U_1(l_1, d_1(\tilde{\pi}, R_1, l_1, y_0'), y_0') \geq U_1(l_2, d_1(\tilde{\pi}, R_2, l_2, y_0'), y_0') \tag{4.47'}$$

(4.46) is a feasibility constraint introduced before. (4.47) and (4.47′) are self-selection constraints analogous to those considered in chapter 1. (4.47) (resp. (4.47′)) say that household 2 (resp. 1) prefers to choose $(l_2, R_2)$ (resp. $(l_1, R_1)$) and hence $d_2(\tilde{\pi}, R_2, l_2, \cdot)$ (resp. $d_1(\tilde{\pi}, R_1, l_1, \cdot)$) rather than $(l_1, R_1)$ (resp. $(l_2, R_2)$) and hence $d_2(\tilde{\pi}, R_1, l_1, \cdot)$ (resp. $d_1(\tilde{\pi}, R_2, l_2, \cdot)$).

Compared with the standard model of this book, the present model has additional degrees of freedom ($R_1, R_2$ here instead of $R$) and additional self-selection constraints.

A number of results obtained in previous chapters of this book could be accommodated here.

*The structure of tax equilibria*

In order to understand the new structure, one should proceed as follows:

Fix $l_1$ and $l_2$ and forget about the self-selection constraints. The structure of the set of $(\tilde{\pi}, R_1, R_2, y_0')$ that satisfy equation (4.46) – or even the more general equation that would obtain if the production set were not a

[19] At a more basic level (see chapter 1) a non-linear income tax schedule is associated with a function $\psi | R = \psi(l)$. However the formulation adopted here does not involve a significant loss of generality (see Guesnerie–Seade (1982) for a discussion of the issue in the pure income taxation model).

hyperplane – can easily be derived from theorems 1–7 in chapter 2. Indeed these theorems characterize the subset $R_1 = R_2$. Furthermore, at fixed $\tilde{\pi}, y_0'$, when $R_1$, $R_2$ are allowed to differ, they relate in a way that is easily characterized. The complication in the structure will be entirely due to the self-selection constraints. For example at fixed $l_1, l_2$ they will restrict the set of feasible states in a complex way: in particular the set of $\tilde{\pi}, R_1, R_2, y_0'$ that meets the constraint has no reason to be connected and every parametrization of the set of equilibria will be defined on a subset of parameters – $\tilde{\pi}, R_1, R_2$ or $\tilde{\pi}, R_1, y_0'$ – that will not in general be connected.

*Tax reform*

The analysis of tax reform in the problem (4.46) (4.47) obtains from variants of the argument used in chapter 3.

If we start from a point where the self-selection constraints do not bind, then a variant of theorem 1 of chapter 3 applies – once one has redefined the demand of each consumer as a function of the real prices $\tilde{\pi}$ and also of the shadow wage and shadow income that supports this initial consumption plan.

At points where one or two self-selection constraints bind, the set of equilibrium-preserving and Pareto-improving directions of change is subject to one or two additional restrictions. The essence of some later properties concerning cost–benefit analysis is however unaffected.

While leaving to the reader to explore further the 'general' tax reform problem, we show now how it simplifies in an extremely well-behaved case. The simplifications comes from two facts.

(i) In the initial situation, only constraint (4.47) is binding.
(ii) $d_2(\tilde{\pi}', R', l_1, y_0') = d_1(\tilde{\pi}', R', l_1, y_0') \; \forall \pi', R'$

In other words, condition (ii) says that if consumption is forced at $l_1$ for both agents their behaviour makes them *indiscernible*. This occurs in particular when both agents have a utility function that is additive in $l$, on the one hand, and in $(\tilde{z}, y_0')$, on the other hand, and when the subutility function depending on $(\tilde{z}, y_0')$ is identical for both of them.[20] We have then

*Proposition 2*
*Allow an initial situation in which (i) and (ii) are true. Let* $\tilde{T} = \tilde{\pi} - \tilde{p}$.
*Then the direction of change* $\dot{\tilde{\pi}} = -\tilde{T}$*, when accompanied by adequate changes* $\dot{R}_1, \dot{R}_2$*, is equilibrium-preserving and Pareto improving.*

[20] Which is the case if they have the same 'basic' utility function and different abilities as in the model of chapter 1.

*Proof* (informal sketch)

From theorem 5 above (assertion 3), it is easily seen that the change under consideration accompanied by a compensating change $\dot{R}_i$ – that leaves $i$'s welfare unchanged – 'releases resources' in each subeconomy consisting of $M{\cdot}i$ alone ($i=1,2$). But from condition (ii), the utility of $M{\cdot}2$ at $l=l_1$ is unaffected. The change then releases resources, leaves individual welfare unaffected and does not affect the self-selection constraint. It can then be transformed into a Pareto-improving change (without changing $l_1$ and $l_2$). □

*Optimization*

Let us consider second-best Pareto optima in which only the self-selection constraint (4.47) binds. We say that such an optimum is **strictly redistributive and well behaved**. Such a second-best optimum is a solution of the following programme ($P$):

$$\max U_1(l_1, d_1(\tilde{\pi}, R_1, l_1, y_0'), y_0')$$

$$U_2(l_2, d_2(\tilde{\pi}, R_2, l_2, y_0'), y_0' \geq \bar{U}_2 \qquad (\mu)$$

$$U_2(l_2, d_2(\tilde{\pi}, R_2, l_2, y_0'), y_0') - U_2(l_1, d_2(\tilde{\pi}, R_1, l_1, y_0'), y_0') \geq 0 \qquad (\lambda)$$

$$\bar{p}\cdot\{d_1(\tilde{\pi}, R_1, l_1, y_0') + d_2(\tilde{\pi}, R_2, l_2, y_0')\} + y_0' - l_1 - l_2 \leq 0 \qquad (-\rho)$$

Some characteristics of such an optimum are summarized in next theorem 6.

**Theorem 6: Characteristics of a strictly redistributive and well-behaved optimum.**

*Let an optimum (*) solution of the above programme (P).*
*Then $\exists \epsilon^* > 0$, such that*

$$\tilde{T}^*(\partial_\pi M)_{(*)} = \epsilon^*(\tilde{z}_1^* - z_2^\bullet) \tag{4.48}$$

*where $\tilde{T}^* = \tilde{\pi}^* - \bar{p}$, $(\partial_\pi M)_{(*)}$ is the truncated aggregate Slutsky matrix (restricted to consumption goods) and*

$$\tilde{z}_1^* = d_1(\tilde{\pi}^*, R_1^*, l_1^*, y_0'^*) \qquad z_2^\bullet = d_2(\tilde{\pi}^*, R_1^*, l_1^*, y_0'^*)$$

*Proof* (sketch)

Consider the Lagrangian associated with ($P$) and consider its derivatives with respect to $\pi_l$; $l=2,\dots n$ and $R_1, R_2$.

$$(\pi_l) \quad -\alpha_1^* z_{1l}^* - (\mu+\lambda)\alpha_2^* z_{2l}^* + \alpha_2^\bullet \lambda z_{2l}^\bullet - \rho\bar{p}\cdot(\partial_{\pi_l} d)_{(*)} = 0 \tag{4.49}$$

$$(R_1) \quad \alpha_1^* - \alpha_2^\bullet \lambda - \rho\bar{p}(\partial_{R_1} d)_{(*)} = 0 \tag{4.50}$$

$$(R_2) \quad \alpha_2^*(\mu+\lambda) - \rho\bar{p}(\partial_{R_2} d)_{(*)} = 0 \tag{4.51}$$

when $\alpha_1^*$, $\alpha_2^*$ are the marginal utilities of incomes of households 1 and 2 at the optimal situation and $\alpha_2^\bullet$ is the marginal utility of income for agent 2 when he mimicks agent 1's pre-income choice.

(4.49) can be rewritten as

$$(-\alpha_1^* + \alpha_2^\bullet \lambda) z_{1l}^* - (\mu + \lambda)\alpha_2^* z_{2l}^* - \rho \bar{p}(\partial_{\pi_l} d)_{(*)} - \alpha_2^\bullet \lambda (z_{1l}^* - z_{1l}^\bullet) = 0$$

and taking into account (4.20) (4.21), and the Slutsky conditions we have

$$\bar{p}\cdot(\partial_{\pi_l} d^c)_{(*)} = -\frac{\alpha_2^\bullet \lambda}{\rho}(z_{1l}^* - z_{2l}^\bullet)$$

which can be rewritten as (4.48). □

Theorem 6 indicates that the optimal taxation formulas still involve indices of discouragement, but here the index of discouragement of commodity $l$ is proportional not to the consumption of commodity $l$ (as in previous sections) but to the difference between consumption of commodity $l$ by agent 1 and agent 2 if he decided to 'mimic' agent 1, i.e., to choose – through labour supply – the same pre-tax and after-tax incomes.[21] In particular this difference is zero if agents 1 and 2 are indiscernible at $l_1 = l_1^*$ (assumption (ii) p. 223). This can be reformulated as corollary 6.

**Corollary 6** *Under the 'indiscernibility' assumption, then* $\tilde{T}^* = 0$.

Note that this corollary is as well a consequence of the reform proposition 1 as of the optimization statement of theorem 6. It is a strong statement since it asserts that, with an optimal non-linear tax schedule, linear taxes are useless. As argued above it holds true in the interpretation stressed in footnote 21, under a separability assumption between, on the one hand, public and private goods and, on the other hand, leisure.

In fact, under these latter conditions the following is also true

*Proposition 3*
*If agents have utility functions that are separable between goods and labour such that the subutility functions for goods are identical, the Samuelson rule governs the optimal supply of public goods.*

*Proof* (sketch)
Under the conditions of proposition 3 – separability between leisure and

[21] If we come back to the (standard) interpretation that the differences of behaviour reflect differences of abilities, then the high ability 'mimicker' 2 supplies less effective labour than agent 1. Then, the index of discouragement is negative whenever a commodity is 'complementary' to leisure.

other goods and identical subutility functions – $d_1$ and $d_2$ do not explicitly depend on $l_1$ and $l_2$. Agents are indiscernible and corollary 6 applies.

Taking into account that $\tilde{T}^* = 0$ and the fact that $\tilde{\pi}.\ \partial_{y'_0} d_i = 0$, the first-order condition with respect to $y'_0$ reduces to

$$(\partial_{y'_0} U_1)_{(*)} + \mu(\partial_{y'_0} U_2)_{(*)} + \lambda[(\partial_{y'_0} U_2)_{(*)} - (\partial_{y'_0} U_2)_{(\bullet)}] - \rho = 0 \tag{4.52}$$

But under the separability assumption $(\partial_{y'_0} U_2)_{(\bullet)} = (\partial_{y'_0} U_1)_{(*)}$, $\alpha_1^* = \alpha_2^\bullet$.

Then, with $\tilde{T}^* = 0$, (4.50) and (4.51) become: $(1-\lambda)\alpha_1^* = \rho$, $(\mu+\lambda)\alpha_2^* = \rho$ and (4.52) can be written $\dfrac{(\partial_{y'_0} U_1)_{(*)}}{\alpha_1^*} + \dfrac{(\partial_{y'_0} U_2)_{(*)}}{\alpha_2^*} = 1$ □

The analysis shows in which directions previous results are changed. Clearly the bird's eye view should be complemented by a more serious exploration. However, the reader should not be misled by the fact that in the case of optimization at least some results are simplified when compared to previous results.

First, the conditions under which a second-best optimum is strictly redistributive and well behaved are much more restrictive than they are in the standard one-dimensional non-linear income tax problem.[22] In particular even when the optimal social welfare function is redistributive enough this property is not necessarily implied by the generalized Spence–Mirrlees conditions used in multi-dimensional screening problems (with one-dimensional hidden information).[23]

Second, the additional separability hypothesis that also implies the no indirect taxation result of corollary 6 provides a nice theoretical reference rather than a plausible stylized description of the world.

## 4.5 Bibliographical note

The general formulation of second-best models considered in section 4.1 has been proposed in Guesnerie (1979b). The analysis proposed in this chapter is not fully rigorous. More rigorous and detailed derivations as well as more general statements (of theorem 1) are indeed found in Guesnerie (1979b). The insights of the latter paper have been systematically used and/or developed in Drèze, J.P. (1982), Drèze, J.P. and Stern (1987).

Theorem 3 elaborates on Diamond–Mirrlees' (1976) who made the simple but important point that the social value of the production plan of constant returns to scale firms should be zero: this is corollary 2 here (for another statement of this fact, see again Guesnerie (1979b)).

22 On this problem, see for example Guesnerie–Seade (1982).
23 See Guesnerie–Laffont (1985).

The analysis of the desirability of quotas of section 4.2 follows my article with K. Roberts (Guesnerie–Roberts (1984)) which built on previous writings of both authors. In particular, the argument of the present text is in essence similar to my previous argument (Guesnerie (1981)) which, however, only concerned redistribution in kind (Roberts' (1978) argument rather concerns questions relative to an optimal income tax problem).

A number of authors have derived, with different techniques, expressions for the derivatives of constrained demand (see Tobin–Houthaker (1950) for an early discussion, Drèze (1977), Guesnerie (1981b)). However, the most systematic treatment is due to Neary–Roberts (1980). The present treatment is that of Guesnerie (1981b). Related to Guesnerie–Roberts, recent articles on the desirability of rationing include Wijkander (1986); Guesnerie–Roberts (1987) using an argument similar to the one of section 2, consider the case for minimum wage legislation.

The results on the Antonelli matrix introduced in the next section are precisely derived in Guesnerie (1980). This concept of the Antonelli matrix is classical as are its properties (see Charette–Bronsard (1975)). However, there are other matrices which have been called the Antonelli matrix: all describe the Jacobian matrix of derivatives of a normal vector to an indifference surface, but they differ in the normalization choice for this vector. Particularly that considered by Deaton (1979) has no simple relationship with the one of this text. The optimal tax formulas for the Ramsey problem, simply derived using this Antonelli matrix, reproduce results found in Atkinson–Stiglitz (1972). The approach through 'composite commodities' seems to have no counterpart in the literature. Feldstein (1973) introduced 'distributional characteristics' of goods and the concept used here with the same name is indeed the same. Work that stress the complexity of the one-consumer case include Blackorby, Davidson–Schworm (1990).

Section 4.3.2 considers the one-consumer economy with offsetting lump-sum income considered in the literature on the reduction of distortions. Following Guesnerie (1980), theorem 5 presents a sample of the main findings of this literature. All these results except perhaps (2) (see theorem 5) are already summarized in Dixit (1975). Additional work that rules out the existence of offsetting lump-sum income in the previous one-consumer economy can be found in Hatta (1986) and Haltiwanger–Hatta (1986).

The simple two-consumer model of section 4 has been studied by Stiglitz (1987) who termed 'normal' the situation leading to the 'redistributive and well-behaved' optimum of theorem 6 (see however the reservations on how 'normal' this situation is at the end of the section). Formulas having the flavour of (4.48) had been derived by Mirrlees (1986) in a more general setting involving a continuum of consumers. Also, Atkinson–Stiglitz (1976) first proved (a more general version of) corollary 6. Given the tractability problem, the most recent work takes place in the Stiglitz two-consumer framework. Little is known on the structure of tax equilibria although the remarks made here suggest that a lot can be derived from the results of chapter 2. The tax reform problem with non-linear taxes has not been much studied. A noticeable exception is Konishi (1992). Recent contributions on the model of section 4 include Boadway–Marchand–Pestieau (1992), Boadway–Keen (1993), Nava (1993). In particular the latter two deal with the problem of valuation of public goods and derive (versions of) proposition 3. Boadway–Keen (1993), who are a priori concerned with the 'fully' non-linear case, discuss in depth the public goods provision rule, extending and clarifying results of Christiansen (1981, 1984).

# 5

# Political economics of taxation

## 5.1 Introduction (*)

The previous chapters have successively considered institutional aspects (chapter 1), positive aspects (chapter 2), and normative aspects of taxation (chapters 3 and 4). Throughout the analysis, the task of implementing fiscal systems is supposed to be accomplished by some central body. The nature of this central body has remained deliberately vague, a fact that is reflected in a hesitant terminology: central fiscal authorities, state, government, planner. Indeed the role of this central body is not necessarily the same across the chapters. It is (implicitly) in charge of implementing the different tax systems which are compared in the positive analysis of taxation of chapter 2. In chapter 1, the central body faces informational constraints that are inherent to the problem and that impose restrictions on its taxation power. The situation is somewhat different in chapter 3, particularly when the emphasis is switched from the Pareto criterion to a social welfare criterion. Endowed with such a social welfare function, the central authorities are no longer a passive coordinating body, but an active institution selecting taxation schemes through discriminatory criteria. This latter assumption raises the question of the nature of the social welfare criteria chosen for the selection of taxation schemes or, equivalently, of the nature of the central body which uses such criteria.

According to one dominant tradition among public economists, the social welfare function is derived from basic equity considerations. The central body internalizes then the society's ethical concerns. This normative conception faces the difficulty of designing a justice criterion which would be evident: utilitarianism leads to a spectrum of candidate social welfare functions depending on the degree of risk aversion imbedded in the individual's cardinal representation of utility and including at the limit the Rawlsian egalitarian criterion of justice. Also, the assumption that agents have the same cardinal utility function – which allows an easy transcription of the precepts of utilitarianism – has less appeal in the multi-commodity, multi-factor world that we are considering here than in the stylized models of income taxation where utilitarian criteria have been popular.[1] Beyond these conceptual and modelling problems, the ethical viewpoint faces the objection of ignoring political bargaining in the determination of the tax system. Indeed the bargaining process which would lead to the adoption of some version of a Benthamite social welfare function (the Rawlsian function being an extreme case) should be held before the agents know the characteristics that will determine their welfare (e.g., productivity). Actual political processes are less idealistic and involve agents who are aware of their characteristics and whose interests differ from what they were behind the veil of ignorance.

It is the purpose of this chapter to propose reflections on political aspects of the choice of tax systems. We still assume the existence of a central body in charge of organizing the fiscal system and facing the incentive constraints described in chapter 1. But instead of relying on the equity axioms underlying Rawlsian or Benthamite criteria, central authorities receive their instructions from the interested agents of the economy (here households) through some 'political' channels. We assume that these instructions lead to the selection of a second-best Pareto optimal outcome,[2] so that the framework of analysis of the previous chapters is unaffected but for one point: the selection between second-best Pareto optima is not made according to an exogenous criterion. Said differently, the purpose of this chapter is to discuss the endogenization of the exogenous social welfare function of chapter 3.

The analysis proceeds as follows.

Section 5.2 analyses the structure of the second best Pareto optimal tax systems. It attempts to shed light on the nature of conflicts (between households) in the choice of tax systems. Section 5.2.1 introduces simple

[1] There has been many discussions on these issues. The concept of fundamental preferences of Tinbergen, Kolm (1972) should play a central role in such discussions.

[2] The fact that the political process leads to a second-best Pareto optimal outcome is, on basic grounds, a debatable hypothesis. An explicit defence of this viewpoint is provided through the game theoretical analysis of the society's taxation decision developed in the second part of the chapter. We may want to note, however, that such an analysis views the central body (the 'state') as some operator whose action is a pure reflection of the conflicting forces of the society.

If instead of being an operator in the game we are considering later, the central body were a player – or a collection of players – having its own interest, then second-best Pareto optimality (in the sense considered in this chapter) would not be guaranteed (even if it were posited as an assumption on the outcome of the extended bargaining process that would have to be considered). This alternative view is both suggested by the modern theory of organizations and by the Public Choice School! Whatever the opinion one may have on the interest of this alternative view, one may conjecture that it is more complement than substitute to the present approach.

examples that are useful reference points for the whole chapter; in particular, the analysis of an economy whose set of tax equilibria is two-dimensional conveys the intuition on which the development of the next section is based. The main purpose of the analysis of section 5.2.2 is to exhibit the 'geometry' of the set of second-best Pareto optima. Theorem 1 and its corollaries – that imply that this set is generically a small set in the set of equilibria when the number of households is small – confirms the conjecture suggested by a former inspection of simple examples.

Section 5.3 first briefly discusses how existing results on voting games would apply. Then it presents a full analysis of the social choice problem induced by taxation when the manifold of equilibria is one-dimensional. In particular, this analysis provides a comprehensive appraisal, within the present model, of what has been called the Laffer controversy.

Section 5.4 introduces the alternative option, developed later in the chapter, of basing the 'political' analysis on game theoretical concepts. This second approach stresses the power given to agents by secession threats of coalitions. It is pursued in section 5.5. The analysis is conducted in the framework of a simple version of our general model where the decision space is one-dimensional.

The analysis of the last two sections shows that in spite of the strength of the standard argument that the per capita cost of public good decreases with the size of the society, the cohesion of a society that uses second-best tools for financing public goods may be vulnerable to credible secession threats from coalitions (cohesion is here tested with the core game-theoretical concept). Increasing returns to size, as reflected in the diminution of per capita cost, have to be compared to decreasing returns to size in decision making due to the increased difficulty in larger, and therefore more heterogeneous, societies, to agree on the (joint) financing and production decisions. This second effect, decreasing returns to size in decision making, disappears when lump-sum transfers are available – since such transfers allow the distribution of any surplus in a Pareto-improving manner — and then has a typically second-best character. Decreasing returns to size in decision making are overcome by increasing returns to size in the use of public good under conditions made clear, in the simple second-best model under consideration, by theorems 5, 6, 7 and 8. When they are not, a stable structure of coalitions may still emerge in the conditions of theorem 1.

## 5.2 The structure of the set of Pareto optimal tax equilibria (***)

A preliminary analysis of examples (2.1) introduces assumptions that will be helpful later on and conveys the intuition of the generic result of section 2.2 (theorem 1).

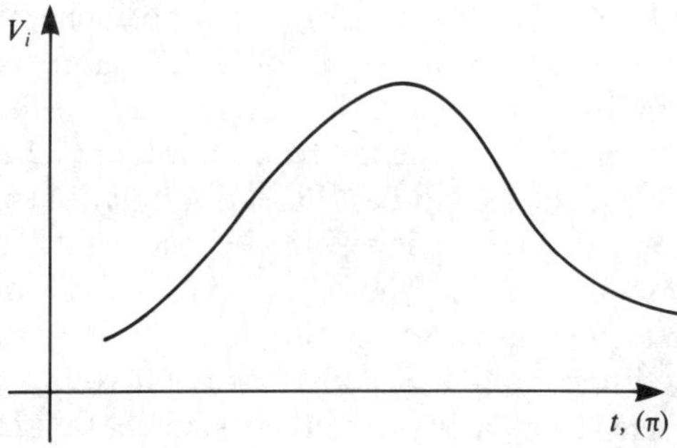


Figure 5.1

### 5.2.1 A preliminary analysis of examples (*)

A preliminary discussion of examples will be most helpful to the understanding of the problem under scrutiny. The first example is a one-dimensional example aimed at discussing indirect preferences of households over the set of equilibria. The second one, a two-dimensional example, conveys the intuition of the analysis of next section.

Let us first come back on example 1 of chapter 2. The economy has two private goods (labour and consumption) and one public good. Households are endowed with one unit of leisure and have Cobb–Douglas utility functions $U_i = \alpha_i \log z_{i1} + \beta_i \log z_{i2} + \gamma_i \log y'_0$. With a constant returns to scale production sector, the set of tax equilibria is easy to compute. If $t$ is the specific tax on the consumption commodity (labour being the numeraire), we have shown that the equation of the set of tax equilibria is $y'_0 = K\dfrac{t}{1+t}$ where $K$ is a number depending upon the coefficients of the agents' utility functions ($K = \sum_i \beta_i$). Remember also that indirect preferences of the agents as a function of $y'_0$ and $t$ are of the form $V_i = \dfrac{(y'_0)^{\gamma_i}}{(1+t)^{\beta_i}}$.

The set of tax equilibria as well as the agents' indifference curves have been visualized on figure 2.2, chapter 2, to which the reader is referred. Let us focus attention here on the household's utility across the set of tax equilibria. The agent's utility along the manifold is visualized in figure 5.1 which plots the agent's indirect utility $V_i$ as a function of the manifold's parameter $t$. Note that the qualitative features of the diagram do not depend upon which variable has been chosen to parametrize the manifold: here it could be $y'_0$ or even the curviline abscissa of a tax equilibrium along the manifold; obviously it could also be $\pi$ the consumption price (cf. chapter 2).

It is left to the reader to show that indirect utility is a quasi-concave function of $t$ (combine $V_i$ above with the equation of the manifold and (for simplicity) take the logarithm of the expression and compute the first and second derivatives with respect to $t$). A given household has a most preferred tax $t_i^* = \gamma_i/\beta_i$; his utility decreases when the tax goes away from this 'bliss' point. In other words, the agent's preferences are *single peaked.*

Note at this stage some additional properties of the set of tax equilibria and of preferences to which the assumptions of sections 5.3, 5.4 will refer.

When the set of agents participating to the economy becomes larger, then $\Sigma\beta_i$ increases and for any given value of $t$, $y_0'$ increases as well as the utility of any given household increases. This property relates to the assumption IRSW of section 5.3.

In the space $(y_0', t)$, at each point, the agents' marginal rates of substitution can be ranked in a way that does not depend upon the bundle under consideration. This is the standard Spence–Mirrlees single crossing condition, associated later with URP.[3]

The ranking is in fact the ranking of $\gamma_i/\beta_i$. Agents with a higher value of $\gamma_i/\beta_i$ have to be compensated by a smaller value of additional public good for a slight given increase in taxes. Note that it is the case that the agents who 'like more tax', in the just defined sense, also have a higher 'most preferred tax'.

Now, as in chapter 2, let us consider the same example but with one more consumption good. We know from the general theorems of chapter 2 that the set of tax equilibria is diffeomorphic to $\mathscr{R}^2$. In fact, we know from the beginning of chapter 2 that the set can be parametrized by $t_2$ and $t_3$, the taxes on the two consumption goods. In order to visualize the 'indirect' indifference surfaces in the plan $t_2$, $t_3$, we can refer to the previous example. For a given tax level ($t_3 = \bar{t}_3$ for example), the computation of chapter 2 shows that the section of the set of tax equilibria is similar to the one-dimensional set of the previous example. Hence indirect preferences restricted to this section should have the qualitative features depicted in figure 5.1. This remark helps us to understand the indirect preferences of figure 5.2.

Again, the figure shows the existence of a bliss point, the 'most preferred' tax system of the household whose indirect preferences have been visualized. With two more households, the picture would look like figure 5.3, where B and C are the bliss points of the two other households.

Consider the curve AB (resp. BC, CA): it is the locus of points in which the indifference curves, of two households whose bliss points respectively

[3] It is well known that such a condition plays a crucial role in incentives theory (see Guesnerie–Laffont (1985)).

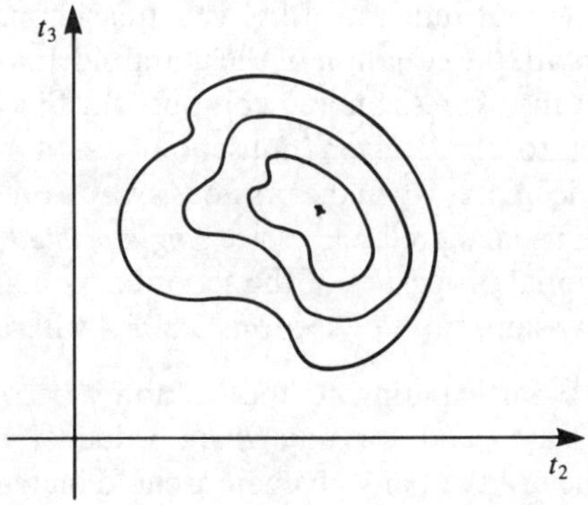


Figure 5.2

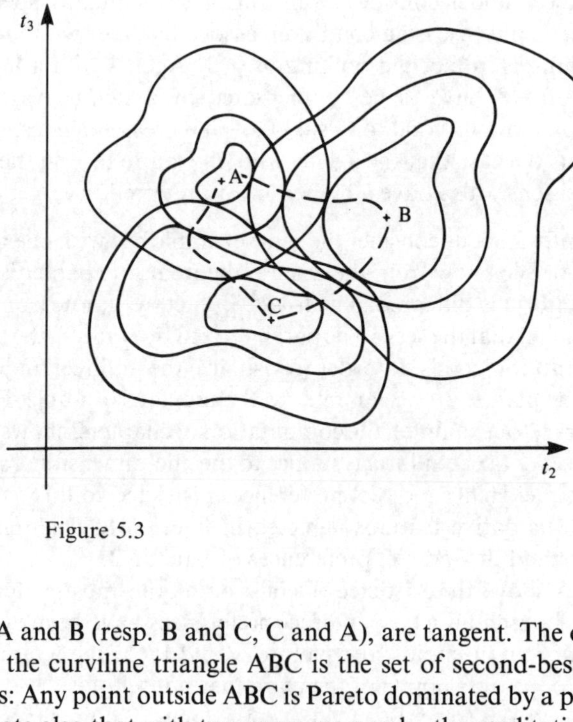


Figure 5.3

are A and B (resp. B and C, C and A), are tangent. The diagram suggests that the curviline triangle ABC is the set of second-best Pareto optimal taxes: Any point outside ABC is Pareto dominated by a point inside ABC.

Note also that with two consumers only, the qualitative features of the diagram would remain unaffected. The set of second-best Pareto optima could reduce for example the curve AB; it would be negligible in the set of tax equilibria. The above examination of our four-good economy calls for a number of remarks:

1 Figure 5.3 suggests that the set of second-best Pareto optima has nice topological properties; i.e., here to be topologically similar to a simplex. As shown elsewhere[4] it is actually true that such a property holds when preferences are convex. When they are not, it is generally more complicated. As the preferences we are considering here are indirect preferences over the manifold of tax equilibria, convexity is unlikely; it is even difficult to identify a large enough class of economies in which such a property would hold. No significant result of the Zeckhauser–Weinstein type can be expected in our framework. We will not pursue this line of investigation here.

2 Roughly speaking, the size of the set of second-best Pareto optima depends upon the diversity of indirect preferences, as visualized by the dispersion of the bliss points and of the number of households: with two households, the set of second-best Pareto optima is negligible when with three it is 'big' in the set of tax equilibria. This intuition will be rigorously formulated in next subsection 5.2.2.

3 The problem of choosing a tax system is isomorphic to a standard social choice problem, the set of alternatives being indentified with $\mathscr{R}^2_+$. The general results of voting theory then apply. Some consequences of this remark will be taken up in section 5.3.

### 5.2.2 The size of the set of second-best Pareto optima (T***)

The above example suggests that the relative number of households and commodities is a key variable for the determination of the size of the set of second-best Pareto optima. The objective of the present section is to provide a more rigorous and general analysis of the graphical intuition that has been developed. Theorem 1 and its two corollaries indeed conveys a message that captures the flavour of the previous argument in a more general setting.

The set of tax equilibria of our economy is again identified with $p, \pi, R, y_0'$, i.e., with previous notation

$$\epsilon = \{(p, \pi, R, y_0') \in A \mid d(\pi, R, y_0') - \eta(y_0', p) = 0\}$$

$\epsilon$ is the set of interior tax equilibria with the terminology of chapter 2. Let us consider the subset of tax equilibria which meets the necessary conditions for second-best Pareto optimality, i.e.

$$p \cdot \partial_\pi d(\pi, R, y_0') + \Sigma \lambda_i d_i(\pi, R, y_0') = 0 \tag{5.1}$$

[4] See Zeckhauser–Weinstein (1974).

$$p{\cdot}\partial_R d(\pi, R, y_0') - \Sigma\lambda_i = 0 \tag{5.2}$$

$$p{\cdot}(\partial_{y_0'} d - \partial_{y_0'}\eta) - \sum_i \lambda_i C_i(\pi, R, y_0') = 0 \tag{5.3}$$

where $C_i(\ )$ is the function of marginal willingness to pay for the public goods (previously defined in chapter 3).

The interior tax equilibria in $\epsilon$ meeting the necessary conditions for second-best Pareto optimality will be called **Pareto equilibria**.

Formally:

$\mathscr{P} \subset \epsilon$, the set of **Pareto equilibria** is the subset of points in $\epsilon$, for which $\exists \lambda_i > 0$, $i = 1 \ldots m$, such that conditions (5.1) to (5.3) hold.

The above examples suggest a property of the size of second-best Pareto optima which could plausibly translate into the following statement.

In the sense of 'generic' to be defined (and with appropriate differentiability assumptions) the following holds:

> 'Generically', the set of Pareto equilibria is a smooth manifold of dimension $d = \min\{m-1, n+n'-1\}$

A fully satisfactory definition of genericity should refer to the basic data of the economy (preferences, production sets). A somewhat less ambitious approach should take as basic objects the supply and demand functions under consideration. The notion of genericity which we will refer to, similar to the one used in chapter 2 for the study of the generic properties of the set of tax equilibria, is still less satisfactory. However, while keeping the argument simple, it goes significantly beyond the 'number of equations, number of unknowns' argument in capturing the relevant ideas.

Let us consider the mapping $\psi$: $A \times \mathscr{R}^m_+ \rightarrow \mathscr{R}^{2n+n'}$

$$\psi_h(p, \pi, R, y_0', \lambda_i) = d_h(\pi, R, y_0') - \eta_h(y_0', p) \qquad h = 1, \ldots n \tag{5.4}$$

$$\psi_{n+h}(p, \pi, R, y_0', \lambda_i) = \frac{1}{\sum_i \lambda_i}\left(\sum_k p_k{\cdot}\partial_{\pi_h} d_k(\pi, R, y_0') - \sum_{i=1}^m \lambda_i d_{ih}(\pi, R, y_0')\right) \tag{5.5}$$

$$h = 1, \ldots n-1$$

$$\psi_{2n}(p, \pi, R, y_0', \lambda_i) = p{\cdot}\partial_R d(\pi, y_0', R) - \sum_{i=1}^m \lambda_i \tag{5.6}$$

$$\psi_{2n+l}(p, \pi, R, y_0', \lambda_i) = p{\cdot}(\partial_{y_0'} d - \partial_{y_0'}\eta) - \sum_{i=1}^m \lambda_i C_i(\pi, R, y_0'), \; l = 1, \ldots n' \tag{5.7}$$

Let us consider $\omega \in \mathscr{R}^n$, $\nu \in \mathscr{R}^n$, $\mu \in \mathscr{R}^{n'}$ and $\alpha = (\omega, \nu, \mu) \in \mathscr{R}^{2n+n'}$. Let $V$ be a neighbourhood of zero and some $\alpha \in V$ such that, $\psi^{-1}(\alpha) \neq 0$. When $\alpha$ is in a neighbourhood of 0, a point in $\psi^{-1}(\alpha)$ is 'almost' a tax equilibrium (market clearing obtains with a vector $\omega$ of exogenous endowments) in which the necessary conditions for second-best Pareto optimality are 'almost' satisfied (the discrepancies being measured by $\mu$ and $\nu$). Slightly differently, we can interpret $\mathscr{P}(\alpha)=\{(p,\pi,R,y_0')|\exists\lambda_i>0 \text{ s.t. } \psi(\cdot)=\alpha\}$ as the set of $\alpha$-(almost) Pareto equilibria in the economy 'close' to the initial economy, whose set of tax equilibria is $\epsilon(\alpha)=\{(p,\pi,R,y_0')|\psi_h(\cdot)=\alpha_h,\ h=1,\dots n\}$.

Both interpretations are compatible with the 'proximity' of the $\alpha$ economy and the initial economy and with the fact that $\epsilon(0)$ and $\mathscr{P}(0)$ are actually the set of interior tax equilibria and of Pareto equilibria in the initial economy: this latter property is easily checked if we note that the (apparently) missing equality in (5.5) when compared to (5.1) obtains from (5.5), (5.6) when the homogeneity of $d_i$ in $\pi$, $R$ is taken into account.[5]

Let us then define the **maximal dimension of** $\mathscr{P}(\alpha)$ as the dimension of the subsets of $\mathscr{P}(\alpha)$ which are of highest dimension. When $\mathscr{P}(\alpha)$ is a smooth manifold, the maximal dimension equals the dimension of the manifold.

One can then show:

**Theorem 1: Generic dimension of Pareto equilibria**

*Assume that $d_i, \eta, C_i$ are $C^\infty$ on the interior of their domain and that there exists a neighbourhood $V$ of 0 in $\mathscr{R}^{2n+n'}$ such that for all $\alpha\in V$, $\mathscr{P}(\alpha)\neq 0$. Then for a set of $\alpha$ in $V$, whose complement is of Lebesgue measure zero, the maximal dimension of $\mathscr{P}(\alpha)$, the set of $\alpha$-(almost) Pareto equilibria is at most*

$$d=\min\begin{Bmatrix}(m-1)\\ n+n'-1\end{Bmatrix}.$$

*Proof* (sketch)

Let us consider $\psi: A\times\mathscr{R}^m_+\to\mathscr{R}^{2n+n'}$ as defined by (5.4) to (5.7). Note that the dimension of $A$ is $2n-1+n'$.

According to Sard's theorem, the set of critical values of $\psi$ in $\mathscr{R}^{2n+n'}$ is of Lebesgue measure zero. Hence, outside this set, it follows from the preimage theorem that $\psi^{-1}(\alpha)$ is a smooth manifold of dimension $2n-1+n'+m-(2n+n')=(m-1)$.

Now, let the projection operator (from $A\times\mathscr{R}^m_+$ on $A$) be denoted Proj. Let us consider its restriction RProj: $\psi^{-1}(\alpha)\to\epsilon(\alpha)$. The image of this mapping is nothing other than the set $\mathscr{P}(\alpha)$. Take an $\alpha$ which is both a regular value of $\psi$ and such that $\epsilon(\alpha)$ is a smooth manifold. The dimension of the starting set ($\psi^{-1}(\alpha)$) is $m-1$ and the dimension of the arrival set ($\epsilon(\alpha)$) is $n+n'-1$. Using theorem 5, chapter 2, this occurs outside a subset of Lebesgue measure zero. Hence the conclusion. □

[5] A fact that was already mentioned in corollary 1 of theorem 1 in chapter 3.

This statement is clearly unsatisfactory on several grounds.

As noted above, this statement provides information on the set of 'almost equilibria' and 'almost Pareto equilibria' rather than on the sets of equilibria and Pareto equilibria for neighbour economies. Also, we have *not* obtained the more appealing statement: $\mathscr{P}(\alpha)$ is a smooth manifold of dimension $d = \min(m-1, n+n'-1)$. Finally, even within the present framework and even assuming the genericity of the manifold property, our conclusion only holds for a dense set of $\alpha$ and not for an open dense set. The more satisfactory statement we would have liked to obtain, i.e., that $\mathscr{P}(0)$ is generically smooth manifold of dimension $d$ would require additional ingredients. At the least, we should use a notion of neighbouring economies more sophisticated than the one we have introduced here, allowing perturbations of the derivatives of the functions under consideration. The more satisfactory option would be to take infinite dimensional basic objects but the analysis would have to then rely upon more abstract transversality theorems.

Directly in line with the previous example of subsection 5.2.1, two corollaries that hold in the weak 'generic' sense stressed in the theorem are worth emphasizing:

**Corollary 1** *If $m < n + n'$, then the set of Pareto equilibria is a null set in the set of interior tax equilibria.*

Also as interior second-best Pareto optima are necessarily included in the set of interior Pareto equilibria, as defined above, the following holds.

**Corollary 2** *If $m < n + n'$, then the set of 'interior' second-best Pareto optima is a null set of the set of tax equilibria.*

Note that in the previous example of section 5.2.1, the uniform lump-sum transfer was not considered a policy variable. It is easy to show that in this case the relevant inequality for finding null sets of Pareto equilibria is $m < n + n' - 1$. We were in the case $m = 2$, $n = 3$, $n' = 1$. The set of second-best Pareto optima was indeed a null set.

## 5.3 Taxation as a social choice or a game theoretical problem (**)

### 5.3.1 The choice between tax systems as a 'social choice' problem (**)

The understanding of the political economics of taxation in a democratic society should benefit from the analysis of the 'voting games' of social choice theory. In this respect, the analysis of this book brings some good news since under the conditions of theorem 6 of chapter 2 voting over the set of tax equilibria can be identified with voting over a $n+n'-1$ dimensional space of alternatives. And voting over a set of alternatives that has the structure of a Euclidean space is a classical problem in social choice theory. The bunch of results of voting theory that apply in this framework[6] can then be transposed to our problem. These results can however be viewed either as 'positive' or 'negative' according to whether they give or do not give an optimistic picture of the voting problem.

Indeed some so-called 'positive' results can be transposed to our problem. For example, section 5.1 focused attention on a one-dimensional set of tax equilibria over which the voting game has a Condorcet winner. However, many other higher dimensional 'positive' results have no easy transcription here. Take as an example, the necessary and sufficient conditions for the existence of a $d$-majority equilibrium;[7] they rely upon a convexity assumption for preferences, and such an assumption should apply here to indirect preferences. It is difficult to identify direct preferences and technologies which would generate such indirect preferences.

The question then arises which subset of 'negative' results of voting theory are relevant to the present analysis. The answer depends on the actual specificities of our taxation problem when compared to a general social choice problem. Is it the case that any social choice problem with an $n+n'-1$ dimensional set of alternatives homeomorphic to $\mathscr{R}^{n+n'-1}$ and any a priori given set of $m$ preference preorderings can be interpreted as a tax problem arising in an economy with $n$ private goods, $n'$ public goods, and $m$ tax payers? Or on the contrary does the taxation problem introduce restrictions on the nature of the social choice problem?

To the best of my knowledge, the answers to these questions are not known in general. But in a paper with M. Jerison[8] we have proved that the taxation social choice problem associated with a one-dimensional manifold of tax equilibria is a general social choice problem in the sense that the indirect preferences over the one-dimensional set of alternatives – as defined in previous subsection – have 'universal domain' (to take the terminology of social choice theory).

I will sketch in the remainder of this subsection a simplified and partial version of the Guesnerie–Jerison argument.

We consider then an economy with two private goods – good 1 is labour and good 2 is the consumption good – and one public good and we assume that the public good is produced from labour following a constant returns

[6] See for example Moulin (1983).

[7] $d$-majority requires the agreement of $d$ voters at least to enforce a change (see Greenberg (1979)). [8] Guesnerie–Jerison (1991).

to scale production technology. (One unit of labour gives one unit of public good.) Also preferences of the consumers are additively separable between public goods and private goods.

We adopt the standard normalization that labour is the numeraire so that the price systems are described by two numbers, $\pi$ the consumption price of the consumption good and $p$ its production price, and a tax equilibrium consists of a triple $p$, $\pi$, $y'_0$.

In this context, our general market-clearing equations take the following form

$$\sum_i d_{i1}(\pi) = \eta_1(p) - y'_0 \tag{5.8a}$$

$$\sum_i d_{i2}(\pi) = \eta_2(p) \tag{5.8b}$$

where the individual budget balance implies that

$$\pi d_{i2}(\pi) = -d_{i1}(\pi)$$

And if $g$ is the cost function associated with the private sector technology, ($g(x)$ is then the quantity of labour required for producing $x$ unit of private good), we have $-\eta_1(p) = g(\eta_2(p))$.[9] The function $g$ is assumed to be strictly convex and 'enough' differentiable.

Taking into account the budget balance and the cost function, equations (5.8) are equivalent to

$$\sum_i \pi d_{i2}(\pi) = g\left(\sum_i d_{i2}(\pi)\right) + y'_0$$

Let us denote, in conformance with previous convention, $\sum_i d_{i2}(\pi) = d_2(\pi)$ as $\tilde{d}(\pi)$; then we have

$$y'_0 = \pi\tilde{d}(\pi) - g(\tilde{d}(\pi)) \tag{5.9}$$

But (5.9) is nothing other than the explicit form of the global parametrization of the manifold of tax equilibria the general validity of which has been shown in theorem 8, chapter 2. With the notation of chapter 2, $y'_0 = \mathcal{Y}(\pi)$ and

$$\mathcal{Y}(\pi) = \pi\tilde{d}(\pi) - g(\tilde{d}(\pi)) \tag{5.10}$$

In the present one-dimensional context, we will adopt a public finance terminology and call $\mathcal{Y}$ the tax-revenue function: indeed $\pi$ is a parameter

9 In fact $g = -\eta_1 \circ \eta_2^{-1}$. In order to see that, one notes that $\eta_2$ is increasing in $p$ and hence invertible: $p = \eta_2^{-1}(x)$. Note also that next formula (5.10) may obtain more quickly from the budget balance (proposition 1, chapter 2).

that indexes the tax system choice and $\mathscr{Y}(\pi)$ the public good level is also the government revenue.

An immediate question comes to mind: what can we say of the shape of the tax revenue function that is not known from the general theorems?

In a first step, we shall point out a number of necessary conditions that have to be fulfilled by the function $\mathscr{Y}$. Then, we will exhibit a large family of functions $\mathscr{Y}$ – satisfying these necessary conditions – that describe the manifold of tax equilibria in economies where the production technology is fixed but where the characteristics of consumer demand are changed. Finally the consequences of this latter fact for the social choice taxation problem will be made explicit.

Consider (5.10) and assume that $\tilde{d}$ is decreasing in $\pi$. The first point to note is that there exists a unique[10] $\pi^*$ such that $\pi^* = g'(\tilde{d}(\pi^*))$. This is the Walrasian price that occurs in the absence of commodity taxes. For such a price, however, the level of public good $\mathscr{Y}(\pi^*)$ is not zero but, since pure profits are taxed, equal to the profit of the private firm $\pi^* \cdot \tilde{d}(\pi^*) - g(\tilde{d}(\pi^*))$ at the Walrasian equilibrium.

Second, consider the profit function of the private firm and call it $\rho$.

$$\rho(p) \overset{\text{def}}{=} \max_{x \geq 0} \{p \cdot x - g(x)\} \tag{5.11}$$

Then it follows immediately from (5.10) that

$$\mathscr{Y}(\pi) \leq \rho(\pi)^{11} \tag{5.12}$$

and we have just shown that

$$\mathscr{Y}(\pi^*) = \rho(\pi^*) \tag{5.13}$$

The inequality (5.12) is strict for every $\pi$ that is not a Walrasian price, i.e., for $\pi \neq \pi^*$.

Also, considering the derivatives of $\mathscr{Y}$, $\rho$ with respect to $\pi$ in $\pi^*$, simple algebra shows that

$$\mathscr{Y}'(\pi^*) = \rho'(\pi^*) = \tilde{d}(\pi^*) \tag{5.14}$$

Limiting our attention to the prices $\pi/\pi \geq \pi^*$, we can summarize our findings as follows by **condition (C)** illustrated on figure 5.4.

*(C) The graph of $\mathscr{Y}$ is strictly below the graph of $\rho$ and tangent to the graph of $\rho$ at $\pi^*$.*

10 As $g'$ is an increasing function (convexity of cost) and $\tilde{d}$ is a decreasing function, the right-hand side of the equality is a decreasing function of $\pi$ and then $\pi^*$ is unique. ($\pi^*$ exists if $g'(0) = 0$ and $d_i(\pi) \to +\infty$, $\pi \to +\infty$ as we implicitly assume).

11 Coming back to the canonical form of equation (5.8) it is easy to see that such a property has general scope (take the inner product of equations (5.8) by the vector $\pi$).

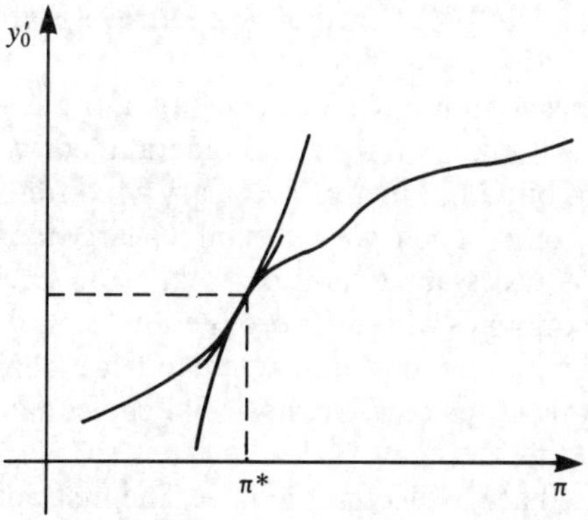

Figure 5.4

Now consider a function $\mathscr{Y}$ that satisfies condition C for some $\pi^*$: we shall say that $\mathscr{Y}$ is a function **compatible** with technology $\rho$.

If we fix the private technology $g$, $\rho$ and vary the aggregate demand function $\tilde{d}$ – while remaining in the set of downward-sloping demand functions – we will generate a family of tax revenue functions $\mathscr{Y}$ that are compatible with the fixed technology $\rho$. We now exhibit such a subset of possible tax revenue functions.

For that consider the following family of functions denoted $SSH$ $(\pi^*)$.

$\phi \in SSH$ $(\pi^*)$ if the set $\{(\pi, y) | y \leq \phi(\pi),\ \pi \geq \pi^*\}$ is **star-shaped** from $\{\pi^*, \phi(\pi^*)\}$.

The set $\{(\pi, y) | y \leq \phi(\pi), \pi \geq \pi^*\}$ is star shaped here if and only if it contains the line that joins the point $\{\pi^*, \phi(\pi^*)\}$ and any point $\{\pi, \phi(\pi)\}$ $\pi \geq \pi^*$ that is on the graph. Equivalently, the slope $\dfrac{\phi(\pi) - \phi(\pi^*)}{\pi - \pi^*}$ is decreasing, i.e., when the function $\phi$ is derivable, $\phi'(\pi) - \dfrac{\phi(\pi) - \phi(\pi^*)}{\pi - \pi^*}$ is negative.

It is remarkable that the graphs of all functions in $SSH(\pi^*)$ can be identified with a manifold of tax equilibria in our given economy. Precisely:

**Theorem 2[12]: Tax revenue functions**

*Consider the economy defined by equation (5.8) where the private production technology g and its corresponding profit function $\rho$ are given but where aggregate demand can vary.*

*Any function $\mathscr{Y}$ that is compatible with the technology $\rho$ (for some $\pi^*$)*

[12] The proof assumes that $y$ and $g$ are $C^2$ but this is sharper than needed. Also we do not explicitly consider some $\pi | y(\pi) = 0$.

*and that belongs to* $SSH(\pi^*)$ *is the tax revenue function for* $\pi \geq \pi^*$ *of an economy (with technology* $\rho$*) with an appropriately chosen downward-sloping aggregate demand function.*

*Proof*

Let us consider such a function $\mathcal{Y}$ and for each $\pi > \pi^*$ consider the equation

$$\mathcal{Y}(\pi) = \pi x - g(x)$$

The left-hand side is a concave function of $x$ that is strictly increasing between 0 and $\eta_2(\pi^*)$, (the optimal supply of the private sector when faced with price $\pi$).

Hence, if as assumed $\mathcal{Y}(\pi) \leq \rho(\pi)$, the above equation has always one and only one solution that belongs to $[0, \eta_2(\pi^*)]$. Let us call $d(\pi)$ such a solution; it is clearly continuous in $\pi$.[13]

But $\mathcal{Y}(\pi) = \pi d(\pi) - g(d(\pi))$ is from equation (5.10) the equation of the manifold of tax equilibria of the economy with technology $g$ (and profit function $\rho$) and demand function $d$ – an economy whose unique Walrasian equilibrium is indeed $\pi^*$.

It remains to show that $d(\pi)$ is decreasing in $\pi$.

Differentiating the above equality yields

$$\mathcal{Y}'(\pi) = [\pi - g(d(\pi))]d'(\pi) + d(\pi) \tag{5.15}$$

But the star shaped inequality $\mathcal{Y}'(\pi) - \dfrac{\mathcal{Y}(\pi) - \mathcal{Y}(\pi^*)}{\pi - \pi^*} < 0$ stressed above implies

$$(\pi - \pi^*)[\pi - g(d(\pi))]d'(\pi) \leq -d(\pi)(\pi - \pi^*) + \mathcal{Y}(\pi) - \mathcal{Y}(\pi^*)$$

But, using equation (5.10) and the fact that $\pi^* = g'(d(\pi^*))$ the right-hand side reduces to $g(d(\pi^*)) - g(d(\pi)) - g'(d(\pi^*))[d(\pi^*) - d(\pi)]$. The latter expression is from the strict convexity of $g$ strictly negative. Since $d'(\pi)$ on the left-hand side is multiplied by a positive number, $d'(\pi)$ is negative. □

Theorem 2 exhibits a large[14] set of possible manifold of tax equilibria (or tax revenue functions) for the simple model under consideration.

In particular as suggested by figure 5.5 it is remarkable that the function may go up and down an arbitrary number of times – although after a

[13] And continuously differentiable if $\mathcal{Y}$ and $g$ are $C^2$.
See Guesnerie–Jerison (1991) for a more careful discussion of all the technical aspects of this subsection.

[14] There are still many possible functions $y$ other than those meeting the star shape condition. See Guesnerie-Jerison (1991) for a necessary and sufficient condition that characterizes such $\mathcal{Y}$.

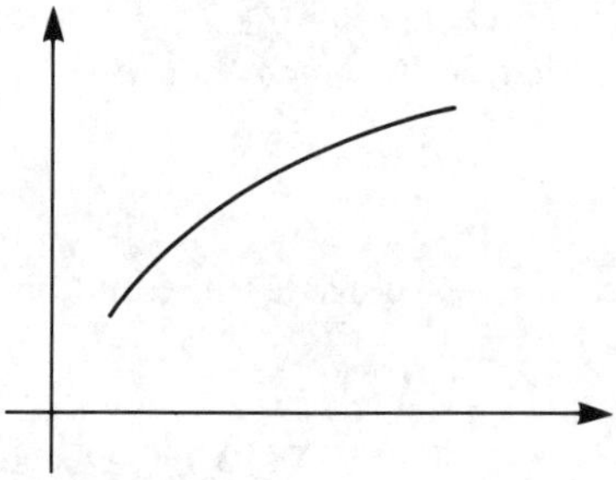

(a)

Figure 5.5a

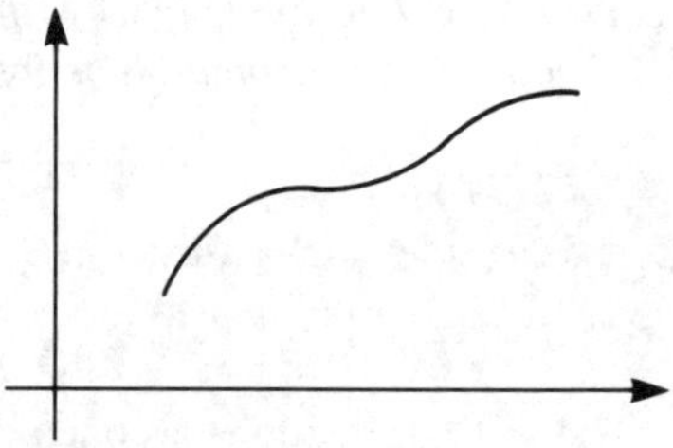

(b)

Figure 5.5b

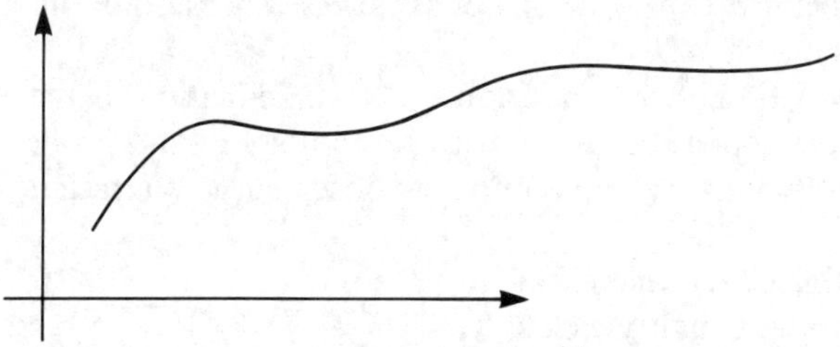

(c)

Figure 5.5c

downturn, the curve must go up more slowly in order to meet the star shape condition.

The above analysis will not be pursued any longer. We will content ourselves with drawing a number of consequences for the social choice problem under consideration.

We should first note that there are many ways to generate a given downward-sloping aggregate demand function from individual demand functions of individual utility maximizers. In fact, we can take any set of $n$ decreasing functions $d_i(\pi)$ such that $\sum_i d_i(\pi) = d(\pi)$.

A straightforward 'surplus' argument shows that $d_i(\pi)$ is the utility-maximizing demand of $i$ when his preferences display separability between public and private goods and his preferences between private goods are represented by the utility function

$$U_i(l, x) = l + \int_0^x d_i^{-1}(\alpha)d\alpha^{15} \qquad (5.16)$$

where $l$ is the amount of leisure and $x$ the amount of the consumption good.

[15] Integration difficulties, if any, could be resolved.

The indirect utility function associated with this direct utility function $U_i$ – call it $V_i$ – satisfies $V_i'(\pi) = -d_i(\pi)$.

Now let us consider the economy $\rho$, with Walrasian price equilibrium $\pi^*$, and some (star shaped) tax revenue function $\phi$ (assumed to be differentiable). Call the points $\pi | \phi'(\pi) < 0$, the **dominated** prices: a dominated price will never be the outcome of a social choice procedure that would select efficient tax systems; decreasing $\pi$ from such a price would allow an increase in the public good level and hence would make everybody better off.

Then consider $m$ utility profiles $w_i(\pi)$ for $\pi \geq \pi^*$ that are subject to only one restriction, i.e., $\frac{w_1'}{\phi'}$ is uniformly bounded from above.

Such $m$ utility profiles can be shown to coincide – over the set of undominated prices – with the indirect utility profile of an $m$-consumer economy that has the tax revenue function $\phi$. In other words, there is no a priori restriction on the set of indirect utility profiles – or at least no restriction to the subset of non-dominated prices[16] – that are associated with a given tax revenue function.

The sketch of proof is the following: consider the following direct utility functions for the $m$ consumers $\mathcal{U}_i(l, x, y_0') = \Lambda_i(U_i(l, x)) + r_i(y_0')$ where $U_i$ is the direct utility function proposed above and $\Lambda_i$, $r_i$ are two increasing functions. Such utility functions do generate the same individual demand functions as those generated by function $U_i$ and hence generate an economy with the tax revenue function $\phi$.

Now $i$'s indirect utility is $\Lambda_i(V_i(\pi) + r_i(\phi(\pi))$ an expression whose derivative is $-\Lambda_i'(\cdot)d_i(\pi) + r_i'(\phi(\pi))(\phi'(\pi))$.

Consider then the equation

$$w_i'(\pi) = -\Lambda_i'(\cdot)d_i(\pi) + r_i'(\cdot)\phi'(\pi) \tag{5.17}$$

By taking $r_i' > 0$ large enough one can have $w_i'(\pi) < r_i'\phi'(\pi)$ (over the set of $\pi / \phi'(\pi) \geqslant 0$). Take one function $r_i$ meeting this (weak) condition.

Then choose $\Lambda_i'$ such that the above equality holds. $\Lambda_i'$ will be positive and by integration will define a function $\Lambda_i$ and hence together with $r_i$ a set of indirect utility functions that have the desired properties. (Note however that the procedure does not work for $\pi / \phi'(\pi) \leqslant 0$.)

The result whose rationale has been sketched is more negative than what we could have expected. The taxation social choice problem has very few restrictions even when considered over set of economies that have the same tax revenue function (a rather 'small' set!).[17] The strongly negative aspect of

[16] In Guesnerie–Jerison (1991) the restriction to non-dominated prices is called a Laffer restriction. The reason for this terminology should be obvious to the reader.

[17] We are a little bit loose here since it is not quite clear that what happens on the dominated region of the manifold of tax equilibria should not matter for social choice.

the result – when one has in view restrictions on the taxation social problem – can however be qualified by noting that the above sketched procedure does not guarantee that the utility functions of consumers are concave in $(l, x, y_0')$. However, as shown in Guesnerie–Jerison, the result still holds if all consumers, except possibly one, have convex preferences.

In conclusion, we get here rather pessimistic prospects for the analysis of the taxation social choice problem. We switch in the next subsection to the analysis of the taxation game.

### 5.3.2 The choice between tax systems as a game theoretical problem (**)

The voting approach does not exhaust the study of the political economics of taxation. It assumes that the power of agents is exerted on a given set of alternatives and results from their voting rights. Such an approach ignores another element of the bargaining power of the agents which relates to the possibilities of 'exit', in Hirschman's sense,[18] which agents have. Indeed we will develop now a model with game theoretical inspiration in which the determination of the tax system is explained from the threat of secession which agents or groups of agents can make. In this approach the 'power' given by voting rights is not taken into account as such, the set of alternatives available to a group of agents varies, in particular according to the endowments of the agents of the group.

Formally, we proceed as follows:

We denote $\epsilon(S)$ the set of tax equilibria which obtains when the society only consists of coalition $S$. When demand and supply functions are single valued, $\epsilon(S)$ is identified with the set of $(p, \pi, R, y_0')$ such that

$$\sum_{i \in S} d_i(\pi, R, y_0') - \eta(y_0', p) = 0 \tag{5.18}$$

Note that the function $\eta$ is the same as in the general model, i.e., we assume that the production technology accessible to coalition $S$ is the same as the production technology accessible to the coalition of all agents (which is denoted $N$ and is referred to as the grand coalition).

Calling $V_i(\pi, R, y_0') = U_i(d_i(\pi, R, y_0'))$ the indirect utility function of agent $i$, a game in characteristic function form is defined as follows

$$v(S) = u = \{(u_1 \ldots u_m) | \forall_i \in S,\ u_i \leq V_i(e) \text{ for some } e \in \epsilon(S)\}^{19} \tag{5.19}$$

Note that $V(S)$ is limited by the second-best utility frontier of the coalition when it can rely upon its own resources. In particular, coalition $S$ is not allowed to cooperate with coalition $N - S$ for the use of public goods.

[18] Hirschman (1970).

[19] Following the notation of Shapley (1972), we associate, with an agent who does not belong to the coalition, any utility level.

This assumption assures the 'orthogonality' of the game and reflects, in the most standard game theoretic tradition, the minimax threat of coalition $S$. A similar assumption is usually made in the game theoretic study of public goods in a first-best context.[20]

The key point – when compared to the full information game theoretical studies of public goods – is that coalition $S$, as well as the society as a whole, is constrained to use incentive compatible tax systems, i.e., linear taxes and uniform lump-sum transfers. This clearly fits the spirit of our present study, but requires some discussion. The fact that the grand coalition is restricted to use tax systems follows from our basic informational assumptions as discussed in chapter 1. By imposing a restriction (on incentive compatible schemes) that is similar for coalition $S$ as for the grand coalition, we implicitly suppose that coalition $S$ is faced with the same informational constraints as the grand coalition $N$, i.e., that the actual distribution of characteristics of agents is public knowledge in coalition $S$, as well as in the grand coalition.[21] It should however be noted that the knowledge of the distribution within the coalition can be exploited only when the coalition is formed and not when the coalition is a subset of another coalition (for example a subset of the grand coalition). We come back on the discussion of this informational assumption when discussing the concept of core and stable solutions later.

At this stage, we can intuitively comment on what makes the strength of a coalition in our game: the coalition is strong first if it has high resources (for example, labour resources – since technological knowledge is the same across coalitions), but a coalition with large labour endowments could be made of agents who strongly disagree about the desirable tax system; such a disagreement cannot be alleviated by the use of personalized lump-sum transfers as in a first-best world. Hence, the homogeneity of opinions among households is a second element of strength of a coalition. As will be seen below, it plays a crucial role in our analysis.

A few words are in order to compare the present contribution with other

[20] For example Champsaur (1975).

[21] The question arises of whether such an assumption is in line with more basic informational assumptions on individual and collective knowledge. This subject would require more formal and more general discussion that is outside the scope of this section. Let us however give some flavour of the issue by considering the case emphasized in section 5 of chapter 1. In this case, agents' characteristics that are privately known are drawn independently from the same box of characteristics and this fact is the only public (common) knowledge.

In this case, the distribution of characteristics of the grand coalition as well as of any large coalition is (almost) public knowledge (by the law of large numbers) but the actual distribution of characteristics of small coalitions is very uncertain, at least if the knowledge of the coalition is assumed to be restricted to the common knowledge of all its members. This is not the assumption made here. We assume that any coalition can acquire at no cost the knowledge of its actual distribution of characteristics – but no more. An alternative, and completely different objection to the present procedure is that the incentive compatibility constraints can be alleviated in a small society where agents know each other better.

contributions to the political economics of taxation that have a similar spirit.

Our game theoretic analysis attempts to analyse the agents' power stemming from the threat of secession which they can make, and ignores the power which, in democratic societies, is associated with voting rights. It is different from the one initiated by Aumann–Kurz,[22] who took an intermediate viewpoint. The Aumann–Kurz characteristic function (which originally was applied in a 'first-best' economy) takes into account both the possibility that coalitions withdraw their resources and the democratic power of majorities. The other important difference with Aumann–Kurz is that we analyse secession threats with game theoretical concepts relating to the core and not with the Shapley value concept.

Our taxation game has now been defined and discussed. The remainder of the subsection introduces definitions and basic properties, the knowledge of which is required for the analysis of a simple version of the taxation game undertaken in the next section.

First, a few definitions are in order:

*Definition: A m-uple of utilities* $u^* = (u.^*, \ldots u^*_m)$ *belongs to the* **core** *of the game with characteristic function* $v$ *if and only if* $u^* \in v(N)$ *where* $N = \{1, \ldots m\}$ *is the grand coalition, and* $\nexists S$ *and* $u' \in v(S)$ *such that* $u' > u^*$ [23]

This is the standard definition of the core which in our context asserts that the grand coalition chooses a tax equilibrium which cannot be blocked by another coalition.

The core concept stresses outcomes which no coalition can object to. A positive interpretation of a core outcome of our game stresses that it is unblocked even under the informational assumptions that are more favourable to secession. A normative interpretation would emphasize the legitimacy of a core outcome since no coalition has 'grievances' that could be sustained even after the coalition has formed and learnt its distribution of characteristics.

However, the core concept is well adapted to superadditive games (when a game is not superadditive, there is no reason why the grand coalition should form). But one of the teachings of the next analysis is that the game under scrutiny is not necessarily superadditive. In this case, one has to consider the superadditive cover of the game $v$. Again, a number of definitions are in order. (Note that these definitions make sense and remain simple thanks to the notational convention stressed in footnote 19).

[22] Aumann–Kurz (1977a, b), (1978).

[23] Again our definition uses the Shapley convention mentioned in footnote 19.

*Definition:* **A structure of coalitions** *is a partition* $\Pi = (S_k)_{k \in K}$ *of the sets of agents N. The set of partitions of N is denoted T(N). For any* $\Pi = (S_k)_{k \in K}$, $\Pi \in T(N)$ *we denote* $v(\Pi) = \cap_{k \in K} v(S_k)$.

*Definition:* **An efficient outcome** *of the game is a vector* $\bar{u} \in \mathscr{R}^m_+$ *such that:*

(a) *There is* $\Pi \in T(N)$ *for which* $\bar{u}$ *belongs to* $v(\Pi)$.
(b) *There is not* $\Pi'$ *and* $u' \in v(\Pi')$ *such that* $u' > \bar{u}$.

*Definition:* **An efficient structure** *is a structure* $\Pi$ *such that there exists an efficient outcome* $\bar{u}$ *belonging to* $v(\Pi)$.

*Definition: A structure* $\Pi$ *is* **universally efficient** *if any efficient outcome* $\bar{u}$ *belongs to* $v(\Pi)$.

*Definition:* **A core-like** *stable solution or* **C-stable solution** *is a vector* $u^* \in \mathscr{R}^m_+$ *which satisfies the following properties:*

*there is a* $\Pi \in T(N)$ *such that* $u^* \in v(\Pi)$.
$\nexists S$ *and* $u' \in v(S)$ *such that* $u' > u^*$.

*A structure* $\Pi$ *associated with a C-stable solution is called a* **stable structure.**

The first definitions make precise a possible extension of standard efficiency concepts to situations where superadditivity is not assured. The fourth definition stresses a case in which some fixed structure is more efficient in a strong sense: this structure dominates other structures on efficiency grounds and should be retained whatever 'social welfare criterion' is retained.[24] In the economic games we are going to consider, it is often the case that there is only one possible candidate for universal efficiency, i.e. the structure consisting of the grand coalition alone.

The last definition provides a plausible extension of the core concept. As the core is, a C-stable solution is immune to secession threats of coalitions. Contrary to the core which is necessarily associated with the formation of the grand coalition, a C-stable solution may involve a 'true' partition of the set of the agents. Even if a C-stable solution is conceptually similar to a core solution, it deserves some specific discussions. One may argue that, as the core does, but in a different way, C-stability both underestimates and

[24] Universal efficiency of the grand coalition can be viewed as a weakening of the property of superaddivity (it necessarily obtains in superadditive games but does not require superadditivity).

overestimates the 'stability' of a partition. C-stability underestimates the stability of a partition, because (positive) externalities between the sets of the partition are ignored when this partition obtains. (In our framework, this means that a coalition is not supposed to be able to cooperate with another disjoint coalition, in exchanging private or public goods.)[25] C-stability overestimates the stability of the partition i.e. because it supposes for example that the knowledge on the distribution of characteristics of two partitions is lost when they merge. Without going further into the discussion, one should note that the concept of stable structure should be interpreted with some care. Absence of positive externalities within the stable structure do not reflect here minimax threats but excludability possibilities that are more likely when elements of a stable structure can be viewed as geographically distinct and isolated cities.

In order to ascertain the formal relationship between the core and the C-stable solution, the reader will immediately check the following properties:

(i) a C-stable solution is an efficient outcome (the stable structure is efficient but not necessarily universally efficient);
(ii) the core is a particular C-stable solution;
(iii) if $N$ is universally efficient, any C-stable solution is necessarily in the core;
(iv) $\Pi = \{N\}$ is a stable structure if and only if the core is non-empty (it is then efficient but not necessarily universally efficient).

The study of the just defined concepts leads us to introduce the concept of the smallest superadditive game associated with $v$:

*Definition* $\tilde{\tilde{v}}$, *the* **superadditive cover** *of the game v is defined by*

$$\tilde{\tilde{v}}(S) = \cup_{\Pi \in T(S)} \cap_{T \in \Pi} v(T), \forall S.$$

A game intermediate between $v$ and $\tilde{\tilde{v}}$ can be defined by:

*Definition the* **intermediate** *game* $\tilde{v}$ *is defined by*

$$\tilde{v}(N) = \tilde{\tilde{v}}(N), \tilde{v}(S) = v(S), S \neq N.$$

The connections between the different concepts introduced here is made clear by the following lemma whose proof will not be repeated here.[26]

[25] Remember, as noted above that the relevance of the core concept is not (entirely) subject to such a restrictive view of the consequences of a partition. (Although the minimax set story may lead to an 'overestimation' of the 'stability' of the core.)

[26] See Guesnerie–Oddou (1979).

**Lemma 1** *$u^*$ is a C-stable solution of v if and only if it belongs to the core of $\tilde{\tilde{v}}$ and if and only if it belongs to the core of $\tilde{v}$.*

The message of the lemma is clear and intuitive; it makes clear that there is no difference of nature between the core concept and the concept of the C-stable solution: the second concept is the transposition of the first one to the superadditive cover of the initial game or even to the 'intermediate' game just considered; as will be seen later the lemma significantly simplifies the analysis of existence of C-stable solutions.

All the concepts that have just been introduced will be lengthily illustrated in the following section.

## 5.4 A one-dimensional version of the taxation game (**)

This section has three parts: the first one presents the one-dimensional version of the taxation game that we are considering, it introduces the assumptions that will be used later on and shows, by means of an example, that the game is not necessarily superadditive (and that the grand coalition is not necessarily universally efficient). Indeed section 5.4.2 provides necessary and sufficient conditions for superadditivity and/or universal efficiency of the grand coalition. It shows that the above properties, the absence of which threatens the society's cohesion, can be checked through a finite number of tests of 'bilateral cohesion' (theorems 3, 4).

Section 5.4.3 focuses attention on the existence of the core of the taxation game. Its main and most surprising result is that universal efficiency of the grand coalition – again a property that is similar but weaker than superadditivity – is sufficient to assure the non-emptiness of the core (theorem 5). Other statements (theorems 6, 7 and 10) provide some idea on the 'location' of the core, i.e. on the nature of the tax decision that assures – in the sense of being unblocked – the society's cohesion.

### 5.4.1 Preliminaries

The taxation game described in the previous section is in general complex. To make the analysis more tractable we focus here on a simple version. In this version, the society's choice set – i.e., in our model, the set of tax equilibria – is one dimensional.

We know that this happens from the following specifications of the general model: (i) there are two private goods and no public goods; (ii) there is one public good and two private goods but no uniform lump-sum transfer (it is zero for everybody). Both our notation and comments in this section refer to this latter case and are in line with the examples presented at the beginning of section 2. However, the reader will easily check that the whole analysis can be transposed, with slight modifications to the case (i).

One of the teachings of the positive theory of taxation is that the consumption price system plays a privileged role in the parametrization of the set of tax equilibria. We will assume that the (weak) conditions of theorem 6, chapter 2, hold so that the one-dimensional set of tax equilibria can be parametrized by $\pi \in \mathscr{R}^+$. In our interpretation of the model, $\pi$ is the consumption price of the non-numeraire commodity. Then the set of tax equilibria is described by one equation $y'_0 = q(\pi)$, $\pi \in \mathscr{R}^+$. In fact this parametrization holds whatever the subeconomy we are considering, so that we will identify the set $\epsilon(S)$ of tax equilibria in coalition $S$ with the graph $y'_0 = q^s(\pi)$, $\pi \in \mathscr{R}^+$. (From now, we use $q$ instead of $y$, for typographical reasons).

With a slight but innocuous change of notation when compared to the previous section, we denote $V_i(\pi, S)$ the household's $i$ utility when he is in coalition $S$ and when the tax equilibrium parameter is $\pi$. Again in the two private goods, one public good and no lump-sum transfer specification of our economy, we have with usual notation, $V_i(\pi, S) = U_i(d_i(\pi, q^s(\pi)), q^s(\pi))$.

We reformulate the characteristic function of the taxation game as follows:

$$v(S) = \{u = (u_1, \dots u_m) | \forall i \in S,\ u_i \leq V_i(\pi, S),\ \text{for } \pi \in [1, \infty]\}$$

Note that, in this definition, $\pi$ is assumed to belong to $[1, \infty]$ rather than to $\mathscr{R}^+$. Remember that a choice of $\pi < 1$ involves a 'negative' production of public good the possibility of which has been allowed in order to simplify the general analysis of the set of tax equilibria. The same simplicity motive here leads us, without loss of economic content, to forget this region of negative production of public good.

Our first assumption is the following:

**(QC)** *For a given coalition $S$, $\forall i \in S$, the function $V_i$ is strictly quasi concave in $\pi$ and is decreasing when $\pi \to +\infty$.*

The second part of the assumption is rather innocuous. The first part of the assumption holds true for the class of examples of the beginning of sections 2. By continuity, it would be true for an open set of economies having a one-dimensional set of tax equilibria. It is not true for all such economies.

QC implies that preferences over $\pi$ are in the terminology of social choice theory 'single peaked'. It is well known then:

*Proposition 1*
*In every coalition with an odd number of agents there is a Condorcet winner taxation scheme.*

We will now introduce two assumptions which reflect the existence of increasing returns to size for coalitions.

**(IRSW)** *(increasing returns to size, weak version)*

$$\forall S \supset S', S \neq S', \forall \pi \in [1, \infty], q^{s}(\pi) > q^{s'}(\pi)$$

Note that an (almost) equivalent statement for IRSW would have been

$$\forall S \supset S', S \neq S', \forall \pi \in [1, \infty], \forall i \in S', V_i(\pi, S) > V_i(\pi, S')$$

The reader is invited to check that weak conditions on the production technology (positive marginal productivity) assure the validity of IRSW in the two private goods and one public good model we are referring to.[27]

A stronger version of the increasing returns to size hypothesis is the following:

**(IRSS)** *(increasing returns to size, strong version)*

*(i)* *IRSW holds true.*
*(ii)* $\forall S \neq S', q^{s}(\pi^{\circ}) > q^{s'}(\pi^{\circ})$ *for some* $\pi^{\circ} \in (1, \infty)$ *implies* $q^{s}(\pi) > q^{s'}(\pi)$ *for every* $\pi \in (1, \infty)$

This condition asserts that for any given two coalitions (and not only for coalitions ordered by the inclusion relationship), an unambiguous ranking of relative efficiency (loosely speaking 'size') can be performed. Given two coalitions $S$ and $S'$, either the set of tax equilibria of $S$ is above the one in $S'$ or the contrary holds; in particular these sets cannot intersect. Again the reader will note that IRSS is true in the class of examples of the beginning of section 5.2, but that it has no reason to hold in every version of our one-dimensional model.

Let us summarize: for every given $\pi$, coalitions can be ordered by the quantity of public goods they can produce. IRSW states that this ordering is compatible with the inclusion ordering of coalitions; IRSS states that this ordering is independent of $\pi$ for every pair of coalitions (and not only for those that satisfy the inclusion relationship). As just noted, IRSW is a very general property of the set of tax equilibria when IRSS is a more demanding one.

[27] Note the role played by the fact that $\pi > 1$, i.e., that there is a positive tax on commodity 2 (whose demand is positive).

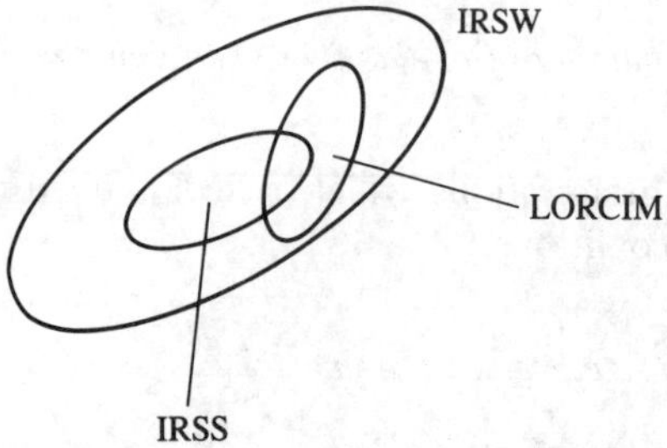


Figure 5.6

The next assumption refers again to the efficiency ordering of coalitions just emphasized. It says that such an ordering for any given $\pi$ can be explained from the identity of agents included in the coalitions.

**(LORCIM)** *(relations between the local ordering of coalitions and the identity of members).*

$\forall \pi \in (1,\infty)\ \exists$ *strictly positive numbers* $w_i(\pi)$, $i=1,\ldots m$, *such that*

$$\sum_{i\in S} w_i(\pi) > \sum_{i\in S'} w_i(\pi) \Leftrightarrow q^s(\pi) > q^{s'}(\pi)$$

*and*

$$\sum_{i\in S} w_i(\pi) = \sum_{i\in S'} w_i(\pi) \Leftrightarrow q^s(\pi) = q^{s'}(\pi).$$

Coming again to the two private goods, one public good specification of our general model, the reader will note that LORCIM holds as soon as the global production set is limited by a hyperplane and preferences between public goods and private goods are separable. If without loss of generality we denote (1,1,1) the normal to this hyperplane, then $q^s(\pi) = (\pi - 1)\sum_{i\in S} d_{i2}(\pi)$ so that $w_i(\pi)$ can be taken as $(\pi - 1)\ d_{i2}(\pi)$.

Note that as $w_i(\pi)$ are positive LORCIM implies IRSW. Also when the $w_i(\pi)$ can be chosen independently of $\pi$, LORCIM implies IRSS. The converse is not true.

The connections between the three assumptions are summarized in figure 5.6.

At this stage, let us give some insights into the model. The set of tax equilibria is visualized in figure 5.7, first for a coalition consisting of agents of one type (A), second for a coalition consisting of agents of another type (B), third for the grand coalition consisting of agents of both types. The equations of these sets are respectively given by $q^A(\pi)$, $q^B(\pi)$, $q(\pi)$. Indiffer-

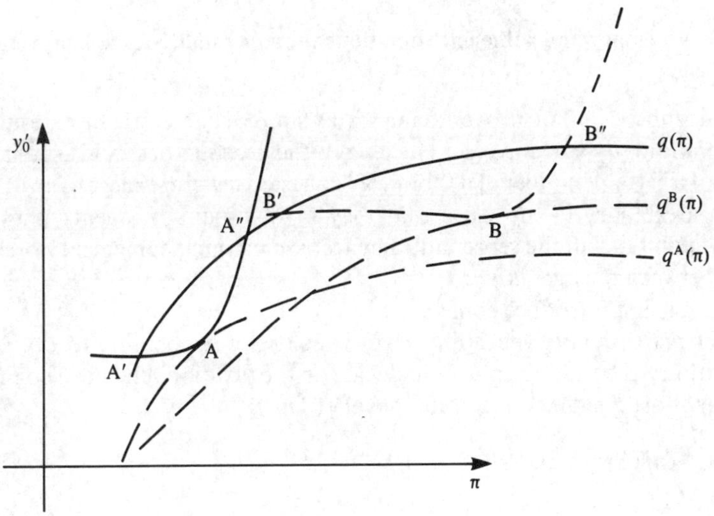


Figure 5.7

ence curves of agents of type A (resp. B) in the space $(\pi, y_0')$ are full lines (resp. dotted lines).

The diagram depicts a situation in which the game is not superadditive. The point A (resp. B) defines a situation in which agents of type A (resp. B) have the highest utility level when the coalition of agents of their type is formed. It gives a utility level $u_A^*$, (resp. $u_B^*$). But agents of type A (resp. B) can obtain a better utility level when the grand coalition forms only if the tax equilibrium which is selected belongs to the portion A′A″ (resp. B′B″) of the set of tax equilibria. As A′A″ and B′B″ have no intersection, the utility levels $u_A^*$ for A, $u_B^*$ for B are not attainable by the grand coalition. (Coming back on the computation of the examples, the reader will convince himself that such a situation is indeed possible.)

The diagram illustrates one phenomenon which has been stressed in the general discussion of the game: Increasing returns to size generated by the presence of the public good can be overcome by the increased difficulty of reaching a decision in a larger group. Hence, the game may not be superadditive. With a non-superadditive game as depicted in figure 5.7, the core stricto sensu is empty.

We are now going to focus on conditions which ensure that the game is superadditive or which ensure the weaker property that the grand coalition is universally efficient (section 5.4.2). When the game is superadditive or universally efficient, we can turn to the examination of the existence of a core outcome (section 5.4.3).

### 5.4.2 Necessary and sufficient conditions for superadditivity and universal efficiency

In this subsection, we prove a remarkably simple characterization result for superadditivity (or universal efficiency): these properties hold true if and only if a certain number of a '"binary" cohesion tests' are successful. (These tests are binary in the sense that they involve pairs of agents, they are 'cohesion tests' in the sense that they test the merging agreement possibilities between the agents.)

Let us first introduce some notation.

Let $u_i^*(S)$ denote the utility level which $i$ would be able to obtain in coalition $S$ if he had the power to decide on the taxation scheme of coalition $S$, for short the **dictatorial** utility level of $i$ in $S$.

$$u_i^*(S) = \max_{\pi} V_i(\pi, S) \stackrel{\text{def}}{=} V_i(\pi_i^*(S), S) \tag{5.20}$$

Associated with a utility level $a$, let us define

$$\Delta(i, a, S) = \{\pi \mid V_i(\pi, S) \geq a\}$$

With $QC$, $\Delta(i, a, S)$ is a closed (convex) interval in $\mathscr{R}^+$. Also it is straightforward that

$$\Delta(i, a, S) \supset \Delta(i, b, S) \text{ for } a < b \tag{5.21}$$

Also,

$$\Delta(i, u_i^*(S), S) = \pi_i^*(S)$$

For the game to be superadditive, the above example suggests that agents should not have too many diverging opinions concerning the desirable tax system. Elaborating on this idea, consider two disjoint coalitions $P, T (P \cap T \neq 0)$ and a couple of agents $i \in P$, $j \in T$. Suppose that $i$ and $j$ respectively obtain their dictatorial utility level $u_i^*(P)$, $u_j^*(T)$. Superadditivity obviously requires that $u_i^*(P)$, $u_j^*(T)$ be feasible in $P \cup T$. In other words if $i$ and $j$ are dictators respectively in coalitions $P$ and $T$, they would find a merging agreement for coalitions $P$ and $T$ favourable to both of them.

Condition $\alpha$ expresses this idea:

> **Condition ($\alpha$) for coalition $S$. Existence of bilateral merging agreements or binary superadditivity.**

*For all $P$ and $T$ such that $P \cup T = S$ and $P \cap T = \varnothing$ for all $i \in P$, for all $j \in T$, $\exists \pi$ such that*

$$u_i^*(P) \leq V_i(\pi, S),\ u_j^*(T) \leq V_j(\pi, S)$$

*Equivalently*

$$\Delta(i, u_i^*(P), S) \cap \Delta(j, u_j^*(T), S) \neq 0$$

Again condition ($\alpha$) has the following economic meaning: take two agents, $i$ and $j$, belonging to two distinct coalitions; suppose that these agents have the power to decide, in their **self interest**, on whether the two coalitions to which they belong should merge and under what conditions. Condition ($\alpha$) says that such a bilateral merging agreement is always possible, whatever the couple of coalitions (in $S$), whatever the couple of agents and whatever their initial situations in the coalitions (and even if they have their dictatorial utility level). Condition ($\alpha$) that asserts that bilateral merging agreements do exist can be viewed as a 'bilateral cohesion test' or as a form of binary superadditivity.

Remarkably enough, this bilateral cohesion test which is necessary for superadditivity is also sufficient.

**Theorem 3: Superadditivity**
*Assume that QC and IRSW hold. Then the taxation game is superadditive if and only if condition ($\alpha$) holds for any coalition S.*

*Proof*

To prove sufficiency, let us consider a coalition $S$, one two-partition of $S$, $\{P, T\}$ and $\bar{v} \in v(P) \cap v(T)$. We have to prove that $\bar{v} \in v(S)$ or equivalently that

$$\cap_{l \in S} \Delta(l, \bar{v}_l, S) \neq 0 \tag{5.22}$$

Note that if $l \in P$, $k \in T$, $\bar{v}_l \leq u_l^*(P)$ and $\bar{v}_k \leq u_k^*(T)$ so that condition ($\alpha$) and (5.21) imply

$$\Delta(l, \bar{v}_l, S) \cap \Delta(k, \bar{v}_k, S) \neq 0. \tag{5.23}$$

Now if $l \in P$ (resp. T) and if $k \in P$ (resp. T) (5.23) is a straightforward consequence of the fact that $\bar{v} \in v(P)$(resp. $v(T)$) and of IRSW. Hence (5.23) holds for any $(l, k) \in S$.

But (5.23) implies (5.22) from the one dimensional version of Helly's theorem: when a finite number of intervals is such that any two of them have a non-empty intersection, all of them have a non-empty intersection.[28] □

The idea behind the proof of theorem 3 is the following: the existence of a global agreement for the realization of $\bar{v}$ in $S$ results from the existence of a large enough set of bilateral merging agreements within $S$.

[28] Cf. for example Berge (1959).

A similar idea applies for the characterization of games with $N$ as a universal efficient structure.

**Theorem 4: Universal Efficiency**
*Assume QC and IRSW.*
*The grand coalition N is universally efficient if and only if condition ($\alpha$) holds for N.*

*Proof*
Necessity is still straightforward. For proving sufficiency let us consider a partition $\mathcal{S}=(S_k)_{k\in K}$ and let $\bar{v}\in \bigcap_{k\in K} v(S_k)$.

Take $l\in S_k$, $l'\in S_{k'}$, $k\neq k'$.
From (5.11) and IRSW we have:

$$\Delta(l', \bar{v}'_{l'}, N)\supset \Delta(l', u^*_l(N\backslash S_k), N) \text{ (since } N\backslash S_k \supset S_{k'}).$$

It follows from condition ($\alpha$) with an argument similar to the one used in the previous theorem 3 that:

$$\Delta(l, \bar{v}_l, N)\cap \Delta(l', \bar{v}_{l'}, N)\neq 0.$$

From Helly's theorem again we conclude:

$$\bigcap_{i\in N} \Delta(i, \bar{v}_i, N)\neq 0$$

$\bar{v}\in v(N)$ and the proposition is proved. □

The necessary and sufficient conditions for superadditivity and universal efficiency are surprisingly simple. Condition ($\alpha$) calls for two remarks:

(i) Condition ($\alpha$) is not a condition which directly bears on what economists consider as the primitives of the problem, i.e., preferences or technologies. However, it is a condition easier to check (and easier to understand by non-economists) than conditions on primitives. One could even argue that the test of existence of bilateral merging agreements is a more primitive test than tests aimed at assessing preferences.

(ii) For a coalition $S$ with $s$ elements, the verification of condition ($\alpha$) requires the implementation of at most $C_s^2\, 2^{s-2}$ different 'experiments'. Each one consists in the search of a bilateral merging agreement for a couple of agents. Hence $\sum_{s=2}^{n} C_s^2\, C_n^s\, 2^{s-2}$ are required for checking superadditivity when $C_n^2\,2^{n-2}$ are sufficient for the test of universal efficiency.

### 5.4.3 The existence of a non-empty core in the taxation game

The previous subsection led to a simple characterization of superadditivity and universal efficiency. Surprisingly enough, it turns out that, in the taxation game under consideration, these properties – and in particular universal efficiency alone – are sufficient to assure the non-emptiness of the core. (Theorem 5). In other words, the 'bilateral cohesion tests' of previous sections are sufficient, when successful, to guarantee a strong form of social cohesion, i.e., the existence of a core outcome (corollary 2).

The remainder of the subsection provides, through theorems 6 to 8, a further assessment of the nature and position of the core outcome.

Let us first state theorem 5.

**Theorem 5: Non-empty core**

*Assume QC and IRSW. Then if the grand coalition N is universally efficient the taxation game has a non-empty core.*

*Proof*

It is a constructive proof which requires some preliminary notation.

Let us consider $\pi_i^*(N)$ the dictatorial taxation scheme of household $i$ in the grand coalition. Without loss of generality, we can assume that agents are ranked as the numbers $\pi_i^*(N)$ so that:

$$i<j \Rightarrow \pi_i^*(N) \leq \pi_j^*(N)$$

Now take some taxation scheme $\pi \in ]\pi_1^*(N), \pi_m^*(N)[$ and denote $i^+(\pi)$ the smallest $i$ such that $\pi_i^*(N) > \pi$ and $i^-(\pi)$ the largest $i$ such that $\pi_i^*(N) < \pi$.

Let us define:

$$I(\pi)=\{1,\ldots,i^-(\pi)\} \qquad J(\pi)=\{i^+(\pi),\ldots,m\}$$

$I(\pi)$ and $J(\pi)$ are respectively the set of agents who in the grand coalition choose a dictatorial consumption price smaller or higher than $\pi$. The sets $I(\pi)$, $J(\pi)$ and $\{i | \pi_i^*(N)=\pi\}$ form a partition of $N$.

Let $\Pi^-$ be the set of $\pi \in [\pi_1^*(N), \pi_m^*(N)]$ which are blocked by some coalition $P \subset I(\pi)$.

Let $\Pi^+$ be the set of $\pi \in [\pi_1^*(N), \pi_m^*(N)]$ which are blocked by some coalition $T \subset J(\pi)$.

From our definition of blocking the sets, $\Pi^+$ and $\Pi^-$ are open in

$$[\pi_1^*(N), \pi_m^*(N)]$$

Moreover, QC (applied to $N$) implies that if $\pi \in \Pi^-$ (resp. $\pi \in \Pi^+$) then $[\pi, \pi_m^*(N)] \subset \Pi^-$ (resp. $[\pi_1^*(N), \pi] \subset \Pi^+$). Hence $\Pi^+$ and $\Pi^-$ are intervals of the form $[\pi_1^*(N), \pi^+[, ]\pi^-, \pi_m^*(N)]$. We show now:

*Assertion 1*

For any $\pi \in [\pi_1^*(N), \pi_m^*(N)]$ there is no blocking coalition $S = P \cup T$ such that $0 \neq P \subset I(\pi)$ and $0 \neq T \subset J(\pi)$ and no blocking coalition contains an $i$ such that $\pi_i^*(N) = \pi$.

To prove the assertion, let us consider such a blocking coalition $S$:$\exists\, \pi^0$ such that $\forall i \in S$, $V_i(\pi^0, S) \geq V_i(\pi, N)$. But if $i \in I(\pi)$, $\pi^0$ must be strictly smaller than $\pi$. (If not IRSW and QC imply $V_i(\pi^0, S) < V_i(\pi^0, N) \leq V_i(\pi, N)$.) Similarly, if $i \in J(\pi)$, $\pi^0$ must be strictly greater than $\pi$, a contradiction which proves the first part of the assertion. The second part is trivial.

*Assertion 2*

There is no $\pi \in [\pi_1^*(N), \pi_m^*(N)]$ simultaneously blocked by two coalitions $P \subset I(\pi)$, $T \subset J(\pi)$.

Suppose that the assertion is wrong, and let $\bar{u}_i$ be the utility levels of agents $i$ in $P \cup T$ in the blocking coalitions $P$ and $T$. From universal efficiency $\exists \bar{\pi}$ such that $V_i(\bar{\pi}, N) \geq \bar{u}_i$, when $\bar{u}_i > V_i(\pi, N)$, $\forall i \in P \cup T$. The same contradiction as above obtains (i.e., $\pi > \bar{\pi}$ and $\pi < \bar{\pi}$ have to hold simultaneously).

Now assertion 2 implies that $\pi^- \geq \pi^+$, and assertion 1 implies that any $\pi$ in $[\pi^+, \pi^-] (\neq 0)$ is in the core of the game. □

Theorem 5 has two corollaries:

**Corollary 3** *If the taxation game is superadditive, then it has a non-empty core.*

Corollary I is a straightforward consequence of theorem 5.
Corollary II combines theorems 4 and 5.

**Corollary 4** *If condition* (α) *for the existence of bilateral merging agreements holds for the grand coalition N, then the taxation game has a non-empty core.*

Let us emphasize again the strong conclusions of theorem 4 and theorem 5 and its corollaries:

Universal efficiency means that the formation of the grand coalition is certainly desirable in terms of efficiency (certainly in the sense that it is not contingent on the specific social welfare function which is used). Hence theorem 5 means that when the formation of the grand coalition is desirable, it is feasible in the sense that it is possible to find a taxation scheme which is immune to the secession threat of coalitions. Universal efficiency itself is equivalent from theorem 4 to the fact that agents do not have too high 'binary' divergences. Hence a finite number of 'bilateral cohesion tests' is enough to check social cohesion in the sense of the core.

Let us come back on the proof of theorem 5. A standard non-constructive proof for the existence of the core consists in showing that the game is balanced in the sense of Scarf. It is known that a balanced game has a non-empty core.[29] However, it does not seem that the assumptions made here are enough to guarantee that the game is balanced. We give in the next section sufficient conditions for ensuring Scarf balancedness.

The constructive proof given here leads to the search for some intermediate taxation scheme which is reminiscent of the intermediate taxation scheme selected by a voting process. Obviously, the core taxation scheme has no reason to be the median voter taxation scheme. The bargaining processes gives to agents weights different from the one involved by voting rights. Also the agents' power reflects more complex considerations than in a voting game. Roughly speaking, it depends both upon their tax contribution or more exactly upon the effect of this contribution on the well being of coalitions, and of their ability to compromise with other agents within coalitions.

However the proof suggests that intermediate taxation schemes are good candidates for being in the core. The next theorem gives a more precise content to this idea. Theorem 6 gives a condition under which the 'Condorcet winner taxation scheme' (that exists from proposition 1, p. 252) is in the core.

**Theorem 6**

*Assume QC and IRSW and assume that the number of households is odd; $m = 2q + 1$. Then if the Condorcet winner taxation scheme in N is not blocked by coalitions with less than (or exactly) q agents, it is in the core.*

*Proof*

According to the proof of theorem 5, $\pi^M$ the Condorcet winner in $N$ has to

[29] Scarf (1967). See the Mathematical appendix for the statements of definitions and theorem.

be blocked either by a coalition in $I(\pi^M)$ or by a coalition in $J(\pi^M)$. Both would have at most $q$ agents, a contradiction. □

For the sake of simplicity, the next theorem will be established and stated for $m = 3q$ (the difficulty for adapting the statement and proof to any $m$ is mainly notational). It asserts that if coalitions with 2/3 of the total population are not 'too attractive' in the sense: (1) that some intermediate taxation scheme in the grand coalition is preferred to the dictatorial position in coalitions comprising 2/3 of the population, (2) bilateral cohesion tests stronger than before and valid for these special coalitions are successful; then the core is non empty and contains one of the intermediate schemes just alluded to.

Suppose that the agents are ranked as in the proof of theorem 5. Call:

$$\pi_{1/3} = \pi^*_{m/3}(N) \text{ and } \pi_{2/3} = \pi^*_{2m/3}(N) \qquad \left(\frac{m}{3} = q, \frac{2m}{3} = 2q\right).$$

**Theorem 7**

*In the same conditions as previously, assume $m = 3q$, and suppose (in addition to QC, IRSW):*

1. *Every agent prefers some $\pi \in [\pi_{1/3}, \pi_{2/3}]$ rather than being dictator in any coalition with $2q$ members, i.e.*

$$\Delta(i, V_i(\pi_i^*(S)), N) \cap [\pi_{1/3}, \pi_{2/3}] \neq \phi, \forall S | \#S = 2q, \forall i \in S.$$

2. *For every couple of agents the following is true: Consider the maximal utility level which each can obtain in coalitions with $2q$ agents to which he belongs. Then, this couple of utility levels is feasible in the grand coalition, i.e.*

$$\Delta(i, V_i(\pi_i^*(S)), N) \cap \Delta(j, V_j(\pi_j^*(S')), N) \neq \phi$$
$$\forall S, S' | \#S = \#S' = 2q$$

*Then the taxation game has a non-empty core with some element in $[\pi_{1/3}, \pi_{2/3}]$.*

*Proof*

Let us consider the associated game $W$ defined as follows: $W(S) = v(S)$ if $S$ is a subset of $I(\pi_{2/3})$ or $J(\pi_{1/3})$

$$W(N) = \{u \in \mathscr{R}^m_+ | \exists \pi \in [\pi_{1/3}, \pi_{2/3}] | V_i(\pi, N) \geq u_i\}$$

$W(S) = \{u \in \mathscr{R}^m_+ | u_i \leq -K, \forall i \in S\}$ for any other $S$ (K is large enough).

To prove that $W$ has a non-empty core we will show that it is Scarf balanced. Let us recall that:

A family of coalitions $\mathscr{T}=(S_k)_{k\in K}$ is balanced if and only if there exists $\delta_{S_k}>0$ $k\in K$ such that

$$\sum_{S_k\ni i}\delta_{S_k}=1,\ \forall i=1,\ldots m$$

A game is Scarf balanced if for every balanced family of coalitions, $u\in\bigcap_{S_k\in\mathscr{T}}v(S_k)$ implies $u\in v(N)$.

So let us consider $\bar{u}\in W(S_k)$, $\forall S_k\in\mathscr{T}$. We have to show that $\bigcap_{i\in N}\Delta(i,\bar{u}_i,N)\cap\{\pi_{1/3},\pi_{2/3}\}\neq 0$ or equivalently from Helly's theorem that for every couple $i,j$ $[\pi_{1/3},\pi_{2/3}]\cap\Delta(i,\bar{u}_i,N)\cap\Delta(j,\bar{u}_j,N)\neq 0$.

Every coalition with fewer than $2q$ agents is dominated in the sense of IRSW by a coalition with $2q$ agents. This fact combined with 5.21 shows that the above condition will be satisfied whenever it holds true with $u_i$ being the maximal dictatorial utility level of $M.i$ across coalitions with $2q$ agents. But assumption 2 and Helly's theorem again show that this latter property is true.

The game $W$ is Scarf balanced. There is $\bar{\pi}$ in $\pi_{1/3},\pi_{2/3}$ which is in the core of $W$. But it is also in the core of $v$. From the proof of theorem 5, blocking coalitions should be subsets of $I(\bar{\pi})$ or of $J(\bar{\pi})$ and hence of $I(\pi_{2/3}), J(\pi_{1/3})$. □

Now, another consequence of the proof of theorem 5, i.e., that only 'small' coalitions can block, can be stressed.

For example, let us suppose that we associate with each consumer a number $\theta_i\in[0,1]$ with $\sum_i\theta_i=1$. (For example, $\theta_i$ could equal $1/n$ or any 'voting weight') Consider the family $\mathscr{S}=\left\{S\subset N\mid\sum_{i\in S}\theta_i>\frac{1}{2}\right\}$. Then we have:

**Theorem 8**

*If blocking coalitions are restricted to the family $\mathscr{S}$, then the core of the taxation game is non-empty.*

*Proof*

Let us come back on the proof of theorem 5 and particularly let us consider assertion 1.

Take a $\bar{\pi}$ such that $\sum_{i\in I(\bar{\pi})}\theta_i\leq\frac{1}{2}$, and $\sum_{i\in J(\bar{\pi})}\theta_i\leq\frac{1}{2}$ (such a $\bar{\pi}$ exists although there is not necessarily only one).

The argument of the above proposition can be transposed to show that such a $\bar{\pi}$ is in the core of the game with restricted blocking power. □

An obvious corollary obtains:

**Corollary 5** *If blocking is allowed only for coalitions of strictly more than* $\frac{m}{2}$ *members, the core is non-empty.*

Theorem 8 and its corollary make clear a fact that was already used in theorem 6, i.e., that blocking coalitions are in some sense 'small' coalitions. This interesting finding is however likely to be related to the special one-dimensional structure of the problem under consideration. In the same way, the existence proof of the non-emptiness of the core as a consequence of universal efficiency crucially exploits the one-dimensional structure: blocking possibilities are richer in a multi-dimensional setting. Indeed if a multi-dimensional extension of the characterization result of universal efficiency, i.e., an extension of theorem 4 exists (see Bibliographical note), there is not such an extension for the core existence result of theorem 5.

## 5.5 Further remarks on the one-dimensional taxation game (****)

The main results of the taxation game already have been obtained. This section proposes further investigation. The first statement (theorem 9) solves a problem already mentioned: until now we have proved that the taxation game has a non-empty core, although we have not proved that it is Scarf balanced. The additional assumption – called above LORCIM – that relates the local ordering of coalitions with the identity of members, assures Scarf balancedness.

The other statements aim at investigating the existence of stable structures. Theorem 11, that uses a Spence–Mirrlees type of condition for indirect preferences – already introduced in section 5.4 – together with the appropriate version of the increasing returns to size assumption (IRSS) provides a (technically non-obvious) neat existence result.

Let us now state and prove theorem 9: the reader is invited to check the role played in the proof by the special assumption LORCIM.

**Theorem 9**

*Assume QC, IRSS and LORCIM.*

*Then if the taxation game v is superadditive, it is Scarf-balanced (and has a non-empty core).*

*Proof*

Consider the taxation game $v$ and consider a balanced set of coalitions $\mathcal{T} = (S_k)_{k \in K}$.

Let us consider $\bar{u} \in v(S_k)$, $\forall S_k \in \mathscr{T}$, i.e. $\forall S_k \in \mathscr{T}$, $\exists \pi_k > 1$ such that $\bar{u}_i \le V_i(\pi_k, S_k)$, $\forall i \in S_k$.

Proving that $\bar{u} \in v(N)$ is equivalent to proving that $\cap_{i \in N} \Delta(i, \bar{u}_i, N) \neq 0$. Again from Helly's theorem this is equivalent to the fact that for every couple $i, j$, $\Delta(i, \bar{u}_i, N) \cap \Delta(j, \bar{u}_j, N) \neq 0$.

To show this latter property, let us distinguish two cases:

Either $i$ and $j$ both belong to some coalition $S_k$ in $\mathscr{T}$, then the property follows from IRSW.

Or there is no coalition in $\mathscr{T}$ which contains both $i$ and $j$. Call $S(i, \mathscr{T})$ (resp. $S(j, \mathscr{T})$) the set of coalitions of $\mathscr{T}$ which contain $i$ (resp. $j$): $S(i, \mathscr{T}) \cap S(j, \mathscr{T}) = 0$. Attach to each household $i$ a strictly positive number $w_i > 0$ and call $w(S) = \sum_{i \in S} w_i$.

Consider the smallest $w(S_c)$ when $S$ is in $S(i, \mathscr{T})$ and the smallest $w(S_d)$ when $S$ is in $S(j, \mathscr{T})$. We have necessarily $w(S_c) + w(S_d) \le w(N)$, or equivalently (with straightforward notation) $w(N|S_d) \ge w(S_c)$. To show this latter assertion consider the balancing weights $\delta_s$, $S \in \mathscr{T}$, such that

$$\sum_{S \ni i} \delta^S = 1 \ \forall i \text{ and consider } \sum_{S \in \mathscr{T}} \delta^S w(S).$$

$$\sum_{S \in \mathscr{T}} \delta^S w(S) = \sum_i \left( \sum_{S \in \mathscr{T} | S \ni i} \delta^S \right) w_i = w(N)$$

But

$$\sum_{S \in \mathscr{T}} \delta^S w(S) \ge \sum_{S \in S(i, \mathscr{T})} \delta^S w(S) + \sum_{S \in S(j, \mathscr{T})} \delta^S w(S)$$

$$\ge \sum_{S \in S(i, \mathscr{T})} \delta^S w(S^c) + \sum_{S \in S(j, \mathscr{T})} \delta^S w(S^d)$$

But balancedness implies that

$$\sum_{S \in S(i, \mathscr{T})} \delta^S = \sum_{S \in S(j, \mathscr{T})} \delta^S = 1$$

Hence the announced property.

Now coming back to the taxation game with LORCIM we can take for $w_i$ the numbers $w_i(\bar{\pi})$ for some given $\bar{\pi}$. With IRSW it follows that $y_0^{N|Sd}(\bar{\pi}) \ge y_0^{Sc}(\bar{\pi})$. Because of IRSS, the inequality holds whatever $\pi$. But then $V_i(\pi, N|S^d) > V_i(\pi, S^c)$.

Now take $\pi_c$ and $\pi_d$, the tax schemes in $S_c$ and $S_d$ associated with $\bar{u}$. We have: $V_j(\pi_d, S_d) \ge \bar{u}_j$, $V_i(\pi_c, N|S_d) \ge \bar{u}_i$.

But then superadditivity implies the conclusion we were looking for. □

Now what happens if the core of the taxation game is empty?

In some sense, there is then no possible stable agreement on taxation schemes within the community. One may here argue that the community will have a tendency to split and the concept of a stable structure attempts to formalize the idea that there is a stable splitting arrangement.

We will now present one result on the existence of stable structures (although, as noted above, one should be careful in the interpretation of 'stable structures'). For that we are now going to present ideas relating to the concept of 'consecutive game'.[30]

Let us consider a ranking of agents $i = 1, \ldots, m$. Let us define a consecutive coalition as a coalition $S$ such that if $i$ and $k$ belong to $S$, every $j | i < j < k$ belongs to $S$. Let us denote $\mathscr{C}$ the set of consecutive coalitions.

The consecutive game[31] associated with $v$, is the game $v^c$ defined by

$$v^c(S) = v(S) \text{ if } S \in \mathscr{C}$$

$$v^c(S) = \{u \in \mathscr{R}^m | u_i = 0, \forall i \in S\} \text{ if } S \notin \mathscr{C}$$

One can show that a consecutive game has necessarily a stable structure of coalitions. The key element of the proof is to show that all relevant balanced families of a consecutive game are partitions.

**Theorem 10**

*Let $v$ be a game such that $\forall S$, $O \in v(S)$.*

*Then $v^c$, the consecutive game associated with $v$, has a stable structure of coalitions.*

*Proof*

Taking the notation of the beginning of section 4, consider the game $\tilde{v}^c$ 'intermediate' between the superadditive cover of $v^c$ ($\tilde{\tilde{v}}^c$) and $v^c$ itself. To show that $v^c$ has a stable structure, it is enough to show that $\tilde{v}^c$ is Scarf balanced (Lemma 1).

We then have to show that for every balanced family $\mathscr{T} = (S_k)_{k \in K}$, $\bar{u} \in v^c(S_k)$, $\forall k \in K \Rightarrow \bar{u} \in \tilde{v}^c(N)$. It is immediate that we can restrict attention to balanced families consisting of consecutive coalitions only.

We will show that such a family $\mathscr{T}$ contains a partition of $N$, a fact which straightforwardly implies the searched property. As $\sum_{S \ni i} \delta^s = 1$, there exists a coalition $S(1)$ which contains 1. As $S(1)$ is consecutive $S(1) = \{1, 2, \ldots p_1\}$. If $p_1 \neq m$ there exists a coalition $S(2)$ which contains $p_1 + 1$ and which does not contain $p_1$. (If not $p_1 + 1 \in S \Rightarrow p_1 \in S$, but $\sum_{S \ni p_1} \delta^s = \sum_{S \ni p_1 + 1} \delta^s + \delta^{s(1)}$ a contradic-

[30] Due to Greenberg–Weber (1986).

[31] Note that the present terminology is somewhat different from the one in Greenberg–Weber. Note that the zero utilities is conventional. We implicitely assume $0 \in v(S)$, $\forall S$

tion with the definition of a balanced coalition.) As $S(2)$ is consecutive $S(2)=\{p_1+1, p_1+2, \dots p_2\}$. If $p_2 \neq m$, we repeat the reasoning to build $S(3)=(p_2+1, p_2+2, \dots)$. We stop when we reach $m$. □

The next step will be to endow agents of the original taxation game with preferences that will have the following consequences: if some taxation scheme is blocked by some coalition, then it is necessarily blocked by some consecutive coalition. For that we are now going to assume that the ranking of individuals reflects some ranking of preferences which has strong properties.

**(URP)** – Unambiguous ranking of preferences
*If* $i<j<k$, *then* $\forall S, \forall S', \forall \pi^0, y_0^{0\prime}$
*If* $a_l = U_l(\pi^0, y_0^{0\prime}, S'), l = i,j,k$
$\Delta(j, a_j, S) \supset \Delta(i, a_i, S) \cap \Delta(k, a_k, S)$

In other words, let us start from a situation where the tax scheme in $S'$ is $\pi^0$, $y_0^{0\prime}$. Consider another coalition $S$ and the set of tax schemes which would be unanimously preferred to the initial situation by two 'extreme' agents $i$ and $k$. It would be also preferred by an intermediate agent.

The reader will check that URP is implied by a Spencian condition on the ranking of marginal rates of substitution between $\pi$ and $y_0'$ (in the space $\pi, y_0'$) and by QC. In particular it holds in our example of the beginning of section 2 where the Spencian condition on marginal rates of substitution is presented and discussed.

Using the unambiguous ranking of preferences assumption URP but also the increasing returns to size assumption, one is going to show:

**Theorem 11: Stable structure**
*With URP, IRSW the game v has a stable structure of coalitions.*

*Proof*
Let a structure $\mathcal{S}$ be: $\mathcal{S}=(S_k)_{k\in K}$ and let $\bar{u} \in \bigcap_K v(S_k)$ a utility vector generated by the structure. We are going to show that if the structure consists of consecutive coalitions and if $\bar{u}$ is blocked by some coalition $T$, it is also blocked by some consecutive coalition $T'$.

Following Greenberg–Weber, let us define for $S$ and $i \in S$

$$m(i,S)=\begin{Bmatrix} 1 \text{ if } \nexists j\in S, j>i \\ \min\{j-i \mid j\in S, j>i\} \end{Bmatrix}$$
$$\text{and } M(S)=\max_{i\in S}\{m(i,S)\}$$

$m(i, S)$ is the distance in terms of our ranking in coalition $S$ between $i$ and the agent 'above' him, $M(S)$ is the maximal distance between agents in $S$.

Now if $\bar{u}$ is blocked by several coalitions $S$ take the one(s) which minimize(s) $M(S)$; if there remains several take the one(s) with the highest number of agents. Call it $T$.

Let $i, k \in T$ be such that $k - i = M(T)$. If $T$ is not a consecutive coalition take $j \notin T$ with $i < j < k$. In the structure $\mathscr{S}$, $j$ belongs to some consecutive coalition $S_{k(j)}$; it is easy to see that

$$M(S_{k(j)} \cup i) < M(T) \text{ and } M(S_{k(j)} \cup k) < M(T) \tag{5.24}$$

Call $\pi_{k(j)}$ the tax scheme (associated with $\bar{u}$) in $S_{k(j)}$.

Let us show $V_i(\pi_{k(j)}, S_{k(j)} \cup i) \leq \bar{u}_i$
and $V_k(\pi_{k(j)}, S_{k(j)} \cup k) \leq \bar{u}_k$.

The inequalities are trivial when $i \in S_{k(j)}$ (resp. $k \in S_{k(j)}$). In the other case, the contrary inequality would mean that $S_{k(j)} \cup i$ (resp. $k$) blocks $\bar{u}$ a contradiction with the definition of $T$ and (5.24).

But if, by abuse of notation, we denote $V_l(\pi, S)$, the utility level of $M.l$ when the consumption price is $\pi$ and the public good level $q^S(\pi)$ (even if $M.l.$ does not belong to $S$) then, either for $S' = S_{k(j)} \cup i$ or $S' = S_{k(j)} \cup k$, we have:

$$V_i(\pi_{k(j)}, S') \leq \bar{u}_i$$
$$V_k(\pi_{k(j)}, S') \leq \bar{u}_k$$

But then starting from $S'$ we can apply URP with $S = T \cup j$ to see that $T \cup j$ blocks $\bar{u}$, a contradiction to the definition of $T$ and $j$. It follows that $T$ is consecutive and the announced property holds.

Now to show that $v$ has a stable structure, take the consecutive game $v^c$. From theorem 10, it has a stable structure $\mathscr{S}$ made of consecutive coalitions. Take $\bar{u}$ the associated utility level. It is unblocked because if it were blocked, it would be blocked by a consecutive coalition (as we have just shown), a contradiction. □

## 5.6 Bibliographical note

The analysis of the size of the set of second-best optima of section 1 closely follows Guesnerie (1979a). The intuition of the results is probably familiar to social choice theorists, particularly those involved in the analysis of dimensionality problems in social choice (such as Kramer (1977), Schofield (1978)). The study of Guesnerie (1979a) was in fact much influenced by the reading of Zeckhauser–Weinstein (1974). Although the subject did not attract the interest of the theoretical optimal taxation literature, it is clearly appraised in some more applied pieces of work such as Gevers–Proost (1978), Gevers–Jacquemin (1987).

The analysis of the one-dimensional taxation social choice problem is entirely extracted from Guesnerie–Jerison (1991). This latter contribution provides a study of the problem that is both more comprehensive and more rigorous and offers a set of references on the Laffer controversy. (See also Malcomson (1986).

The subsequent analysis of the taxation game relies heavily on the work of Guesnerie–Oddou (1979), (1981), (1982), (1987). The difference between this approach and the work of Aumann–Kurz (1977a and b), (1978) which has similar motivations has been explained in the chapter. Either extensions of the work of Guesnerie–Oddou or work in a similar spirit are due to Greenberg–Weber (1982), (1986a), (1986b) and Weber–Zamir (1985) who show that stable structures may not exist in the Guesnerie–Oddou model). A partnership problem has also been studied in a simpler setting by Farell–Scotchmer (1986). More recent work in the spirit of section 4 include Berliant (1992). Also recent literature that refers to the concept of a stable structure include Henriet–Demange (1988). Perez (1991) discusses the non-cooperative foundations of the concept of a stable structure.

Going into the details, more precise references can be given.

A careful examination of the concepts of C-stable solution, stable structure, universally efficient structure and of the relationships between the three games, $v$, $\tilde{v}$, $\tilde{\tilde{v}}$, can be found in Guesnerie–Oddou (1979). Earlier analysis of related concepts in games with transferable utility can be found in Aumann–Drèze (1975).

The existence of a Condorcet winner for the taxation game of the type considered here has been well known from the literature on median voter with a linear income tax, for example Roberts (1977), Romer (1975).

Theorems 4, 5, 6, 7, 8 on superadditivity and universal efficiency and non-emptiness of the core are taken from Guesnerie–Oddou (1981). Theorem 9 is adapted from Greenberg—Weber (1982).

Theorem 10 is taken from Greenberg–Weber (1986b), and Theorem 11 is a variant, with maybe more appealing assumptions, of a theorem due again to Greenberg–Weber (1986b). Guesnerie–Oddou (1987) provide an extension of the results on superadditivity and universal efficiency to an $n$-dimensional partnership game that is not necessarily orthogonal. (For that they use the $n$-dimensional version of Helly's theorem.)

# Conclusion

This conclusion successively considers four points: it first attempts to analyse the main shortcomings of the study while remaining within the justificatory framework of Chapter 1 (A); it then provides a critical assessment of the polar assumptions of chapter 1 (B); third, it shows that our 'monist' option stressing theoretical unity has led us to interpret the results in a much too restrictive way (C); finally it discusses some of the most promising directions of research in the theory of second-best taxation (D).

**(A)** The model under consideration in chapters 2, 3 and 5 has features which fit the conclusions of chapter 1 except in one respect: there are a number of commodities for which taxation should be **non-linear** rather than linear. Whatever the merits of the linearity assumption, non-linear taxation of, for example, labour income is suggested both by theoretical analysis and real world observation. Even taking into account the detailed analysis of quotas policies – that introduce non-linearities in the tax system, albeit of a special kind – in the section 4.2 of chapter 4, and the discussion of the non-linear taxation model of section 4.4, the treatment of non-linearities in this book is incomplete. This is an obvious shortcoming. Two different but related points concerning the nature and extent of the shortcomings are however in order:

First, considering the case where the analysis is restricted to some fixed non-linear tax schedule the simplification may be less significant than a superficial glance suggests.

In that case the only modelling change concerns the definition of the consumer's demand function, that has to take into account the coexistence of linear prices with a fixed non-linear part of the budget set. Such a 'modified' demand function has no longer some competitive symmetry properties that are used in the optimality analysis of chapter 3 (although they fit the model of section 4.1 in chapter 4) but this is unimportant for the positive analysis of chapter 2, as soon as the (fixed) non-linear budget set delimitates a convex region. When the non-linear scheme generates a non-convex choice problem, the corresponding function is no longer necessarily continuous; the local analysis of chapter 2 remains true outside the points of discontinuity even if the global analysis is significantly affected. When the non-linear part of the scheme is not subject to change, the tax reform analysis is likely not to be affected at continuity (and differentiability) points. In the same setting, however, optimization might face new phenomena such as those detected in a (related) second-best setting where the agents' responses are discontinuous: second-best optimization may systematically select discontinuity points at which first-order conditions for optimal taxes analogous to those of theorem 1 in chapter 3, will be invalid.[1]

Second, the study of the general case where the non-linear schedule is no longer fixed would greatly benefit both from previous results in this book and from what has just been suggested. In particular, section 4.4, illustrated, from a special case, how the results on linear taxation can serve as building blocks to get results on the structure and on tax reform problems. Some suggestions have been exploited in the context of section 4.4, others have only been mentioned. All provide some of the basic ingredients for a more systematic analysis in line with that of this book. The only missing ingredients are probably those that relate with a careful analysis of the self-selection constraint in a multi-dimensional setting (see the bibliographical note to chapter 4).

**(B)** The second emphasis of this conclusion concerns the assessment of the **polar assumptions** on which the institutional analysis of chapter 1 relies. Let me list again the most significant of these assumptions: (i) individual characteristics are private rather than public knowledge; (ii) there is no asymmetric information between the government and the production sector; (iii) transactions between the production and the consumption sectors are costlessly observed.

The precise form of (i) adopted for the analysis of chapter 1 is clearly extreme: all relevant characteristics are supposed unobservable, or, at least, the discovery cost is supposed to be too high to make it worthwhile. The assumption has obvious weaknesses: some characteristics that are part of

[1] This discontinuity phenomenon has been noted independently by Guesnerie–Laffont (1978) in a second-best taxation framework and Mirrlees (1975) in a moral hazard context. There is a large literature to determine conditions under which the difficulty disappears in a moral hazard context (then, the 'first-order approach' is valid – see for example Guesnerie (1989) for a brief assessment). In the problem of taxation of a monopolist considered by Guesnerie–Laffont, only very strong assumptions on technologies and demand will rule out the phenomenon: in other words, optimization may often select taxation schemes that lead to potentially unstable situations (because the monopolist's reactions function is discontinuous around the optimum).

(or that are correlated with) the vector of basic characteristics are observable either costlessly or with low cost (let us think about family status and size ...) and such possibilities of cheap observation are indeed exploited by 'real' tax systems. Much of the theory seems to be affected in a rather straightforward way by this complication; however, as underlined in section 4 of chapter 1, the analysis of this problem here is clearly insufficient.

The most serious theoretical questions are associated with the correlation issue and have been lengthily discussed in chapter 1: would then sophisticated incentive devices be superior to tax systems? Roughly speaking the answer has been shown to be negative unless incentives devices can exploit the correlation between the characteristics of different (groups of) agents. But neither the theoretical nor the empirical significance of the answer is fully elucidated: theoretically, mechanisms that rely on cross checking of characteristics may be more vulnerable to manipulations by coalitions, a subject that was outside the scope of the analysis of chapter 1; empirically, the circumstances under which such correlations might indeed be exploited are somewhat unclear.

Another and maybe deeper theoretical question, that does not directly relate with the correlation issue, lies in the assessment of the nature of the hidden characteristics of each agent: to what extent are such characteristics really known by the agents? If they are (even partly) why cannot they be detected at low expected cost by using powerful devices with very low frequencies?[2] These basic questions are not specific to our taxation problem but are behind all the so-called adverse selection models of contract theory; their classical discussion within a principal–agent framework (again, see footnote 2) provides guidelines, rather than full answers, for their assessment in the present setting; also they have – here as well as in a standard principal agent model – a time dimension that cannot be fully captured in a static model.

Pushing further the critical assessment of the polar assumptions will more fundamentally stress the polar character of our option. Using again the terminology and concepts of contract theory, this option can concisely be described in one sentence: adverse selection, rather than moral hazard, is the basic justification for the taxation systems considered in this book. In fact, a tax system does not only distribute income or allocate financing

[2] Such a question is meaningful for every adverse selection problem and the question of high penalties has received attention in the contracts literature both for adverse selection and moral hazard problems. The objections to the use of high penalties in a moral hazard context (as briefly assessed in my New Palgrave entry Guesnerie (1989)) have relevance for the adverse selection framework. Their discussion is obviously outside the scope of the present conclusion.

between people of different abilities and tastes but provides insurance for risky investments – education ... – that cannot be fully insured *ex ante*. To put it briefly, a tax system acts as an insurance as well as a distribution device,[3] and we have here deliberately ignored this aspect. This option might be justified in chapter 1 since the moral hazard viewpoint could be straightforwardly included, but mixing both viewpoints could create more confusion than clarity; the option is however kept in the following and in particular in chapter 3 where the analysis crucially reflects an income redistribution rather than an insurance viewpoint. This limitation of the scope of the analysis appears as a deliberate, even if debatable, effect of the theoretical option presented in the introduction. This option has led us to stick to a polar and coherent but limited world i.e. without uncertainty.

Non insurable uncertainty may exist, not only because of moral hasard but also because of the incompleteness of markets due to transactions costs. Although we have mentioned in the introduction that the methods of second best are most relevant for the welfare analysis of incomplete markets, this latter subject has remained outside the scope of the present analysis. Naturally, incompleteness provides an additional and specific justification for taxation, that deserves careful scrutiny.

The asymmetric treatment of production and consumption (ii), that allows the government to indirectly or directly control the production sector, has already been lengthily discussed in chapter 2 where alternative separation options have been shown inadequate. In some sense the analysis of section 5.3 of chapter 3 (concerning the nature of second-best optimal rules and the separability allowed by the consideration of social values of commodities) gives further support to such a separation option: we will not go back over this point.

Assumption (iii), according to which all transactions between the production and the consumption sector are costlessly observed is much more debatable; clearly, examination of real world situations suggests not only that the production–consumption frontier may not be well defined and that the observation of flows through this frontier may be costly and inaccurate – particularly when these flows determine taxes so that people have an interest in hiding them: this is the standard tax evasion problem. Indeed, many characteristics of actual of tax systems – for example the fact that there are few commodity tax rates – may be explained by such observability costs. Even if those costs are often referred to as administrative costs, the analysis of their implications for the appropriate tax discrimination between commodities is a problem of theoretical and

[3] For an early public finance viewpoint on these questions, see Varian (1980). Recent work includes, Cremer–Gahvani (1992).

practical interest on which the present theory – and this monograph in particular – is almost silent.[4]

Having acknowledged the lacunae and emphasized the needs (and promises?) for future research on the administrative costs issue, one should be careful in not qualifying too much the interest of the present perspective. The analysis of the end of chapter 2, deals with given tax systems, whatever their specific attributes, and is not concerned with the above remarks. Even if the actual limited number of tax categories make impossible a literal interpretation of the reform and optimization results of chapter 3, they provide the right guidelines for an aggregate analysis where commodities are grouped in categories within which the same tax rate applies. Nevertheless, the zero observation cost assumption is an unsatisfactory feature of the present model, the reconsideration of which seems to be an unavoidable subject of future research.

**(C)** We have just emphasized some of the limitations of the present analysis while remaining within the logic of the polar world that we have chosen to explore (i.e., in (subjective) order of increasing importance the absence of non-linearities in the tax system, the insufficient investigation of the correlation issue – either between observable or between unobservable characteristics – the silence on the nature and implications of administrative costs); one should now stress the **variety of possible interpretations** outside the 'monist' scheme of interpretation we have stuck to until now.

I have already mentioned that the analysis of chapter 2 remains useful for analysing the structure of tax equilibria in a world where linear taxation schemes coexist with a non-linear one or when the tax system only discriminates between broad groups of commodities. One should more generally stress that this positive analysis applies to taxation schemes fairly independently of the actual justifications of those taxation schemes. In a world where (linear) tax schemes would be used for insurance purposes rather than, as here, for redistributive ones – i.e., when moral hazard rather than adverse selection justifies taxation – the positive analysis of chapter 2 would remain valid.[5]

The normative analysis of chapter 3 has certainly less claim to generality: if the tax reform methodology conveys messages of general interest, and if as argued above, optimization can be more operationally reinterpreted at some aggregate level, the optimization formulas are sensitive to the exact hypothesis and problematic that are adopted. However, even in the

[4] A systematic attempt at the theoretical comparison of two different tax bases is Maskin–Riley (1985) who compare an income-based and a wage-based tax scheme.

[5] As well, as noted in the bibliographic note of chapter 2, the model is relevant for the discussion of profit taxes along the lines of an earlier public finance tradition.

normative case, a significant flexibility in interpretation still exists and, for example, some of the results would remain useful in understanding the insurance aspects of taxation, in a stylized one-consumer, two periods model.

Finally, it goes without saying that the message of the first two sections of chapter 4 is very general when chapter 5 has a somewhat different status: most of its results are exploratory and more illustrative than general; its only possible claim to generality is through the scope of its concepts and methodology.

**(D)** What are the prospects for **future research in the theory of taxation?** Again, when looking at this question, I rule out the important segment of taxation, the design of which is explained mainly by considerations relative to the firm's behaviour. A number of open questions the examination of which does not imply a significant departure from the polar world problematic of this monograph have already been discussed. Then I will limit myself to discuss some possible research avenues that do involve a more significant departure while again not basically interfering with the issues of the production sector's modelling.

The present polar world is a static and closed world. Much remains to be done. Forgetting about the open economy problem (not because it is unimportant!) the most obvious extension obtains with the introduction of the time dimension of the problem. Such a suggestion may reflect either partly theoretical naivety or real potential innovation. Theoretical naivety has two dimensions. On the one hand, one must remember that a static model may be reinterpreted in a dynamic context: a standard Arrow–Debreu reinterpretation of commodities as dated commodities would allow to introduce savings into the analysis. On the other hand, at a deeper level, one has to realize that the solutions of a number of difficulties due to the incorporation of time into the analysis have to rely on the development of other fields: this is true for the treatment of expectations, as well as for example for the analysis of the role of savings in growth – a question that is crucial for the question of taxation of savings, but whose solution has to be expected from growth theory rather than from taxation theory. Indeed, a number of results interesting for the theory of taxation have been imported from other fields and already complement in a useful way the static perspective: I am thinking here for example of the role of the commitment hypothesis in intertemporal contexts and its applications to the repeated taxation problem.[6]

[6] The solution of Brito-Hamilton-Slutsky-Stiglitz (1990) to the repeated income tax problem is closely similar of the standard solution of a repeated adverse selection principal agent problem (see Caillaud–Guesnerie–Rey–Tirole (1988)).

The inclusion of the time dimension might be innovative if it were the occasion of a theoretically sounder reassessment of the conditions of what was called earlier the institutional economics of taxation. For example, the reflection on the temporal dimension might give the opportunity to reassess the nature of asymmetric information: the problem is neither of a purely adverse selection type (agents themselves have neither accurate information on their characteristics, nor time-independent characteristics and learning is present), nor a purely moral hazard problem (taxation is not only an insurance device but also a screening device). An elucidation of the actual mix of the different types of asymmetric information and of their time dimension and evolution, together with a better understanding of the administrative constraints would serve to develop better intellectual tools for the assessment of the performance of actual tax systems.[7]

Clearly, the last word of theory will not be said in the near future. Sceptics might argue that tax systems that are observed are usually the products of the tatonnement of history rather than of the a priori effort of the human brain. Others may hope for a radical breakthrough in the design of tax policies emerging from the progress of theory. Arguing that a better understanding of fiscal tools will serve to improve tax policies may leave us on safer grounds.

[7] This might in particular allow to reevaluate, within an improved perspective, some of their a priori most irrational characteristics – such as the yearly tax base etc... –.

# Mathematical appendix

The following mathematical appendix does not aim at a systematic presentation of – or an even introduction to – the mathematical tools used in this book. It only recalls, for the sake of completeness, definitions and statements that are not necessarily standard in formalized economic theory. Mathematical appendix 1 borrows (mainly from Milnor (1965)) key definitions and theorems in differential topology that serve to the analysis of chapter 2. Mathematical appendix 2 gathers a (somewhat arbitrary) selection of definitions and statements that are referred to in other chapters.

## 1 Differential topology (from Milnor 'Topology from the differentiable viewpoint')

Let $U \subset \mathscr{R}^k$ and $V \subset \mathscr{R}^l$ be open sets. A mapping $f$ from $U$ to $V$ (written $f$: $U \to V$) is called *smooth* if all of the partial derivatives $\partial^n f / \partial x_i \ldots \partial x_{i_n}$ exist and are continuous.

More generally let $X \subset \mathscr{R}^k$ and $Y \subset \mathscr{R}^l$ be arbitrary subsets of Euclidean spaces. A map $f$: $X \to Y$ is called *smooth* if for each $x \in X$ there exists an open set $U \subset \mathscr{R}^k$ containing $x$ and a smooth mapping $F$: $U \to \mathscr{R}^l$ that coincides with $f$ throughout $U \cap X$.

*Definition* A map $f$: $X \to Y$ is called a *diffeomorphism* if $f$ carries $X$ homeomorphically onto $Y$ and if both $f$ and $f^{-1}$ are smooth.

*Definition* A subset $M \subset \mathscr{R}^k$ is called a *smooth manifold of dimension m* if each $x \in M$ has a neighbourhood $W \cap M$ that is diffeomorphic to an open subset $U$ of the Euclidean space $\mathscr{R}^m$.

Now let $f$: $U \to \mathscr{R}^k$ with $U$ open in $\mathscr{R}^k$.

**Inverse Function Theorem** *If the derivative* $df_x$: $\mathscr{R}^k \to \mathscr{R}^k$ *is non-singular, then f maps any sufficiently small open set U' around x diffeomorphically on to an open set f(U').*

**Implicit Function Theorem** *Let* $f$: $U_1 \times U_2 \subset \mathscr{R}^k \times \mathscr{R}^l \to \mathscr{R}^l$ *be* $C^r$ *differentiable (note: not* $C^\infty$ *here) where* $U_1$ *and* $U_2$ *are two open sets. If* $f(x_0, y_0) = 0$ *and if* $(\partial_y f)_{(x_0, y_0)}$ *is of rank l, there exist two open sets* $U_1' \subset U_1$, $U_2' \subset U_2$ *with* $x_0$ *in* $U_1'$, *and* $y_0$ *in* $U_2'$ *and a* $C^r$ *differentiable function* $\psi$: $U_1' \to U_2'$ *such that,* $\forall x$, *in* $U_1'$, $f(x, \psi(x)) = 0$ *and* $\psi(x_0) = y_0$.

## Sard's theorem

**Theorem.** *Let* $f$: $U \to \mathscr{R}^n$ *be a smooth map, defined on an open set* $U \subset \mathscr{R}^m$, *and let*

$$C = \{x \in U | \text{rank } df_x < n\}.$$

*Then the image* $f(C) \subset \mathscr{R}^n$ *has Lebesgue measure zero.*

We say that $x \in M$ is a *regular point* of $f$ if the derivative $df_x$ is non-singular. In the case $m = n$, it follows from the inverse function theorem that $f$ maps a neighbourhood of $x$ in $M$ diffeomorphically on to an open set in $N$. The point $y \in N$ is called a *regular value* if $f^{-1}(y)$ contains only regular points.

If $df_x$ is singular, then $x$ is called a *critical point* of $f$, and the image $f(x)$ is called a *critical value*. Thus each $y \in N$ is either a critical value or a regular value according as $f^{-1}(y)$ does or does not contain a critical point.

More generally consider a smooth map $f$: $M \to N$ from a manifold of dimension $m$ to a manifold of dimension $n$. Associating with each $x \in M$, (resp. $y \in N$), a linear subspace of dimension $m$ (resp. $n$) called the tangent space of $M$ at $x$ (resp. $N$ at $y$) one can define the derivative $df_x$ as a linear mapping from $TM_x$ to $TN_y$ where $y = f(x)$.

The concept of regular or critical values is immediately transposed in this case. We have:

**Corollary** *The set of regular values of a smooth map* $f$: $M \to N$ *is everywhere dense in N. If in addition f is proper (the inverse image of a compact set is a compact set) then the set of regular values is open and dense.*

The following is important for exploiting Sard's theorem.

**Preimage Theorem** *If $f$: $M \to N$ is a smooth map between manifolds of dimension $m \geq n$, and if $y \in N$ is a regular value, then the set $f^{-1}(y) \subset M$ is a smooth manifold of dimension $m-n$.*

**Homotopy**

Given $X \subset \mathscr{R}^k$, let $X \times [0,1]$ denote the subset of $\mathscr{R}^{k+1}$ consisting of all $(x, t)$ with $x \in X$ and $0 \leq t \leq 1$. Two mappings

$$f, g: X \to Y$$

are called *smoothly homotopic* if there exists a smooth map $F$: $X \times [0,1] \to Y$ with

$$F(x,0) = f(x), \; F(x,1) = g(x)$$

for all $x \in X$. This map $F$ is called a *smooth homotopy* between $f$ and $g$.

The mod 2 degree of a map depends only on its smooth homotopy class:

**Homotopy Lemma** *Let $f, g$: $M \to N$ be smoothly homotopic maps between manifolds of the same dimension, where $M$ is compact and without boundary. If $y \in N$ is a regular value for both $f$ and $g$, then*

$$\#f^{-1}(y) \equiv \#g^{-1}(y) \text{ (mod 2)}.$$

Assume that $M$ is compact and boundaryless, that $N$ is connected, and that $f$: $M \to N$ is smooth.

**Theorem** *If $y$ and $z$ are regular values of $f$ then*

$$\#f^{-1}(y) \equiv \#f^{-1}(z) \text{ (modulo 2)}.$$

*This common residue class, which is called the* mod. 2 degree *of $f$, depends only on the smooth homotopy class of $f$.*

The compactness assumption on the manifold $M$ can be removed if the function $f$ is proper.

**Brouwer degree and Poincare Hopf theorem**

**Brouwer degree** Now let $M$ and $N$ be oriented $n$-dimensional manifolds without boundary and let

$$f: M \to N$$

be a smooth map. If $M$ is compact and $N$ is connected, then the degree of $f$ is defined as follows:

Let $x \in M$ be a regular point of $f$, so that $df_x$: $TM_x \to TN_{f(x)}$ is a linear isomorphism between oriented vector spaces. Define the *sign* of $df_x$ to be $+1$ or $-1$ according as $df_x$ preserves or reverses orientation. For any regular value $y \in N$ define

$$\deg(f; y) = \sum_{x \in f^{-1}(y)} \operatorname{sign} df_x.$$

This integer $\deg(f; y)$ is a locally constant function of $y$. It is defined on an open dense subset of $N$.

**Theorem a** *The integer* $\deg(f; y)$ *does not depend on the choice of regular value* $y$. (It is called the degree of $f$ (denoted $\deg f$)).
**b** *If f is smoothly homotopic to g, then* $\deg f = \deg g$.

Consider now an open set $U \subset \mathscr{R}^m$ and a smooth vector field

$$v: U \to \mathscr{R}^m$$

with an isolated zero at the point $z \in U$. The function

$$\bar{v}(x) = v(x)/\|v(x)\|$$

maps a small sphere centred at $z$ into the unit sphere. The degree of this mapping is called the index $i$ of $v$ at the zero $z$.

Let $M$ be a compact manifold and $w$ a smooth vector field on $M$ with isolated zeros. (If $M$ has a boundary then $w$ is required to point outwards at all boundary points.)

**Poincaré-Hopf Theorem** *The sum* $\sum i$ *of the indices at the zeros of such a vector field is equal to the Euler number which is a topological invariant of M: it does not depend on the particular choice of the vector field.*

We will be mainly interested in the case of a compact domain of $\mathscr{R}^m$.

**Corollary** *Let* $X \subset \mathscr{R}^m$ *be a compact m-manifold with boundary. If v:* $X \to \mathscr{R}^m$ *is a smooth vector field with isolated zeros and if v points outwards, along the boundary, the sum* $\sum i$ *does not depend on the choice of v.*

*In particular if X is the disc* $D^m$*, the sum is* $+1$.

In order to compute the index at some zero, consider a vector field $v$ on an open set $U \subset \mathscr{R}^m$ and consider $v$ as a mapping $U \to \mathscr{R}^m$ and consider $dv_x$.

*Definition* The vector field $v$ is *non-degenerate* at $z$ if the linear transformation $dv_z$ is non-singular.

It follows that $z$ is an isolated zero.

**Lemma 4** *The index of $v$ at a non-degenerate zero $z$ is either $+1$ or $-1$ according as the determinant of $dv_z$ is positive or negative.*

## 2 A brief reminder of other useful results

### 1. Theorem: Separation of convex cones

*Let $K_0, \ldots K_{p-1}$ be $p$ open convex cones and let $K_p$ be a convex cone*

$$\bigcap_{0\ldots p} K_i = \varnothing$$

*if and only if there exists $q_0, \ldots q_i \ldots q_p$ (some of them non zero) such that* $\sum_{i=0}^{p} q_i = 0$ and $q_i \cdot x \leq 0, \forall x \in K_i$.

### 2. Theorem: Existence of solutions of differential equations

*Let the differential equation be*

$$\frac{dx}{dt} = F(x(t)) \qquad (x \in \mathscr{R}^n)$$

*Let $t_0 \in \mathscr{R}$ and $x_0 \in \mathscr{R}^n$*

*Assume that $F$ is $C^1$ in a neighbourhood of $x_0$. Then $\exists h > 0$ such that the differential equation has a solution defined on $[t_0, t_0 + h]$ such that $x(t_0) = x_0$.*

### 3. Theorem: Real symmetric matrices

*Every matrix real and symmetric has real eigenvalues, is diagonalisable (in $\mathscr{R}$) and has an orthogonal basis of eigenvectors.*

### 4. Theorem: Core of games without transferable utility

The players are denoted $i = 1 \ldots m$

$v(S) \subset \mathscr{R}^m$ denotes the set of feasible utilities for coalition $S$ (with the Shapley convention – cf. chapter 5, p. 246).

A collection of coalitions $\mathscr{T} = \{S_1 \ldots S_p\}$ is **balanced** if

$$\forall S_k \in \mathscr{T}, \exists \delta_{S_k} > 0 \text{ such that}$$
$$\sum_{S_k \in \mathscr{T}, S_k \ni i} \delta_{S_k} = 1 \ \forall i = 1 \ldots m$$

($S_k \ni i$ designates a coalition to which player $i$ belongs).
A game is **balanced** if

$$\forall \mathscr{T}, \text{ a balanced family, } \bigcap_{S_k \in \mathscr{T}} v(S_k) \subset v(N)$$

**Theorem: (Scarf)**
*Every balanced game has a non-empty core.*

# Bibliography


Ahmad, S. and N. Stern (1981), 'On the Evaluation of Indirect Tax Systems: An Application to India', mimeo.

(1983), 'Effective Taxes and Tax Reform in India', DERC Discussion Paper.

(1984), 'The Theory of Tax Reform and Indian Indirect Taxes', *Journal of Public Economics*, 25: 259–98.

Allais, M. (1977a), *L'impot sur le capital*, Paris: Hermann.

(1977b), 'La Théorie générale des surplus', *Cahiers de L'ISMEA*, serie EM, n°8.

Arnott, R. and J.E. Stiglitz (1988), 'Randomization with Asymmetric Information: A Simplified Exposition', *Rand Journal of Economics*, 19: 344–62.

Arrow, K. and F. Kahn (1971), *General Competitive Analysis*, San Francisco: Holden Day.

Artzner, P. and W. Neuefeind (1978), 'Boundary Behaviour of Supply: A Continuity Property of the Maximizing Correspondence', *Journal of Mathematical Economics*, 5: 133–52.

Atkinson, A. and N. Stern (1974), 'Pigou, Taxation and Public Goods', *Review of Economic Studies*, 41: 119–28.

Atkinson, A. and J. Stiglitz (1972), 'The Structure of Indirect Taxation and Economic Efficiency', *Journal of Public Economics*, 97–119.

(1976), 'The Design of Tax Structure: Direct versus Indirect Taxation', *Journal of Public Economics*, 6: 55–75.

(1980), *Lectures in Public Economics*, New York: MacGraw Hill.

Aumann, R. and J. Drèze (1975), 'Cooperative Games with Coalition Structure', *International Journal of Game Theory*, 3(4): 217–37.

Aumann, R. and M. Kurz (1977a), 'Power and Taxes in a Multicommodity Economy', *Israel Journal of Mathematics*, 27: 185–233.

(1977b), 'Power and Taxes', *Econometrica*, 45: 1135–61.

(1978), 'Taxes and Power in a Multicommodity Model', *Journal of Public Economics*, 9: 139–62.

Baccouche R. and F. Laisney (1986), 'Analyse microéconomique de la réforme de la TVA de juillet 1982 en France', *Annales d'Economie et Statistique*, 2: 37–74.

Balasko, Y. (1976), 'L'équilibre du point de vue différentiel', Thesis.

Barre, R. (1973), *La Politique du Logement*, La Documentation Française, Paris.

Berge, C. (1959), *Espaces topologiques. Fonctions multivoques*, Paris: Dunod.

Berliant, M. (1992), 'On Income Taxation and the Core', *Journal of Economic Theory*, 56: 121–41.
Besley, T. and I. Jewitt (1991), 'Decentralizing Public Good Supply', *Econometrica*, 59: 1769–78.
Besley, T. and J. Coates (1992), 'The Design of Income Maintenance Programs', mimeo.
Bewley, T. (1980), 'Stationary Monetary Equilibrium with a Continuum of Independently Fluctuating Consumers', mimeo.
Blackorby, C. (1990), 'Economic Policy in a Second Best Environment', Innis Lecture, *Canadian Journal of Economics*, 23: 748–71.
Blackorby, C., R. Davidson and W. Schworm (1990), 'Use and Misuse of Single Consumers Results in a Multiconsumer Economy: The Optimality of Proportional Commodity Taxation' in *Measurement and Modelling in Economics*, G.D. Myles (ed.), Amsterdam: North-Holland, pp. 425–54.
Blackorby, C. and D. Donaldson (1988), 'Cash versus Kind, Self Selection and Efficient Transfers', *American Economic Review*, 78: 691–700.
Boadway, R. (1975), 'Cost Benefit Rules in General Equilibrium', *Econometrica*, 42: 361–74.
Boadway, R. and R. Harris (1977), 'A Characterization of Piecemeal Second Best Policy', *Journal of Public Economics*, 8: 169–90.
Boadway, R. and M. Keen (1993), 'Public Goods, Self Selection and Optimal Income Taxation', *International Economic Review*, 34: 463–78.
Boadway, R., M. Marchand and P. Pestieau (1992), 'Towards a Theory of the Direct-Indirect Tax Mix', Core D.P. 9226.
Brito, D. Hamilton, Slutsky S. and J. Stiglitz (1990), 'Randomisation in Optimal Income Tax Schedules', mimeo.
Bruno, M. (1972), 'Market Distortions and Gradual Reform', *Review of Economics Studies*, 39: 373–83.
Caillaud, B., R. Guesnerie, P. Rey and J. Tirole (1988), 'Government Intervention in Production and Incentives Theory: a Review of Recent Contributions, *Rand Journal of Economics*, 19: 1–26.
Castaing, C. (1966), 'Sur les équations différentielles multivoques', *C.R. Acad. Sci.*, Paris, 263: 63–6.
Champsaur, P. (1975), 'How to Share the Cost of a Public Good', *International J. Game Theory*, 4: 113–29.
(1989), 'Information, Incentives and General Equilibrium' in 'Contribution to Operations Research and Econometrics', in B. Cornet and H. Tulkens (eds.), Cambridge, Mass.: MIT Press.
Champsaur, P. and G. Laroque (1981), 'Fair Allocations in Large Economies', *Journal of Economic Theory*, 49: 627–35.
Charette, L. and C. Bronsard (1975), 'Antonelli Hicks Allen et Antonelli Allais Barten. Sur l'utilisation des conditions d'intégrabilité d'Antonelli', *Recherches Economiques de Louvain*, 41: 25–34.
Christiansen, V. (1981), 'Evaluation of Public Projects under Optimal Taxation', *Review of Economic Studies*, 48: 447–57.
(1984), 'Which Commodity Taxes should Supplement the Income Tax', *Journal of Public Economics*, 24: 195–200.

Cooper R. and A. John (1989), 'Coordinating Coordination Failures in Keynesian Macroeconomics', *Quarterly Journal of Economics* 103: 441–63.

Cremer, H. and F. Gahvani (1992), 'Uncertainty, Optimal Taxation and the Direct Versus Indirect Tax Controversy', VPI Discussion Paper.

Dasgupta P. and J. Stiglitz (1972), 'On Optimal Taxation and Public Production', *Review of Economic Studies*, 39: 87–103.

D'Aspremont, C., J. Cremer and L.A. Gerard-Varet (1993), 'Correlation, Independance and Bayesian Implementation', mimeo IDEI.

D'Aspremont, C., H. Tulkens (1980), 'Commodity Exchanges as Gradient Processes', *Econometrica*, 48: 387–400.

Deaton, A. (1979), 'The Distance Function in Consumer Behaviour with Applications to Index Numbers and Optimal Taxation', *The Review of Economic Studies*, 46: 391–405.

(1981) 'Optimal Taxes and the Structure of Preferences', *Econometrica*, 49: 1245–60.

Diamond, P.A. (1975), 'A Many Person Ramsey Tax Rule', *Journal of Public Economics*, 4: 335–42.

Diamond, P.A. and J. Mirrlees (1971), 'Optimal Taxation and Public Production', *American Economic Review*, 61: 8–27, 261–78.

(1976), 'Private Constant Returns and Public Shadow Prices', *Review of Economic Studies*, 43: 41–7.

Dierker, E. (1972), 'Two Remarks on the Number of Equilibria of an Economy', *Econometrica*, 40: 951–3.

(1976), 'Regular Economies: A Survey', *Frontier of Quantitative Economics* III A, edited by M. Intriligator, 167–189. Amsterdam: North-Holland.

Dierker, E. and H. Haller (1990), 'Tax Systems and Direct Mechanisms in Large Finite Economies', *Journal of Economics*, 52(2): 99–116.

Dieudonné J. (1969), *Eléments d'analyse*, vol. I Paris: Gauthiers-Villars.

Diewert, W.E. (1979), 'Optimal Tax Perturbations', *Journal of Public Economics*, 10: 139–77.

(1983), 'Cost Benefit Analysis and Project Evaluation', *Journal of Public Economics*, 265–302.

Dixit, A.K. (1970), 'On the Optimum Structure of Commodity Taxes', *American Economic Review*, 60: 295–301.

(1975) 'Welfare Effects of Tax and Price Changes', *Journal of Public Economics*, 4: 103–23.

(1979), 'Price Changes and Optimum Taxation in a Many-Consumer Economy', *Journal of Public Economics*, 11: 143–57.

(1987), 'On Pareto Improving Redistribution of Aggregate Economic Gains', *Journal of Economic Theory*, 41: 133–53.

Drèze, J.H. (1977), 'Demand Theory under Quantity Rationing', Core D.P.

(1984), 'Second Best Analysis with Markets in Desequilibrium: Public Sector Pricing in a Keynesian Regime', in *The Performance of Public Enterprises*, M. Marchand, P. Pestiau and H. Tulkens (eds.) Amsterdam: North-Holland.

Drèze, J.H. and D. de la Vallée Poussin (1971), 'A Tatonnement Process for Public Goods', *Review of Economic Studies*, 38: 133–50.

Drèze, J.P. (1982), 'On the Choice of Shadow Prices for Project Evaluation',

University of Warwick D.P.

Drèze, J.P. and N. Stern (1987), 'The Theory of Cost Benefit Analysis', *The Handbook in Public Economics*, (A. Auerbach, M. Feldstein eds.) Amsterdam: North-Holland, vol 2, 909–89.

Farell, J. and S. Scotchmer (1986), 'Partnerships', mimeo, Berkeley.

Feldstein, M. (1973), 'Distribution Equity and the Optimal Structure of Public Prices', *American Economic Review*, 63: 16–32.

(1975), 'On the Theory of Tax Reform', *Journal of Public Economics*, 6(1/2): 77–104.

Fogelman, M., R. Guesnerie and M. Quinzii (1978), 'Dynamic Processes for Tax Reform Theory', *Journal of Economic Theory*, 17: 200–25.

(1979), 'A Stable Path to Optimal Taxation', in *New Trends in Dynamic System Theory and Economics*, Academic Press, pp. 365–75.

Foster, E. and H. Sonnenschein (1970), 'Price Distortions and Economic Welfare', *Econometrica*, 38: 281–97.

Fuchs G. (1974), 'Private Ownership Economies with a Finite Number of Equilibria', *Journal of Mathematical Economics*, 2: 141–58.

Fuchs, G. and R. Guesnerie (1983), 'Structure of Tax Equilibria', *Econometrica*, 51: 403–34.

Gantmacher, F. (1986), *Théorie des matrices*, Paris: Dunod.

Gevers, L. and R. Jacquemin (1987), 'Redistributive Taxation, Majority Decisions and the Minmax Set', *European Economic Review*, 31: 202–11.

Gevers, L. and S. Proost (1978), 'Some Effects of Taxation and Collective Goods in Postwar America: A Tentative Appraisal', *Journal of Public Economics*, 9: 115–37.

Gibbard, A. (1973), 'Manipulation of Voting Schemes: A General Result', *Econometrica*, 41: 587–602.

Green, J. and J.J. Laffont (1978), *Incentives in Public Decision Making*, Amsterdam: North Holland.

Greenberg, J. (1979), 'Consistent Majority Rules over Compact Sets of Alternatives', *Econometrica*, 47: 627–36.

Greenberg, J. and S. Weber (1982), 'The Equivalence Superadditivity and Balancedness in the Proportional Tax Game', *Economic Letters*, 9: 113–17.

(1986a), 'Strong Tiebout Equilibrium under Preferences Domain', *Journal of Economic Theory*, 38: 101–10.

(1986b), 'Stable Coalitions Structures in Consecutive Games', mimeo.

Greenwald, B. and J. Stiglitz (1986), 'Externalities in Economies with Imperfect Information and Incomplete Markets', *Quarterly Journal of Economics* (May): 229–64.

Guesnerie, R. (1975), 'Production of the Public Sector and Taxation in a Simple Second-Best Model', *Journal of Economic Theory*, 10: 127–56.

(1977), 'On the Direction of Tax Reform', *Journal of Public Economics*, 7: 179–202.

(1979a), 'Financing Public Goods with Commodity Taxes: The Tax Reform View Point', *Econometrica*, 47(2): 393–421.

(1979b), 'General Statements on Second Best Pareto Optimality', *Journal of Mathematical Economics*, 6: 169–94.

(1980a), *Modèles de l'économie publique*, Monographies du Séminaire d'Econométrie, Editions du CNRS, Paris.

(1980b), 'Second Best Pricing Rules in the Boiteux Tradition, Derivation, Review and Discussion', *Journal of Public Economics*, 13: 51–80.

(1981a), 'On Taxation and Incentives; further Remarks on the Limits to redistribution', Bonn Discussion Paper 89.

(1981b), 'La gratuité outil de politique économique?', *Canadian Economic Review*, 14: 232–60.

(1989), 'Hidden Actions, Moral Hazard and Contract Theory', in *The New Palgrave, Allocation, Information and Markets*, edited by J. Eatwell, M. Milgate and P. Newman, London: MacMillan.

Guesnerie, R. and M. Jerison (1991), 'Taxation as a Social Choice Problem, The Scope of the Laffer Argument', *Journal of Public Economics*', 44(1): 37–64.

Guesnerie, R. and J.J. Laffont (1978), 'Taxing Price Makers', *Journal of Economic Theory*, 19(2): 423–55.

(1985), 'A Complete Solution to a Class of Principal–Agent Problem with an Application to a Self-Managed Firm', *Journal of Public Economics*, 25: 329–69.

Guesnerie, R. and C. Oddou (1979), 'On Economic Games which are not Necessarily Superadditive. Solution Concepts and Application to a Local Public Good Problem with Few Agents', *Economic Letters*, 3: 301–6.

(1981), 'Second Best Taxation as a Game', *Journal of Economic Theory*, 25: 67–91.

(1982), 'Les rendements croissants dus à la taille et leurs limites', *C.E.Q.D.*, DP. – English version: next reference.

(1987), 'Increasing Returns to Size and Their Limits', *Scandinavian Journal of Economics*, 90(3): 259–73.

Guesnerie, R. and K. Roberts (1984), 'Effective Policy Tools and Quantity Controls', *Econometrica*, 52: 59–86.

(1987), 'Minimum Wage Legislation as a Second Best Policy', *European Economic Review*, 31: 490–8.

Guesnerie, R. and J. Seade (1982), 'Non Linear Pricing in a Finite Economy', *Journal of Public Economics*, 17: 146–57.

Guillaume, H. (1973), *Prix Fictifs et calcul économique public*, Monographie du Séminaire d'Econométrie, Editions du CNRS, Paris.

Guillemin, V. and A. Pollack (1974), *Differential Topology*, Englewood Cliffs, NJ: Prentice Hall.

Hahn, F. (1973), 'On Optimum Taxation', *Journal of Economic Theory*, 6: 96–106.

Haller, H. (1984), 'Some Facts Concerning the Law of Large Numbers with a Continuum of Random Variables', Bonn Discussion Paper.

Haltiwanger, J. and T. Hatta (1986), 'Tax Reform and Strong Substitutes', *International Economic Review*, 27: 303–15.

Hammond, P. (1979), 'Straightforward Incentive Compatibility in Large Economies', *Review of Economic Studies*, 46: 263–82.

(1983), 'Approximate Measure of the Social Welfare Benefits of Large Projects', Stanford D.P., 410.

(1985), 'Project Evaluation by Potential Tax Reform', *Journal of Public Economics*, 30: 1–36.

(1987), 'Markets as Constraints: Multilateral Incentive Compatibility in Continuum Economies', *Review of Economic Studies*, 54: 399–412.

(1990), 'Theoretical Progresses in Public Economics: A Provocative Assesment', *Oxford Economic Papers*, 42: 6–33.

Harberger, R. (1962), 'The Incidence of Corporation Income Tax', *Journal of Political Economy*, 215–40.

Harris, C. (1986), 'On Strategic Taxation', Nuffield College D.P.

Harris, R. (1978), 'On the Choice of Large Projects', *Canadian Journal of Economics*, 11: 404–23.

(1979), 'Efficient Commodity Taxation', *Journal of Public Economics*, 12: 27–40.

Harris, R. and J.G. MacKinnon (1979), 'Computing Optimal Tax Equilibria', *Journal of Public Economics*, 11: 197–212.

Hatta, T. (1977), 'A Theory of Piecemeal Policy Recommendations', *Review of Economic Studies*, 1–22.

(1986), 'Welfare Effects of Changing Commodity Tax Rates towards Uniformity', *Journal of Public Economics*, 29: 99–112.

Heady, C. and P. Mitra (1977) 'The Computation of Optimum Linear Taxation', *Review of Economic Studies*

(1982), 'Restricted Redistribution, Taxation, Shadow Prices and Trade Policy', *Journal of Public Economics*, 17: 1–22.

Heal, G.M. (1972), *The Theory of Economic Planning*, Amsterdam: North Holland.

Hellwig, M. (1986), 'The Optimal Linear Income Tax Revisited', *Journal of Public Economics*, 31: 163–80.

Henriet, D. and G. Demange (1988), 'Sustainable Oligopolies', *Journal of Economic Theory*, 54: 417–28.

Hirschman, A.O. (1970), *Exit, Voice and Loyalty*, Cambridge, Mass. Harvard University Press.

Hurwicz, L. (1973), 'The Design of Mechanism for Resource Allocation', *American Economic Review (Papers and Proceedings)*, 63: 1–30.

(1979), 'On Allocations Attainable through Nash Equilibria', *Journal of Economic Theory*, 21: 140–65.

Kemp, M. and H. Wan (1986), 'Gains from Trade With and Without Compensation', *Journal of International Economics*, 16: 99–110.

King, M. (1983), 'Welfare Analysis of Tax Reforms Using Household Data', *Journal of Public Economics*, 21: 183–214.

(1986a), 'A Pigovian Rule for the Optimum Provision of Public Goods', *Journal of Public Economics*, 30: 273–91.

(1986b), 'The Empirical Analysis of Tax Reforms', NBER Working Paper.

Kolm, S.C. (1970), *Le Service des masses*, Paris: Dunod.

(1972), *Justice et Equité*, Monographies du Séminaire d'Econométrie.

(1987), 'Public Economics', in *The New Palgrave: A Dictionary of Economics*, J. Eatwell, M. Milgate and P. Newman (eds.), London, Macmillan.

Konishi, H. (1993), 'A Pareto Improving Commodity Tax Reform under a Smooth Non Linear Income Tax', mimeo University of Rochester.

Kramer, G. (1977), 'A Dynamical Model of Political Equilibrium', *Journal of Economic Theory*, 16: 310–34.

Kwan Koo Yun (1989), 'On the Welfare Effects of Reducing Price Distortions – A Global Analysis', Albany Discussion Paper 13.

Lau, L., E. Sheshinsky and J. Stiglitz (1978), 'Efficiency in the Optimum Supply of Public Goods', *Econometrica*, 46: 269–84.

McLure C.E. (1975), 'General Equilibrium Incidence Analysis: The Harberger Model after Ten Years', *Journal of Public Economics*, 4: 125–61.

Malcomson, J. (1986), 'Some Analytics of the Laffer Curve', *Journal of Public Economics*, 29: 263–86.

Malinvaud, E. (1971), 'Procedures for the Determination of a Program of Collective Consumption', *European Economic Review*, 2: 187–217.

Mantel R. (1975), 'General Equilibrium and Optimal Taxes', *Journal of Mathematical Economics*, 2: 187–200.

Mas Colell, A. (1978), 'An Axiomatic Approach to the Efficiency of Non Cooperative Equilibria in Economies with a Continuum of Traders', mimeo IMSS.

Mas Colell, A. and X. Vives (1993), 'Implementation in Economies with a Continuum of Agents', *Review of Economic Studies*, 60(3): 613–30.

Maskin, E. (1980), 'On First Best Taxation', in R. Lecomber and M. Slater (eds.), *Income Distribution: The Limits to Redistribution*, Bristol: Scientechnica.

(1985), 'The Theory of Implementation in Nash Equilibrium', in *Social Goals and Social Organization*, L. Hurwicz, D. Schmeidler and H. Sonnenschein (eds.), Cambridge Univerity Press.

Maskin, E. and J. Riley (1985), 'Input versus Output Incentives Schemes', *Journal of Public Economics*, 28: 1–25.

Mieszkowski P.M. (1967), 'On the Theory of Tax Incidence', *Journal of Political Economy*, 75: 250–62.

(1969), 'Tax Incidence Theory: The Effects of Taxes on the Distribution of Income', *Journal of Economic Literature*, 7: 1103–24.

(1972), 'The Property Tax: An Excise Tax or a Profit Tax?', *Journal of Public Economics*, 1: 73–96.

Milnor, T. (1965), *Topology from the Differentiable View Point*, University Press of Virginia, Charlottesville.

Mirrlees, J. (1971), 'An Exploration in the Theory of Optimum Income Taxation', *Review of Economic Studies*, 38: 175–208.

(1972), 'On Producer Taxation', *Review of Economic Studies*, 39: 105–11.

(1975a), 'Optimal Commodity Taxation in a Two-Class Economy', *Journal of Public Economics*, 4: 27–33.

(1975b), 'The Theory of Moral Hazard and Unobservable Behaviour', Part 1, mimeo Nuffield College, Oxford.

(1976), 'Optimal tax theory: a synthesis', *Journal of Public Economics*, 6: 327–58.

(1986), 'The Theory of Optimal Taxation', *Handbook of Mathematical Economics*, vol. 3, Amsterdam: North-Holland.

Moore, J. (1992), 'Implementation in Environments with Complete Information', in *Advances in Economic Theory*, J.J. Laffont (ed.), Cambridge University Press.

Moulin, H. (1983), *The strategy of Social Choice*, Amsterdam: North-Holland.

Munk, K.J. (1978), 'Optimal Taxation and Pure Profit', *Scandinavian Journal of*

*Economics*, 80: 1–19.

Nava, M. (1993), 'Optimal Taxation and Optimal Provision of Public Goods: The Case of Non Linear Direct and Linear Indirect Taxes', CORE mimeo.

Neary, J.P. and K. Roberts (1980), 'The Theory of Household Behaviour under Rationing', *European Economic Review*, 113: 25–42.

Osborne, M. (1981), 'On Explaining the Tax System: Why Do Some Goods Bear Higher Taxes than Others?', Columbia D.P.

Perez-Castillo, D. (1991), 'Cooperative Outcomes through Non Cooperative Games', Delta Discussion Paper.

Piketty, T. (1993), 'Essais sur la Redistribution des Richesses', Thesis EHESS, Paris.

Ramsey, F.P. (1927), 'A Contribution to the Theory of Taxation', *Economic Journal*, 37: 47–61.

Rawls, J. (1971), *A Theory of Justice*, Cambridge, Mass. Harvard University Press.

Roberts, K. (1977), 'Voting Over Income Tax Schedules', *Journal of Public Economics*, 8: 329–40.

(1978), 'The Treatment of the Poor under Tax-Transfer Schemes', MIT.

(1984), 'The Theoretical Limits to Redistribution', *Review of Economic Studies*, 51: 177–95.

Roell, A. (1985), 'A Note on the Marginal Tax Rate in a Finite Economy', *Journal of Public Economics*, 28: 267–72.

Rochet, J.C. (1986), 'Le Contrôle des Equations aux Dérivées Partielles Issues de la Théorie des Incitations', Thesis Université Paris IX.

Rockafellar, T. (1970), *Convex Analysis*, Princeton, NJ: Princeton University Press.

Romer, T. (1975), 'Individual Welfare, Majority Voting and the Properties of a Linear Income Tax', *Journal of Public Economics*, 4: 163–85.

Sandmo, A. (1974), 'A Note on the Structure of Optimal Taxation', *American Economic Review*, 64: 701–6.

Scarf, H. (1967), 'The Core of an N-Person Game', *Econometrica*, 35: 50–69.

Schofield, N. (1978), 'Instability of Simple Dynamic Games', *Review of Economic Studies*, 45: 575–94.

Shafer, W. and H. Sonnenschein (1976), 'Equilibrium with Externalities, Commodity Taxation and Lump Sum Transfers', *International Economic Review*, 17: 601–11.

Shapley, L.S. (1972), 'On Balanced Games without Side Payments', The Rand Corporation, Santa Monica, Calif.

Sheshinsky, E. (1972), 'The Optimal Linear Income Tax', *Review of Economic Studies*, 39: 297–302.

Shoven, J.B. (1974), 'A Proof of the Existence of a General Equilibrium with ad valorem Commodity Taxes', *Journal of Economic Theory*, 8: 1–25.

Shoven, J.B. and J. Whalley (1973), 'General Equilibrium with Taxes: A Computational Procedure and an Existence Proof', *Review of Economic Studies*, 40: 475–89.

Sjöström, T. (1991), 'Implementation in Undominated Nash Equilibrium without Integer Games', mimeo Harvard University.

Smith, A. (1983), 'Tax Reform and Temporary Inefficiencies', *Journal of Public Economics*, 12: 171–89.

Snyder, J.M. and G.H. Kramer (1988), 'Fairness Self Interest and the Politics of the Progressive Income Tax', *Journal of Public Economics*, 36: 197–230.

Sontheimer K. (1971), 'An Existence Theorem for Second Best', *Journal of Economic Theory*, 3: 1–22.

Stern, N. (1986), 'A Note on Commodity Taxation: The Choice of Variables and the Slutsky, Hessian and Antonelli Matrices', *Review of Economic Studies*, 173: 293–300.

Stiglitz, J. (1987), 'Pareto Efficient and Optimal Taxation and the New Welfare Economics', in *Handbook of Public Economics*, vol. II, A. Auerbach and M. Feldstein (eds.) Amsterdam: North Holland, pp. 991–1042.

Stiglitz, J. and P. Dasgupta (1971), 'Differential Taxation, Public Goods and Economic Efficiency', *Review of Economic Studies*, 38: 151–74.

Tirole, J. and R. Guesnerie (1981), 'Tax Reform from the Gradient Projection Viewpoint', *Journal of Public Economics*, 15: 275–93.

Tobin, J. and H. Houthaker (1950–1), 'The Effects of Rationing on Demand Elasticities', *Review of Economic Studies*, 18: 140–53.

Varian, H. (1975), 'A Third Remark on the Number of Equilibria of an Economy', *Econometrica*, 43: 985.

(1978), *Microeconomic Analysis*, San Francisco: Norton.

(1980), 'Redistributive Taxation as Social Insurance', *Journal of Public Economics*, 14: 49–68.

Weber, S. and S. Zamir (1985), 'Proportional Taxation; Non Existence of Stable Structures in Economy with a Public Good', *Journal of Economic Theory*, 35: 178–85.

Weitzman, M. (1977), 'Is the Price System or Rationing More Effective in Getting a Commodity to those who Need it Most', *Bell Journal of Economics*, 8: 517–25.

Westhof, F. (1975), 'Existence of Equilibria in Economies with a Local Public Good', *Journal of Economic Theory*, 14: 84–112.

Weymark, J. (1978), 'On Pareto Improving Price Changes', *Journal of Economic Theory*, 19: 294–320.

(1979), 'A Reconciliation of Recent Results in Optimal Taxation', *Journal of Public Economics*, 7: 171–90.

(1981a), 'Undominated Directions of Tax Reform', *Journal of Public Economics*, 16: 343–69.

(1981b), 'On Sums of Production Sets Frontiers', *Review of Economic Studies*, 48: 179–83.

(1984), 'Majority-Rule Directions of Income Tax Reform and Second Best Optimality', *Scandinavian Journal of Economics*, 86(2): 194–213.

Wibaut, S. (1986), 'Fiscal Reform and Disequilibrium', CORE Discussion Paper.

Wildasin, D. (1984), 'On Public Good Provision with Distortionary Taxation', *Economic Inquiry*, 22: 227–43.

Wijkander, H. (1988), 'Equity and Efficiency in Public Sector Pricing: a Case for Stochastic Rationing', *Econometrica*, 56(6): 1455–66.

Zeckhauser, R. (1977), 'Taxes in Phantasy or Most Any Tax on Labour Can Turn out to Help the Labourer', *Journal of Public Economics*, 8: 133–50.

Zeckhauser, R. and M. Weinstein (1974), 'The Topology of Pareto Optimal Regions of Public Goods', *Econometrica*, 42: 643–66.

# Index